YOU

CAN

COOK

EVERYTHING

YOU

CAN

A contemporary guide
to perfect home cooking
every time

COOK

EVERYTHING

ABOUT THIS BOOK

Welcome to *You Can Cook Everything*, an invaluable contemporary cooking guide with more than 275 recipes and techniques. Whether you are a kitchen novice or a more experienced cook who wants to brush up on skills and master essential techniques, this book is an indispensable kitchen companion.

Learn everything from the basic principles of boiling an egg and making a cheese sauce to perfect fish and meat cooking. *You Can Cook Everything* covers all bases with specific recipes for those who don't eat dairy or eggs as well as lots of vegetarian and vegan options. The inspiring combination of recipe classics and modern dishes allows you to build on your culinary repertoire and learn valuable key techniques at the same time.

The chapters are organized by both type of ingredient—good-quality ingredients are at the heart of a successful recipe—as well as type of dish. For instance, you'll find chapters on Eggs & Alternatives, Chicken, Meat, Seafood, Dairy & Alternatives, Beans & Pulses, Rice & Grains, Nuts & Seeds, and Vegetables as well as Bread; Pasta, Noodles & Dumplings; Pickles & Ferments; and of course Desserts.

At the heart of the book are culinary techniques—the building blocks of cooking. These are clear and easy-to-follow with step-by-step photographs showing each stage and complemented by a detailed recipe method. Many of the techniques are supported by additional recipes showing you how to use your newly learned skill as part of a dish or meal. For instance, find out how to make perfect fresh pasta (see p.230), then learn to roll (see pp.232–233) and cut (p.234) your fresh pasta to make Lemony Ricotta & Spinach Ravioli (see p.236), and finally how to pair it with a brown butter and hazelnut sauce (see p.238)—a culinary journey packed with valuable skills to learn. Other techniques are more simple, Frying Eggs (see p.25), for example, then using your fried egg to make the classic Vietnamese sandwich, Bánh Mi (see p.26).

Each recipe comes with an introduction to whet the appetite, providing background on the dish, its origins, preparation and serving suggestions. There are also plenty of tips, freezing and storage ideas, and advice on how to make simple changes to the recipe to create a brand-new dish. You are guided through each process, allowing you to practice and develop your cooking skills on the way. Enjoy!

Using the recipes

Before you start making the recipes in this book, the following pages will help you get the most from your cooking journey. The Cook's Notes (see p.8) take you through the basics, covering everything from the importance of accurate measuring, preparation and cooking guidelines, useful ingredient information, as well as hygiene and safety, to ensure you're armed with all the essentials you need. Cooking terms, unfamiliar techniques, and less-common ingredients can be confusing, particularly for the new cook, and you'll find them explained in the Cooking Terms & Glossary at the back of the book (see p.468).

COOK'S NOTES

Before you start to make a recipe, it's always a good idea to read through it first to ensure you have all the necessary ingredients and equipment. It is also best to weigh, measure, and prepare the ingredients before you start cooking, unless there is a period of chilling, marinating, or similar featured as part of the method. In each recipe, the ingredients are listed in the order that they are used within the method. You will also find an overall preparation/cooking time at the top of each recipe. Preparation includes the time is takes to chop, slice, and measure, and any general steps required to prepare the recipe, while the cooking time is the accumulative time it takes to make the recipe, whether that be on the stove, oven, or under the broiler. Use these timings as a guide—everyone cooks at a different pace with varying kitchen skills, and the efficiency of ovens, stoves, etcetera, can be different.

When a recipe can be partly or fully prepared in advance, instructions are given at the appropriate stage in the method. Follow the stages for chilling, marinating, rising, storing, and finishing, where mentioned in the method.

Weights and measures: these are given in both imperial and metric. Use one or the other in the recipe (rather than a mixture of both), because they may not always be exact conversions. Spoons refer to measuring spoons (not table cutlery) and these should be level unless otherwise stated.

Oven temperatures: ovens should be preheated to the temperature specified in the recipe and at the appropriate point during the preparation. The method will tell you when to turn the oven on. Ovens can vary in their accuracy, not only from brand to brand but from the front to the back of the oven as well as top to bottom. It's worth investing in an oven thermometer if you can.

Method timings: use these as a guide. These can vary depending on the ingredients, such as ripeness, or the individual oven or equipment, for example, the type of pan, or even the weather when it comes to the time it takes for a dough to rise or yogurt to ferment. Check the preparation/cooking progress at the suggested time, or at intervals during preparation/cooking.

Ingredients

The quality of the ingredients you use will reflect in the finished dish. Fresh ingredients, such as fruit, vegetables, meat, poultry, eggs, dairy, and seafood should be in the best condition possible for the best results. If possible, buy ingredients when they are in season; they will not only taste better and be more readily available but should be cheaper to buy. Keep an eye on the use-by date and store fresh ingredients as recommended, whether that be in a cool place, the fridge, or in the freezer.

Fruit and vegetables: follow the instructions in the recipe on the choice of ingredients, such as the size of a fruit or vegetable and the level of ripeness. All vegetables and fruit are assumed to be medium in size unless otherwise stated in the recipe. They should be washed, scrubbed, and/or peeled unless alternative instructions are given. Essential preparation, such as slicing or chopping, are given in the ingredients list. When the preparation is mentioned before the ingredient, this should be done before measuring. For instance, if chopped herbs are listed in tablespoons, then measure after preparation for accuracy.

When a recipe calls for lemon or lime zest, it's preferable to use unwaxed fruit. However, if you find it hard to find unwaxed, place the fruit in a colander and pour over just-boiled water from a kettle or scrub with soapy water, rinse well and dry with paper towel to remove the waxy residue.

Eggs and dairy: the size of the egg to be used is stated in each relevant recipe and should be at room temperature (see p.18). If you store your eggs in the fridge, remove them 30 minutes to 1 hour before using. Some recipes may contain raw or lightly cooked egg. It is recommended that babies, young children, pregnant women, the elderly, or the vulnerable should avoid these recipes.

Whole milk and full-fat cream, crème fraîche, and yogurt are used, unless otherwise specified.

Dried and pantry ingredients: these include beans, dried herbs, spices, flour, and grains, and should be in good condition and stored in a cool, dry place. Discard any that are stale, have lost their aroma, or are past

their use-by date. Oils and vinegars can deteriorate in flavor when stored in very warm or light conditions, or are past their use-by date. Similarly, dried herbs and spices will lose their flavor and potency if kept in transparent jars in a light room.

Use the type or flour, sugar, yeast, oil, or vinegar as specified in the recipe, unless alternatives are given. Using a different type of ingredient may affect the success of the finished dish.

Allergies or special diets: you'll find many recipes that state alternatives to dairy and eggs but please be aware that some recipes contain allergens. Check before you make them for yourself and others.

Accurate measuring

Electronic scales tend to be more accurate than balance scales, especially when weighing very small or large quantities. When measuring liquids, use a clear measuring cup or spoons—some electronic scales can also measure volume (fl oz, ml). Do not pour liquids into a measuring spoon over the food you are preparing in case it overflows into the mixture.

It is also wise to crack eggs into a separate bowl, in case any stray bits of eggshell find their way into your dish. This is especially important when separating eggs, since even the smallest trace of yolk can detrimentally affect how fluffy and light your egg whites will whip up.

Hygiene and safety

A knowledge of how to prepare and store food is essential in the kitchen. You'll find each chapter and ingredient comes with storage guidelines and hygiene advice throughout the book where relevant.

Wash your hands and ingredients, such as fruit and vegetables, prior to starting a recipe. Any cutting boards, knives, or utensils used in the preparation of raw meat, poultry, or seafood should be sprayed with a disinfectant or sanitizer and scrubbed thoroughly with hot, soapy water after use and ideally before being used again.

Many professional cooks and chefs color code their cutting boards to avoid the risk of cross contamination, using a different one for meat, poultry, seafood, and fruit/vegetables.

KITCHEN EQUIPMENT

It's not necessary to go overboard and fill your kitchen with every type of gadget, but a well-equipped kitchen with a good range of basic equipment and utensils will set you up for success and just make cooking that much easier and more enjoyable. As a general rule, the simpler the tool and the more frequently it is used, the better quality it should be: pots, pans, knives, baking/roasting pans, and cutting boards are used most frequently. With care, good-quality items will last you many years. Spatulas, spoons, graters, and smaller utensils are not so expensive and usually need replacing more frequently. Of course, the kitchen equipment you choose all comes down to personal choice—it should feel comfortable and practical to use, and suit your budget, skills, and experience in the kitchen. Start with a few good-quality essentials and build on these with time and as your cooking repertoire grows.

Saucepans and pots

When buying a selection of saucepans or pots, check that they are compatible with your cooking equipment, stove, or oven in size, shape, and type. Check the manufacturer's instructions since some materials don't work on certain types of stove. If you intend to use the pan or pot in the oven, for a casserole or pot-roast, for instance, make sure the handle and lid are also ovenproof. Quality is key when buying saucepans and pots; you don't have to invest in the most expensive, but buying cheap is a false economy—they won't last long or be efficient to use or easy to maintain.

Firstly, pans are made in different materials. Those made from cast-iron, aluminum (with or without a nonstick coating), copper, stainless steel, or enamel are the most popular, and the one you opt for is really down to personal choice and budget. Look for one that has a heavy base, so heat is distributed evenly, sturdy handle(s) riveted to the side, and a well-fitting lid. They can have a straight or sloping side, and a small one with a pouring lip is useful for liquids and sauces.

For the recipes in this book, it's not necessary to have a large collection of pans, but two to three of varying sizes—small, medium, and large, plus a skillet is a good starting point.

Other pans to consider (but not essential):

Dutch oven: useful for slow- cooking, such as braising and stewing. It conducts heat well, and a good-quality one will last for years if properly maintained. A large Dutch oven can be heavy, though, so pick it up and make sure it's not beyond your strength!

Grill pan: recommended in some of the recipes for grilling vegetables, seafood, poultry, and meat. It is best to choose a heavy-based, sturdy one that will heat efficiently to a high temperature without buckling. Cast-iron grill pans also last well, but will need to be kept oiled to prevent rusting, then dried after use.

Sauté pan: similar to a skillet but usually with straight, deeper sides and a lid (useful if your skillet doesn't come with a lid). This is for sautéing and tossing small pieces of meat, poultry, seafood, or vegetables in fat and makes a good alternative to a wok.

Steamer: perfect for cooking vegetables and fish, there are many types to choose from—a perforated basket, like a flat-based colander, that sits on top of a pan; an unfolding basket, useful for pans of differing sizes; or a bamboo steamer basket for a wok.

Wok: choose one with high-sides and a rounded, heavy base to make easy work of stir-frying. A lid and Chinese steamer basket are also useful for steaming.

Knives

There is a vast choice of types and sizes available, but the starting point is to choose one that feels suited to the shape and size of your hand with a well-balanced ratio of blade to handle that is a good weight, not flimsy. A good-quality knife is not cheap (though you don't need to go top of the range here), but it should last you for years. A poor-quality, blunt knife is frustrating to use and makes hard work of chopping and slicing, while a good-quality knife makes preparation that much more pleasurable and efficient.

The best knives are made from one piece of metal that runs from the blade all the way through the length of the handle. A large chef's knife (about 8 in/20 cm long), a smaller chef's knife (about 4 in/10 cm long), a

medium serrated knife for fruit and vegetable preparation, and a long serrated bread knife, makes a good basic starting point.

The safest knife is a sharp knife; a blunt one is far more dangerous and clunky to use. Make sure you regularly sharpen your knives (with a steel or stone) and take care of the blade, washing and drying it well after use. A wooden block or drawer separator are good ways to store knives, rather than loose in a drawer where blades can become damaged.

Scales and measures

A set of digital weighing scales tend to be more accurate and useful than balance scales—most now offer various units of measure, plus their small size means they can be tucked away in a kitchen cabinet without taking up valuable worktop space. A clear measuring cup and measuring spoons are both valuable (see p.9 on Accurate Measuring).

Baking/roasting pans

A heavy-duty steel baking sheet will last longer and is less likely to buckle in the heat of the oven. A cookie sheet has a lip on one side but is otherwise flat and is useful for baking foods, such as pastries and cookies, while a baking sheet has shallow sides and is perfect for baking/roasting foods that may otherwise slip off a flat cookie sheet, like vegetables. Roasting pans tend to be rectangular in shape with sides low enough to allow direct heat to reach whatever you are cooking but deep enough to contain the juices or fats. They come in varying sizes for roasting meat, fish, and poultry—stainless steel or coated aluminum is best for efficiency and quality.

For simplicity, the layered cake recipes in this book use two standard-size springform cake pans (8 in/20 cm), a square brownie pan (8 in/20 cm), and a 2 lb (900g) loaf pan. For more specialized cakes, you will need a shallow-sided Swiss roll pan and a tube pan. A springform pan has sides that unclip to release it from the base, making removing the cake from the pan that much easier, but you can also use regular cake pans.

A flan/tart pan can be made of ceramic or metal with straight or fluted sides. Metal may not look as appealing as ceramic, but it is better for browning and cooking the base of a crust.

Other kitchen tools

Cutting boards: use to protect your worktop when cutting and chopping. Available in wood or hardened plastic and often color coded to be used for different types of foods.

Colander: a deep, perforated metal or enameled bowl, perfect for draining pasta and vegetables. Choose a colander with feet and handles so it can be lifted easily and stand in the sink for safe, efficient draining, especially of hot foods.

Grater: there are some fancy graters available but you can't go wrong with a good old box (four-sided) grater with its mix of fine and large holes to cover all bases. The very fine holes are for zesting citrus fruit and grating nutmeg.

Kitchen scissors/shears: choose a sturdy pair in a size appropriate for the task at hand—a small pair for snipping herbs or larger shears for spatchcocking poultry or cutting through fish skin.

Mandolin: perfect for thinly slicing potatoes for a gratin. These come in different forms, but one with a metal frame, adjustable cutting blades, and a hand guard is a good choice. Use it to cut vegetables and potatoes into thin, round slices, crinkle-cut fries, or matchsticks.

Mixing bowls: available in many sizes and materials. A heatproof, heavy-duty glass or ceramic bowl can be used in a water bath, or bain-marie, for melting chocolate or making hollandaise, for instance.

Pastry brush: this short-bristled brush is useful for applying glazes, such as an egg wash, to pastry and dough to give it a golden appearance after baking, as well as brushing marinades over meat and fish to coat. Ideally, have a couple for different uses.

Pestle and mortar: not essential but a traditional tool for pounding and crushing herbs and spices. Marble is a good option because it does not absorb flavors and is sturdy on the worktop.

Potato masher: invaluable for mashing potatoes and crushing beans. A ricer or mouli may also be useful.

Rolling pins: wooden ones with or without a handle at either end are a good choice for rolling out pastry and dough, while those without a handle can also be used to bash/flatten meat steaks or chicken breasts. Pasta rolling pins tend to be smaller with tapered ends.

Strainers: smaller than a colander with a fine mesh bowl and long, thin handle, a strainer is ideal for getting rid of lumps in flour, powdered sugar, and cocoa powder; straining liquids; and puréeing. Stainless steel strainers are easier to clean than nylon ones and tend to last longer.

Spoons, spatulas, and tongs: for mixing, stirring, lifting, and turning. Wood does not conduct heat so can be useful for prolonged stirring, but there are also silicone alternatives. Some have a flat edge to make getting into the edge of a pan that much easier. A ladle has a long handle and a bowl-shaped head and is useful for transferring liquids, soups, and sauces between pans or for serving. A long-handled slotted spoon or skimmer is perfect for lifting cooked foods out of oil, water, or stock, allowing any excess liquid to drain at the same time.

Thermometers: there are many types to choose from with varying functions, but a digital one is useful for safe and accurate cooking. A deep-fry or sugar thermometer measures temperatures up to 400°F (200°C) and allows you to tell when fat is at the correct temperature for frying or when sugar has reached the desired heat for making caramel. A meat thermometer comes with a probe for inserting into a cut of meat to assess whether it has reached the recommended internal cooking temperature. An oven temperature gauge is also worth considering. Over time, the internal oven thermometer can change or deteriorate, meaning an overall drop or rise in temperature. An internal oven temperature gauge will tell you how accurate your oven is.

Vegetable peeler: available with a fixed or rotary blade, a peeler makes easy work of removing the skin from fruit and vegetables, or use to slice cheese.

Whisks: a balloon whisk, with its bulbous, rounded end and thin metal wires, is useful for whipping small amounts of cream, eggs, or sauces, rather than using an electric alternative.

Wire cooling rack: a mesh or open metal framed platform makes cooling cakes and cookies that much easier, allowing the steam/heat to escape while maintaining a crisp bottom.

Specialized equipment

It's tempting—and easy—to get carried away when choosing kitchen equipment, such as blenders, food processors, ice cream makers, pasta machines, stand mixers, and more .... The first consideration before making a purchase is how often are you likely to use it? For instance, realistically, is that ice cream machine worth the investment? This may be obvious—you love ice cream and sorbets and are likely to make them often. In that case, an ice cream maker would be an asset in the kitchen, making easy work of churning smooth and creamy ice creams, especially if it freezes too. Another consideration is kitchen space. Many pieces of equipment are large, taking up a lot of room in a kitchen cabinet or on a worktop, so it pays to buy wisely and well and not be swayed by fads or impulse.

Blender: useful for puréeing liquids, soups, sauces, smoothies, fruits, and vegetables. You can choose from a static one, with a pitcher, that sits on the worktop or an immersion blender that makes easy work of puréeing sauces and soups.

Food processor: depending on its size, this chops, purées, blends, kneads, and crumbles, although it is not efficient at creaming or whisking. Disks for slicing, shredding, and grating are often a feature, and the machine may come with other accessories too. A mini food processor is useful for handling smaller quantities of ingredients, such as when making breadcrumbs or grinding spices.

Pasta machine: the options are either a hand-cranked or electric machine for kneading, rolling, and cutting fresh pasta (see p.233).

Stand mixer: useful for mixing and creaming cakes and batters, kneading pastry and dough, whipping cream, beating mixtures, and whisking egg whites, depending on the range of attachments. It can be bulky, so often a handheld electric mixer may be enough to cater for your recipe requirements.

EGGS

&

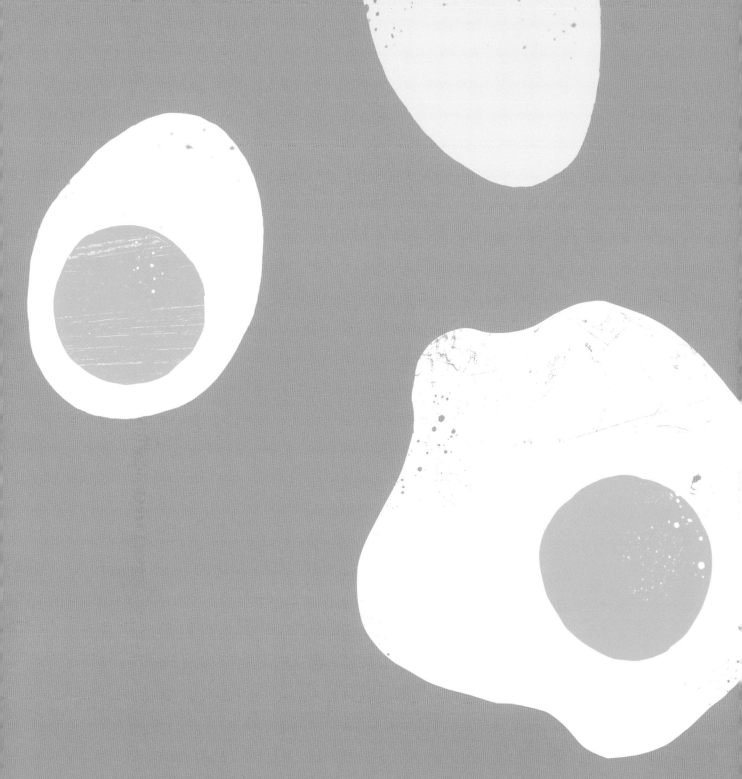

ALTERNATIVES

EGGS

Versatile, nutritious and economical to buy, eggs are one of the most useful ingredients in the kitchen. The ultimate convenience food, they can be eaten on their own—boiled, poached, scrambled, fried, or baked—or used as an ingredient to enrich cakes, thicken sauces, bind pasta, or glaze pastry.

A good source of protein, vitamins, and minerals, it is best to opt for organic free-range eggs, if your budget allows, as these are produced following strict welfare regulations with the hens fed a pesticide-free diet.

Chicken eggs are the most popular type, but also look for quail, duck, and goose eggs which differ in size from the very small to the large, as well as in flavor.

Storage

Advice on whether eggs are best stored in the fridge or not differs depending on the country you live in—either way eggs need to be kept at a constant temperature, below 68°F (20°C).

If you store your eggs in the fridge, keep them away from strong smelling foods because the shells are porous. Remove them 30 minutes before cooking for the best results. Room temperature eggs are less likely to crack when submerged in boiling water, combine more readily when beaten, and achieve a better rise when used in pancake batters or baking than those that are fridge-cold.

BOILING EGGS

Prep 5 minutes

Cook 5–10 minutes

Serves 3

Boiling an egg is often touted as the simplest technique in cooking, whereas in reality, it can be easy to get wrong, resulting in an over- or under-cooked egg. There are many different ways to boil an egg but this failsafe method is simple to follow.

3 large eggs, at room temperature

1 | Bring a saucepan filled two-thirds with water to a boil, then turn down the heat to a simmer (this is what they never tell you—you don't want to boil the egg). Using a spoon, carefully lower the eggs into the simmering water to completely cover, then set a timer for your preferred egg (right).

2 | Once cooked, use a slotted spoon to transfer the eggs to a bowl of cold water. This prevents them from cooking any further, unless you are making soft- or hard-boiled eggs, in which case you can serve them right away.

3 | To peel an egg, gently tap both ends on a work surface (this is where any air pockets will be), then gently roll the egg to loosen the shell. Using your thumbs, peel the shell and membrane away from the egg white. Dipping the egg into the bowl of cold water as you peel will help get rid of any stubborn bits of shell.

BOILING TIMES FOR A LARGE EGG

4½ minutes
Egg with a runny yolk and just-set white.

6 minutes
Set white and soft yolk, liquid in the center and just setting around the edges.

7 minutes
Set white and softly set sticky yolk.

10 minutes
Hard-boiled egg with set white and yolk

Soft-boiled egg, broccolini, & tomato salad

Prep 5 minutes

Cook 10 minutes

Serves 2

This is a simple summery salad that's fresh and vibrant, with a zingy dressing and an umami creamy depth from the eggs, which are cooked until the whites are set and the yolks remain soft.

¼lb (100g) long-stem broccolini, each cut in half so you have a separate stem and floret
4 large eggs, at room temperature
¼lb (100g) cherry tomatoes, quartered
½ small red onion, finely chopped
3oz (85g) arugula
1 tbsp capers, drained
1 tbsp balsamic vinegar
2 tbsp extra-virgin olive oil
1oz (30g) Parmesan cheese
¼ cup (30g) sliced almonds, toasted (see p.288)
salt and freshly ground black pepper

1 | Put the broccolini into a pan of boiling water and cook for 2–3 minutes, until just tender. Using tongs, lift the broccolini out of the pan, letting any water drain off, and place onto a plate, leaving the pan of water on the heat.

2 | Follow steps 1–3 from Boiling Eggs (see p.18), cooking the eggs for 6 minutes in the same pan of water, until the whites are set and the yolks are slightly soft and jammy.

3 | Place the broccolini into a large serving bowl with the tomatoes, red onion, arugula, capers, vinegar, and oil. Using a vegetable peeler, slice the Parmesan into thin shavings, then season lightly with salt and pepper and toss well. Divide the salad between two plates and top with the toasted almonds.

4 | Cut the eggs in half, season with some extra salt and pepper, then place on top of the salad and serve.

Soy-marinated egg on jazzed-up packaged ramen

Prep 10 minutes + marinating

Cook 10 minutes

Serves 1 (makes eggs for 3)

The softly set boiled eggs are marinated in a mix of soy sauce, honey, garlic, and chili flakes, which lend both flavor and color. For an easy, go-to lunch, serve them on top of packaged ramen with added veggies.

For the soy-marinated eggs
4 large eggs, at room temperature
5 tbsp dark soy sauce
3 tbsp honey
3 garlic cloves, crushed
2 green onions, finely chopped
1 tsp dried chili flakes

For the ramen
1 package instant ramen
1 small bok choy, quartered lengthwise
1 tsp toasted sesame seeds
1 green onion, thinly sliced
few fresh cilantro leaves
1 tsp chili oil

1 | Follow steps 1–3 from Boiling Eggs (see p.18), cooking the eggs for 7 minutes, until the white is set and the yolk is softly set and sticky.

2 | In a small container with a lid or bowl, mix together the soy sauce, honey, garlic, green onions, chili flakes, and 3 tablespoons of water. Add the peeled eggs, turning to coat them fully, but don't worry if they're not completely submerged.

3 | Put the lid on or cover the bowl with plastic wrap. Leave the eggs to steep in the soy sauce marinade in the fridge for at least 3 hours, turning halfway.

4 | Cook the ramen following the package instructions, adding the bok choy to the pan 2 minutes before the end of the cooking time and cook until just tender.

5 | Ladle the ramen and bok choy into a serving bowl. Top with the sesame seeds, green onion, cilantro, and the chili oil. Cut one of the soy-marinated eggs in half and place on top of the ramen, along with 1 tablespoon of the marinating liquid. Serve while still warm.

TIP

These soy-marinated eggs will keep in the fridge for up to 3 days, just remember to turn them now and again so they are evenly marinated. They make a quick meal with some steamed rice and extra chili oil.

POACHING EGGS

Prep 10 minutes

Cook 5 minutes

Serves 1

Mastering the skill of poaching an egg is easy when you know how, but it can take a little practice. One of the keys to perfection is to use the freshest eggs since the whites are thicker and hold their shape better around the yolks as they cook.

1 tbsp white wine vinegar
1 large egg, at room temperature

1 | Bring a small, deep saucepan of water to a boil, you want at least 5 in (12 cm) of water. Once boiling, add the white wine vinegar (this helps the poaching egg hold its shape) and turn the heat down so the water is barely simmering.

2 | Crack a room-temperature egg into a small bowl or ramekin, taking care not to break the yolk. Using a wooden spoon, create a vortex in the water by stirring it in a circular motion until a gentle whirlpool forms. The whirlpool will help the whites gather around the yolk when you drop in the egg.

3 | Carefully lower the egg into the center of the whirlpool. Simmer for 3–4 minutes, until the white is completely set and the yolk remains runny but is warm.

4 | Using a slotted spoon, lift out the poached egg, then drain on a plate lined with paper towel before serving as desired.

TIPS

You can poach 2 eggs at the same time. Lower one egg into the gentle whirlpool, then once the white starts wrapping around the yolk, lower in the second egg and cook as above.

Try to lower the eggs into the water as close to the surface as possible. This will ensure the white fully encases the yolk.

Perfect poached egg
& garlicky tomato toast

Prep 10 minutes

Cook 15 minutes

Serves 2

Sizzling cherry tomatoes in garlicky oil concentrates their flavor and sweetness. Pile them on top of toast with a perfectly poached egg for a winning brunch. When you cut into the poached egg, the yolk combines with the tomatoes to make the most delicious sauce.

2 tbsp extra-virgin olive oil
2 garlic cloves, thinly sliced
½lb (225g) whole cherry tomatoes
salt and freshly ground black pepper
1 tbsp sherry vinegar
2 large eggs, at room temperature
2 slices of sourdough bread
1 handful of parsley leaves

1 | Heat the olive oil in a small skillet over medium heat and add the garlic. Cook, stirring with a spatula, for 1–2 minutes, until fragrant.

2 | Add the cherry tomatoes and continue to cook, stirring occasionally, for another 4–5 minutes, until they start to burst. Season with salt and pepper. Pour in the sherry vinegar, taking care as the vinegar may spit, stir, then turn the heat to the lowest setting to keep the tomatoes warm while you poach the eggs.

3 | Follow steps 1–4 from Poaching Eggs, using the tip on how to poach a second egg.

4 | Meanwhile, toast the sourdough bread and place on two serving plates. Pile on the garlicky tomatoes and any oil from the pan, then top each serving with a poached egg. Season with extra salt and pepper, if you like, then finish with a few parsley leaves.

Leek, spinach, & za'atar shakshuka

Prep 10 minutes

Cook 15 minutes

Serves 2

Poaching eggs in a sauce is one of the easiest ways of mastering this technique. Here, the classic tomato-based shakshuka is swapped for one heavily packed with greens for a comforting, spiced, veggie one-pan meal. Za'atar (see p.449) is a Middle Eastern herb and spice mix made with sesame seeds, dried oregano and/or thyme, and sumac. It brings a zesty, earthy flavor to the dish.

2 tbsp olive oil, plus extra to serve

1 medium leek, washed, halved lengthwise and finely sliced

pinch of salt

3 fat garlic cloves, peeled and finely sliced

1 tbsp cumin seeds

3½oz (100g) baby spinach leaves

3½oz (100g) frozen peas

1 large handful of parsley and/or dill, roughly chopped, divided

1 tbsp za'atar (see p.449) or store-bought, plus extra to serve

4 large eggs, at room temperature

2 tbsp (30g) salted butter

½ tsp smoked paprika

⅓ cup (50g) feta cheese

toasted pita bread, to serve

1 | Heat the oil in a deep nonstick skillet, about 11 in (28 cm) in diameter, with a lid, over medium heat. Add the leek and a pinch of salt, then cook, stirring occasionally, for 6 minutes, until softened.

2 | Add the garlic and cumin seeds to the pan. Cook for a further minute, stirring, until the garlic is golden, then add the spinach, peas, and half of the herbs. Add the za'atar and 1 cup (250 ml) of water to create your shakshuka sauce.

3 | Cook, stirring until the spinach wilts into the sauce, about 2–3 minutes, then create four holes in the mixture. Crack in the eggs. Cover the pan with the lid and poach the eggs in the sauce for 3–5 minutes, until the whites set and the yolks are still runny.

4 | Meanwhile, melt the butter in a second small saucepan over low heat. Once melted, stir in the smoked paprika, then remove the pan from the heat.

5 | Spoon the spiced butter on top of the shakshuka, crumble over the feta and sprinkle with the remaining herbs. Finish with a little more za'atar and serve with toasted pita bread on the side.

FRYING EGGS

Prep 5 minutes

Cook 5 minutes

Serves 1

This method of frying an egg results in a frilly, crispy edge around the outside of the just-set white and a runny yolk. It may seem like a lot of oil but this helps achieve the right texture and fully cook the egg white, leaving the yolk soft, without drying it out. The cooked egg is drained before serving to remove any excess oil.

1 tbsp vegetable oil
1 large egg, at room temperature
salt and freshly ground black pepper

1 | Heat the oil in a small nonstick skillet over medium-high heat for 2–3 minutes—you want the egg to go into a hot pan. Crack the egg firmly and confidently onto a flat surface or the edge of the pan, then use your thumbs to prize open the shell and drop the egg into the pan.

2 | Let the egg cook for 2 minutes, until the white starts to crisp around the edge. Gently tip the pan and spoon some of the hot oil over the top of the uncooked egg white to help it cook. Repeat this several times until the egg white is set and the edge starts to crisp but the yolk remains runny.

3 | Season the egg with salt and pepper, then use a spatula to lift the egg onto a plate lined with paper towel before serving.

Flavor variations

Cumin-spiced fried egg: add 1 teaspoon of cumin seeds for the final minute of frying to give the egg a spicy, earthy kick.

Fried egg with feta: crumble in ¼ cup (30g) of drained feta cheese as you heat the oil, then crack the egg on top. The feta becomes a little crisp on the bottom and adds umami creaminess to your egg.

Fried egg with nduja: crumble in ¼ cup (30g) of nduja and let it heat in the oil, then follow the steps for frying the egg. The nduja turns the oil and egg a vibrant red and adds a savory umami spiciness.

TIP

If you prefer your yolk more cooked, follow the steps to the end of step 2, then flip the egg over and cook for 30 seconds on the yolk side. If you prefer a less crispy fried egg, reduce the heat to medium and put on the lid so the egg almost poaches as it cooks for a set white and runny yolk.

Breakfast bánh mì

Prep 10 minutes

Cook 5 minutes

Serves 2

A crispy fried egg in a soft and crunchy baguette with pickled, zingy veggies and added oomph from hoisin sauce and crispy chili oil—this take on the classic Vietnamese sandwich is an absolute winner of a breakfast.

2 tbsp rice vinegar
large pinch of sugar
pinch of salt
1 carrot
¼ cucumber
2 large eggs, at room temperature
1 medium baguette
2 tbsp mayonnaise
2 tbsp hoisin sauce
1 handful of cilantro leaves
Crispy Chili Oil (see p.452) or store-bought,
    to serve

1 | To make a quick pickle, mix together the rice vinegar, sugar, and a pinch of salt in a small bowl. Using a vegetable peeler, cut the carrot and cucumber into ribbons, discarding/eating the seeded core. Put the vegetables into the bowl with the dressing and toss well. Set aside.

2 | Follow steps 1–3 from Frying Eggs (see p.25).

3 | Cut the baguette in half lengthwise, then slice it in half horizontally. Spread the bottom halves with the mayonnaise and the top halves with the hoisin. Top the bottom half with the cucumber and carrot ribbons and then the fried egg.

4 | Add the cilantro, then spoon on as much crispy chili oil as you dare. Finish each with the top half of the baguette.

SCRAMBLING EGGS

Prep 5 minutes

Cook 5 minutes

Serves 2

Nothing beats soft, creamy, perfectly scrambled eggs. Unlike some recipes, this version does not whisk a small amount of milk into the eggs, which can dilute the intensity of flavor—it's all about using melted butter and taking the eggs off the heat before they're fully cooked. Remember to have your buttered toast ready and waiting in the wings.

4 large eggs, at room temperature
salt and freshly ground black pepper
3 tbsp (40g) unsalted butter

1 | Crack 4 eggs into a bowl, season well with salt and pepper, then use a balloon whisk to beat together for 1–2 minutes, until combined and frothy, this will ensure even-textured eggs without clumps of white.

2 | Place a medium nonstick skillet over medium-low heat and melt the butter.

3 | Once the butter is bubbling, pour the eggs into the pan and leave to set for 30 seconds, before stirring gently and leaving again. As the eggs start to cook further, keep stirring and folding gently and slowly with a spatula or spoon, moving the eggs around the pan to ensure they cook evenly and don't stick to the bottom. Keep stirring until the eggs are almost fully set, but still have a bit of liquid and wobble, this takes 2–3 minutes.

4 | Remove the pan from the heat and stir the eggs gently for another minute until just set.

Scramble variations

Soy scramble: replace the salt with **1 tablespoon soy sauce** for a deep umami saltiness.

Herby truffle scramble: add a **handful of chopped chives** to the beaten egg. Replace 1 tbsp (10g) of the butter with **1 tablespoon of truffle oil** or cook the eggs as per the recipe and grate over some fresh truffle just before serving.

Spicy scramble: whisk **1 tablespoon of chipotle paste** into the beaten egg for a spicy, smoky twist.

TIPS

Good scrambled eggs are all about patience, so don't be tempted to turn the heat up too high or you may end up with rubbery, overcooked eggs. If you think your eggs are cooking too fast, take the pan off the heat and add a few cubes of diced, cold butter to slow down their cooking time.

If you don't eat eggs, silken tofu makes a great alternative (see Indian Scrambled Tofu on p.37).

A CLASSIC FOLDED OMELET

Prep 5 minutes

Cook 5 minutes

Serves 1

A classic French omelet and a technique that showcases eggs in all their glory: fluffy, soft curds wrapped up in a soft, yellow, buttery, eggy blanket. Once you've mastered the basics you can fill the omelet with all kinds of deliciousness. This is an omelet for one because it's easier and more manageable to make successfully.

3 large eggs, at room temperature
salt and freshly ground black pepper
1 tbsp (15g) unsalted butter

1 | Crack the eggs into a bowl and season well with salt and pepper. Using a balloon whisk, beat the eggs for 1–2 minutes, until combined and frothy to ensure an even texture without clumps of white.

2 | Melt the butter in a medium nonstick skillet over medium-low heat, swirling the pan so the butter evenly coats the base.

3 | Once melted, pour in the seasoned eggs. Let cook for 30 seconds, until thinly set on the bottom.

4 | Stir the egg mixture with a spatula, drawing it into the center and allowing the raw egg to run to the sides, so soft curds start to cover the base of the pan.

5 | Leave the omelet to cook gently for 1–2 minutes, until the egg has firmed slightly and is set underneath (you can gently lift the edge with a spatula to have a look). The top will be glossy and moist but not wet.

6 | Use the spatula to free the edge of the omelet, then carefully roll three-quarters of it, leaving about 1½ in (4 cm) of the omelet unfolded.

7 | Fold the omelet in the opposite direction so you have a seam running along the top.

8 | Carefully flip the omelet out onto a serving plate with the seam facing downward and season with extra pepper, if desired.

Filling variations

Follow steps 1–5, then add your filling. You're unlikely to be able to roll the omelet if it's filled, so put the filling over one half of the omelet, then fold the other half over to encase it. Let the filling heat through briefly before sliding the omelet out of the pan onto your plate. Here are a few quick filling ideas:

Simple cheese: grate over a generous amount of Cheddar for a classic cheesy omelet. You could add a few chopped fresh chives too.

Herby garlic mushrooms: sauté sliced mushrooms with garlic and parsley separately, then spoon on top of the omelet. Finish with a nutty cheese, like Comté, grated over the top.

Smoky pepper: sauté sliced peppers, onions, and garlic in olive oil with a little smoked paprika and spoon on top of the omelet before folding.

Crispy bacon: fry chopped bacon until crisp, then set aside and make the omelet in the same pan before sprinkling with the crispy bacon.

Spanish onion
& potato omelet

Prep 15 minutes,
+ resting

Cook 40 minutes

Serves 4–6

**A classic Spanish omelet—or tortilla—should
be golden on the outside with well-seasoned
caramelized onions, soft potato, and just-cooked
egg in the middle. You'll ideally need two 10 in
(25 cm) skillets for this recipe).**

¾ lb (300g) waxy potatoes, such as Yukon Gold
3 tbsp extra-virgin olive oil
1 onion, halved and thinly sliced
8 large eggs, at room temperature
salt and freshly ground black pepper

1 | Peel the potatoes and cut them in half lengthwise.
Cut the halved potatoes into ⅛-in- (3-mm-) thick slices.

2 | Heat the oil in a deep, nonstick skillet, about 10 in
(25 cm) in diameter, over medium heat. Add the onion
and cook for 5 minutes, until beginning to soften, then
add the potato slices. Cook for another 20 minutes,
stirring often, until soft and caramelized.

3 | Crack the eggs into a large bowl and lightly whisk
with a fork—the more you whisk the eggs the thinner
they will become, you want to just break the yolks
and lightly combine them with the whites. Add the
cooked onion, potatoes, and any residual oil in the
pan to the eggs, season well with salt and pepper and
mix gently until combined. The eggs will immediately
cool the filling and the flavors will mingle. Leave to sit
for 10 minutes.

4 | Put the pan over medium-low heat. Pour the
egg mixture back into the pan, spreading the potatoes
and onions out to an even layer.

5 | Gently cook the omelet for 6–8 minutes, until
the bottom is set and light golden and the top is soft,
wobbly, and runny in the center (you can gently lift
the edge with a spatula to take a look). Run a spatula
around the sides and underneath the omelet to ensure
it hasn't stuck to the pan. Put a second 10-in (25-cm)
skillet over the top of the omelet and, in one
movement, flip it over quickly so the cooked side is
facing upward in the clean pan.

6 | Cook the other side for 2–3 minutes on medium
heat, until the bottom is lightly golden and the center
is a little runny (you don't want to overcook it). Use
a spatula to plump the outer edge, pressing the sides
toward the center of the pan slightly to prevent the
omelet from becoming flat and to give it a rounded
edge. Free the bottom with a spatula, then slide out
onto a serving plate. Cut into wedges to serve.

TIP

*If you don't have a second, similarly
sized pan, slide the tortilla out onto a
plate, slightly larger than the pan. Put
the pan back over the top of the tortilla,
then in one swift movement, flip the
plate and tortilla back into the pan so
the uncooked side is bottom-down.*

Persian herb frittata

Prep 5 minutes

Cook 15 minutes

Serves 4

This is a take on *kuku sabzi*, a vibrant green Persian frittata served at Nowruz or Iranian/Persian New Year. It's packed full of fragrant herbs, nuts, and dried fruit for extra texture and flavor.

½ cup (50g) walnuts
3 tbsp extra-virgin olive oil
1½ cups (30g) cilantro, leaves and stalks, chopped
1½ cups (30g) flat-leaf parsley, leaves and stalks, chopped
1¼ cups (20g) dill, leaves and stalks, chopped
6 green onions, finely chopped
pinch of salt, plus extra for seasoning
1 tsp ground cumin
½ tsp ground cinnamon
½ tsp turmeric powder
1 tsp baking powder
½ cup (50g) dried barberries or cranberries
6 large eggs, at room temperature, lightly beaten
freshly ground black pepper
plain yogurt and a crisp green salad, to serve (optional)

1 | Add the walnuts to an 11-in (28-cm) ovenproof skillet over medium heat and toast for 2–3 minutes, until they start to turn golden and smell toasted. Remove them from the pan and roughly chop. Set aside until needed.

2 | Pour the olive oil into the same pan over medium heat, add the herbs, green onions, and a pinch of salt. Cook for 3–4 minutes, until softened but still vibrant green, then move everything into a large bowl. Add the spices, baking powder, berries, and chopped toasted walnuts, then pour in the beaten eggs. Season with salt and pepper and mix until everything is combined.

3 | Preheat the broiler to medium-high.

4 | Meanwhile, pour the egg mixture into the skillet and return it to medium-low heat. Cook the frittata for 3–4 minutes, until golden and set on the bottom and sides, with the center still runny, then slide the pan under the broiler for 2–3 minutes to cook the top.

5 | Loosen the sides of the frittata with a spatula, then slide it out of the pan onto a large serving plate. Serve with plain yogurt and a crisp green salad, if you like.

TIP

The cooked frittata will keep for up to 3 days in the fridge, slice into wedges and serve at room temperature, or reheat in a hot oven for 6–8 minutes, or in a microwave for 2 minutes.

SEPARATING EGGS

Prep 5 minutes

No cook

Serves 1

There are many different ways to separate an egg, from cracking it in your hand over a bowl and letting the white run through your fingers underneath to cracking the whole egg into a bowl and using a spoon to fish out the yolk. This method is the least messy and creates the smallest amount of washing up.

1 large egg, at room temperature

1 | Firmly tap the egg onto a flat work surface to crack it around the middle. Cracking the egg on a work surface, rather than over the bowl, helps ensure the shell breaks cleanly. Working over the bowl for the egg white, carefully prize the cracked egg into two halves. As you do this some of the egg white will naturally drip into the bowl—take care to avoid any shell falling into the bowl.

2 | Using a see-saw action, pass the egg yolk from one half of the shell to the other, allowing more of the white to fall into the bowl and taking care not to split the yolk.

3 | Once all of the egg white is in the bowl, pour the egg yolk into a second bowl. Both are now ready to use (see Tip, below).

TIPS

Once separated, the egg white and yolk can be used in different ways: the yolk adds richness and thickens (see Custard, p.394); while the white can be whisked into peaks (see Black Forest Gateau Pavlova, p.400).

Freeze separated egg whites for up to 3 months in an airtight container. Defrost in the fridge overnight.

Separated egg yolks are best used the same day. Cover their surface with plastic wrap to prevent a skin forming and keep in the fridge.

Hot sauce eggs benedict

Prep 10 minutes

Cook 25 minutes

Serves 2

Many regard hollandaise sauce as the pinnacle of home cooking, perhaps one not to be attempted by the faint-hearted. This recipe proves how simple it is to make hollandaise and how easy it is to fix if it does split. It's a super-buttery, egg-based sauce, so we've spiked ours with a piquant hot sauce to cut through the richness, but a good squeeze of lemon juice works just as well.

4 large eggs, at room temperature
2 English muffins, split in half
4 slices of thick smoked ham, fat removed and cut into rounds a similar size to the muffins

For the hot sauce hollandaise
2 egg yolks (see Separating Eggs, left)
½ cup (125g) melted Clarified Butter (see p.50)
2 tbsp hot sauce of your choice
1 tbsp just-boiled water

1 | Start by making the hot sauce hollandaise. Half-fill a small saucepan with boiling water and place a heatproof mixing bowl on top to create a double boiler. Put the pan on low heat so the water is now barely simmering. Add the egg yolks and 1 tablespoon of water to the bowl and whisk with a balloon whisk for 2–3 minutes, until light and frothy.

2 | Very slowly, pour the melted clarified butter over the eggs, whisking constantly, with the pan over low heat. Keep slowly pouring in the butter, whisking until incorporated and you have a sauce with a thick, mayonnaise-like consistency.

3 | Whisk in the hot sauce and the just-boiled water to loosen slightly. Turn the heat off under the pan, but keep the bowl over the hot water while you poach the eggs, whisking the hollandaise now and again.

4 | Follow steps 1–4 from Poaching Eggs (see p.22), cooking 4 eggs in total. Toast the English muffins, then put them on two serving plates. Top each with a slice of ham and a poached egg. Spoon over plenty of the hot sauce hollandaise and serve immediately.

TIPS

You don't have to make hollandaise with clarified butter, you can use regular butter instead. This does, however, make the sauce slightly less stable because the higher water content of butter increases the chance of the sauce splitting.

If your hollandaise splits, don't panic — simply set it aside and put a clean bowl over the hot water in the pan. Add 1 egg yolk and 1 tablespoon of just-boiled water to the bowl and whisk for 1 minute, until combined. Next, very slowly whisk in the split hollandaise, followed by any remaining clarified butter, as above.

JAPANESE SOUFFLÉ PANCAKES

Prep 10 minutes

Cook 20 minutes

Serves 2

With their light, fluffy texture and not-too-sweet flavor, these pancakes are the perfect vessel for your favorite toppings. When cooking the pancakes, have patience; you want the pan to be over a lowish heat as you are steaming the pancakes to create the desired fluffy texture, rather than frying them.

4 large eggs, at room temperature, separated
(see p.32)
½ tsp vanilla extract
3 tbsp whole milk
½ cup (60g) all-purpose flour
1 tsp baking powder
pinch of salt
¼ cup (50g) sugar
vegetable/sunflower oil spray, for cooking

To serve (choose from a choice of toppings)
whipped cream and fresh sliced berries
butter and maple syrup
whipped cream with matcha and grated
white chocolate

1 | Put the egg yolks into a large bowl. Add the vanilla extract and milk and whisk until combined and frothy. Using a fine mesh strainer, sift in the flour, baking powder, and salt and whisk again to combine, set aside.

2 | In a separate mixing bowl, add the sugar to the egg whites. Using an electric hand whisk, beat until the mixture turns opaquely white, glossy, and holds firm peaks.

3 | Add one-third of the whisked egg whites to the yolk batter. Making a figure-eight motion with a spoon or rubber spatula, confidently fold the egg whites into the yolks until there are no visible pockets of egg white left. Repeat with the remaining egg whites until you have a light, fluffy pancake batter.

4 | Put a large nonstick skillet (with a lid) over medium-low heat. You want it high enough that when the pancakes go in they ever so slightly sizzle, but low enough for them to steam and not burn. Spray the base of the pan with a generous amount of cooking spray. Using a large dessert spoon, add 3 scoops of batter, about 3-in (7.5-cm) in diameter, to the pan, making sure to leave space between each one. Add another scoop of batter on top of each pancake so they are now double in height. Add 1 tablespoon of water to the pan. Put the lid on and steam-fry the pancakes for 2 minutes.

5 | After this time, place a final spoonful of batter on top of each pancake—you want them to be high, rather than wide. Add another tablespoon of water to the pan, return the lid and cook for a further 2–3 minutes. By this point, you should have used up half of your pancake batter.

6 | Using a spatula, carefully flip the pancakes. They should come away from the pan easily and be evenly golden brown on the cooked side (if they won't flip, cook them for a minute more). Once flipped, add a final tablespoon of water to the pan, cover and cook for a further 2–3 minutes, until the second side is nicely browned. Remove from the pan and keep warm in a low oven.

7 | Repeat steps 4–6 with the remaining batter to make 3 more pancakes. Transfer the cooked pancakes to two plates and serve with the toppings of your choice—see some ideas (left).

EGG ALTERNATIVES

In cooking, eggs have the ability to bind, leaven, and thicken sauces, cakes, pancakes, baked goods and more, but for those who don't eat eggs, whether that is due to dietary or health reasons, there are many readily available substitutes. Commercially made egg alternatives created from some form of starch, pea protein, or other plant-based ingredient can be found in most large supermarkets, health food stores, or online. It is also easy to make your own alternatives and be safe in the knowledge that you aren't adding any unwanted ingredients or additives. We have included a guide (below) on easy-to-make egg substitutes, but also consider mashed potato, flour, potato starch, cornstarch, avocado, and pumpkin puree as useful binding/thickening ingredients. Egg replacers vary in their use so make your choice depending on what you are making. Except for tofu, which can be used as a direct replacement for eggs to make omelets, fritters, scrambles, custards, quiches, and mousses, the other substitutes work best as a binding, thickening, or leavening ingredient.

Storage
Follow the instructions on the package if using store-bought egg substitutes or refer to the guide below for other alternatives.

EGG SUBSTITUTE	HOW TO USE	PERFECT FOR ...
Ground flaxseeds	1 tbsp flaxseed + 3 tbsp water = 1 egg. Whisk until gelatinous and leave to sit for 5 minutes before use	Great as a binder. Use in baking and for fritters, pancakes, and burgers.
Aquafaba (chickpea liquid)	1 tbsp = 1 egg yolk 2 tbsp = 1 egg white 3 tbsp = 1 whole large egg. Whisk until fluffy and light	Use to make egg-free meringue and as an egg substitute in sweet and savory baked goods, mousses, mayonnaise, creamy dressings, and sauces.
Tofu (silken, medium-firm)	Break into small or large pieces, cut into cubes, coarsely grate, or whisk to aerate	Use to mimic the soft, fluffy texture of eggs, to make Indian Scrambled Tofu (right), omelets, fritters, and dairy-free mousses.
Chia seeds	1 tbsp chia + 3 tbsp water = 1 egg. Mix together and leave to sit for 15 minutes	Use as a binder in baking, burgers, pancakes, and fritters.
Banana	½ ripe banana = 1 egg. Mash and use right away	Use as a binding ingredient in cakes and cookies.
Apple sauce	¼ cup (60g) apple sauce = 1 egg. Make your own or buy ready-made	Use as a binding ingredient in cakes and pancakes.
Agar agar	1 tbsp powder + 1 tbsp water = 1 egg. Mix together and use right away	Use as a thickener/binder for mousses, icing, jellies, and blancmange.
Xanthan gum	Check the package for instructions	Add as a binder or thickener to baked goods, cakes, biscuits, ice cream, sauces, dressings.
Buttermilk/yogurt	¼ cup (60g) = 1 egg	A useful leavening agent in cakes, biscuits, pancakes, fritters.

Indian scrambled tofu

Prep 15 minutes

Cook 15 minutes

Serves 4

This is based on the classic Indian scrambled egg dish, *akoori*, although here silken tofu replaces the egg to make soft, creamy curds. Warmly spiced and silky, this vegan twist on scrambled eggs is a breakfast winner. For a more traditional *akoori* made with eggs, follow the tip (below).

2 tbsp vegetable oil
1 onion, finely chopped
pinch of salt, plus extra to taste
4 garlic cloves, crushed

2-in piece of fresh ginger, peeled
    and finely grated
½–1 green chile, finely chopped (depending
    on how spicy you like it)
1 tbsp cumin seeds
1 tsp turmeric powder
1 tsp coriander seeds
4 Roma tomatoes, diced
2 (10oz/300g) packages silken tofu, drained and
    broken into pieces
freshly ground black pepper
1 handful of fresh cilantro
warmed chapatis or toast, to serve

1 | Heat the vegetable oil in a large skillet over medium-high heat. Add the onion and a pinch of salt and cook, stirring regularly, for 5–6 minutes, until softened and lightly golden.

2 | Turn the heat down to medium, add the garlic, ginger, and green chile and cook, stirring for another minute until starting to color.

3 | Sprinkle in the spices and cook, stirring for a further minute, before adding the tomatoes and tofu. Cook, stirring and folding with a wooden spoon or spatula, for 3–4 minutes, until the tomatoes soften and the tofu breaks down into soft curds. Taste for seasoning, adding extra salt and pepper, if needed.

4 | Divide between four serving plates and sprinkle with the cilantro. Serve with warmed chapattis or toast.

TIP

You can swap the tofu for 8 eggs, at room temperature, seasoned and lightly beaten. Add to the pan in step 3 with the tomatoes and cook, stirring for 3–4 minutes, until scrambled.

DAIRY

&

ALTERNATIVES

MILK

Milk has long been a staple part of diets around the world, as a drink; the foundation of butter, cheese, and yogurt; as well as an ingredient in cooking. Valued for its versatility and nutritional value, milk can come from goats, sheep, and even camels, although in Western cuisines cow's milk is the most commonly used type.

Ideally, use whole milk in cooking since it contains a good amount of fat for a rich, creamy flavor and texture. Containing around 3.5 percent fat per scant ½ cup (100g), whole milk makes a good base for many sauces, such as a white sauce, béchamel, or cheese sauce. Other milks can have fat content of 1 or 2 percent and while they can be substituted for whole milk they don't have the same level of rich creaminess and consistency. Skim milk, containing around 0.3 percent fat, is suitable for when you want to keep fat levels to a minimum and can be a useful ingredient in baking. When using milk in cooking, it's important to heat it gently, because the milk solids quickly sink to the bottom of the pan and can burn if heated too quickly or if not stirred regularly enough. Overheating milk or letting it boil can lead to curdling.

Storage

Keep all milk stored in the fridge to avoid spoiling and to preserve its nutrient levels.

MAKING A WHITE SAUCE

Prep 5 minutes

Cook 15 minutes

Makes about generous 2 cups (500ml)

One of the fundamental skills of learning to cook, a white sauce contains just three main ingredients: butter, flour, and milk. To make the sauce, equal quantities of butter and flour are cooked together to create a stable thickening base called a roux, which when combined with hot milk transforms into a rich sauce with a velvety consistency. A white sauce can be used in many different ways, from the baked Veggie Lasagna (see p.178) to the Ultimate Fish Pie (see p.44) and, of course, a favorite: Mac & Cheese (see p.42).

3 tbsp (45g) salted butter
5 tbsp (45g) all-purpose flour
2 cups (500ml) whole milk
salt and freshly ground black pepper

1 | Melt the butter in a medium saucepan over medium-low heat.

2 | Once the butter melts and begins to foam, use a balloon whisk to mix in the flour and cook for 1–2 minutes, whisking continuously, until it forms a golden-colored paste or roux—this will thicken your sauce. It shouldn't brown at all, but it's important to sufficiently cook the flour in the butter to prevent the finished sauce from tasting floury.

3 | Next, gradually add the milk, about a fifth at a time, to the pan, whisking constantly. The sauce will be thick after the first addition of milk, but will gradually become looser and thinner the more you add. Keep whisking to get rid of any lumps and to make a smooth, silky sauce.

4 | Once all the milk has been added, simmer the white sauce, stirring regularly with a wooden spoon, for 5–10 minutes, until thickened to the consistency of thick cream. Season to taste, then use in the recipes on the following pages.

TIP

If not using the white sauce right away, pour it into a container and cover the surface with plastic wrap to stop a skin from forming on the top and to keep your sauce nice and smooth. Let cool to room temperature, then place in the fridge. It will keep in the fridge for up to 3 days.

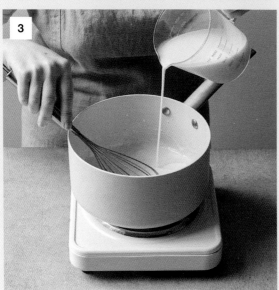

White sauce variations

Classic béchamel: gently heat the milk in a small saucepan with ½ of a peeled onion and 3 bay leaves until steaming, then turn off the heat and allow the flavorings to infuse the milk for 10 minutes. Continue to make the white sauce, following steps 1–4 (left). Once the sauce has thickened, season with a good grating of nutmeg along with salt and pepper. Use this béchamel sauce in the Veggie Lasagna (see p.178) or as a base for a creamy chicken pasta sauce.

Cheese sauce: follow steps 1–4 from Making a White Sauce (left). Once the sauce has thickened and is ready to use, stir in 2 cups (225g) grated hard cheese of your choice (a mixture of mature Cheddar and Gruyère or Emmental is good) and 1 heaped teaspoon of English mustard. Once the cheese melts, season the sauce to taste with salt and pepper. Use this sauce for Mac & Cheese (see p.42) or to make cauliflower and cheese or other vegetable or pasta bakes.

All-in-one white sauce: this is a great alternative to the roux method (see Making a White Sauce, left), especially if you're making a smaller quantity. It's also much quicker and more straightforward. Add 1¼ cups (300ml) whole milk to a medium saucepan with 1 tbsp (20g) butter and 2 tbsp (20g) all-purpose flour and place over medium heat. Using a balloon whisk, stir constantly and vigorously until the sauce is smooth, around 2 minutes. Continue to whisk and cook for a further 3 minutes, until thickened to the consistency of thick cream. Season to taste with salt and pepper.

Mac & cheese

Prep 10 minutes

Cook 25 minutes

Serves 3–4

This favorite classic features a cheese sauce made with two different types of cheese for extra depth of flavor. The dish is finished with herby, crisp breadcrumbs, then broiled, rather than baked, to retain the sauciness and add a bit of crunch to the top. Once you've mastered the cheese sauce, try the flavor variations suggested below.

1 garlic clove, peeled
3 tbsp panko breadcrumbs
1 small handful of flat-leaf parsley, leaves finely chopped
1 recipe quantity of Cheese Sauce (see p.41)
1 tbsp Worcestershire sauce (optional)
½lb (225g) dried macaroni pasta
salt and freshly ground black pepper

1 | To make the topping, crush the garlic into a small bowl, stir in the breadcrumbs and parsley, then season with salt and pepper. Set aside.

2 | Follow steps 1–4 from Making a White Sauce (see p.40) using the cheese flavor variation and adding the Worcestershire sauce with the mustard, if you like.

3 | Fill a medium saucepan three-quarters full of water. Season generously with salt and bring it to a boil. Once boiling, drop in the macaroni, stir, and cook for 2 minutes less than instructed on the package. Drain the macaroni, then add it into the pan containing the cheese sauce off the heat. Stir so the pasta is completely coated in the sauce.

4 | Preheat your broiler to high. Put the macaroni and cheese into a small baking dish, about 6 x 9 in (25 x 18 cm). Sprinkle over the parsley breadcrumbs and slide the dish under the broiler for 1–3 minutes, until deeply golden, crisp, and bubbling, watching to make sure the breadcrumbs don't burn—broilers can vary in temperature so keep an eye on it. The ultimate comfort food—enjoy.

Flavor variations

Caramelized onion: sauté 2 finely sliced onions in oil until caramelized (see p.194). Make the Mac & Cheese recipe (above), omitting the breadcrumb topping. Pour the macaroni and cheese into a baking dish, along with the caramelized onions, mix well, then top with 1 cup (100g) grated Cheddar. Bake at 425°F (220°C) for 15–20 minutes, until crisp, golden, and bubbling.

Chorizo breadcrumb topping: fry ½ cup (100g) diced, peeled chorizo sausage in 1 tablespoon olive oil over medium-high heat until crisp. Remove the chorizo with a slotted spoon, then set aside. Make the Mac & Cheese recipe (above), using the same pan as the chorizo for extra flavor. Leave out the parsley from the breadcrumbs, then stir in the crisped chorizo before topping. Swap the Worcestershire sauce in the cheese sauce with ½ teaspoon sweet smoked paprika. Broil following the method in step 4 (above).

COOKING
IN MILK

Due to its mild, creamy flavor and rich fat content, whole milk makes a great base for poaching. A classic dish that uses this technique is smoked haddock poached in milk—the creaminess complements the richness of the fish, while the milk takes on both the smokiness of the fish and the aromatics. Infusing hot milk with flavorings is something that also works well with sweet dishes, such as Custard (see p.394).

POACHING SMOKED
HADDOCK

Prep 5 minutes

Cook 10 minutes

Serves 2

Opt for undyed smoked haddock here because the fish is naturally smoked without the use of artificial bright-yellow colorings and flavorings. Save both the poaching milk and the haddock to use in the Ultimate Fish Pie (see p.44) or serve alongside Scrambled Eggs (see p.27), wilted spinach, and hot buttered toast as a great breakfast for two people.

3 cups (750ml) whole milk
2 bay leaves
1 tsp whole black peppercorns
½lb (250g) undyed smoked haddock fillet, skin-on, bones removed

1 | Pour the milk into a medium, deep sauté pan and add the bay leaves and peppercorns. Bring the milk to a light simmer over medium-low heat, stirring occasionally with a wooden spoon to avoid the milk burning on the bottom of the pan. Once lightly simmering, lay the smoked haddock flat in the pan so it is completely submerged in the milk and gently poach for 5 minutes, until the fish is opaque and readily flakes into large pieces.

2 | Put a fine mesh strainer over a medium bowl, then carefully strain the cooking milk, catching the fish in the strainer above.

3 | Allow the fish to cool slightly, then break it into large chunks, discarding any skin or bones, and keeping both the milk and fish for the Ultimate Fish Pie (see p.44) or serve the poached fish as part of a hearty breakfast or brunch.

Ultimate fish pie

Prep 20 minutes

Cook 50 minutes

Serves 4

Perfectly poached fish in a creamy white sauce with little pops of flavor from the cornichons and capers, this fish pie is hard to beat. For an added twist, you could top the pie with salt and vinegar potato sticks for the perfect crunchy finish.

For the mashed potatoes
2¼lb (1kg) Russet potatoes, peeled and quartered
generous pinch of salt, plus extra to season
½ cup (125g) salted butter, diced
freshly ground black pepper
½ cup (125g) whole milk

For the pie filling
4 tbsp (60g) salted butter
½ cup (60g) all-purpose flour
1 recipe quantity of Poached Smoked Haddock (see p.43), saving 3 cups (750ml) of the poaching milk
½ cup (125g) full-fat crème fraîche
1 tbsp Dijon mustard

½ cup (75g) cornichons, drained and chopped
2 tbsp capers, drained
1 small bunch of dill, fronds and stalks, chopped
salt and freshly ground black pepper
⅓lb (175g) raw peeled large shrimp
½lb (225g) skinless salmon fillets, cut into bite-size chunks, bones removed
buttered peas, to serve

1 | Start by making the mashed potatoes. Put the potatoes into a large saucepan of cold water with a generous pinch of salt. Bring to a boil over medium-high heat and cook for 12–15 minutes, until very tender (a table knife should be able to pierce the center of the potato with no resistance).

2 | Drain the potatoes in a colander and leave to steam-dry for 5 minutes, then place them back into the pan. Using a potato masher, mash until completely smooth. Add the butter and plenty of salt and pepper and mash again, then gradually pour in the milk, mashing well between each addition. Set to one side.

3 | Preheat the oven to 400°F (200°C).

4 | To make the pie filling, using the butter, flour, and poaching milk, follow steps 1–4 from Making a White Sauce (see p.40).

5 | Remove the pan from the heat and whisk in the crème fraîche, mustard, cornichons, capers, and dill. Season with salt and pepper to taste. Add the shrimp and salmon. Mix well, then gently stir in the poached smoked haddock.

6 | Spoon the fish pie mix into a deep, ovenproof dish, about 9 x 13 in (30 x 20 cm), then spoon over the mashed potatoes and spread out in an even layer.

7 | Put the dish onto a baking sheet (this will catch any drips) and bake for 30 minutes, until bubbling and golden on top. Leave the pie to rest for 5 minutes, then serve with buttered peas.

BUTTERMILK

Buttermilk is the slightly sour liquid left as a result of making butter with cultured cream. This tangy liquid adds a richness to baked goods, cakes, pancakes, and, because of it's high acidity, marinades. When combined with baking soda, it also works as a yeast replacement to leaven bread, such as in soda bread, as well as a meat tenderizer when used as a base for a marinade. Buttermilk is easily found at your local grocery store, but if you don't have any on hand, you can make your own version at home using whole milk.

Storage
Make as and when needed—any leftover buttermilk will keep in the fridge in a covered container for up to 2 days. Buttermilk can be frozen in portions and kept for up to 3 months in the freezer.

MAKING BUTTERMILK

Prep 10 minutes

No cook

Makes 1 cup (250ml)

It is very quick and easy to make buttermilk at home using whole milk and an acid, such as lemon juice or vinegar. The combination of the two creates a chemical reaction causing the milk to thicken and develop a tangy taste. It is slightly different and perhaps not as creamy as traditional cultured buttermilk, but can be used in much the same way.

1 cup (250ml) whole milk
1 tbsp lemon juice or white wine vinegar

1 | Put the milk in a measuring cup, then add the lemon juice or white wine vinegar and mix well with a spoon until combined. It may look a little curdled at this point, this is normal and it won't affect the finished dish when you use it.

2 | Leave at room temperature for around 6 minutes, until the mixture thickens. Use as desired or in the Buttermilk Chicken Tenders (see p.46) or Pickled Jalapeño Cheese Biscuits (see p.47). It will keep in the fridge, covered, for up to 2 days.

Buttermilk chicken tenders

*Prep 30 minutes
+ 6 hours
marinating*

Cook 20 minutes

Serves 4

These super-crispy, spice-coated chicken tenders are unbelievably delicious. The secret is the light, spiced buttermilk marinade, which simultaneously tenderizes the chicken (the acid changes the structure of the surface of the meat), while adding flavor. This cooking method is an easy introduction to deep-frying; use a digital thermometer or a cube of bread to test the temperature of the oil—it should brown in 20 seconds.

1 recipe quantity of Buttermilk (see p.45) or store-bought
2 tsp sweet smoked paprika
2 tsp garlic powder
1 tsp dried oregano
½ tsp cayenne pepper
salt and freshly ground black pepper
1½lbs (750g) skinless, boneless chicken tenderloins
vegetable oil, for frying
Ranch Dressing (see p.432) or ketchup, to serve

For the coating
1½ cups (200g) all-purpose flour
1 tbsp baking powder
2 tsp sweet smoked paprika
2 tsp garlic powder
1 tsp dried oregano
½ tsp cayenne pepper
salt and freshly ground black pepper

1 | To make the marinade, follow steps 1–2 from Making Buttermilk (see p.45). Pour the buttermilk into a large bowl with all the spices, then season with plenty of salt and pepper and mix well—you want to season the marinade generously so it permeates the meat. Add the chicken pieces and stir well so they are completely coated in the marinade. Cover and chill in the fridge for at least 6 hours.

2 | When you're ready to cook, mix together all the coating ingredients in a separate medium bowl. Season with plenty of salt and pepper.

3 | Line a baking sheet with parchment paper and, one at a time, remove the chicken pieces from the marinade, shaking gently to remove any excess, then add to the spiced flour bowl and toss until lightly coated all over. Place on the lined baking sheet and repeat until all the chicken tenders are coated.

4 | Fill a deep skillet, about 11 in (28 cm) in diameter, with 1½ in (4 cm) of vegetable oil and place over medium-high heat. Heat the oil until it reaches 350°F (180°C) on a cooking thermometer or until a cube of bread browns in 20 seconds; it will take about 8–10 minutes to heat up. (If the oil becomes too hot, simply turn off the heat, leave it to cool for a few minutes, then test the temperature again.)

5 | Meanwhile, line a second baking sheet with paper towel for draining the fried chicken when cooked.

6 | Once the oil is at the correct temperature, carefully lower half of the chicken pieces into the oil. Fry for 3–4 minutes, until crisp, golden, and cooked through, turning them halfway for an even color. Using a slotted spoon, scoop onto the paper-towel-lined tray and sprinkle with salt. Repeat with the remaining chicken. Serve with ranch dressing or go for ketchup, if you like.

Pickled jalapeño cheese biscuits

Prep 25 minutes

Cook 15 minutes

Makes 7

A cheese biscuit is a simple thing of beauty, especially when eaten warm and buttered it's a joy. The acidity of the buttermilk reacts with the baking powder to make for the best rise and a light biscuit. Try to handle the dough as little as possible, confidently and firmly patting and stamping out the biscuits for even more rise. You will need a 2½-in (6-cm) fluted round cutter, a pastry brush, and a wire rack for this recipe.

⅓ cup (80ml) Buttermilk (see p.456) or store-bought
1¾ cups (225g) all-purpose flour, plus extra for dusting
3 tsp baking powder
1 tsp salt
4 tbsp (60g) cold salted butter, cut into cubes
1 large egg, at room temperature
½ cup (75g) grated mature Cheddar cheese
6–8 pickled sliced jalapeños, drained and finely chopped
butter, at room temperature, to serve

1 | Follow steps 1–2 from Making Buttermilk (see p.456).

2 | Preheat the oven to 425°F (220°C). Lightly dust a baking sheet with flour.

3 | Using a fine mesh strainer, sift the flour, baking powder, and salt into a large mixing bowl. Add the butter, then use your fingertips to rub it into the flour until the mixture resembles wet sand or breadcrumbs.

4 | Crack the egg into a bowl and whisk in the buttermilk with a fork until well combined.

5 | Add the cheese and pickled jalapeños to the flour and butter mixture. Mix together with a pastry cutter, then while slowly stirring, pour in three-quarters of the buttermilk-egg mixture until the dough just comes together and away from the sides of the bowl. If the dough is a little dry and not coming together, add a splash more of the buttermilk-egg mixture and stir again.

6 | Working as quickly as possible, dump the dough out onto a lightly floured work surface and use your hands to lightly flatten it into a rectangle, about 1–1¼-in (2.5–3-cm) thick. Lightly flour a 2½-in (6-cm) fluted round cutter, then cut out 7 biscuits. Gather the dough trimmings and pat out again if you have extra.

7 | Place the biscuits on the floured baking sheet. Using a pastry brush, lightly brush the tops with the remaining buttermilk mixture. Bake for 12 minutes, until risen and golden. Leave to cool for a few minutes on a wire rack, then slice in half and slather with butter to serve. The biscuits will keep in an airtight container for 2–3 days at room temperature, if they last that long.

TIP

To freeze, transfer whole or halved biscuits to an airtight freezer bag and freeze for up to 3 months. Defrost the whole biscuits before eating, the halved ones can be toasted from frozen.

BUTTER

The building block of so many dishes and cooking techniques, butter is a staple ingredient in many cuisines and one of the earliest types of preserved food, being a way of extending the life of cream. Around 80 percent fat, butter is a versatile ingredient, contributing to the texture and consistency of a dish, and generally making everything taste more delicious. From being a foundation ingredient in cakes and baked goods to sauces and perfectly basted meat, poultry, fish, and vegetables, butter is equally useful in both sweet and savory dishes.

Using salted or unsalted butter is a matter of personal preference, depending on the level of seasoning you like. Salted butter will bring a rounded saltiness, whereas unsalted obviously allows you to control the level of salt and is usually best used in baking.

Storage
Butter is best kept wrapped in the fridge away from strong-smelling food. It can turn rancid if left out of the fridge for too long, especially in hot weather. It also freezes well for up to 6 months.

MAKING FLAVORED BUTTERS

Sweet-spiced butter
Put 1 cup (225g) of softened salted butter into a medium bowl and add the finely grated zest of 1 orange, plus a squeeze of juice, 1 teaspoon of ground cinnamon, and ¼ cup (50g) of turbinado sugar, then beat to combine. Shape the flavored butter into a log in a sheet of parchment paper and chill or freeze. Use for baking fruit or in cakes in place of regular butter, or melt on top of Pancakes (see p.349).

Herby garlic butter
Put 1 cup (225g) of softened salted butter into a medium bowl and crush in 6 peeled garlic cloves, then add the finely grated zest of 1 unwaxed lemon and a small bunch of finely chopped flat-leaf parsley. Season with salt and freshly ground black pepper, then beat to combine. Shape the flavored butter into a log in a sheet of parchment paper and chill or freeze. Use for the Homemade Chicken Kiev (see p.78) or melted into hot cooked spaghetti for a quick and easy dinner.

Miso-ginger butter
Put 1 cup (225g) of softened salted butter into a medium bowl and finely grate in a 2-in piece of fresh, peeled ginger. Add 2 tablespoons of white miso, the juice and finely grated zest of 1 lime, a handful of finely chopped fresh cilantro, then beat to combine. Shape the flavored butter into a log in a sheet of parchment paper and chill or freeze. This is great on a grilled cheese or spread over Corn-on-the-Cob (see p.190).

Smoked paprika & lemon butter
Put 1 cup (225g) of softened salted butter into a medium bowl and add 1 tablespoon of sweet smoked paprika and the juice and finely grated zest of 1 unwaxed lemon. Season with salt and freshly ground black pepper, then beat to combine. Shape the flavored butter into a log in a sheet of parchment paper and chill or freeze. Use for the Whole Roasted Sea Bream (see p.130), or over roasted chicken thighs, adding it to the roasting tray for the final 5 minutes of cooking.

Sweet-spiced butter

Miso-ginger butter

Herby garlic butter

Smoked paprika
& lemon butter

MAKING CLARIFIED BUTTER

No Prep

Cook 5 minutes

Makes ½ cup (100ml)

A variation on butter is clarified butter, or ghee, which is used widely in cooking across the Indian subcontinent. Clarifying raises the smoke point of butter, or the temperature at which it would normally burn, allowing you to use it instead of cooking oil. It has a rich, slightly nutty flavor and can be used to make the Hot Sauce Eggs Benedict (see p.33) or for sautéing fish and vegetables, roasting potatoes, or in curries and stews in place of vegetable or sunflower oil.

1 cup (225g) salted or unsalted butter

1 | Put the butter in a small saucepan and melt very gently over low heat, stirring occasionally with a spatula until melted.

2 | Once melted, spoon off any white scum that has risen to the surface and discard.

3 | At this point, the milk solids will have sunk to the bottom of the pan, leaving clear clarified butter on top.

4 | Gently pour the clarified butter into a jar, leaving the milk solids behind in the bottom of the pan—they can be discarded. Use right away or store in the fridge in a lidded container for up to 6 months.

BROWN BUTTER & CAPER ASPARAGUS

Prep 5 minutes

Cook 10 minutes

*Serves 2
(as a side)*

This may sound complicated, but browning butter is much easier than you think. All it requires is a little patience and continuous whisking until the milk solids caramelize and you're left with an amber-colored, nutty-tasting butter. There are many ways to use brown butter, including pan-frying fish or meat, or in place of regular butter in cakes and bakes (see p.365 and p.373) or in this asparagus side dish (below).

6 tbsp (100g) salted butter
½lb (225g) asparagus, woody ends snapped off
2 tbsp capers, drained
juice and finely grated zest of ½ unwaxed lemon
1 handful of flat-leaf parsley leaves
salt and freshly ground black pepper
Simple Salted Roast Chicken (see p.69) and crusty
   bread, to serve

1 | Melt the butter in a small saucepan over medium-high heat. With the pan still on the heat, once the butter melts and has stopped foaming (this will take a couple of minutes), use a balloon whisk to beat continuously for 3–4 minutes, until the milk solids start to turn golden on the bottom of the pan.

2 | Keep cooking and whisking for a few minutes until the butter smells nutty and the milk solids darken to a deep amber caramel color.

3 | Meanwhile, fill a large saucepan with water and bring to a boil over medium-high heat. Once the water is boiling, drop in the asparagus and cook for 2–3 minutes, until vivid green and tender, then drain well through a strainer. Put the cooked asparagus into a serving dish and add the capers, lemon juice and zest, and parsley, then toss well. At this point, remove the brown butter from the heat and carefully spoon it over the asparagus mixture, tossing well with tongs to combine.

4 | Season the asparagus with salt and pepper to taste and serve as a side to roast chicken with chunks of crusty bread instead of roast potatoes.

YOGURT

The milk from cows, goats, and sheep can all be transformed into yogurt, and each comes with its own characteristic flavor, texture, and varying fat content. Yogurt is made by fermenting whole or cultured skim milk with beneficial bacterial cultures and sometimes yeast, which in turn converts the lactose (sugars) present in the milk into lactic acid. This acidic environment prevents other more harmful strains of bacteria from spoiling the yogurt, meaning it keeps longer than regular milk. It also gives the yogurt a delicious tang to balance out the rich creaminess. Greek yogurt, made from sheep's or cow's milk, has a higher fat content than most other plain yogurts, giving it a thick consistency that is more stable in cooking.

Yogurt is an excellent ingredient to use in cooking. Its slightly acidic taste and creamy, silky texture make it perfect for many types of dishes, like tenderizing and marinating meat, as an alternative to cream in cakes and icings, or as a cooling addition to spicy dishes.

From a health perspective, yogurt is more digestible than regular cow's milk, which is good news for those who suffer from lactose intolerance. Additionally, the beneficial bacteria works as a probiotic and is good for the health of the gut.

Storage
Keep yogurt covered in the fridge for up to 2 weeks if using store-bought and 1 week for homemade.

EASY HOMEMADE YOGURT

Prep 5 minutes + cooling, 8 hours fermenting and chilling

Cook 20 minutes

Makes 1lb 2oz (500g)

Making yogurt at home is straightforward—it's all about hitting the right temperatures, so you'll need a digital thermometer for this recipe, as well as an insulated container to keep the milk and yogurt mix warm so it can work its magic. This is a great one to make when you have some milk and a few spoons of leftover yogurt in the fridge. Make sure the yogurt says "live" on the label, since this means it still contains beneficial bacterial cultures, which are essential for the fermentation process.

2 cups (500ml) whole milk
3 tbsp good-quality live natural yogurt

1 | Gently warm the milk in a medium saucepan on low heat for 15–20 minutes, stirring regularly to prevent it burning on the bottom of the pan. Regularly check the temperature of the milk, you want it to reach 185°F (85°C) on a digital cooking thermometer and it must not reach a simmer or boil. Remove the pan from the heat and cover with a lid. Leave the milk to cool slightly until it reduces to 113°F (45°C), stirring now and again to prevent a skin from forming and checking the temperature as you do—this will take around 30 minutes to 1 hour, depending on the temperature inside your kitchen.

2 | Once the milk has reached the right temperature, put the natural yogurt into a small bowl and add 4 tablespoons of the warm milk, then stir well until combined.

3 | Pour the yogurt mixture back into the pan containing the rest of the warm milk and mix again to combine.

4 | Pour the milk mixture into an insulated container, seal with the lid and leave at room temperature for around 8 hours, until thickened and soured. You can wrap the container in a thick towel or place it in a warm airing cupboard to keep in the heat while the yogurt ferments.

5 | Pour the yogurt into a bowl, cover, and chill in the fridge for at least 2–3 hours, until it thickens further and is the consistency of natural yogurt. The yogurt will keep covered in the fridge for up to 1 week.

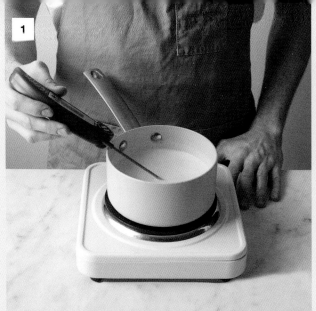

TIP

If the yogurt looks a little split once it has chilled in the bowl, give it a good stir with a balloon whisk and it will become smooth and luscious again.

Mango lassi

*Prep 10 minutes
+ cooling
fermenting
and chilling*

No cook

Serves 4

This cooling, creamy drink is loved across the Indian subcontinent. When the yogurt and mango are blended together they create the most luxurious texture with fruity sweetness, spice from the cardamom, and a nice tang from the yogurt and lime.

½ recipe quantity of Easy Homemade Yogurt (see p.52)
    or store-bought
1lb (450g) diced ripe mango (peeled weight)
2 tsp honey
juice of 1 lime
½ tsp ground cardamom

1 | Follow steps 1–5 from Easy Homemade Yogurt (see p.52). Reserve half of the yogurt for another dish.

2 | Blend the yogurt, mango, and honey in a high-powered blender until smooth (you can leave a few chunks of fruit, if you like). Add half of the lime juice, then mix and taste. Depending on the ripeness and sweetness of the mango, add more lime to taste. Fill four glasses with ice, pour over the lassi and top with a sprinkling of ground cardamom, to serve.

TIP

If more convenient, this lassi can be made with canned mango pulp or frozen mango chunks, which are readily available in supermarkets.

Slow-cooked zucchini & lemon yogurt conchiglie

Prep 5 minutes

Cook 20 minutes

Serves 2

Yogurt is used here to make a creamy, tangy pasta sauce that works perfectly with the soft sweetness of the caramelized zucchini. If cooking for one, see the Tip (below).

2 tbsp olive oil
2 medium zucchini, coarsely grated
2 garlic cloves, crushed or finely grated
pinch of dried chili flakes (optional)
½lb (225g) dried conchiglie pasta (or another smallish shape, such as farfalle or orecchiette)
4 tbsp Greek yogurt
juice and finely grated zest of 1 unwaxed lemon
1 handful of basil leaves, chopped
2 tbsp pine nuts, toasted (see p.288)
salt and freshly ground black pepper
Parmesan cheese (or vegetarian alternative), finely grated, to serve (optional)

1 | Heat the olive oil in a medium skillet over medium heat. Add the grated zucchini, along with a pinch of salt. Cook, stirring regularly with a wooden spatula, for 12–15 minutes, until the zucchini has collapsed and is completely soft—it will turn lightly golden in color.

2 | Add the garlic to the zucchini and cook, stirring for another minute, then add the chili flakes, if using. Turn the heat down to the lowest setting.

3 | Meanwhile, fill a deep medium saucepan with water and salt generously. Bring to a boil. Once boiling, drop in the conchiglie or pasta shape of your choice, cook for a minute less than the package instructions say, then drain into a strainer, saving a cup of the pasta cooking water.

4 | Put the cooked pasta into the pan containing the zucchini. Turn the heat to the lowest setting, add the yogurt, lemon juice and zest, and most of the basil, saving some to serve at the end. Stir so each piece of pasta is coated in the sauce, adding as much pasta cooking water as needed to give a silky, creamy consistency. Season to taste with salt and lots of black pepper. You need to keep the heat low to allow the sauce to combine without the yogurt splitting.

5 | Divide the pasta between two bowls, top with the remaining basil, toasted pine nuts, and some grated Parmesan, if you like, to serve.

TIP

Stir 1 (15-oz/400-g) can of drained lima beans into the zucchini and yogurt sauce and gently warm through. Serve with or without pasta.

CREAM

Cream is the fat skimmed off the top of fresh unpasteurized cow's milk before it is homogenized. Rich and indulgent, it is a highly versatile ingredient and can be used in many dishes, both sweet and savory, from mousses and ice creams to sauces and bakes. We cover the different types of cream in more detail in Desserts (see p.402–405), including tips on how to whip cream. For savory dishes that involve cooking/heat, heavy cream is best. With its high fat content, around 48 percent, it is more stable when heated than whipping cream and is less likely to split. Look too for crème fraîche and sour cream, which are both cultured milk products, hence the slightly sour, rich tang they give to cooked and uncooked dishes. Crème fraîche is more heat stable than sour cream so is perfect for sauces, but opt for the full-fat option.

Storage
Cream, crème fraîche, and sour cream will keep for up to 10 days in the fridge before opening (check the use-by date). Once opened, use within 3 days.

POTATOES AU GRATIN

Prep 30 minutes

Cook 1 hour 40 minutes

Serves 6–8

One of the most loved ways to use cream is in the classic French potato dish, dauphinoise, or potatoes au gratin—thinly sliced potatoes baked with heavy cream and garlic, sometimes with the addition of cheese. There are many ways to make this dish: some slice and then lightly boil the potatoes in the cream mixture before layering, but the easiest method, which also results in the best texture, comes from adding the ingredients cold and letting them bake together in the oven. Milk and cream are used in equal measure here to balance the richness with sauciness. A mandolin makes easy work of slicing the potatoes, although a sharp chef's knife also works well. If using a mandolin, take care and use the guard to protect your fingers.

2 tbsp (30g) softened salted butter
3¼lbs (1.5kg) Yukon Gold potatoes, peeled
2 cups (500ml) whole milk
2 cups (500ml) heavy cream
3 garlic cloves, crushed
salt and freshly ground black pepper
1 cup (100g) grated Gruyère cheese (optional)

1 | Preheat the oven to 350°F (180°C). Grease the base and sides of a 10 x 14 in (35 x 25 cm) baking dish with butter. Very finely slice the potatoes into ¹⁄₈-in- (3-mm-) thick rounds using a mandolin or a sharp chef's knife.

2 | Once sliced, layer the potatoes in the buttered baking dish, seasoning each layer as you go. You don't need to make the bottom layers neat because you won't see them once baked, just the top one.

3 | Once all the potatoes are layered, use a balloon whisk to whisk the milk and heavy cream together, add the garlic and season generously with salt and pepper. Pour the milk and cream mixture over the potatoes.

4 | Using a spatula, press the potatoes down to completely submerge them in the sauce, then sprinkle over the cheese, if using.

5 | Cover the dish with foil and bake for 1 hour, until the potatoes are almost tender, testing them with the tip of a knife. After 1 hour, remove the foil and bake for a further 30–40 minutes, until the potatoes are cooked through and the top is bubbling and golden brown. The point of a knife should slide into the center of the potatoes easily.

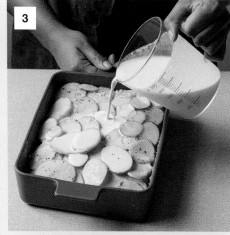

TIPS

If you want a little more color on the top, slide the dish under a hot broiler for a final couple of minutes. Serve as a side dish to roast meats or on its own with a big, crisp, French-dressed green salad (see p.429 for French Dressing).

The dish can be part-cooked in advance. Simply bake it, covered with foil, for 1 hour, then leave to cool. Place the covered dish in the fridge and keep for up to 3 days. To reheat, remove the foil and bake for 45 minutes, until cooked through, bubbling, and golden.

Flavor variations

Cheddar & chile jam: swap the Gruyère for 2 cups (225g) grated extra-mature Cheddar cheese. Follow steps 1–4 (left) for layering the potatoes, adding a small teaspoon of chile jam every so often and sprinkling over half of the Cheddar as you go. Top with the remaining Cheddar and bake as instructed (left).

Anchovy & caramelized onion: before starting the recipe, caramelize 3 onions (see p.194). Once caramelized, add a drained 2-oz (55-g) can of anchovies and cook for 2 minutes, stirring, until melted into the onions. Follow steps 1–4 (left), for layering the potatoes, using the Gruyère and adding caramelized onions between each layer. Reduce the quantity of salt you use because the anchovies are salty. Bake as instructed (left).

CHEESE

There are more than 1,800 different types of cheese in the world and what is incredible is that they all come from milk, whether that be from cows, sheep, goats, or water buffalo. They range from fresh, soft cheeses such as the Homemade Labneh (right) and ricotta and fromage blanc to be eaten within a few days of making, to paneer, a pressed fresh cheese from the Indian subcontinent to hard-pressed cheese, such as English Cheddar, which is traditionally matured in caves to give it depth of flavor and extend its keeping properties. While at the far end of the scale are very hard-pressed cheeses, including Parmesan, which is aged for an average of 2 years, possibly longer, to give a strong-tasting distinctive cheese with a complex nutty flavor and slightly crumbly texture.

Storage

The keeping properties of cheese vary tremendously depending on the type: fresh soft cheese will only keep for a few days in the fridge, while hard, mature cheeses will keep for much longer, about 1 month, even longer if unopened. It is advisable to check the use-by dates and keep cheeses well wrapped in the fridge to avoid cross-contamination. Hard and semi-hard cheeses can also be frozen for up to 6 months. For optimum flavor and texture, especially when serving as part of a cheeseboard, bring the cheese out of the fridge about 1 hour before serving.

COOKING WITH CHEESE

Cheese + heat = magical reaction. Who doesn't love that cheese pull, from melted mozzarella on pizzas and Monterey Jack on nachos to the gooey inside of a whole baked Camembert and the saucy cheesiness of Mac & Cheese (see p.42)—nothing beats the flavor and texture of melted cheese. The table (below) gives some ideas of different cheese cooking techniques and highlights some of the ones that work best.

CHEESE	COOKING METHOD	WHY ...	PERFECT FOR ...
Halloumi and paneer	Frying	Retains shape during frying with a crisp outside and soft inside	Use in salads, vegetable stews, curries, or as a filling for rolls and pita bread (see p.63).
Mozzarella, Cheddar, Gouda, raclette, and Gruyère	Melting	Can withstand high heat, becoming stretchy and elastic when melted	Use to top pizzas, bakes or gratins, in a grilled cheese, or on top of toast.
Parmesan and pecorino	Bubbling crust	Creates a thick, crunchy crust when finely grated	Use to top gratins, open pies, savory bakes.
Camembert and Brie	Baking	Holds its shape when baked, while the center becomes gooey	Serve with vegetable sticks, chips, and crackers for dunking.

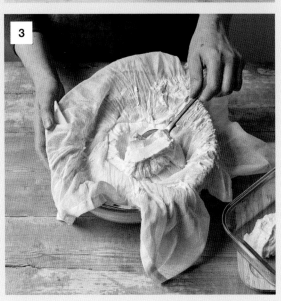

HOMEMADE LABNEH

Prep 10 minutes + overnight chilling

No cook

Makes 1lb 5oz (600g)

Making your own fresh cheese from strained yogurt is easier than you may think. Labneh has been made in the Middle East for thousands of years. It is often served as part of a mezze, drizzled with olive oil, flavored with herbs and spices, or even as a spread on bread. It has a soft, creamy, and slightly tangy taste that works with stronger flavored ingredients. When making it, you will need a piece of cheesecloth to strain the yogurt through, but you can use a clean kitchen towel instead. An elastic band or piece of string is recommended to tie the yogurt bundle up so it hangs with ease.

2lb (900g) thick cow's or sheep's milk Greek yogurt
large pinch of sea salt

1 | Line a large fine mesh strainer, placed over a deep bowl (that will fit in your fridge) with a rectangle of doubled cheesecloth—it should entirely cover the strainer with a generous overhang. Mix the yogurt with a large pinch of sea salt, then spoon it into the center of the cloth in the lined strainer.

2 | Gather the cloth up around the yogurt to encase it in a round parcel. Tie with an elastic band or piece of string to secure the yogurt mixture in a bundle. Leave the yogurt to hang, draining in the strainer over the bowl, for 12 hours in the fridge.

3 | The next day, lift the yogurt bundle out of the strainer, the bowl underneath will contain water (whey) that has drained from the yogurt. Squeeze the cheese in its cloth to get rid of any extra excess water or whey.

Untie and open the cloth bundle to reveal a ball of fresh cheese or labneh inside. It is now ready to use and will keep for up to 5 days stored in an airtight container in the fridge.

TIP

Serve the labneh as part of a mezze with Falafel (see p.274) or with the Harissa Sticky Chicken (see p.71). To flavor the labneh, stir in the finely grated zest of 1 unwaxed lemon and some cracked black pepper, or add 1 tablespoon Za'atar (see p.449) for an herby, spicy kick.

Roast squash with chili-honey dressing & labneh

*Prep 20 minutes
+ overnight
chilling*

Cook 30 minutes

Serves 4

The soft, rich creaminess of labneh is the perfect mild-tasting foil for spice-roasted vegetables, such as these wedges of cumin-crusted butternut squash that come with a hot chili and honey dressing. Making this salad along with your own fresh cheese is great for showing off to friends, although you can use a ready-made labneh if more convenient.

1 butternut squash, skin left on, seeded and
   cut into 1-in- (2.5-cm-) thick wedges
2 tbsp extra-virgin olive oil
2 tbsp cumin seeds
salt and freshly ground black pepper
3 tbsp honey
½ tsp dried chili flakes
10oz (300g) Labneh (see p.59) or store-bought
1 large handful of mixed herbs, such as dill, flat-leaf
   parsley, and mint, leaves picked
½ cup (50g) unsalted shelled nuts of your choice, such
   as hazelnuts or almonds, toasted (see p.288) and
   roughly chopped

1 | Follow steps 1–3 from Homemade Labneh (see p.59). You will need to start making this a day ahead.

2 | To make the salad, heat the oven to 425°F (220°C). Line a large baking sheet with parchment paper. Toss the butternut wedges in the olive oil and cumin seeds with plenty of salt and pepper on the baking sheet. Spread out the squash in a single layer so it cooks evenly and roast for 25 minutes, until tender and slightly caramelized.

3 | Add the honey and chili flakes to a small pan and gently heat, stirring, to combine and loosen. Spoon half of the chili-honey dressing over the roasted squash and return it to the oven for another 5 minutes to caramelize further.

4 | Spread the labneh across the base of a large platter or over four serving plates. Pile on the roasted squash, sprinkle over the herbs and nuts, then drizzle with the rest of the chili-honey dressing, to serve.

TIP

Instead of the toasted nuts, sprinkle 2 tbsp Dukkah (see p.303) over the salad for an additional spicy, nutty kick.

Kimchi grilled cheese

Prep 5 minutes

Cook 10 minutes

Serves 2

A mixture of grated mozzarella and Cheddar ups the flavor with that enviable melted cheese pull. When buying kimchi, look for a fresh chilled variety as it will be funkier, contain fewer preservatives, and have more flavor, or see p.464 to make your own.

4 thick slices of crusty bread (like sourdough)
2 tbsp Mayonnaise (see p.420) or store-bought
2 tbsp sesame seeds
2 tbsp (30g) salted butter
1 cup (150g) ready-grated mozzarella and
　　Cheddar mix
3½oz (100g) Kimchi (see p.464) or store-bought

1 | Spread each slice of bread evenly with mayonnaise, then sprinkle over the sesame seeds so the mayonnaise side is covered.

2 | Melt the butter in a large nonstick skillet over medium heat.

3 | Once melted, lay two of the bread slices sesame-seed side down in the pan. Top each slice with half of the cheese, all of the kimchi, then the remaining cheese. Finally, sandwich together with the remaining bread, sesame seed-side up.

4 | Fry the sandwiches for 2–3 minutes, occasionally pressing down with a spatula to help melt the cheese, until the undersides are deep golden with a sesame crust, then carefully flip over and cook for a further 2–3 minutes on the other side, until the cheese is melting and oozing in the middle. Remove the sandwiches from the pan and cut in half to serve.

Sabich-style halloumi pitas

Prep 10 minutes

Cook 20 minutes

Serves 4

Sabich is a popular Israeli sandwich with a filling of hard-boiled eggs; fried eggplant; chopped salad; hummus; tahini; and amba sauce, which is made from pickled mangoes, all stuffed inside a pita bread. This features the added salty chewiness of fried sliced halloumi and uses mango chutney in place of amba for a more accessible version.

2 large eggs, at room temperature
½ cucumber, finely chopped
2 vine-ripened tomatoes, chopped to the same size
   as the cucumber
½ red onion, finely chopped
1 handful of flat-leaf parsley and/or mint leaves, picked
juice of ½ lemon
1 large eggplant, cut into ½-in- (2-cm-) thick rounds
2 tbsp olive oil, plus 1 tsp
8oz (225g) halloumi, patted dry and cut into ½-in-
   (2-cm-) thick slices
2 tbsp mango chutney

To serve
4 large pita breads
8 tbsp Hummus (see p.xx) or store-bought
salt and freshly ground black pepper

1 | Follow steps 1–3 from Boiling Eggs cooking the eggs for 7 minutes, until the white is set and the yolk is slightly soft and sticky. Drain, then peel and set aside.

2 | Meanwhile, mix the cucumber, tomatoes, red onion, and most of the herbs in a small bowl. Season to taste with salt, pepper, and lemon juice.

3 | Heat a large nonstick skillet over high heat. Drizzle the eggplant slices with 2 tablespoons of the olive oil and season with salt and pepper. Place in the pan and sauté for 3–4 minutes on each side until deeply golden and soft. Remove onto a plate.

4 | Drizzle the remaining 1 teaspoon of olive oil over the halloumi slices. Turn the heat down to medium, place the halloumi in the pan, and cook for 2 minutes on each side until evenly golden—at first some water will leak out of the halloumi, then the slices will turn crisp and golden.

5 | Once the halloumi is browned on both sides, take the pan off the heat and add the mango chutney. Using a dessert spoon, toss the halloumi in the chutney so each slice is coated in the glaze.

6 | Toast the pita breads, then slice each one in half lengthwise to open up. Cut the eggs into round slices.

7 | Spread the inside of each pita evenly with the hummus, then stuff in the eggplant, egg slices, and chopped salad. Top with the halloumi and remaining herbs, to serve. There may be more filling than can fit into each pita, so serve any remaining as a salad on the side.

DAIRY-FREE ALTERNATIVES

Ingredients as diverse as nuts, oats, rice, potatoes, beans, and seeds can be turned into a plant-based milk, and make a tasty, nutritious, and versatile alternative to those made with dairy products. Starting with dairy-free milk, making your own is both simple and economical, and you have the luxury of it being freshly made. And where there is dairy-free milk, there are also alternatives to yogurt, butter, cheese (see recipe right), and cream to try.

Storage
Store in the same way as dairy milk (see p.40).

ALMOND MILK

Prep 10 minutes + overnight soaking and straining

No cook

Makes 1¼ pints (750ml)

This recipe for plant-based milk uses almonds, but you can use other types of nut, such as hazelnuts, cashews, and pecans, or grains, like oats and rice. The almonds need to soak overnight, but you'll be rewarded with a rich, creamy milk packed with almond flavor. You'll need a high-powered blender to achieve smoothness and if you can't find cheesecloth for straining the milk, a clean kitchen towel works just as well.

½lb (225g) whole blanched almonds
pinch of sea salt
1–2 tsp maple syrup (optional)

1 | Put the almonds into a bowl and pour over 3 cups (750ml) of water. Cover and let soak overnight. The next day, place the nut mixture into a blender, add a pinch of salt and the maple syrup, if you prefer a sweetened nut milk. Blend until completely smooth.

2 | Place a fine mesh strainer over a large bowl and line the strainer with cheesecloth or a clean kitchen towel so it is completely covered. Pour the blended nut mixture into the center and leave it to drip through the cloth and strainer into the bowl underneath. You can stir the mixture with a spoon to speed up the process.

3 | Gather up the cloth into a bundle and squeeze the remaining liquid from the pulp, discarding the nut pulp (or see the next step) in the cloth and keeping the liquid milk in the bowl underneath. Pour the almond milk into sterilized bottles (see p.456) and chill until ready to serve. The almond milk will keep for up to 5 days in the fridge.

4 | If you don't want to throw away the nut pulp after blending, use it to enrich smoothies or when making porridge for an added nutty texture.

Cashew nut cheese

Prep 10 minutes + overnight soaking

No cook

Makes 9oz (250g)

While not technically a cheese, this delicious, creamy, plant-based alternative has a similar texture and flavor to soft cheeses made with dairy milk and can be used in much the same way.

½lb (225g) unroasted, unsalted cashew nuts
1 tbsp nutritional yeast flakes
juice of ½ lemon
1 tsp garlic powder
1 tsp onion powder
salt and freshly ground black pepper

1 | Put the cashews in a bowl and cover with plenty of cold water. Cover and leave overnight to soak.

2 | Drain the cashews through a strainer over a bowl. Once drained, reserve ⅓ cup (100ml) of the soaking liquid, discarding the rest.

3 | Put the cashews into a high-powered blender or food processor with the nutritional yeast, lemon juice, and garlic and onion powders. Blend until smooth-ish.

4 | With the motor running, slowly pour in the reserved water, until you have a thick dipping consistency (you may not need all of it).

5 | Season with salt and pepper to taste, then spoon into a small bowl to serve or into an airtight container to be used later. It will keep for up to 5 days in the fridge.

TIP

The cashew cheese works great as a swap for soft cheese in cooking, or as a dip with pita chips and crudités, or as a creamy spread.

CHICKEN

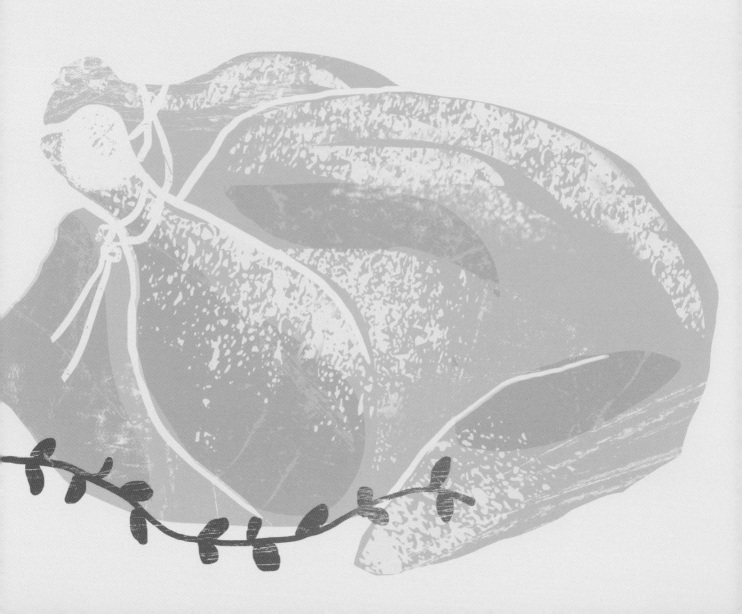

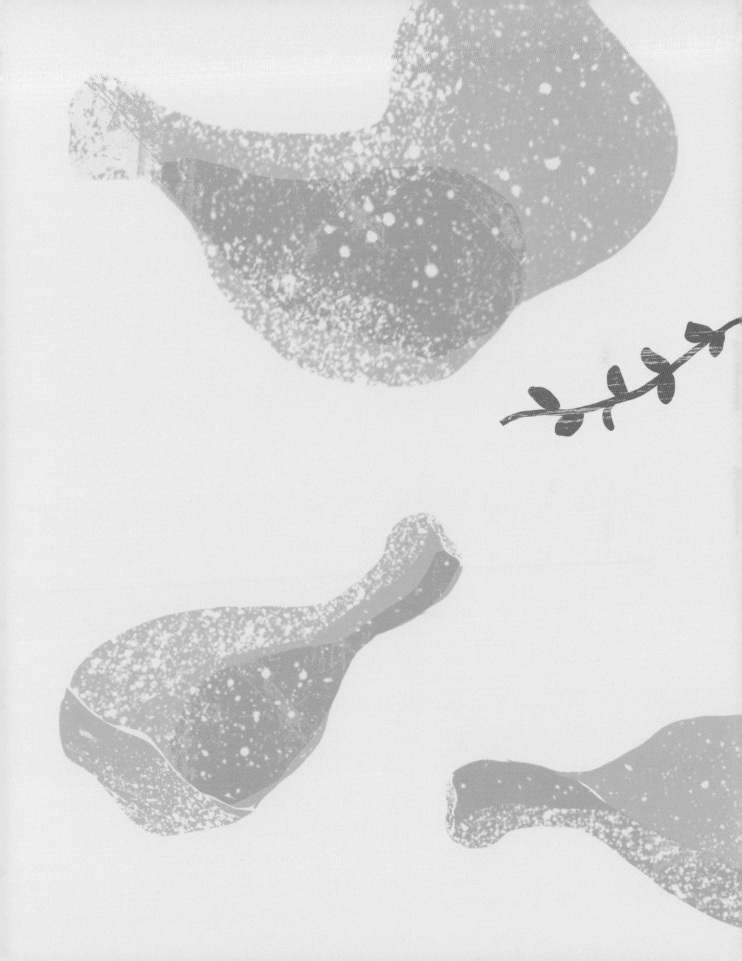

CHICKEN

The most popular type of poultry eaten worldwide, a whole chicken comprises predominantly lean white breast meat and richer-tasting dark leg meat. The high-protein, comparatively low-fat meat is incredibly versatile, equally suited to quick cooking methods, such as grilling or frying, as well as those that adopt a more relaxed style, including slow-roasting or braising. Its relatively mild flavor makes chicken a great vehicle for strong marinades, herbs, spices, and sauces, yet the whole bird can still shine when simply seasoned and roasted until the skin is crisp and golden (right). A chicken can be cooked whole, spatchcocked (see p.80), or jointed (see p.76) and we have covered these useful techniques in the following chapter. For the best flavor, choose the highest-quality bird you can afford. Organic birds tend to be reared longer, with a better diet and more space to grow, resulting in well-developed, more tasty meat than a non-free-range bird. When buying a whole chicken, look for one that looks plump with firm, dry skin.

Always wash your hands and any kitchen equipment and surfaces thoroughly with hot, soapy water and a kitchen sanitizer after handling raw chicken.

Storage

Store uncooked chicken in the fridge for up to 2–3 days, depending on its use-by date. Remove chicken from its packaging and use paper towels to pat it dry to remove as much moisture as possible, then keep it covered with plastic wrap on a plate—or in a large airtight container if spatchcocked because it will fit better in your fridge this way. To defrost a frozen chicken, place it on a plate or in a shallow bowl in the fridge for about 5 hours or overnight, until defrosted. Make sure raw meat is kept separate from cooked food, preferably at the bottom of the fridge, to avoid cross-contamination.

Cooked chicken will keep for up to 4 days, covered, in the fridge, then eat cold or reheat thoroughly until piping hot.

ROASTING A CHICKEN

When cooked correctly, a roast chicken is a simple, delicious pleasure. Getting it right can be a fine balance between cooking the meat thoroughly to avoid the risk of food poisoning and not allowing it to become dry in the process. Cooking temperatures, timing, and methods can vary depending on which recipe you follow, but the roast chicken recipe (right), ensures that perfect combination of golden, crisp skin and succulent, juicy meat. A chicken benefits from rubbing with olive oil or butter before roasting to keep it moist as well as resting the bird after cooking to allow the juices to redistribute in the meat.

CHICKEN	ROASTING TIMES (450°F/230°C)
Whole bird	15 minutes per 1lb (450g)
Breast	15 minutes per 1lb (450g)
Legs	40–45 minutes
Thighs (bone in, skin on)	30–40 minutes
Wings	30–45 minutes

SIMPLE SALTED ROAST CHICKEN

Prep 5 minutes + resting

Cook 50 minutes

Serves 4

This method of roasting chicken is high and fast, ensuring you get crisp, golden skin and juicy, succulent meat. Some people prefer the low-and-slow method; however, this can lead to the chicken drying out before the skin gets a chance to crisp up. The table (left) will help you work out the cooking time of your chicken according to its weight—this 3lb (1.5kg) chicken takes roughly 50 minutes to roast and feeds 4 people, so is an excellent starting point.

3lb (1.5kg) whole chicken, removed from the fridge 15 minutes before roasting
1 tbsp olive oil
1 tbsp sea salt flakes
1 tsp freshly ground black pepper

1 | Preheat the oven to 450°F (230°C). Put the whole chicken, breast-side up, in a large roasting pan, rub the olive oil all over, then sprinkle with the salt and pepper.

2 | Put the roasting pan in the center of the oven for 50 minutes, basting the chicken with the pan juices halfway. Check to see if your oven has a noticeable hot spot at the same time and turn the tray if needed. Roast the chicken until a meat thermometer reads 160°F (70°C) and the juices run clear when the thickest part of the thigh is pierced with a skewer or small knife; there should be no sign of any blood or pinkness. If the chicken hasn't reached the correct temperature inside or the juices aren't running clear, return it to the oven and test again after 10 minutes.

3 | When ready, the chicken should be cooked through but still remain juicy and succulent. Cover the chicken loosely with foil (you don't want the steam to soften the crispy skin) and leave it to rest for 15 minutes before carving (see p.70) This allows the juices in the chicken to redistribute, which means relaxed, succulent meat. Save the chicken juices from the roasting pan to make the Gravy (see p.418).

CARVING A ROAST CHICKEN

Carving is a great technique to learn so your lovingly roasted chicken can be neatly presented without fear of waste. A large chef's knife works well so you can get good purchase on the bird and make long precise cuts.

1 | Put the roasted chicken on a cutting board with the legs nearest you. Using a large, sharp chef's knife, cut along the skin between the leg and the breast, gently prizing the leg away from the breast, until you can slice around the leg joint, cutting it neatly away from the body of the chicken. Repeat with the second leg. Put the leg onto the cutting board and cut down on the joint between the drumstick and thigh.

2 | To remove the wings, pull each one out from either side of the breast and cut through the joint that attaches them to the body of the chicken.

3 | Run your finger along the breastbone, which runs from top to bottom, then make a long cut parallel to the bone down one side to free the breast from the bone. Holding the breast in one hand, and gently teasing it away from the bone, keep cutting until you have completely removed the breast. Repeat on the other side to remove the second breast.

4 | Cut the breast into equal slices on the diagonal, then arrange on a warmed serving dish with the legs and wings and take to the table. Keep the carcass and any juices for Chicken Stock (see p.414) and leftover meat recipes (below).

Leftover roast chicken

Roasting a whole chicken potentially provides you with multiple meals. This technique explains how to strip any leftover roasted chicken meat off the carcass.

1 | Place the carved chicken carcass, breast-side up and facing you, on a cutting board. Run your fingers along one side of the breastbone and use your thumbs to press lightly yet firmly onto the bone to prize away any leftover white meat. Repeat on the other side.

2 | Flip the chicken so that the breast faces downward on the cutting board. Feel along the backbone for two small pockets where the main body of the chicken once joined the legs. Push gently down into the pockets to remove the oyster meat.

3 | Continue to work your way around the carcass, concentrating on the areas where the joints meet the body of the chicken to remove any leftover meat with your fingertips. If you have a thigh or drumstick left from your roast chicken, peel away the chicken skin then hold the main bone in one hand and use a downward pulling action to strip away all the meat, leaving the bone behind.

4 | Once you've removed all visible strips of meat, either use it right away or keep, covered, in the fridge for up to 2 days. Place the remaining carcass in a large saucepan and follow the recipe on p.414 for making Chicken Stock. Use the leftover chicken in the recipes on pp.72–75.

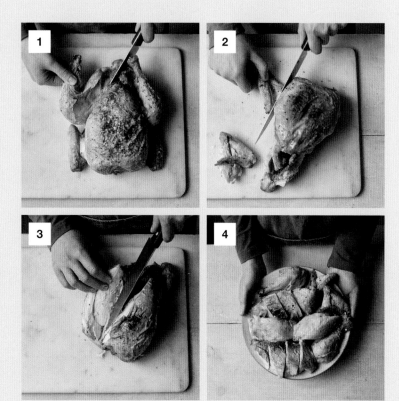

Harissa sticky chicken thighs

Prep 5 minutes

Cook 45 minutes

Serves 4

These chicken thighs are sure to become one of your recipe staples. Once roasted, they have a crispy, sticky skin with soft, unctuous meat. This recipe calls for longer, slower cooking at a lower oven temperature than that of the Simple Salted Roast Chicken (see p.69) because the harissa and honey coating can burn if the oven is too high. Harissa is a chili paste originating from North Africa and gives the thighs a spicy, sweet flavor.

8 whole skin-on, bone-in chicken thighs
1 tbsp vegetable oil
salt and freshly ground black pepper
3 tbsp harissa paste
1 tbsp honey
Roast Squash with Chili-Honey Dressing & Labneh
  (see p.60), to serve

1 | Preheat the oven to 400°F (200°C). Place the chicken thighs into a large roasting pan, drizzle over the oil and season generously with salt and pepper. Put the tray in the oven for 20 minutes, until the skin begins to crisp.

2 | Remove the chicken thighs from the oven and add the harissa. Mix well until the chicken is evenly coated in the oil and harissa, then put the tray back into the oven for 20 minutes, until the chicken skin is crisp and golden.

3 | Drizzle the honey over the thighs and roast for another 5 minutes, until they are sticky and glazed. Serve with the squash and labneh salad.

Chicken, preserved lemon & chickpea soup

Prep 15 minutes

Cook 30 minutes

Serves 4

Once you've stripped any leftover roast chicken meat from its carcass (see p.70) and perhaps made your stock (see p.414), what better way to use your leftovers than in a spiced soup? Don't be put off by the number of ingredients, this soup utilizes your pantry, with fragrant warmth coming from the ground spices. Serve topped with a spoonful of an optional, but highly recommended, super-zingy parsley Gremolata (see p.443).

2 tbsp olive oil

1 large onion, peeled and chopped

2 medium carrots, peeled and chopped

½lb (200g) Tuscan kale, stalks finely sliced and leaves stripped and sliced

pinch of salt, plus extra to season

3 garlic cloves, peeled and finely chopped

2 tsp sweet smoked paprika

2 tsp ground cumin

1 tsp ground turmeric

½ tsp ground cinnamon

2 tbsp tomato paste

4¼ cups (1 liter) Chicken Stock (see p.414), or store-bought

2 (15.5oz/400g) cans chickpeas, save the liquid

10oz (300g) leftover cooked chicken meat from Simple Salted Roast Chicken (see p.69), cut into strips

3 Preserved Lemons (see p.460) or store-bought, flesh removed and pith finely chopped

freshly ground black pepper

1 recipe quantity of Gremolata (see p.443), optional, to serve

1 | Heat the olive oil in a large saucepan over medium heat. Add the onion, carrots, and Tuscan kale stalks with a pinch of salt. Cook, stirring regularly for 10–12 minutes, until the vegetables soften.

2 | Add the garlic and cook, stirring, for 1 minute, then add the spices and tomato paste. Cook, stirring constantly, for another minute until the onion is coated in the spices and the tomato paste, then pour in the chicken stock.

3 | Bring the soup to a simmer, add the chickpeas along with the liquid from the cans and the Tuscan kale leaves. Simmer, stirring occasionally, for 10 minutes, until the kale is tender.

4 | Add the cooked chicken and the preserved lemons to the soup. Simmer for a further 3–5 minutes, until the chicken is warmed through.

5 | Season the soup to taste with extra salt and pepper, then ladle into four bowls and top with a spoonful of gremolata, if using, to serve. The soup will keep for up to 2 days in the fridge or freeze for up to 3 months. Reheat thoroughly after defrosting.

TIP

This soup is great for using up whatever leftovers you have in the fridge or pantry, so if you have white beans rather than chickpeas, feel free to use them instead. Similarly, rainbow chard, spinach, or regular kale make a great substitute for the Tuscan kale.

Chicken, leek & mustard pie

*Prep 10 minutes
+ cooling*

Cook 50 minutes

Serves 4

Pie is the ultimate comfort food and using roasted chicken meat is a winning shortcut for both time and effort. Here, the quality of your chicken stock will also make a big difference, so it's a great recipe to try if you've made your own. Flour is added to the buttery leeks to create a roux to thicken the filling, much like the one used to make the White Sauce (see p.40). If you don't have leftover roast chicken, you could use ready-cooked meat.

3 tbsp (50g) salted butter
2 medium leeks, halved lengthwise and finely sliced
pinch of salt, plus extra to season
4 garlic cloves, peeled and finely sliced
1 handful of thyme, leaves stripped
1 tbsp all-purpose flour
1½ cups (350ml) Chicken Stock (see p.414) or
  store-bought
10oz (300g) leftover cooked chicken meat from Simple
  Salted Roast Chicken (see p.69), shredded

1½ tbsp wholegrain mustard
⅔ cup (150g) full-fat crème fraîche or sour cream
1 large egg, at room temperature, lightly beaten
1 sheet pre-rolled puff pastry
freshly ground black pepper
Mashed Potatoes (see p.171) and veggies, to serve

1 | Melt the butter in a large, deep skillet over medium heat. Add the leeks and a pinch of salt and cook, stirring regularly, for 8 minutes, until softened. Add the garlic and thyme and cook, stirring, for a further 2 minutes, then sprinkle over the flour. Cook for 1 minute, stirring constantly so the leeks are evenly coated in the flour, then pour in the chicken stock.

2 | Bring the stock to a simmer, then add the cooked chicken to the pan along with the mustard and crème fraîche. Give everything a good stir, then remove the pan from the heat. Season to taste with extra salt and pepper. Leave the filling to cool if time allows.

3 | Preheat the oven to 400°F (200°C). Spoon the chicken pie filling into a medium pie dish, about 9 x 13 in (30 x 20 cm). Brush the beaten egg along the edge of the dish (this will help the pastry lid stick to the dish). Place the sheet of puff pastry on top, pressing it down to seal and leaving a ½-in (1-cm) overhang around the edge. Brush the pastry top with beaten egg. Using a small, sharp knife, cut a ¾-in (2-cm) cross in the center of the pastry lid (this will allow steam to escape and help the pastry crisp).

4 | Bake the pie for 20–25 minutes, until the pastry is well risen and deep golden brown. Leave to cool for a few minutes, then serve with mashed potatoes and your choice of vegetables.

TIP

For a crisp, golden pie, make the filling ahead, then leave it to cool and chill for 30 minutes (or even up to a day ahead), before topping with the pastry lid—this will ensure the pastry doesn't become soggy underneath.

Sesame chicken salad

Prep 15 minutes

No cook

Serves 2

Fresh, zingy, and vibrant, this salad shows how you can take a roast chicken and turn it into something entirely different. Texturally, this recipe benefits from some crispy roast chicken skin, so if you can, save a whole thigh or drumstick. To crisp up the skin, place it in a roasting pan in the oven preheated to 425°F (220°C). You can even reheat the dark meat for 15 minutes at the same time.

½lb (250g) leftover cooked chicken meat from Simple Salted Roast Chicken (see p.69), shredded
1 celery stalk, finely sliced
1 small carrot, peeled and cut into julienne (see p.163)
1 shallot, peeled and thinly sliced into rounds
1 cup (100g) red cabbage, very finely sliced
1 butter lettuce, roughly sliced
1 garlic clove, peeled and crushed
1½ cups (30g) cilantro, chopped
1 tbsp sesame seeds
juice of 1 lime

For the dressing
2 tbsp sesame oil
2 tbsp tamari or light soy sauce
2 tbsp rice wine vinegar
½ tbsp red chili paste

1 | Mix all the ingredients for the dressing in a small bowl, whisking with a fork until well combined.

2 | Mix all the salad ingredients in a large serving bowl, pour the dressing over, and toss together with tongs so everything is evenly coated. Eat right away or allow the flavors to mingle, covering the bowl and chilling in the fridge. This can be done the day before—just allow the salad to come to room temperature before serving.

TIP

For a more substantial salad, add 3½oz (100g) of cooked rice noodles before tossing together.

JOINTING
A CHICKEN

Prep 15 minutes

No cook

Makes 1 chicken

This classic French technique shows you how to cut a whole chicken into 8 pieces to serve 4 people, so each person gets a piece of dark leg meat and a piece of white breast meat cooked on the bone. It is especially useful when braising a chicken for a stew or curry, or the pieces can be roasted, marinating them first if liked.

1 whole chicken, patted dry with paper towel

1 | Place the chicken, breast-side up, on a cutting board with the legs nearest you. Using a large, sharp chef's knife, cut along the skin between the leg and the breast. Using your hands, gently prize the leg away from the body, until you can cut around the ball and socket joint near the backbone, separating it from the crown, ensuring you cut around the oyster—a small, soft, round of meat on either side of the backbone at the top of the leg, keeping it attached to the leg. Repeat with the second leg.

2 | Put the leg onto the cutting board and cut down through the joint between the drumstick and thigh. Repeat with the other leg so you now have 4 chicken leg pieces.

3 | Place the chicken breast-side up with the neck end facing you, and use your fingers to locate the breastbone. Using the knife, cut along one side of the breastbone, freeing the meat from the bone.

4 | Now use large kitchen scissors or poultry shears to cut along the breastbone, following the cut you initially made along the breast, cutting from the tail end through to the wishbone. Use a small chef's knife to remove the wishbone.

5 | Put the chicken on its side and use a pair of scissors or poultry shears to cut through the ribs following a line of fat, down the body to the neck and around the wing joint. You will now have a single chicken breast on the bone with the wing attached. Repeat on the other side.

6 | Put both chicken breasts, skin-side up, on the cutting board and cut each breast in half, making a slight diagonal cut for a neater appearance. Repeat with the remaining breast piece to give 8 pieces of on-the-bone chicken to use as you wish. The chicken can be marinated at this point (see p.81), braised, roasted, or cooked to your liking.

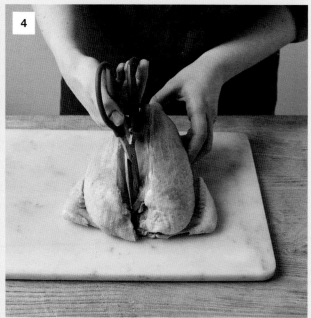

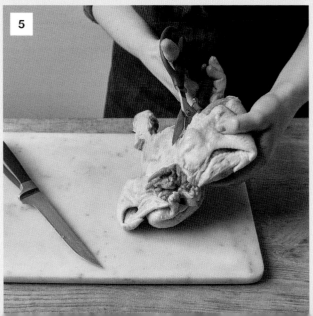

CHICKEN KIEV

Prep 30 minutes
+ freezing

Cook 20 minutes

Serves 2

The secret to a good Kiev is keeping all that garlicky, buttery filling inside the chicken while it cooks, and this magic combination of cooking methods ensures perfect results. First, fry the chicken breast until the outside is crisp and golden, then bake it in the oven until the meat is cooked through and the butter melts. Freezing the butter first also helps, allowing you the time to get a good crust on the outside of the chicken without the butter melting and escaping, effectively sealing it inside. It's also important to roll the breast tightly and secure with toothpicks (just remember to remove them before eating). While the butter melts, it helps poach and steam the chicken from the inside out, keeping it juicy and succulent.

¼ recipe quantity of Herby Garlic Butter (see p.48), softened
2 boneless, skinless chicken breasts
½ cup (50g) all-purpose flour
1 large egg, at room temperature, lightly beaten
½ cup (75g) panko breadcrumbs
salt and freshly ground black pepper
vegetable oil, for frying
Homemade French Fries (see p.192) and ketchup and/ or steamed broccoli and peas, to serve

1 | Beat the Herby Garlic Butter until soft using a wooden spoon, then place it on a piece of plastic wrap and shape into a rectangle, about 3 in (7.5 cm) wide and ¾ in (2 cm) thick. Wrap the butter in parchment paper and put it in the freezer for 1 hour, until firm.

2 | To butterfly the chicken breast (to open it out so it's an even thickness), place it on a cutting board with the thicker end away from you. Place one hand on the chicken breast and with the other use a sharp medium-size chef's knife to gently cut the chicken breast lengthwise down the middle of one side, taking care not to cut it all the way through.

3 | Open out the chicken breast and place a sheet of parchment paper on top to cover. Using the end of a rolling pin, pound the chicken breast out so it is an even ½ in (1 cm) thick. Repeat with the second chicken breast.

4 | Once the butter is really hard, carefully cut it in half. Put one portion of butter onto the widest end of the flattened chicken breast. Fold in the sides of the chicken breast to wrap around the butter, then tightly roll it up, so you have a cylindrical shape.

5 | Secure the chicken into a tight parcel and seal in the butter with 2 or 3 toothpicks. Repeat with the second chicken breast and portion of butter.

6 | Put the flour, beaten egg, and panko breadcrumbs into 3 separate, shallow bowls. Season the flour with salt and pepper. Roll each chicken breast first in the flour, shaking off any excess, then dip it into the egg until completely covered. Finally, place the chicken in the breadcrumbs, really pressing it into the crumbs to coat evenly. Repeat with the second breast.

7 | Meanwhile, fill a large, deep skillet with 1¼ in (3 cm) of oil and heat to 350°F (180°C) on a cooking thermometer, or until a cube of bread browns in 20 seconds. Once the oil is at the correct temperature, gently lower the chicken breasts into the hot oil and fry for 3 minutes, until well browned. Carefully turn the chicken over with a slotted spoon and cook for another 3 minutes, until brown and crisp. Carefully lift out onto a paper-towel-lined plate to drain, then season with salt and remove the toothpicks.

8 | Meanwhile, line a baking sheet with parchment paper and heat the oven to 400°F (200°C). Place the fried chicken on the lined baking sheet into the oven for 8–10 minutes, depending on the size of your chicken breasts, until golden brown and crisp on the outside and the inside is cooked through, succulent, and juicy. Serve right away with fries and ketchup and/ or steamed broccoli and peas.

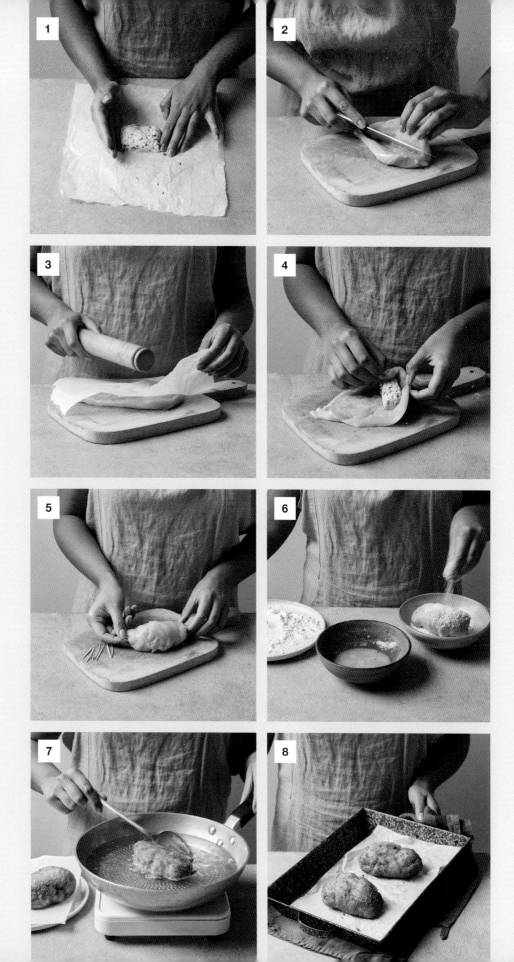

SPATCHCOCKING A CHICKEN

Prep 10 minutes

No cook

Makes 1 chicken

Spatchcocking involves removing the spine or backbone of a chicken to create a large, flat, even cooking surface, resulting in a bird that takes much less time to roast or grill than normal as well as one that is much easier to cook to perfection—two great reasons to try this useful technique.

1 whole chicken, patted dry with paper towel

1 | Place the chicken, breast-side down, on a large cutting board, with the tail end away from you. At the base of the chicken body you will see a fleshy stub known as the parson's nose.

2 | Hold the parson's nose firmly in one hand and using a large chef's knife, sharp kitchen scissors, or poultry shears, cut closely along one side of the backbone, up to the chicken's neck, and cutting through the ribcage.

3 | Repeat on the other side to completely remove the spine.

4 | Turn the chicken over, so it is now breast-side up on the cutting board, and open it out. Gently press the breastbone with your hands to flatten the chicken to an even thickness.

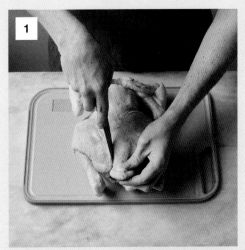

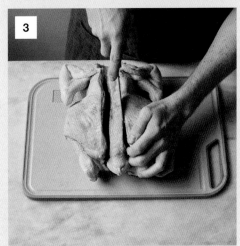

TIP

To hold a spatchcocked chicken flat while cooking, insert two diagonal skewers through the chicken. To do this, place the chicken, breast-side up on a cutting board with the legs nearest you. Take one skewer and from the outside of the right leg, pierce through, continuing through the leg and up to the left-hand breast, and exiting the chicken by the wing on the left-hand side. Repeat on the other side.

MARINATING CHICKEN

Due to its neutral taste and light color, chicken is perfect for marinating, becoming extra tender and readily taking on the flavor of the marinade it is bathed in. It's best to leave the chicken to marinate for at least 1 hour to work its magic, but 8 hours or overnight is even better. Adding an acidic ingredient to a marinade will help tenderize the chicken, as here with the use of citrus and yogurt in the Spiced Yogurt Marinade. This is a technique that is also used in the Buttermilk Chicken Tenders (see p.46).

Easy marinades

Cajun marinade

In a large mixing bowl, mix 1 tablespoon ground cumin with 1 tablespoon sweet smoked paprika, 2 teaspoons garlic powder, 1 teaspoon dried oregano, the juice and finely grated zest of 1 unwaxed lemon, and 2 tablespoons extra-virgin olive oil. Season well with salt and pepper and add 8 chicken thighs or 1 spatchcocked chicken (left) or 1 whole chicken, jointed into 8 pieces (see p.76). Mix well to combine and coat the chicken in the marinade. Cover and leave to marinate for at least 1 hour or ideally overnight.

Soy & ginger marinade

In a large mixing bowl, finely grate in 4 peeled garlic cloves and a 2-in piece of peeled fresh ginger. Cut 1 red chile in half and add to the bowl with 2 green onions, cut into 1-in (2.5-cm) pieces. Add 4 tablespoons of dark soy sauce and 2 tablespoons of light brown sugar. Add 1 tablespoon toasted sesame oil and the juice and finely grated zest of 1 lime. Season well with salt and pepper and add 8 chicken thighs or 1 spatchcocked chicken (left) or 1 whole chicken, jointed into 8 pieces (see p.76). Mix well to combine and coat the chicken in the marinade. Cover and leave to marinate for at least 1 hour or ideally overnight.

Spiced yogurt marinade

In a large mixing bowl, add ½ cup (100g) of Greek yogurt. Finely grate in 4 peeled garlic cloves and a 2-in piece of peeled fresh ginger. Add 2 teaspoons each of ground cumin, ground coriander, sweet smoked paprika, and turmeric powder. Mix in 1 tablespoon of garam masala, ½ teaspoon of cayenne pepper, and the juice and finely grated zest of 1 unwaxed lemon. Season well with salt and pepper and add 8 chicken thighs or 1 spatchcocked chicken (left) or 1 whole chicken, jointed into 8 pieces (see p.76). Mix well to combine and coat the chicken in the marinade. Cover and leave to marinate for at least 1 hour or ideally overnight.

Peri-peri spatchcock chicken

Prep 20 minutes + marinating and resting

Cook 40 minutes

Serves 4

This gives you two techniques in one recipe: spatchcocking chicken and marinating. Peri-peri is hugely popular and for good reason, the spicy chile sauce packs a serious flavor punch and works perfectly as a marinade. Here, the chicken is marinated then broiled, rather than roasted, for maximum smoky flavor and crispy golden skin. There is also a barbecue option. Serve the chicken with the Lemony Pesto Potato Salad (see p.170) and/or the Alabama White Sauce Slaw (see p.165).

1 tbsp sweet smoked paprika
2 tsp dried oregano
2 red chiles, chopped, seeded if preferred
3 roasted red peppers from a jar, drained
juice of 2 limes
4 green onions, chopped
3 garlic cloves, peeled and roughly chopped
salt and freshly ground black pepper
1 Spatchcocked Chicken (see p.80)
1 tbsp olive oil

1 | Into the pitcher of a high-powered blender, add the paprika, oregano, chiles, roasted red peppers, lime juice, green onions, and garlic. Season with plenty of salt and pepper, then blend until smooth.

2 | Follow steps 1–4 from Spatchcocking a Chicken (see p.80). Put the spatchcocked chicken, breast-side up, in a large mixing bowl or a large ovenproof dish and pour over the marinade. Mix well so the chicken is completely coated. Cover and chill in the fridge for at least 1 hour or overnight.

3 | When ready to cook the chicken, preheat the broiler to medium-high, about 425°F (220°C), and place the rack underneath in the middle of the oven. Uncover the chicken and turn it so it is breast-side down in a large roasting pan. Stir 1 cup (250ml) of water into the pan. Broil the chicken for 20 minutes, checking regularly, until golden and blackened in places.

4 | Turn the chicken so the breast is facing upward and then drizzle with the olive oil. Broil for another 15–20 minutes, until the skin is bubbling, golden, and crisp and the chicken is cooked through. Leave the chicken to rest for 5 minutes before serving.

Barbecue variation

To cook the marinated spatchcocked chicken you will need a grill with a lid.

1 | Heap the coals to one side of the grill and light. You are ready to cook once the flames have died down and you are left with red-hot coals. Put the grill rack roughly 12 in (30 cm) above the coals. Remove the chicken from the marinade, gently brushing it to remove any excess. Save the remaining marinade in the bowl or dish.

2 | Put the chicken, breast-side up, on the grill rack over the half without the coals underneath. Put the lid on and cook for 30–45 minutes, rotating the chicken now and again so it cooks evenly and basting with some of the marinade in the bowl.

3 | Turn the chicken, breast-side down, and place it directly over the hot coals. Cook for 10–15 minutes, basting it regularly with some of the marinade, until the skin is crisp and the chicken is cooked through.

4 | Meanwhile, pour any remaining marinade into a small saucepan and heat gently over medium heat for 10 minutes. Serve the peri-peri sauce spooned over the chicken.

Jerk chicken wings

*Prep 10 minutes
+ marinating*

*Cook 1 hour
10 minutes*

Serves 4

Although it's not the national dish of Jamaica, jerk chicken has emerged as one of the most recognized foods of the country. Traditionally cooked in a smoky fire pit with pimento wood, this version sacrifices authenticity for a more readily accessible high oven, so this popular street food can be made in the home kitchen.

2¾lb (1.25kg) chicken wings
3½ tbsp ready-made wet jerk seasoning (heat of choice), divided
1 green onion, white and green parts separated, finely chopped
1 tsp onion powder
1 tbsp garlic powder
½ tbsp coarsely ground black pepper
3 tbsp barbecue sauce
2 limes, cut into quarters

1 | Using a large, sharp chef's knife, make 1 or 2 diagonal incisions into each chicken wing and place in a large mixing bowl.

2 | Add 3 tablespoons of the jerk seasoning, the white part of the green onion, onion powder, garlic powder, and black pepper to the bowl. Using your hands (wear disposable gloves, if you prefer), massage the marinade into the chicken wings, ensuring you get the mixture into all of the cuts. Cover the bowl and leave to marinate in the fridge for at least 1 hour, preferably overnight.

3 | When ready to cook, preheat the oven to 400°F (200°C). Line a large baking sheet with parchment paper (or use a roasting tray with a rack) and place the marinated wings in the tray. It doesn't matter if they can't be spread out completely or if they are touching. Keep any remaining marinade for later. Once the oven is hot, roast the wings for 30 minutes.

4 | Meanwhile, add the barbecue sauce and remaining ½ tablespoon of wet jerk seasoning to the leftover marinade in the bowl and stir to combine.

5 | After 30 minutes, remove the tray from the oven. Using a pastry brush or spoon, coat the top of the wings with half of the marinade mixture. Place the tray back in the oven for 20–25 minutes, until the chicken is turning brown and glossy.

6 | Remove the tray from the oven, turn the wings over, then coat them with the remaining marinade mixture. Return to the oven and cook for another 10 minutes. The wings should now be deep brown and starting to char in places.

7 | Turn the oven up to 425°F (220°C), turn the chicken wings over again and cook for a final 5 minutes, until dark brown and sticky all over.

8 | Remove the wings from the baking sheet, place on a wire rack and leave to cool for a few minutes. Serve the wings topped with the remaining green part of the green onion and lime wedges for squeezing over.

POACHING CHICKEN

This gentle method involves slowly cooking the chicken in liquid on a low temperature, which keeps the meat succulent and tender while imparting flavor from the poaching liquid. This method is best suited to lean white meat, such as chicken, because it is less likely to toughen once cooked. Be sure to monitor the temperature throughout because boiling the bird will lead to overcooked dry meat.

CHICKEN IN BROTH

Prep 15 minutes

Cook 1½ hours

Serves 4

This is a two-for-one recipe in that you get a perfectly tender poached chicken as well as a beautifully light and flavorful chicken broth/stock. Win-win! The chicken can be served simply in the clear broth, perhaps with some fresh herbs sprinkled over, or in the Chicken Orzo Soup (see p.86), or each used separately.

2 white or red onions, peeled and roughly chopped
1 medium carrot, peeled and roughly sliced
2 celery stalks, roughly sliced
1 garlic bulb, halved horizontally
1 tsp whole black peppercorns
3 bay leaves (fresh or dried)
1 handful of flat-leaf parsley, leaves and stalks
1 whole chicken, about 3½lb (1.6kg), patted dry
    with paper towel
pinch of salt

1 | Put all of the ingredients into your largest saucepan or Dutch oven, add a big pinch of salt and pour in enough cold water to cover, about 8–10 cups (2.5 liters). Bring to a boil over medium-high heat, skimming off and discarding any white foam that rises to the surface of the water with a spoon. Reduce the heat to medium-low so the water is just simmering. Gently poach the chicken, uncovered, occasionally skimming off any foam that rises to the surface, for 1 hour, until the juices run clear when the chicken is pierced with a skewer into the thickest part of the leg.

2 | Carefully transfer the chicken to a plate with the help of 2 spatulas, cover with foil, and leave it to rest for 20 minutes.

3 | Carve the chicken (see p.70), removing the skin, then use two forks to shred the meat into pieces. Strain the chicken broth through a metal strainer into a medium saucepan, discarding the solids in the strainer, then put the pan back on high heat and let it bubble away for 15 minutes, until reduced by a third, about 6½ cups (1.5 liters) of broth/stock. Use right away or store in the fridge for up to 3 days, or freeze.

Chicken orzo soup

Prep 30 minutes

Cook 1¾ hours

Serves 4

This simple chicken and pasta soup feels super nourishing and healthy. The poached leftover chicken and stock are the stars of the show, while the orzo adds sustenance for a more substantial meal. To save time, you can use precooked chicken and a good-quality store-bought chicken stock, if preferred.

1 Chicken in Broth (see p.85)—you will need 10oz (300g) of shredded cooked chicken and 6½ cups (1.5 liters) of broth
5oz (125g) dried orzo pasta
½lb (200g) baby spinach leaves
juice and finely grated zest of 1 unwaxed lemon
salt and freshly ground black pepper
½ cup (50g) finely grated Parmesan cheese
1 handful of basil, leaves picked
extra-virgin olive oil, to drizzle

1 | Follow steps 1–5 from Chicken in Broth (see p.85), saving 10oz (300g) of the shredded chicken meat for this recipe and 6½ cups (1.5 liters) of the poaching broth/stock.

2 | Bring the poaching broth to a boil in a large saucepan over high heat. Add the orzo and cook for 6–8 minutes, stirring occasionally to stop the pasta sticking to the bottom of the pan, until it is just tender.

3 | Add the spinach and poached chicken meat and cook for 2–3 minutes, stirring, until the spinach wilts and the chicken is warmed through, then squeeze in the lemon juice and season with salt and pepper to taste.

4 | Ladle the soup into four bowls and top with the lemon zest, Parmesan, basil leaves, a drizzle of olive oil, and extra black pepper before serving.

TIP

The soup will keep for up to 2 days in the fridge or can be frozen in individual portions (save takeout containers for this) for up to 3 months. Defrost the soup in a pan on the lowest heat with an extra ⅔ cup (150ml) of water, then cook on high for 10 minutes.

FRYING & GRILLING CHICKEN

Chicken lends itself wonderfully to frying, whether that's in a skillet, in a grill pan, or deep-fried. Since it is such a lean, low-fat meat, these quick methods of cooking allow the chicken to retain its juicy, tender texture, while developing a slightly caramelized, golden exterior. Cooking in a grill pan additionally lends a slight grilled flavor and characteristic stripes from the ridged pan.

Deep-frying can be a little intimidating for beginner cooks, but there are plenty of tips in the Homemade Crispy Fried Chicken (see p.90) recipe to help you feel as reassured as possible. For starters, only pour in enough oil to half-fill your pan. Adding uncooked food to hot oil causes it to bubble and splatter, so you don't want to overfill the pan. Make sure you have everything set up before you start frying—the food ready to go into the hot oil, a slotted spatula or scoop, and a paper-towel-lined tray or plate for draining. A multi-function digital cooking thermometer or a deep-fry thermometer is a real asset because it will help you heat the oil to the right temperature for deep-frying, ensuring that whatever you're cooking becomes crisp and golden, rather than soggy, or at the other end of the scale burned, and overcooked.

GRILLED CHICKEN SANDWICHES

Prep 10 minutes

Cook 15 minutes

Serves 2

Chicken breasts in particular lend themselves to this hard-and-fast method of cooking, ensuring the lean white meat remains juicy and the outside becomes golden brown and lightly caramelized. This chicken burger comes with all the extras and hits all the right spots, as well as making a healthier option than most takeout alternatives.

2 boneless, skinless chicken breasts
salt and freshly ground black pepper
2 tsp ground cumin
1 tbsp olive oil
2 tsp honey

To serve
2 seeded brioche burger buns, halved
2 tbsp Mayonnaise (see p.420) or store-bought
4 tbsp Zhoug (see p.445) or store-bought
1 butter lettuce, leaves separated
½ cucumber, peeled into ribbons
2 green onions, green and white parts, finely
   sliced

1 | Put the chicken breasts on a sheet of parchment paper on a cutting board, placing them slightly apart to allow room for spreading. Cover the chicken breasts with a second sheet of parchment paper.

2 | Using the end of a rolling pin, pound the chicken breasts between the layers of parchment paper until they are an even ¾ in (2 cm) thick.

3 | Place a grill pan or large nonstick skillet over high heat. While the pan heats, season the chicken generously on both sides with salt, pepper, and ground cumin, then drizzle with the olive oil.

4 | Once the pan is visibly hot and smoking, place the chicken breasts in the grill pan and cook for 3–4 minutes on each side, without moving them too much, until cooked through, juicy, and nicely charred.

5 | Once the chicken is cooked, turn the heat off underneath the pan and spoon over the honey. This will lightly caramelize one side of the chicken, then transfer the chicken breasts to a plate to briefly rest, loosely covered in foil.

6 | Using the residual heat of the pan, toast the cut sides of the brioche buns. To assemble, spread the mayonnaise across the bottom of each bun and half of the zhoug on the underside of each bun top. Place the lettuce on the mayonnaise, then top with the chicken and the remaining zhoug, the cucumber, and green onions, then finish with the bun tops.

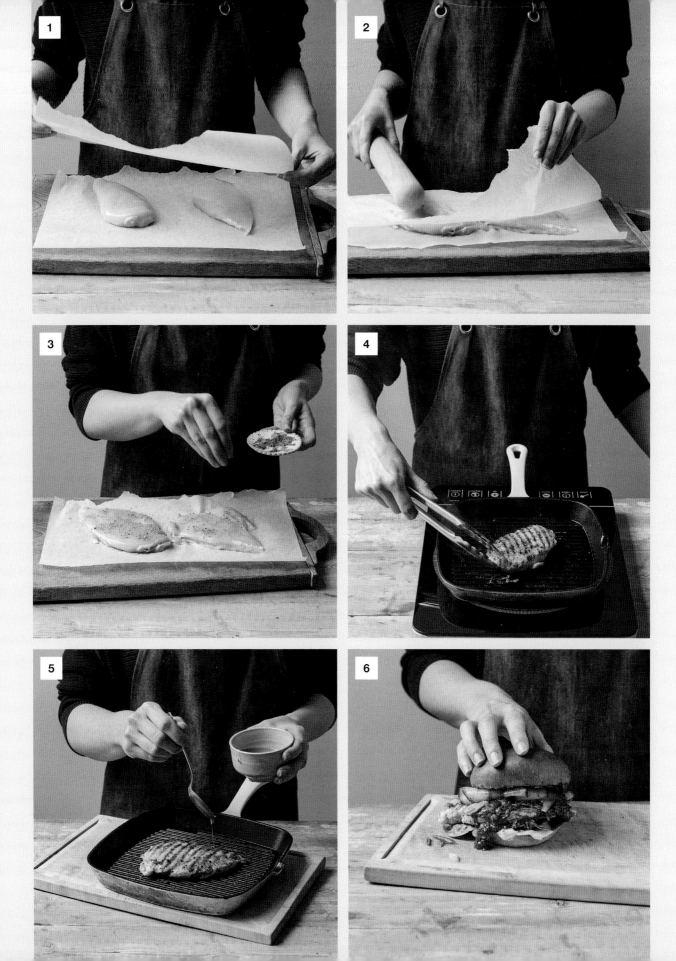

HOMEMADE
CRISPY FRIED CHICKEN

*Prep 10 minutes
+ marinating*

Cook 30 minutes

Serves 4

Once you've made this at home, you'll never settle for the fast-food alternative again. The buttermilk marinade helps tenderize the chicken, while the dusting of herb-and-spice flour becomes a flavorful crispy, golden crust when fried. If you don't have buttermilk on hand, you can make your own (see p.456). Traditional fried chicken is on the bone, but boneless, skinless chicken thighs make a good alternative because they are easier and quicker to cook and still keep their juiciness. This recipe goes perfectly with the Alabama White Sauce Slaw (see p.165).

8 boneless, skinless chicken thighs
1¼ cups (300ml) buttermilk
4 tbsp cornichon or dill pickle brine
1¼ cups (150g) all-purpose flour
2 tsp dried oregano
2 tsp dried basil (optional)
1 tbsp garlic powder
1 tbsp onion powder
1 tbsp mustard powder
3 tbsp paprika (not smoked)
2 tsp ground ginger
1 tsp fine sea salt, plus extra for seasoning
2 tbsp freshly ground black pepper, plus extra for
   seasoning
vegetable oil, for deep-frying

1 | Put the chicken thighs on a sheet of parchment paper on a cutting board. Open them out, then put a second piece of parchment paper on top to cover, and use the end of a rolling pin to pound the thighs so they are an even ¾ in (2 cm) thick.

2 | Pour the buttermilk into a medium mixing bowl, spoon in the pickle brine, and season with salt and pepper. Add the chicken thighs and mix well until they are coated. Cover and chill in the fridge for at least 1 hour or overnight.

3 | When you are ready to cook the chicken thighs, mix together the flour with all the herbs and spices, salt, and pepper in a wide, shallow bowl. Line 2 baking sheets with parchment paper and a large plate with paper towel.

4 | Working one piece at a time, remove a chicken thigh from the buttermilk and gently shake to remove any excess marinade. Put the chicken straight into the spiced flour, pressing it into the mixture to ensure it is coated all over. Arrange the chicken in a single layer on one of the lined baking sheets and repeat with the remaining chicken until all 8 thighs are coated.

5 | Meanwhile, half-fill a large, deep skillet or wok with oil, place over medium-high heat, and heat to 350°F (175°C) on a digital cooking thermometer or until a cube of bread browns in 30 seconds. Heat the oven to 325°F (160°C).

6 | Carefully lower 4 of the chicken pieces into the hot oil and cook for 3–4 minutes, until crisp and golden.

7 | Using tongs, turn the chicken in the pan and cook for another 3–4 minutes, until deeply golden brown and crisp. To test whether the chicken is cooked, cut into a thigh to make sure the inside is completely white with no traces of blood, or check with a meat thermometer—the inside should read 160°F (70°C) when ready.

8 | Using a slotted spoon or tongs, lift the chicken out of the pan onto the lined plate to drain briefly, sprinkle with salt, then move onto the clean parchment-paper-lined tray into the oven to keep warm while you fry the second batch of chicken.

Air-fryer variation
To air-fry the chicken instead of deep-frying, follow steps 1–3 until you have coated the thighs in the spiced flour mix. Heat the air-fryer to 350°F (180°C) and spray the basket well with cooking spray. Put 4 of the chicken thighs into the basket and spray with more oil, then cook for 10 minutes. Turn the chicken, spray again with oil and cook for another 8 minutes, until the chicken is cooked through and super crisp. Repeat with the remaining 4 chicken thighs.

TIP

When coating the chicken in the seasoned flour, use one hand to pick the chicken out of the wet marinade (your "wet" hand) and the other to dredge it in the flour (your "dry" hand), this will make the process more efficient and prevent your hands from getting covered in a sticky mass of flour.

BRAISING CHICKEN

This classic French technique involves what is known as combination cooking—you start by browning or searing the chicken to add color and flavor, then liquid is added to give moisture and allow the meat to cook slowly and gently. The secret is not to let the liquid boil for too long because this can toughen and dry out the chicken (the same applies to red meat).

When cooked at a gentle simmer, you will be rewarded with a richly flavored sauce that slowly intensifies as the chicken softens. Braising can be done on the stove top or in the oven, and it is usual for the ovenproof casserole or Dutch oven to be covered with a lid for some part of the cooking to avoid the liquid evaporating too much—you don't want it to be too dry.

CHICKEN CACCIATORE

Prep 25 minutes

Cook 1 hour 5 minutes

Serves 4

This rustic Italian dish, known as hunter's stew, is the perfect braise and great for using a whole jointed chicken because everyone can choose the cut of meat they prefer. If more convenient for you, use chicken thighs instead for an equally economical yet delicious meal. The sauce is rich from tomatoes and the chicken cooking juices and comes with a slight salty burst from the capers and olives. Serve with Ultimate Roast Potatoes (see p.174) or tagliatelle tossed in butter.

1 Jointed Chicken (see p.76) or 8 skin-on, bone-in chicken thighs
2 tbsp olive oil
salt and freshly ground black pepper
1 onion, peeled and cut into ½-in (1-cm) thick slices
1 red bell pepper, seeded and cut into ½-in (1-cm) thick slices
1 green bell pepper, seeded and cut into ½-in (1-cm) thick slices
4 garlic cloves, peeled and finely chopped
8 sprigs of thyme
1 tsp dried chili flakes (optional)
1 cup (250ml) red wine
2 (12oz/375g) cans cherry tomatoes
1 tsp sugar
2 tbsp capers, drained and rinsed
1 cup (100g) green olives, pitted and left whole
1 handful of flat-leaf parsley, leaves picked
Ultimate Roast Potatoes (see p.174) or tagliatelle tossed in butter, to serve

1 | Follow steps 1–7 from Jointing a Chicken (see p.76) or use 8 chicken thighs. Heat the olive oil in a large ovenproof casserole or Dutch oven over medium-high heat. Season the chicken with salt and pepper and brown it in batches of 3–4 pieces, depending on the size of your pan. Cook each thigh for 6–8 minutes, turning once, until the skin is crisp and golden. Place on a plate and set aside.

2 | Add the onion and peppers to the pan along with a pinch of salt and cook for 6–8 minutes over medium-high heat, stirring regularly, until the onion starts to soften and turn light golden.

3 | Add the garlic, thyme, and chili flakes, if using, and cook for 1 minute, stirring, then pour in the red wine. Bring to a boil and bubble for 2 minutes, then add the cherry tomatoes, sugar, capers, and olives and stir until combined.

4 | Add the browned chicken pieces back to the pan, along with any juices from the plate, then when the sauce starts to bubble, reduce the heat to low and simmer gently, uncovered, for 45 minutes, stirring every 15 minutes, until the chicken is cooked through. It should almost start to come away from the bone, and the sauce reduces to a rich tomato gravy.

5 | Sprinkle with parsley and serve with the roast potatoes or spooned over buttered tagliatelle.

TIP

This stew freezes well. Leave to cool, then divide into individual portions and freeze for up to 3 months. Defrost thoroughly before reheating in a small pan, covered with the lid, on medium heat until hot.

OTHER POULTRY

Chicken is the most popular type of poultry, but there are many others, including turkey, duck, and game birds, that offer cooks a multitude of cooking options. Turkey is typically the star of the meal during Thanksgiving as well as the festive season in many parts of the world. Like chicken, turkey is a lean form of protein and is available as a whole bird or as various cuts, including breast, legs, and ground. For recipes that call for ground turkey or chicken, they are interchangeable and will cook in the same length of time. Since a whole turkey is much larger than a chicken it requires a slightly different method of

roasting (below/right). Unlike chicken and turkey, duck contains a generous amount of fat with a rich flavor, which is perhaps more akin to red meat (see p.97).

Storage
As with chicken (see p.68), raw poultry should be handled and stored carefully. Always scrub the work surface or board and any knives you use to prepare or cut poultry with hot, soapy water and a kitchen sanitizer. When storing poultry in the fridge, make sure it is kept away from cooked food—the bottom half of the fridge is preferable.

ROASTING TURKEY

Before you embark on roasting your turkey (right), here are a few tips to help ensure you have a delicious, succulent bird with crisp, golden skin.

Preparation
To help dry the skin and ensure well flavored, juicy meat, season the bird with salt, inside and out, and leave uncovered in the fridge overnight. Turkeys are big birds so they need plenty of seasoning and time for it to penetrate the flesh.

On the day
Remove the turkey from the fridge 1 hour before roasting and spread butter under the skin. Turkey breast meat is very lean, so putting butter under the skin helps keep it juicy and succulent, basting the meat as it cooks. If your turkey is larger than 8lb (4kg), increase the butter and flavorings by 1½ times.

Roasting
A whole turkey is a large bird, so starting the oven on high, then reducing it will help the heat penetrate the meat and ensure the skin crisps up. Large sheets of foil placed over the bird during roasting help trap this heat and keep in moisture in the way of steam, making for a more gentle cook. For the best bird, test if the turkey is ready using a meat thermometer to probe the thickest part of the thigh—it should read 160°F (70°C). If you don't have a thermometer, pierce the thickest part of the turkey thigh using a metal skewer—the juices should run clear, not pink.

Resting
Turkey needs time to rest after roasting to allow it to relax and for any juices to redistribute, giving evenly juicy meat. A whole turkey will need around 45 minutes of resting time, whereas a turkey breast (boneless or bone-in) requires about 30 minutes.

TURKEY	ROASTING TIMES
Whole bird	Weigh the turkey and calculate 20 minutes + 30 minutes of cooking time per 2¼lb (1kg). Cook for 20 minutes at 425°F (220°C), then reduce the heat to 375°F (190°C) for the remaining cooking time.
Breast	Weigh the turkey breast and calculate 20 minutes + 40 minutes of cooking per 2¼lb (1kg). Cook for the full cooking time at 375°F (190°C).

ROASTING A TURKEY

Prep 15 minutes
+ overnight
chilling and
resting

Cook 2½ hours

Serves 6–8

Whether it is to do with its large size or the pressure of the occasion, preparing and roasting a turkey seems to strike fear into even the most confident of home cooks, but these steps for stress-free and successful roasting will result in a well-flavored and juicy bird. This recipe is for an 8lb (4kg) bird, serving 6–8 people, but do adapt according to the number you are cooking for, using the roasting chart (left) to calculate the roasting time.

8lb (4kg) whole turkey
½ cup (200g) salted butter, softened
salt and freshly ground black pepper
2 garlic cloves, peeled and finely grated
1 small bunch of flat-leaf parsley, finely chopped
3 onions, peeled and thickly sliced
vegetable oil, for rubbing
2 cups (500ml) white wine

1 | The night before roasting, remove all packaging from the turkey, pat dry with paper towel, and season really well with salt and pepper. Put the turkey onto a large plate or in a large roasting tray and leave uncovered in the bottom of the fridge overnight.

2 | Preheat the oven to 425°F (220°C). Put the softened butter into a small bowl and season with a little salt and pepper. Add the garlic and parsley, then beat with a wooden spoon until evenly combined and very soft. Starting from the neck, use clean hands to gently and carefully prize the skin away from the breast meat. Run your hands under the skin to create a pocket between the two, being careful not to tear the skin. Spread the seasoned butter evenly underneath the skin over the breast meat.

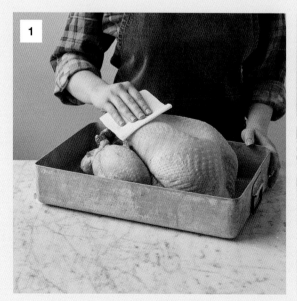

3 | Lay the onion slices in an even layer in the bottom of a large roasting tray, then put the turkey, breast-side-up, on top to raise it off the bottom of the tray. Rub the bird all over with vegetable oil and pour the wine around the turkey.

4 | Tear off 2 large sheets of foil and use this to create a tent over the turkey, making sure the foil doesn't touch the skin but it is tightly sealed around the edges of the tray. This will trap any steam and moisture around the bird as it roasts.

5 | Roast for 20 minutes, baste the turkey with pan juices, then reduce the heat to 375°F (190°C) for the remaining cooking time, about 2 hours. Remove the foil for the final 30 minutes of cooking, baste again, then cook to allow the skin to brown and crisp up.

6 | To test if the turkey is cooked through, use a digital meat thermometer to probe the thickest part of the thigh, it should read 160°F (70°C). Alternatively, pierce the thickest part of the turkey thigh using a metal skewer—the juices should run clear with no traces of pink.

7 | Move the turkey onto a large platter, cover with foil and leave to rest for 45 minutes. After resting, carve the turkey following the instructions for Carving a Roast Chicken (see p.70). Save the turkey juices from the roasting tray to make the Gravy (see p.418).

Pan-fried duck breast with five-spice plums

Prep 10 minutes

Cook 25 minutes

Serves 2

Fruit and duck is a classic combination and with good reason—the slight sharpness of the plums helps cut through the richness of the duck meat, while contributing to the sweet, sticky sauce.

2 skin-on duck breasts
salt and freshly ground black pepper
4 plums, halved and stones removed
2 tsp Chinese five-spice powder
1 cup (200ml) Chicken Stock (see p.414) or
  store-bought

3 tbsp red wine vinegar
3 tbsp light brown sugar
Sesame Green Bean & Sugar Snap Salad
  (see p.168), to serve

1 | Using a small, sharp knife, score the skin of each duck breast, making shallow cuts across the skin on a diagonal at ½-in (1-cm) intervals, taking care not to cut into the meat. Season well with salt and pepper.

2 | Heat the oven to 400°F (200°C). While the oven is heating, put the duck breasts, skin-side down, in a cold, medium, ovenproof skillet and place over medium-high heat. Once the pan is hot, you should be able to hear the fat from the duck starting to sizzle. Cook the duck for 5–6 minutes, until the skin is crisp and deeply golden brown. Take the pan off the heat.

3 | Put the duck breasts, skin-side up, on a rack over a baking sheet—this helps the air circulate around the duck as it roasts, ensuring even cooking. Put the tray in the oven and roast the duck for 12 minutes.

4 | Meanwhile, put the ovenproof skillet with the fat from the duck, back on medium-high heat. Add the plums, cut-side down, with the five-spice powder and cook for 2 minutes. Mix together the chicken stock, red wine vinegar, and sugar, then carefully pour the liquid into the pan and let it bubble away for 2 minutes, until reduced slightly. Put the pan in the oven.

5 | When ready, remove the duck from the oven. Each breast will have shrunk in size slightly and feel firm but with a little give when pressed. If using a meat thermometer, it should read between 115–120°F (45–50°C) when inserted into the middle. Leave to rest for 5 minutes on a plate, skin-side-up. Don't cover the breasts—you want the skin to remain crisp.

6 | After 10 minutes, remove the plums from the oven; they should be soft and jammy at this point. Thinly slice the duck breasts and pour any resting juices into the plums. Serve the sliced duck with the plums and the sauce spooned over with the sesame green bean and sugar snap salad on the side.

MEAT

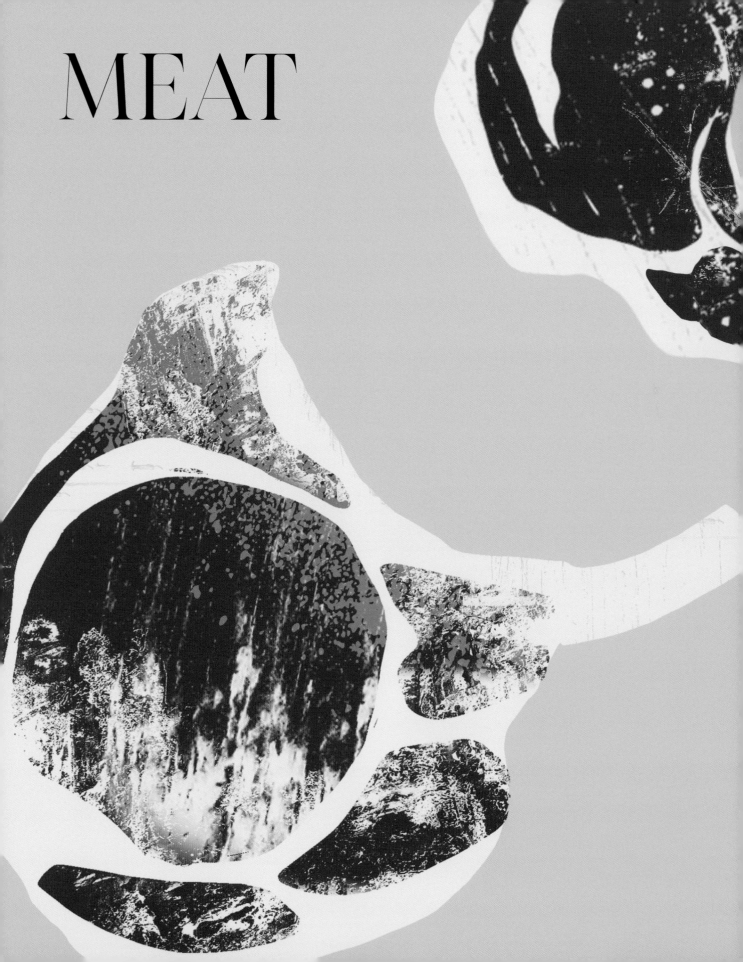

MEAT

Nothing impresses quite like a large cut of beautifully roasted meat, ready for carving into tender, juicy slices and served with gravy and all the trimmings. It's a classic technique to learn and straightforward when you know the basics. All bases are covered in this chapter for the main meat types—beef, pork, and lamb—and there are cooking guides for a wide range of techniques, starting with roasting and moving through marinating and frying to grilling and braising. Before you start on your cooking journey, all cuts of meat benefit from being removed from the fridge 30 minutes to 1 hour (depending on size) before cooking for the best results.

Storage

Uncooked meat should be kept in the refrigerator, ideally in the bottom and away from cooked food. Keep an eye on the use-by date. After handling meat, rinse all kitchen equipment and work surfaces well, first in cold water, then wash in hot, soapy water.

ROASTING MEAT

You've bought your cut of meat, prepared it, and now it's in the oven, but how do you know when it's ready without over- or under-cooking it? The simplest recommendation for perfectly roasted meat is to invest in a digital cooking thermometer or meat thermometer. When taking the internal temperature of the meat after roasting, it's important to remember that it continues to rise for a short time once it is out of the oven—and the meat carries on cooking at the same time. To test, insert the thermometer into the thickest part of the meat, then leave for 1 minute for an accurate reading.

The following internal temperature roasting guide should help: the numbers on the left are the desired temperature when the meat is first taken out of the oven, depending on whether you want your meat rare, medium, or well done. The temperatures in parentheses on the right are after resting for 20–30 minutes.

Resting is important for most cooked meats, especially those that have experienced the fiery heat of the oven. It allows the muscles to relax and the juices to redistribute, as well as ensuring the meat reaches the correct internal temperature. When roasted, lift the meat onto a warm plate and cover loosely with foil (the only exception is if there's crackling, which will soften if you cover it). It's best to rest all large cuts of meat for around 20–30 minutes, depending on their weight; 15 minutes should be plenty for smaller cuts.

When carving, some cuts of meat will be easier to slice if removed from the bone first, such as a rib of beef. Start by removing the bone by cutting down and around the bone(s) with a large, sharp chef's knife. For all boneless cuts, secure the meat with a carving fork, then cut it into slices against the grain of the meat to ensure tender, regular slices.

MEAT	INTERNAL TEMP AFTER ROASTING	INTERNAL TEMP AFTER RESTING
Beef & Lamb	105–110°F (40–45°C) for rare 115–120°F (45–50°C) for medium 120–130°F (50–55°C) for medium-well done	125–130°F (50–55°C) 130–140°F (55–60°C) 140–150°F (60–65°C)
Pork	125–130°F (50–55°C) for medium-well done (with a pink blush) 140–150°F (60–65°C) for well-done (juicy meat with no pink)	140–150°F (60–65°C) 160°F (70°C)

CUT OF BEEF	ROASTING TIMES	ROASTING METHOD
Boneless topside and boneless top rump	Medium rare: 15 minutes per 1lb (500g) Medium: 20 minutes per 1lb (500g) Well done: 25 minutes per 1lb (500g)	Heat 2 tbsp of neutral oil in a large skillet over high heat. Season the meat well, then brown for 2 minutes on each side. Put the meat in a roasting pan in the oven at 450°F (230°C) and immediately reduce the temperature to 375°F (190°C) for the remaining calculated cooking time.
Bone-in rib of beef	Medium rare: 20 minutes + 8 minutes per 1lb (500g) Medium: 20 minutes + 10 minutes per 1lb (500g) Well done: 20 minutes + 15 minutes per 1lb (500g)	Heat 2 tbsp of neutral oil in a large skillet over high heat. Season the meat well, then brown for 2 minutes on the meat sides and 3 minutes on the fat cap. Put the meat in a roasting pan in the oven at 450°F (230°C) for 20 minutes. Reduce the temperature to 375°F (190°C) for the remaining calculated cooking time.
Boneless sirloin roast	Rare: 15 minutes per 1lb (500g) Medium: 20 minutes per 1lb (500g)	Heat 2 tbsp of neutral oil in a large skillet over high heat. Season the meat well, then brown for 2 minutes for the meat sides and 3 minutes for the fat cap. Put the meat in a roasting pan in the oven at 375°F (190°C) for the remaining calculated cooking time.
Boneless fillet	Rare: 10 minutes per 1lb (500g)	Heat 2 tbsp of neutral oil in a large skillet over high heat. Season the meat well, then brown for 2 minutes on each side. Put the meat in a roasting pan in the oven at 375°F (190°C) for the remaining calculated cooking time.

CUT OF LAMB	ROASTING TIMES	ROASTING METHOD
Bone-in leg of lamb	30 minutes per 2¼lb (1kg) for medium rare	Season and roast at 400°F (200°C) for the calculated cooking time.
Boneless shoulder of lamb	30 minutes + 4–5 hours slow-cooking, depending on size	Season and roast at 400°F (200°C) in a roasting pan, tightly covered with foil for 30 minutes. Reduce the temperature to 325°F (160°C) for the remaining cooking time.

CUT OF PORK	ROASTING TIMES	ROASTING METHOD
Boneless pork belly	30 minutes + 1 hour per 1lb 10oz (750g)	Season and roast for 30 minutes at 450°F (230°C). Reduce the temperature to 325°F (160°C) for the remaining cooking time.
Rolled boneless pork shoulder	30 minutes + 30 minutes per 1lb (500g)	Season and roast for 30 minutes at 450°F (230°C). Reduce the temperature to 350°F (180°C) for the remaining cooking time.
Skinless, boneless pork loin	25–27 minutes per 1lb (500g) 25 minutes will give you blushing meat; 27 minutes ensures cooked-through but juicy meat	Heat 2 tbsp of neutral oil in a large skillet over high heat. Season the meat well, then brown for 2 minutes on each side. Put the meat in a roasting pan in the oven at 350°F (180°C) for the calculated cooking time.

ROASTING
BEEF

Top rump, topside, and sirloin have similar cooking times, because they are single-muscle cuts of meat, while a rib of beef requires slightly different roasting instructions. Firstly, it is made up of several muscles, which have both fat and connective tissue around them, meaning it conducts heat differently and needs longer cooking to render the fat. It's also on the bone, which initially protects the meat from the fierce heat of the oven, but as the bone warms up will radiate heat into the meat through conduction, influencing the timings. For these cuts, after an initial browning in a hot pan, roast them in a high oven to build a deep delicious crust, before reducing the temperature and slowly cooking the meat to perfection (see p.101). Don't be tempted to cut the fat off—it adds flavor and moisture to the meat.

ROAST TOP
RUMP OF BEEF

*Prep 10 minutes
+ resting*

*Cook 1½ hours,
depending on
preference*

Serves 4–6

Top rump has a good balance of lean, tender meat with a cap of fat that helps baste the beef as it roasts, keeping the meat moist and juicy. It's also generally an affordable cut to buy and a straightforward one to roast and carve because it is boneless. So a win on all fronts! Use the pan juices to make a Gravy (see p.418) and serve with all your favorite trimmings. Yorkshire Puddings (see p.347) are especially good.

3¼lb (1.5kg) boneless top rump, topside
    or silverside
salt, for seasoning
2 tbsp vegetable oil
1 onion, peeled and thickly sliced
1 carrot, peeled and cut into chunks
1 celery stalk, cut into chunks
1 garlic bulb, cut in half horizontally
Gravy (see p.418), Yorkshire Puddings (see p.347)
    and your choice of vegetables, to serve

1 | Remove the beef from the fridge 1 hour before roasting to allow it to come to room temperature. Season the meat all over with salt, patting to ensure it sticks to the meat.

2 | Preheat the oven to 450°F (230°C). Pour the vegetable oil into a large skillet over high heat. Using tongs, carefully lower the seasoned meat, fat-side down, into the oil. Brown the fat for 2 minutes, until golden, then turn the meat in the pan to sear each side for 2 minutes, until browned all over.

3 | Put the onion, carrot, celery, and garlic in a large roasting pan, about 9 x 13 in (35 x 25 cm), in a single layer—there should be space around the beef to allow airflow. Place the beef on top of the vegetables, then put the pan into the oven. Immediately turn the heat down to 375°F (190°C) and roast for 45 minutes for medium-rare; 1 hour for medium; and 1 hour 15 minutes for well-done (see temperature guide on page 100).

4 | Move the beef and vegetables onto a warm serving plate, very loosely cover with foil and let the meat rest for 30 minutes while you make the gravy, using any fat and juices in the roasting pan.

5 | To carve, secure the roast beef with a carving fork, then cut it into thick slices against the grain of the meat. Serve the beef with Yorkshire puddings, gravy, and your choice of vegetables on the side.

TIP

Roast beef, pork, or lamb will keep covered in the fridge for up to 3 days and can be used as sandwich fillings, or added to a simple dressed salad or Asian noodle salad for added protein. Roast pork is great added to stir-fries, while roast lamb or beef can be diced and used to make a shepherd's or cottage pie.

ROASTING PORK

Roast pork has an unfounded reputation for being one of the trickiest meats to cook well. While pork has a high level of external fat, most cuts have little internal fat, which can lead to dry meat with a layer of unrendered, chewy fat on the top. Following the useful cooking guide (see p.101) makes it much easier to cook pork well every time. Additionally, the one thing everyone around the table will be looking out for is super-crisp and golden crackling, so make sure you check the tips (right).

ROAST PORK BELLY WITH CREAMY CIDER SAUCE

Prep 5 minutes + overnight salting and resting

Cook 3½ hours

Serves 6

The combination of crispy golden crackling with juicy meat is what makes roast belly pork so popular. When buying belly pork look for a cut that has a good ratio of meat to fat—50:50 is ideal. This recipe shows how to score the skin before roasting, but you can ask your butcher to do this for you or buy ready-scored pork if easier. The secret to a perfect pork belly roast is low, slow cooking, after an initial quick blast in a high oven, to ensure the fat renders into the meat, keeping it moist and tender.

4½lb (2kg) boneless pork belly, fat scored (right)
1 tbsp vegetable oil
1 celery root, peeled and cut into 2½-in (6-cm) chunks
2 onions, peeled and thickly sliced
salt and freshly ground black pepper

For the creamy cider sauce
4 apples, such as Braeburn, Granny Smith, or Pink Lady, cored and each cut into 8 pieces
2 cups (500ml) dry cider
2 cups (500ml) Chicken Stock (see p.414) or store-bought
2 tbsp wholegrain mustard
⅔ cup (150ml) heavy cream

1 | The day before roasting, follow the tips For the Best Crackling (right) for scoring the skin, if needed, as well as preparing the pork. The next day, remove the pork from the fridge 1 hour before cooking. Place the celery root and onions into a large roasting pan and season with salt and pepper. Sit the pork on top, skin-side up.

2 | Preheat the oven to 450°F (230°C). Drizzle the oil over the pork and season well with salt. Put the pork in the oven and roast for 30 minutes, then reduce the heat to 325°F (160°C) and continue to cook for 2 hours 45 minutes, until tender. A knife should slide easily into the pork with little resistance. Move the pork and vegetables onto a warm plate or platter, cover very loosely with foil and leave to rest for 30 minutes.

3 | If the pork skin still needs to crisp up, preheat the broiler to high. Cut off the skin and fat, place it on a baking sheet, and broil for 4–5 minutes, until the crackling is crisp and golden, keeping an eye on it so it doesn't burn. Alternatively, put it in a high oven (right).

4 | While the meat is resting make the sauce. Put the roasting pan with any fat from the cooked pork over medium-low heat, add the apple wedges and cook for 3–4 minutes, until starting to caramelize. Meanwhile, pour the cider into a medium saucepan over medium-high heat and cook until reduced by two-thirds. Pour the reduced cider over the apples, scraping the pan to loosen any crusty bits.

5 | Pour everything from the roasting pan back into the saucepan, then add the chicken stock and let it bubble away for 15 minutes. Add the mustard and cream and cook until you have a glossy sauce the consistency of light cream.

6 | Cut the pork meat and crackling into slices with a long serrated knife and serve with the creamy cider sauce spooned over.

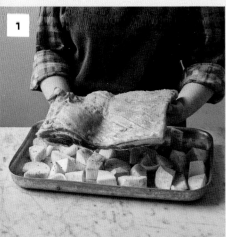

For the best crackling

The day before roasting
Score the skin of your pork belly (or buy it ready-scored) to allow the fat to render and crisp up during cooking. To do this, use a small sharp chef's knife to make diagonal cuts into the skin, spaced about ½ in (1 cm) apart. Carefully pour a kettle of just-boiled water over the pork belly, then drain and pat dry completely. This technique helps lift the skin and fat from the meat. Alternatively, a good rubbing of salt into the scored fat the night before cooking will help. The salt draws moisture out of the skin, which can then be dried with paper towel before cooking.

Chill overnight to dry the skin
If you can, leave the meat uncovered overnight in the fridge. Modern fridges are made to be moisture-free environments, so this will help remove any moisture, ideally drying out the skin too. Pat the pork belly down with paper towel before roasting.

Start by roasting the pork in a high oven
Preheat the oven to 450°F (230°C) at the start of cooking to give the crackling a good head start. A quick blast of heat will render the fat and start to crisp the skin.

If your crackling isn't crisp
Never fear! Turn the broiler to high and use a sharp knife to remove the skin and fat from the pork. While the meat is resting, covered with foil, put the skin on a baking sheet under the broiler for 4–5 minutes to crisp. Alternatively, increase the oven to 450°F (230°C). Put the skin on a baking sheet and return it to the hot oven to crisp up.

ROASTING LAMB

With its distinctive flavor and high-fat content, lamb is perhaps not as popular as other meats, but when cooked well these characteristics can be to the cook's advantage. Lamb is one of the most tender meats and benefits from either fast cooking or long, slow cooking, depending on the cut. Like most meat, the cuts tend to fall into two categories: muscles that have worked hard and require long cooking such as shoulder, or those that have worked less and require faster cooking, such as the lamb chop recipe on p.112.

SLOW-ROASTED ANCHOVY & ROSEMARY LAMB SHOULDER

*Prep 15 minutes
+ resting*

Cook 4½ hours

Serves 6–8

Roasted slowly until the meat literally falls off the bone, this lamb shoulder is a small-effort, high-reward dish. Lamb shoulder is ideal for low, slow cooking, as it becomes increasingly tender, to the point of not needing a knife, the longer it cooks. Serve with the classic Fresh Mint Sauce (see p.445) and Couscous (see p.217) as a side.

10 fresh rosemary sprigs
1 (2oz/50g) can anchovies in olive oil
salt and freshly ground black pepper
2 red onions, peeled and sliced into rounds
1 garlic bulb, halved horizontally
1 boneless lamb shoulder, around 1¾–2¼lb (800g–1kg)
1¼ cups (300ml) Chicken Stock (see p.414) or
    store-bought
Fresh Mint Sauce (see p.445) and Couscous (see
    p.217), to serve

1 | Heat the oven to 400°F (200°C). While the oven is heating, strip half of the rosemary from the sprigs and finely chop. Pour the anchovy oil into a small bowl and add the chopped rosemary. Finely chop the anchovies, then add them to the oil. Stir and season with lots of pepper. Cut the remaining rosemary into 1-in (2.5-cm) sprigs. Set aside.

2 | Put the red onions and garlic into a large, deep roasting pan, about 12 x 14 in (40 x 30cm). Season the lamb all over and place it on top of the onions—you want it to fit comfortably but snugly in the tray.

3 | Using the point of a small, sharp chef's knife, make ¾-in (2-cm) deep incisions across the top of the lamb shoulder, leaving a ¾-in (2-cm) gap between each one.

4 | Insert the remaining rosemary sprigs into the cuts made in the lamb.

5 | Using a teaspoon, spoon the anchovy and rosemary oil all over the lamb shoulder, making sure to open each incision with the back of the spoon so the marinade gets inside the cuts.

6 | Pour the chicken stock into the tray around the meat and over the onions.

7 | Place a sheet of parchment paper over the lamb and cover tightly with foil, sealing the edges so there are no gaps. Roast the lamb in the center of the oven for 30 minutes, then turn the temperature down to 325°F (160°C). Roast the lamb for a further 4 hours or until the meat readily comes away from the bone.

8 | Transfer the lamb and onions to a warm plate or platter, cover loosely with foil and leave it to rest for 15 minutes before slicing. Alternatively, shred the lamb with two forks. Squeeze the garlic out of its skin into the tray and mix it with the lamb juices before serving. Serve the lamb with the garlicky pan juices, mint sauce, and couscous (see the Tip, right) on the side.

TIPS

This is a great roast to make the day before. Leave the shredded lamb shoulder to cool, then chill the meat overnight. The next day, place the lamb in a roasting tray with ¾ cup (200ml) chicken stock, cover tightly with foil, and reheat in an oven preheated to 350°F (180°C) for 30 minutes.

Follow the method for cooking Couscous (see p.217), using half the lamb juices from the roasting tray and making up the amount of liquid needed with just-boiled water from a kettle.

Sriracha beef short ribs

Prep 10 minutes

Cook 4½ hours

Serves 6

If you've never cooked beef short ribs before, this recipe is for you. Short ribs are best cooked low-and-slow in the oven to allow the meat to tenderize and the marbled fat to render down and add succulence. Once roasted to meltingly soft, the ribs benefit from grilling hard-and-fast to caramelize the meat's exterior in the spicy, sticky, sweet sauce.

6 fat garlic cloves, 2 peeled, and 4 left in their skins and smashed with the back of a knife
2-in piece of fresh ginger, ½ sliced in its skin, ½ peeled
salt and freshly ground black pepper
6 on-the-bone short ribs
4¼–5 cups (1–1.2 liters) Beef Stock (see p.415) or store-bought
4–5 tbsp sriracha (depending on how spicy you like it)
1½ tbsp light brown sugar
juice of 1 lime, plus 1 lime, cut into 6 wedges, to serve
3 green onions, green and white parts, finely sliced
1 handful of salted roasted peanuts, roughly chopped
1 handful of cilantro, leaves picked
cooked jasmine rice (see p.202) and Quick Pickled Cucumbers (see p.459), to serve

1 | Preheat the oven to 325°F (160°C). You will need a large, deep roasting pan that the short ribs can fit into snugly, about 12 x 14 in (40 x 30 cm). Put the smashed garlic cloves and sliced ginger into the bottom of the pan, then nestle the short ribs on top and season generously with salt and pepper.

2 | Finely grate the remaining peeled garlic and ginger into a bowl with the beef stock. Whisk in the sriracha, brown sugar, and lime juice with a fork until combined.

3 | Pour the liquid around and over the short ribs until fully submerged. Cover with a sheet of parchment paper, followed by a sheet of foil, securing it around the edges of the pan so there are no gaps. Put the pan in the oven and roast the ribs for 3½–4 hours, until the meat is meltingly tender. The meat should almost be falling off the bone. Leave the ribs to cool enough to handle, then transfer them to a baking sheet.

4 | Meanwhile, strain the liquid in the roasting pan through a metal strainer into a medium saucepan— this will become the glaze/sauce. Put the pan on high heat and let it reduce for 15 minutes, stirring occasionally until glossy and the consistency of heavy cream.

5 | Preheat the broiler to high. Slide the short ribs under the broiler for 3–4 minutes, until the ribs are nicely browned and becoming slightly blackened in places, then spoon over three-quarters of the sriracha glaze. Slide the tray back under the broiler for 3–4 minutes, until the ribs are burnished, bubbling, and sticky.

6 | Meanwhile, reheat any leftover sauce in the pan. Arrange the ribs on a serving platter or plate, spooning over the remaining warmed sauce. Top with the green onions, peanuts, and cilantro, then serve with the lime wedges, jasmine rice, and the pickled cucumbers.

MARINATING
MEAT

Marinating is a surefire way to make your meat extra delicious. Meat is extremely good at taking on flavors, from wet marinades using oil or yogurt to spice-heavy dry rubs. The latter imparts flavor, which penetrates the meat, as well as drying the surface allowing a thick, caramelized crust to form when the meat is cooked. As well as adding plenty of flavor, marinades have a tenderizing effect. They work by breaking down the proteins in the meat, allowing the marinade to penetrate as well as making it more tender when cooked. Acidic ingredients, such as citrus, yogurt, buttermilk, and vinegar, work wonders in a marinade, while some fruit, such as pineapple and mango, contain enzymes that also have a tenderizing effect.

It is important to marinate meat for the correct length of time as well as use the right balance of ingredients; too long and the acid in the marinade can have a negative effect, turning the meat mushy or even tough. Overnight marinating is usually perfect for flavor penetration and tenderizing, but if time is tight then marinating for an hour will still make a difference to the taste. Bear in mind, the smaller the cut of meat, the less time you need to marinate it for, and the greater the influence it will have on its flavor. Before choosing a marinade, it's important to consider how you're going to cook your meat. Dry-spice rubs are much better if the meat is seared before it's braised. This toasts the spices, preventing a raw spice flavor.

GREEK YOGURT–MARINATED
LAMB SKEWERS

Prep 20 minutes + marinating

Cook 15 minutes

Serves 2

Lamb leg steaks are perfect for taking up the flavor of the herbs and spices, while the yogurt and lemon in the marinade work in unison to tenderize the meat. The skewers are cooked until burnished on the outside and juicy pink in the middle—a high grill or broiler is the perfect quick way to achieve this. Serve the skewers with Watermelon Greek Salad (see p.166) and crusty bread. You'll need 6 metal skewers for this recipe, or if you only have wooden ones see the Tip (right).

¾lb (350g) lamb leg steaks, cut into 1½-in (4-cm) pieces
1 red onion
2 red bell peppers
Watermelon Greek Salad (see p.166) and crusty bread, to serve

For the marinade
1½ cups (150g) Greek yogurt
1 tbsp dried mint
1 tsp sweet smoked paprika
1 tsp ground cumin
3 garlic cloves, peeled and finely grated
juice and finely grated zest of 1½ unwaxed lemons, divided
salt and freshly ground pepper

1 | To make the marinade, put the yogurt into a medium bowl, large enough to hold the lamb, with the dried mint, paprika, cumin, garlic, the juice of 1 lemon and all the zest, then season well with salt and pepper.

2 | Add the lamb to the marinade and use a spatula to mix everything together. Cover the bowl and chill in the fridge for at least 1 hour, but preferably overnight.

3 | When ready to cook, trim the onion and cut it in half through the root end. Peel and cut each onion half into 3 wedges, then separate the layers. Trim and seed the peppers and cut them into chunks.

4 | Line a baking sheet that is just slightly smaller than the length of your skewers with foil. Thread a piece of lamb onto one metal skewer, pushing it all the way down to the bottom. Follow this with a piece of red pepper and a few slices of onion. Repeat until you have finished all of the meat, peppers, and onions, split evenly between the 6 metal skewers. Place on the lined baking sheet. Spoon over any remaining marinade.

5 | Preheat the broiler to high with the rack in the middle of the oven. Broil the lamb skewers for 5–6 minutes on each side, until caramelized and blackened in places. Squeeze over the remaining half of lemon and serve with the watermelon Greek salad and crusty bread.

TIP

If using long wooden skewers instead of metal ones, soak them first in cold water for 30 minutes to prevent them from burning. Do keep an eye on them while cooking as the skewers may still blacken.

BROILING & GRILLING MEAT

Whether under the broiler or on the stove top in a grill pan, both methods of cooking are great for more tender or thinner cuts of meat, such as steaks, loins, or chops, and for several reasons. Both utilize a very high intense heat, meaning you maximize the outer crust or char on the meat due to what's called the Maillard reaction (see p.414), and give it a boost of flavor. It's also a great method for rendering any fat—no one wants chewy, undercooked fat surrounding their meat! When fat is rendered, it bastes and adds moisture to the meat, while any excess can be discarded, meaning you're eating less of it too.

When using the broiler, it's essential to give it plenty of time to heat up to its highest setting before cooking because you want the meat to brown and sear, not stew in its juices. Once hot, place the meat on a baking sheet, about 3 in (7.5 cm) below the heat source. Turn it halfway through cooking to ensure it cooks evenly and baste occasionally to keep it moist.

Similarly, preheat the grill pan until smoking hot. As with broiling, basting with fat or a marinade will help prevent the meat from drying out. The ridges of a grill pan give characteristic charred stripes to the outside of the meat and lend a slightly grilled flavor.

GRILLED LAMB CHOPS

Prep 5 minutes

Cook 10 minutes

Serves 2

A chop, sometimes called a cutlet, is one of the most tender cuts of lamb so it may seem paradoxical to blast it over high heat, yet it requires fierce, hot cooking to build a caramelized crust quickly without drying out. These lamb chops go perfectly with Sauce Vierge (see p.426) and a crisp green salad.

2 large lamb chops
1 tsp vegetable oil
sea salt flakes
Sauce Vierge (see p.426) and a crisp
   green salad, to serve

1 | Heat a large grill pan over high heat. Rub the lamb chops evenly all over with the oil, then season well with salt.

2 | Put the chops, side-by-side and fat-side down, in the pan and hold in place with tongs for 1–2 minutes, until caramelized and slightly blackened in places.

3 | Lay each chop onto its side and cook for 2–4 minutes, depending on the thickness, then flip and repeat on the other side. This will give the chops a browned outer crust and blushing pink meat inside. For well done chops, cook them for 4 minutes on each side.

4 | Serve immediately to retain the moisture in the chops (there is no need to allow them to rest) with the sauce vierge spooned over the top.

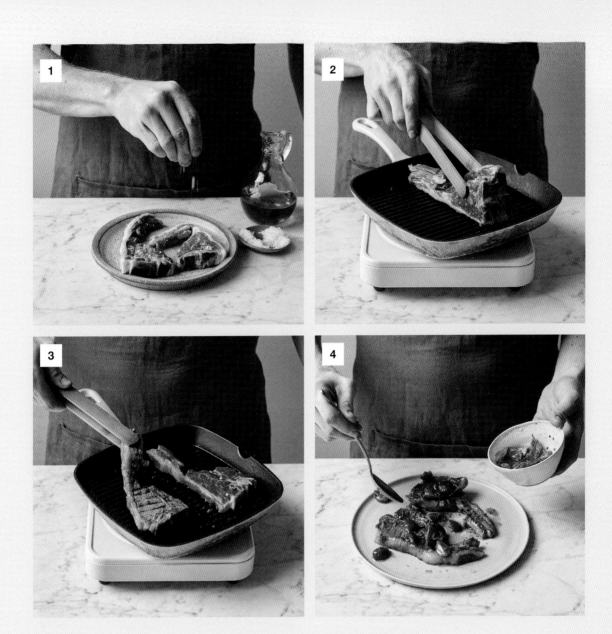

TIP

To cook in the oven, preheat the broiler to high and while heating, rub the lamb chops evenly all over with the oil and season well with salt. Put an oven rack above a foil-lined baking sheet. Put each lamb chop on its flat side onto the rack. Broil for 4–6 minutes, depending on their thickness, then flip and repeat on the other side until golden and caramelized on the outside and blushing pink inside. For well done, broil for 7–10 minutes on each side. Serve as left.

FRYING MEAT

This quick method of cooking suits steak, cutlets, thin strips, and especially leaner tender cuts of meat. For successful shallow-frying you need to start with a decent wide, shallow pan. The fat you use should either be heated before adding the meat, or added to the meat once the pan has been heated, depending on preference. Both will ensure the meat sears and browns, developing a golden crust. It's important to choose your cooking fat wisely because it will influence the taste of the meat and the finished dish—you also want one that is stable when heated. Butter has a delicious flavor but can burn or split when heated, while vegetable oils are milder in flavor but are more stable, so a combination of the two is often a good solution.

Along with shallow-frying, this speedy cooking method also includes sautéing and stir-frying. The former typically uses very little fat and the strips or cubes of meat are tossed frequently in the pan until browned, which is particularly useful for preparing meat for slow-cooking, such as a stew. Stir-frying involves cooking small, even-size pieces or strips of meat in a little oil in a wok or large skillet over high heat. The meat is tossed constantly so it cooks evenly and quickly.

THE PERFECT STEAK

Prep 10 minutes + resting

Cook 15 minutes

Serves 2

This recipe uses rib eye steak, chosen for its tenderness and rich marbling of creamy-white fat, ensuring lots of flavor and succulent meat. Resting the steak is vital after frying to allow the juices to redistribute through the meat, ensuring it is tender and juicy. The steak comes with a peppercorn sauce, but you could try the herby, spicy salsa Chimichurri (see p.444) instead.

1¼lb (500g) rib eye steak, about 2½in (6cm) thick
½ tbsp sea salt flakes, plus extra to taste
1 tbsp black peppercorns
2 tsp vegetable oil
4 tbsp (50g) butter
2 garlic cloves, skin on and smashed
1 shallot, finely chopped
3 tbsp brandy
⅔ cup (150ml) strong beef stock
3 tbsp heavy cream

1 | About 1 hour before cooking, remove the steak from the fridge so it comes up to room temperature. Season the steak with sea salt flakes.

2 | When ready to cook, toast the black peppercorns in a medium skillet over high heat, tossing them occasionally, for 1 minute, then put into a pestle and mortar and roughly crush. Set aside until needed.

3 | Put the pan back on high heat and continue to heat until it is smoking hot. Pour the vegetable oil over both sides of the steak and place in the pan, fat-side down, holding it in place with tongs for 1 minute, until the fat is crisp and golden.

4 | Carefully lay the steak on one of its sides and cook for 2½ minutes, until browned.

5 | Turn the steak and cook for a further 2 minutes, then add the butter and garlic. Spoon the garlicky butter over the meat for the final 30 seconds. It should have a golden crust and a pink interior at this point. Test the internal temperature with a digital meat thermometer, it should read 115°F (45°C), which will increase to 120–130°F (50–55°C) after resting.

6 | Move the steak onto a plate to rest for 5 minutes while you make the sauce, keeping the buttery juices in the pan. With the pan off the heat, add the shallot and cook for 2 minutes, stirring, until softened.

7 | Put the pan back on low heat and carefully pour in the brandy. Let it bubble for 30 seconds (be careful because it may ignite—if it does, add the beef stock right away). Pour in the stock and add the peppercorns.

8 | Simmer the sauce for 2 minutes, then pour in the cream and simmer for another minute, stirring. Pour in any resting juices from the steak and season with salt to taste. Serve the steak with the sauce spooned over.

TIPS

When buying steak, it's important to look for well-marbled meat; this is the internal, thin lines of fat that will make the steak even juicier once cooked.

Steak may come with a date denoting how long it has been aged or hung for. Aging ranges from 14–100 days—the longer the meat is hung, the greater the depth of flavor. Most butchers and supermarkets will go up to around 21 days, which provides a balance of tender meat with a slightly aged intensity of flavor.

Pork chops with miso lime-butter shallots

Prep 5 minutes

Cook 40 minutes

Serves 2

This recipe is all about rendering that delicious pork fat. Initially holding the chop upright on its fatty side while it cooks draws the fat out, basting the meat once it is placed on its flat side in the pan, becoming crisp and golden at the same time. Don't be scared of getting the pan super hot—the high heat chars the pork adding to its flavor. The lime helps cut through the richness of the pork fat, while the buttery miso sauce holds everything together. Serve with the Sesame Green Bean & Sugar Snap Salad (see p.168), if you like.

1 tbsp olive oil
4 shallots, trimmed, peeled, and cut
    in half lengthwise
4 tbsp (50g) salted butter, melted
1 cup (250ml) Chicken Stock (see p.414) or
    store-bought
2 tbsp white miso
2 bone-in pork chops
salt and freshly ground black pepper
juice of 1–2 limes
Sesame Green Bean & Sugar Snap Salad
    (see p.168), to serve

1 | Preheat the oven to 400°F (200°C).

2 | Pour half the olive oil into a medium skillet set over medium-high heat. Add the shallots to the pan, cut-side down, and fry for 4–5 minutes, until charred and golden. Flip the shallots over and repeat on the other side, then place in a small, deep roasting pan.

3 | Whisk together the melted butter, stock, and miso, then pour the mixture over the shallots. Roast in the oven for 25 minutes.

4 | Meanwhile, pour the remaining oil over the pork chops and season well with salt.

5 | Place the skillet back on high heat. Using tongs, hold the pork chops fat-side down in the pan for 1 minute, until caramelized. Lay each pork chop onto one side and fry for 2 minutes, then flip and repeat until golden.

6 | Remove the shallots from the oven, squeeze in the juice of 1–2 limes, depending on preference, and season with salt and pepper. Nestle in the pork chops and return the pan to the oven to roast for 5 minutes, until the pork is cooked through.

7 | Remove the pan from the oven and allow the pork to rest for a few minutes. Serve the pork with the roast shallots and any sauce left in the pan along with the sesame green bean and sugar snap salad on the side, if you like.

Curried lamb koftas

Prep 15 minutes

Cook 20 minutes

Serves 3–4

Ground lamb is ideal for making koftas because its high fat content means the meat retains its juiciness when cooked. After frying, which browns the outside and seals in the juices, the kofta are glazed in mango chutney to enhance their caramelized exterior and then finished in the oven. Once you've mastered this simple recipe, you can change the flavorings in the lamb—harissa and feta also make a great combination, or even swap for ground chicken or pork instead. Serve with the Gujarati Carrot Salad (see p.167) and flatbreads for an epic meal.

1lb (400g) ground lamb
1 red onion, peeled and coarsely grated
3 garlic cloves, peeled and finely grated
2-in piece of fresh ginger, peeled and finely grated
1 green or red chile, finely chopped (seeded if you
    don't like it too hot)
2 tbsp medium curry powder

1 large handful of cilantro, stalks and
    leaves, finely chopped
salt and freshly ground black pepper
2 tbsp vegetable oil
2 tbsp mango chutney
⅔ cup (150ml) plain yogurt
Gujarati Carrot Salad (see p.167) and warmed
    naan or pita bread, to serve

1 | Put the ground lamb into a large bowl. Add the onion, garlic, ginger, chile, curry powder, all the cilantro stalks and most of the leaves, saving some to serve. Season with plenty of salt and pepper, then use clean hands to mix and distribute the flavorings evenly throughout the meat.

2 | Divide the lamb mixture into 12 equal pieces. Lightly wet your hands with water, then take each piece of meat and roll it in the palm of your hand to create an oval cylindrical shape, about 1¼ in (3 cm) diameter and 3½ in (8 cm) long. Place it on a baking sheet and repeat until you have made 12 koftas.

3 | Preheat the oven to 375°F (190°C).

4 | Put a large nonstick skillet over high heat. Once hot, pour in half of the oil and add 6 koftas to the pan. Fry the koftas for 4 minutes, turning them occasionally with tongs, until browned all over, then transfer to a roasting pan. Pour the rest of the oil into the skillet and repeat with the remaining koftas.

5 | Dot an equal amount of the mango chutney over each browned kofta. Put the pan in the oven for 6–8 minutes, turning halfway, until the koftas are glazed, caramelized, and cooked through, but still juicy in the middle. To check they are ready, there should be no sign of pink when cut into.

6 | Spread the yogurt across the base of a serving plate, pile the koftas on top and sprinkle over the remaining cilantro leaves. Serve with the Gujarati carrot salad and some warmed torn naan or pita bread, if you like.

BRAISING & STEWING MEAT

Braising and stewing are methods of cooking that somehow always feel like magic—you take humble ingredients and with a little preparation, effort, and time you can create truly special meals. While the terms are often used interchangeably, braising involves slow-cooking larger pieces of meat partially covered in liquid, while stewing relates to smaller pieces of meat slow-cooked while immersed in liquid.

The best cuts of meat for both methods are the ones that work hardest on the animal. The harder the muscle has worked, the tougher and more sinewy it will be, which means it needs lots of gentle slow cooking to make it tender. With time, the collagen and fat in the meat eventually start to break down to make the sauce unctuous and the meat meltingly tender.

When stewing and braising, it's best to sear the meat first in hot oil to increase the depth of flavor and enrich the color of your final dish. To do this, heat a tablespoon of oil in an ovenproof casserole or Dutch oven over medium-high heat. Add the cubes or chunks of meat (beef, lamb, or pork) and cook, turning occasionally, for about 5–10 minutes, until browned all over. It is best to cook the meat in batches to avoid over-crowding the pan which can lead to it steaming in its own juices. Once all the meat has been browned, carry on with the rest of the steps in the recipe.

BEEF CUTS FOR STEWING/BRAISING	LAMB CUTS FOR STEWING/BRAISING	PORK CUTS FOR STEWING/BRAISING
Chuck	Shoulder	Shoulder
Shoulder/chuck	Leg	Neck
Flank	Belly	Leg
Blade	Neck	Belly
Brisket	Shank	Ribs
Short rib		
Oxtail		
Shank		

BEEF BOURGUIGNON

Prep 15 minutes
+ soaking

Cook 4 hours

Serves 4–6

This hearty French stew is a classic for a reason. The beef is slowly cooked until meltingly tender so not a single drop of flavor is lost, and you can taste this in its rich, full-bodied red wine sauce. The stew is finished with fried bacon lardons, pearl onions, and mushrooms. Pure comfort food! Beef shoulder is perfect for slow cooking at a low temperature because it's a hard-working muscle that needs time to tenderize and for the fat to render down, but it's so worth the effort. This is perfect served with Mashed Potatoes (see p.171) and the Five-Spice Braised Red Cabbage (see p.184).

1lb (500g) pearl onions
4 tbsp olive oil, divided
½lb (200g) smoked pancetta or bacon, cut into lardons
1lb (450g) button mushrooms, halved and large ones quartered
pinch of salt, plus extra to season
2¼lb (1kg) boneless beef shoulder or chuck roast, cut into 1½-in (4-cm) chunks
freshly ground black pepper
2 medium carrots, peeled and cut into chunks
2 onions, chopped
1 heaped tbsp all-purpose flour
2 tbsp tomato paste
1 bottle (750ml) red wine
2 bay leaves
1 handful of flat-leaf parsley, chopped
Mashed Potatoes (see p.171) and Five-Spice Braised Red Cabbage (see p.184), to serve

1 | Put the pearl onions into a medium bowl and pour over just-boiled water to cover. Let soak for 15 minutes, then drain through a metal strainer. Trim the ends and peel—soaking loosens the skin, making them easier to peel.

2 | Heat 1 tablespoon of the olive oil in an ovenproof casserole or Dutch oven over medium-high heat. Add the lardons and cook for 5 minutes, turning occasionally, until crisp and golden. Using a spatula, scoop them into a medium bowl.

3 | Add the pearl onions and mushrooms with a pinch of salt and sauté for 8–10 minutes, until softened and beginning to brown. Scoop the vegetables into the bowl containing the lardons.

4 | Preheat the oven to 350°F (160°C). Add another tablespoon of oil to the pan. Season the beef well with salt and pepper, then cook in two or three batches to avoid over-crowding the pan for 3–4 minutes on each side, until browned all over. Add a drizzle of oil between each batch, if needed, to prevent the meat sticking to the bottom of the pan. Once browned, scoop the beef into a separate bowl.

5 | Reduce the heat to medium-low, add a drizzle more oil, then add the carrots and onions with a pinch of salt and cook for 2–3 minutes, until softened slightly. Add the flour and tomato paste and cook for a few minutes, stirring, to cook out the flour, then add the red wine and bay leaves.

6 | Return the browned beef to the pan, stir, scraping to remove any bits stuck to the bottom of the pan, and bring up to a boil. Cover with a lid and move into the preheated oven. Cook for 1½ hours, until bubbling and slightly browned on top. The meat won't be tender at this point. Remove the lid and stir in the pearl onions, mushrooms, and lardons.

7 | Put the pan back in the oven, without the lid, for another 1½ hours, until the beef is meltingly tender and the sauce has reduced and thickened. Season with salt and pepper to taste and finish with a sprinkling of chopped parsley. Serve with mashed potatoes and five-spice braised cabbage.

TIPS

Most stews, this one included, taste even more delicious the next day as the flavors continue to improve, marinate, and merge. Leave the stew to cool, then transfer to the fridge and chill overnight. Simply reheat in the oven at 350°F (180°C) for 40–45 minutes, until bubbling hot.

The stew can be frozen in individual portions for up to 3 months. Defrost thoroughly before reheating in a small covered saucepan over medium heat.

THE BEST
SPAGHETTI BOLOGNESE

Prep 15 minutes

Cook 2½ hours

Serves 4

The combination of ground pork and beef with smoky pancetta gives this bolognese sauce plenty of flavor, which is boosted by browning the meat before slow cooking. And the secret ingredient? Milk! This adds to the velvety, creamy texture of the sauce and also helps tenderize the meat. If you don't eat pork, skip the first step and simply double the amount of ground beef, choosing one with a high percentage of fat. If you have a leftover Parmesan rind, add it to the sauce to give a savory depth to the dish.

2½oz (75g) diced pancetta
1 tbsp olive oil
2 tbsp (30g) salted butter
1 onion, peeled and finely chopped
1 carrot, peeled and finely chopped
1 celery stalk, finely chopped
pinch of salt, plus extra to season
2 fat garlic cloves, peeled and finely chopped
½lb (250g) ground pork
½lb (250g) ground beef
1¼ cups (300ml) whole milk
1¼ cups (300ml) red wine
1 (28oz/800g) can crushed tomatoes
2 tbsp tomato paste
1 tsp dried Italian herbs
freshly ground black pepper
1 Parmesan rind (optional)
dried spaghetti or tagliatelle pasta and Parmesan
    cheese, finely grated, to serve

1 | Put the pancetta into a large, deep, dry saucepan with a lid over medium heat. Cook for 4–5 minutes, stirring very occasionally, until the fat has rendered and the meat is crisp and golden.

2 | Add the olive oil and butter with the onion, carrot, celery, and a pinch of salt. Cook for 10–12 minutes, stirring occasionally, until softened. Add the garlic and cook, stirring for another minute.

3 | Turn the heat up to high. Add the ground meats and cook for 5–8 minutes, stirring regularly with a wooden spatula to break up the meat, until browned.

4 | Pour in the milk, stir, and cook for 3–4 minutes, until there is no visible liquid left in the pan, then pour in the red wine and repeat.

5 | Add the tomatoes, tomato paste, and Italian herbs, stir, mashing the tomatoes with a wooden spatula to break them down. Season with salt and pepper and add the Parmesan rind, if using. Give everything a good stir.

6 | Turn the heat down to the lowest setting, part-cover the pan with the lid, leaving it ajar so steam can escape while it slowly cooks. Cook the bolognese sauce for 2 hours, stirring every 20 minutes, until thick and luscious. Season to taste with salt and pepper. Serve with the pasta shape of your choice and finely grated Parmesan sprinkled over.

Bolognese variations

Cottage pie: add 2 tablespoons of Worcestershire sauce and 1 teaspoon of English mustard to a half quantity of the bolognese sauce. Spoon into a small baking dish and top with creamy Mashed Potatoes (see p.171). Sprinkle ¾ cup (75g) of coarsely grated Cheddar over the top and bake at 400°F (200°C) for 35–40 minutes, until piping hot and the cheese is bubbling and golden.

Chili con carne: sauté 1 chopped red bell pepper in 1 tablespoon of olive oil in a medium saucepan over medium heat for 8–10 minutes, stirring occasionally, until softened. Add 1 teaspoon of smoked paprika, 1 teaspoon of ground cumin, and 3 teaspoons of chipotle paste and cook, stirring, for 30 seconds, then add a half quantity of bolognese sauce. Add in a 15.5oz/400g can of drained kidney beans. Bring the mixture to a simmer and cook for 10–15 minutes, stirring occasionally, until thick and unctuous. Season with salt and pepper to taste. Serve with rice and/or tortilla chips and some smashed avocado.

Meat lasagna: use 1 recipe quantity of the spaghetti bolognese sauce in place of the lentil ragu in the Veggie Lasagna (see p.178).

TIPS

It's worth making a double batch of this bolognese to use as the base of a chili or cottage pie (left).

Freeze the bolognese in individual portions for up to 3 months. Defrost thoroughly in the fridge before reheating in a small saucepan, letting it bubble away, covered with a lid, for 10 minutes.

Chorizo & zucchini bean stew

Prep 10 minutes

Cook 25 minutes

Serves 4

The chorizo gives this simple tomato-based bean and vegetable stew a lovely smokiness and heat, boosted by the smoked paprika and chili flakes.

2 tbsp olive oil
½lb (225g) chorizo, sliced into ½-in (1-cm) rounds
1 large red onion, peeled and finely sliced
2 medium zucchini, halved lengthwise and sliced into half moons
pinch of salt, plus extra to season
4 fat garlic cloves, peeled and finely sliced
2½ tsp sweet smoked paprika, divided
large pinch of dried chili flakes
1 (12oz/375g) can cherry tomatoes
2 (15.5oz/400g) cans white beans, saving the liquid
1½ cups (150g) Greek yogurt
freshly ground black pepper
2 tbsp capers
1 handful of dill, stalks and fronds, roughly chopped
1–2 tbsp sherry vinegar

1 | Heat the olive oil in a large saucepan over medium-high heat. Add the chorizo and cook, stirring occasionally, for 5 minutes, until crisp and most of the fat has rendered out. Add the onion and zucchini with a pinch of salt and cook, stirring occasionally, for 6–8 minutes, until softened and starting to caramelize.

2 | Add the garlic and cook, stirring, for another minute, then add 2 teaspoons of the paprika and the chili flakes. Cook, stirring, for a further 30 seconds, then add the canned cherry tomatoes and the beans with their liquid. Give everything a good stir, reduce the heat to medium and cook for 10 minutes, stirring occasionally, until the sauce thickens.

3 | Meanwhile, mix the remaining smoked paprika into the Greek yogurt in a small bowl and season with salt and pepper to taste.

4 | Stir the capers and most of the dill into the stew. Add the sherry vinegar, to taste, along with salt and pepper, then divide between four serving bowls. Spoon over the paprika yogurt and top with the remaining dill.

TIPS

This stew will keep in the fridge for up to 3 days or freeze in individual portions for up to 3 months. Defrost thoroughly before reheating in a saucepan, adding a splash of water.

You can easily swap the chorizo for other types of sausage—simply slice or leave whole and cook in the same way. Try a Toulouse pork sausage or even a spicy lamb sausage, such as merguez. If using whole sausages, brown them first, then return to the stew with the beans in step 2. Let the stew simmer away for 15–20 minutes, covered with the lid, until the sausages are cooked through.

Cochinita pibil tacos

Prep 15 minutes

Cook 2 hours

Makes about
20 tacos

Pib is a Mayan word that means "to cook in a pit," while *cochinita pibil* is a traditional pork dish from the Yucatán peninsula. It has changed over time, and with the arrival of the Spaniards people started to cook this dish with a particular breed of pig from the area, hence the name *cochinita* (little pig). The recipe typically uses *achiote*, a red paste mix with annatto seeds, spices, and *naranja agria* (bitter orange), a fruit also from the region, which is used to flavor the pork before cooking it on top of a banana leaf. If you can't find banana leaf, then use parchment paper instead. The dish makes a perfect Mexican feast served with soft corn tortillas, pickled onions, and a sprinkling of fresh chile.

1 large banana leaf or parchment paper
juice of 2 large oranges, about 1 cup (250ml)
juice of 1 lemon, about 3 tbsp
1½ tbsp (25g) achiote paste

2¾lb (1.25kg) boneless pork shoulder, cut
    into 4-in (10-cm) cubes
¼ white onion, thinly shredded
1 garlic clove, minced
1 tbsp sea salt flakes
pinch of freshly ground black pepper

To serve
about 20 corn tortillas, warmed
Pink Pickled Onions (see p.459)
1 habanero or Scotch bonnet chile, finely chopped
    (seeded if you prefer it less spicy)

1 | Preheat the oven to 400°F (200°C).

2 | Wipe the banana leaf clean with a wet sheet of paper towel. Place the leaf in a large dry skillet and heat slightly until flexible, then use it to line a large cast-iron pot (or use parchment paper) and set aside.

3 | Put the orange and lemon juice with the achiote paste in a blender and blitz until combined.

4 | Place the pork shoulder pieces on top of the banana leaf in the pot. Sprinkle the onion over the pork and add the garlic, salt, and pepper. Pour in the achiote mixture and stir to coat the pork until thoroughly combined. Fold the banana leaf (or parchment paper) over the pork to cover. Put the lid on the pot and cook in the oven for 2 hours, until the pork is tender and starting to fall apart.

5 | Using two forks, shred the cooked pork in the pot, then transfer it to a warm serving plate.

6 | To serve, place the warm tortillas and other accompaniments in serving bowls on the table to allow everyone to help themselves. To assemble, spoon some of the shredded pork over a warm corn tortilla, top with a spoonful of the pickled onions and finely chopped habanero to add some heat, and eat right away.

SEAFOOD

SEAFOOD

A lot of people avoid cooking seafood—which includes fish and shellfish—believing it's difficult to prepare or tricky to cook well, but with a little attention to detail and a knowledge of the basics, you can create impressive, delicious seafood dishes in mere minutes.

A valuable source of protein, along with vitamins, minerals, and beneficial fats, there are several types of fish, broadly split into freshwater and seawater. White fish, such as haddock, bream, and cod, have a light-flavored, flaky flesh, while oily fish, like tuna, sardines, and mackerel, can take stronger flavors and more intense heat. Whatever you buy, be it fish or shellfish, it's wise to shop mindfully, checking that the seafood is responsibly sourced, is not on the endangered list, and is in season.

Storage

Fish and shellfish have a short shelf life so are best eaten soon after buying, or within 24 hours. Do check the use-by date, or ask at your fish counter if buying unpackaged, and store in the coolest part of the fridge (the bottom section). Fillets should be kept in their packaging, a container, or shallow bowl covered with plastic wrap, while whole fish are best stored on crushed ice, again covered. Store shellfish in the same way, in its packaging or in a covered container, and avoid direct contact with water or ice. Defrost frozen fish and shellfish in the fridge overnight.

DESCALING A FISH

Before gutting and filleting your whole fish, the first step is to remove the scales. Scaling the fish will make the skin much more pleasurable to eat, but it can be a messy job, so if you have the option of a fishmonger doing it for you, go for it.

1 gutted round fish, such as sea bream, sea bass, mackerel, or red mullet

1 | Put a clean plastic grocery bag onto a cutting board. Put the gutted fish into the bag, head first. If it's a small fish, you can do this in the sink.

2 | Holding the tail of the fish with paper towel, use a fish scaler or the back of a large, sharp chef's knife to scrape away the scales. Start from the tail end of the fish and scrape along the flesh toward the head. Flip the fish and repeat on the other side.

3 | Rinse the fish under cold running water to remove any stray bits of scale and pat dry with paper towel. Your fish is now ready to be gutted, if needed.

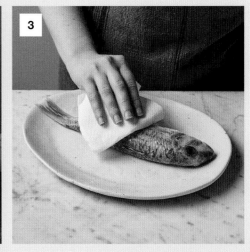

GUTTING A FISH

Before cooking a whole fish, it's important to remove the internal organs. You can ask your fishmonger to do this for you or follow the guide (below) for gutting a round fish. (If gutting a flat fish, the stomach is on the central underside of the fish, below the throat, rather than there being a noticeable belly.)

1 round fish, such as a sea bream, sea bass, mackerel, or red mullet

1 | Put the fish on a cutting board with the belly facing you. Using a small, sharp chef's knife or kitchen scissors, cut into the skin from the head end down the center of the belly to the central base fin.

2 | Working from the head end, remove the guts of the fish with an upturned spoon, gently but firmly pulling them out to remove, then discard.

3 | Lift the flap at the base of the head and remove the bright orange gills with a pair of kitchen scissors.

4 | Rinse the cavity of the fish under cold running water, ensuring it is clean and free from any remnants. Pat dry with paper towel and your fish is now ready for cooking.

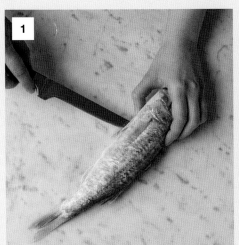

TIP

After gutting and descaling your round fish, you can slash the sides before cooking to help it cook evenly and more quickly. Use a sharp chef's knife to make 2–3 diagonal cuts into each side, about 1 in (2.5 cm) apart, although this depends on the size of the fish.

ROASTING &
BAKING SEAFOOD

There are few culinary highlights that rank above the promise of the soft, pearly white flesh and crispy skin of a whole roasted fish. The dry, hot heat of the oven cooks whole fish, such as sea bream, sea bass, mackerel, trout, or salmon, beautifully, and the cavity can also be stuffed with heady aromatics to steam and perfume the fish from within. And for those who are fearful of cooking fish, there's no tricky pre-roast filleting or removing the skin to worry about.

Roasting (or baking, the terms are interchangeable) is also an easy, convenient way to cook fish fillets or steaks with minimum fuss and effort. Oily fish, like salmon or trout, remain moist when roasted, although more delicate fillets of white fish, including plaice and sole, benefit from basting occasionally with melted butter or oil to prevent them drying out.

There are other ways to cook fish that also need to be done in the oven, such as "en papillote," when the fish is cooked in a parchment paper or foil parcel, as well as fish baked in pastry or a salt crust. These methods of cooking seal in both the flavor and juices of the fish, keeping it moist and tender.

WHOLE ROASTED SEA BREAM
WITH PAPRIKA BUTTER

Prep 15 minutes

Cook 20 minutes

Serves 2

This recipe is such a wonderful way to cook fish. It's golden on the outside with flaky flesh within and the most wonderful smoky, buttery juices to baste the fish as it cooks, preventing it from drying out. If you've never cooked a whole fish before this simple recipe is a great place to start—not only does it look impressive, roasting it on the bone will help lock in flavor.

1 whole sea bream, about 1¼lb (500g), scaled and gutted (see pp.128–129) or buy ready-prepared
2 tsp olive oil
salt and freshly ground black pepper
1 lemon, ½ sliced, ½ cut into quarters
½ recipe quantity of Smoked Paprika Butter (see p.48), melted
Easy Homemade French Fries (see p.192) and vegetables, to serve

1 | Preheat the oven to 425°F (220°C). Put the fish on a cutting board and use a large, sharp chef's knife to make 3 diagonal cuts, ½ in (1 cm) deep, into each side of the fish.

2 | Put the fish into a roasting pan, lined with parchment paper, and drizzle with the olive oil. Season all over with salt and pepper, both inside and out, then put the lemon slices into the cavity of the fish.

3 | Roast in the oven for 15 minutes, until the skin starts to crisp. Spoon the melted paprika butter over the top of the fish (you may not need all of it) and roast for a final 5 minutes, until the flesh is pearly white and readily flakes into large chunks. Baste the fish with the melted butter.

4 | To fillet, using a small, sharp chef's knife, make a cut down the center of one side of the cooked fish as well as at the head and tail end—this will create two fillets on each side of the fish.

5 | Starting at the head end, use a spoon to gently lift the meat away from the body, prizing it gently from the bones. Repeat with the second fillet on the same side. Turn the fish and repeat on the other side.

6 | Lift the skin of the cheek from the fish and remove the cheek meat. The chef's treat! Serve the fish with fries, your choice of vegetables, and wedges of lemon.

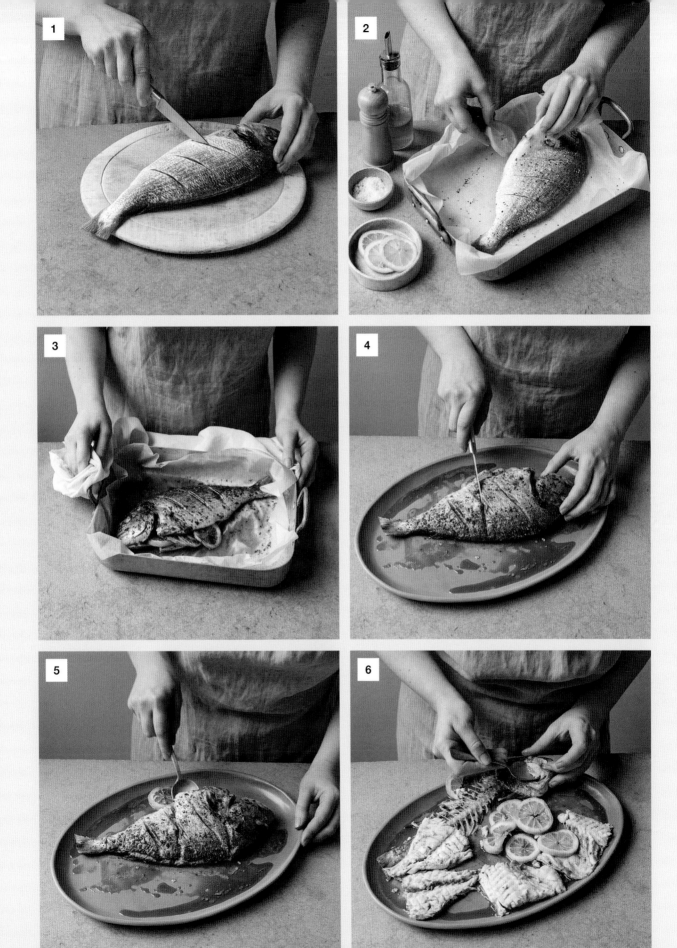

Sheet pan turmeric cod & chickpeas

Prep 15 minutes

Cook 20 minutes

Serves 2

This one-pan fish dinner is speedy and packed with protein and vegetables. Thick cod fillets are perfect for baking because the meaty yet flaky flesh can withstand the high temperature and dry heat of the oven and they readily take on the flavors of the ingredients they're cooked with. If you can't get cod, haddock, pollock, or hake fillets make a great alternative.

2 tbsp vegetable oil
2 garlic cloves, peeled and finely grated
2-in piece of fresh ginger, peeled and
    finely grated
2 tsp ground turmeric
1 (15.5oz/400g) can chickpeas, drained and rinsed
½lb (200g) cherry tomatoes, halved
2 boneless, skinless cod fillets, about ⅓lb
    (150g) each
salt and freshly ground black pepper
2 handfuls of baby spinach leaves
½lb (200g) sugar snap peas
1 lime, juice of ½, ½ cut into quarters
4 tbsp plain or coconut yogurt
1 small handful of cilantro, leaves picked

1 | Preheat the oven to 400°F (200°C).

2 | Pour the oil into a small bowl, add the garlic, ginger, and turmeric, then stir to combine.

3 | Put the chickpeas and cherry tomatoes onto a greased baking sheet, about 10 x 14 in (35 x 25cm), pour over one-third of the spice oil, and mix well. Season both sides of the cod with salt and pepper, then nestle the fillets into the middle of the tray so everything is roughly in a single layer.

4 | Spoon the remaining spice oil over the cod and bake in the center of the oven for 8 minutes. Carefully remove the tray from the oven and sprinkle the spinach leaves and sugar snap peas over the chickpeas and tomatoes, but not the cod.

5 | Return the tray to the oven for 7–8 minutes, until the spinach wilts and the cod is cooked to your liking. It should have turned opaque white and readily flake into large chunks when prodded with a fork.

6 | Lift the cod onto two serving plates, then stir the wilted spinach and sugar snap peas into the chickpeas and spoon onto the plates.

7 | Squeeze the lime juice over everything and season with salt and pepper to taste. Drizzle over the yogurt and sprinkle with the cilantro. Serve with the remaining lime wedges for squeezing over.

CURING SEAFOOD

A method of preserving a valuable, nutritious, and tasty food source, curing can be traced back over many hundreds of years and to countries all over the world. It remains a popular technique and incorporates various methods, including air-drying, fermentation, smoking, pickling, marinating, and dry-salting.

The two easiest ways to cure fish at home are creating a rub with salt and sugar, which over time draws out the moisture in the fish, or using acid to marinate and lightly "cook" the fish without adding heat, such as the Cilantro & Jalapeño Ceviche (see p.137). Both are celebrated in the recipes that follow.

BEET & ORANGE CURED SALMON

Prep 20 minutes
+ 36 hours curing

No cook

Serves 6–8

Using beets, spices, and orange as part of a cure made from equal parts sugar and salt lends both a gorgeous color and flavor to the salmon. The floral sweetness of the orange and earthiness of the coriander seeds work well with the oily fish, enhancing its flavor. Curing looks impressive, but it is a simple process that requires just a handful of ingredients, plus time and patience. Make sure you buy the best-quality salmon you can—one which is plump, firm, and with an even thickness because this will give a uniform cure and ensure the best results.

1 skin-on, boneless side of salmon, about 1¾–2¼lb (800g–1kg)

For the cure
1 tbsp coriander seeds
½lb (250g) skin-on raw beets, coarsely grated
finely grated zest of 1 orange
1¼ cups (20g) dill, ½ roughly chopped, ½ picked, to serve
¾ cup (150g) sea salt flakes
¾ cup (150g) sugar

To serve (optional)
Bagels (see p.320), split in half and lightly toasted
cream cheese
cornichons, sliced
lemon wedges

1 | To make the cure, toast the coriander seeds in a small dry skillet over medium heat for 2–3 minutes, until they smell floral and fragrant. Remove the seeds into a large bowl.

2 | Add the grated beets, orange zest, and chopped dill to the coriander seeds and add the salt and sugar. Give everything a good stir to combine.

3 | Place a piece of plastic wrap large enough to completely wrap the salmon fillet on your work surface, then repeat so you have a double layer of plastic wrap on top of one another. Spoon one-third of the cure mixture down the center of the plastic wrap, pressing it down with the back of a spoon into a single layer roughly the same size and shape as the salmon fillet.

4 | Place the salmon fillet, skin-side down on top. Spoon the remaining two-thirds of the cure mixture on top of the salmon, letting it fall down the sides so the fish is completely covered in the cure mixture.

5 | Bring the sides of the plastic wrap over the salmon to wrap it into a parcel, then carefully use an extra sheet of plastic wrap to tightly wrap it again.

6 | Put the wrapped salmon on a baking sheet, then place a smaller baking sheet on top and weigh it down with three heavy cans (the weight of the cans will help the salmon cure). Refrigerate the salmon for 12 hours. (Continued overleaf.)

7 | Turn the salmon, replace the small baking sheet and cans and return it to the fridge for a further 12 hours. Repeat this once more, curing the salmon for a further 12 hours, so 36 hours in total. After the salmon has cured, unwrap it and discard the plastic wrap and cure. Rinse the salmon under cold running water to get rid of any remaining cure, then pat dry with paper towel.

8 | To serve the salmon, place it skin-side down on a cutting board and slice it thinly on the diagonal with a large, sharp chef's knife, cutting it away from the skin.

9 | Gently lift the salmon slices and place them on a bagel with cream cheese, extra dill, cornichons, and lemon wedges for squeezing over, if you like.

TIPS

Once cured, the salmon will keep in the fridge, tightly wrapped in plastic wrap, for up to 1 week. Slice just before serving.

The cured salmon makes an ideal appetizer with mascarpone, spiked with lemon zest and chopped capers and served on toasted brioche or eaten as part of a rice bowl or in a salad.

To keep the remaining dill fresh, cover it with a damp sheet of paper towel in the fridge while the salmon cures.

Cilantro & jalapeño ceviche

Prep 15 minutes + curing

No cook

Serves 4 as a starter

Popular in Peruvian and Mexican cuisines, ceviche is the process of lightly marinating and "cooking" fish by gently curing it in citrus juice. Since the fish is effectively raw, make sure to seek out the freshest fillets you can find for this recipe. If buying from a fishmonger, ask for fish that is fresh in that day, or sushi grade. If buying at the supermarket, look for plump, firm fillets that haven't been frozen, with no residue water and the longest best-before date.

½lb (250g) boneless, skinless sea bass or sea bream fillets, any bones removed
1 small red onion, peeled, halved, and very finely sliced
salt and freshly ground black pepper
1 small garlic clove, peeled and finely grated or crushed
1 green jalapeño chile, seeded and finely chopped
juice and finely grated zest of 2 limes
1 handful of cilantro, leaves picked
tortilla chips, to serve

1 | Cut the fish into ¾-in (2-cm) cubes using a sharp chef's knife. Add to a serving bowl, along with the red onion. Season with salt and pepper.

2 | Put the garlic into a second small bowl, add the jalapeño and lime juice and zest. Stir together to create a wet cure.

3 | Pour the cure over the fish and give everything a gentle yet confident stir with a large spoon. Leave the fish in the cure for 10 minutes at room temperature to lightly "cook" the fish, then stir through the cilantro. Serve right away with tortilla chips for scooping.

TIP

If you can't get fresh jalapeños, use a regular red or green chile instead. Try the very point of the chile before chopping to establish how spicy it is and adjust the quantity accordingly.

GRILLING & BROILING SEAFOOD

The smoky aroma of seafood cooking on a grill or under a broiler may revive memories of hot summer days and sunny vacations. These are high-temperature, dry-heat methods of cooking so it is important to select the right type of seafood and avoid ones that are very delicate or likely to overcook and fall apart. Grilling and broiling are great ways of cooking whole fish, in particular, because you get the double whammy of crispy skin and being on the bone so the flesh is less likely to dry out or overcook. Just remember to turn the fish halfway through cooking and add a bit of oil or butter to moisten, if needed.

Thick fish fillets and steaks also respond well to these cooking methods, especially meaty-textured or oil-rich varieties like salmon, mackerel, or tuna because their high-fat content helps keep them moist during cooking, while the outside sears and chars. If using more delicate or thin fillets of white fish, brushing them occasionally with a marinade or fat will ensure they remain moist and prevent drying out. They don't need turning—they are more fragile than whole fish and will cook a lot quicker, about 5 minutes in total.

Shellfish, such as squid (below), scallops, shrimp, and lobster, are also perfect for grilling or broiling. You are looking for them to be just cooked in the center with a slightly golden caramelized exterior to get the ideal balance of a smoky flavor and sweet, juicy meat.

PREPARING SQUID

Prep 15 minutes

No cook

This is not as technical or tricky as it may first appear, in fact preparing a whole squid is pretty straightforward. There are two main parts—the body (mantle) and the tentacles (arms)—which need separating, gutting, and cleaning before cooking. Squid is best cooked high-and-fast, like the recipe for Grilled Squid with Nuoc Cham (see p.140) or low-and-slow to keep it tender—anything between and it can become rubbery and tough.

1 whole squid, about ½lb (200g)

1 | Put the squid on a cutting board and hold the tentacles in one hand and the body in the other. Confidently pull apart, the eye, beak, and ink sac will pull away with the tentacles.

2 | Feeling along the inside of the squid, find the transparent long quill—you will know when you find it because it feels kind of like plastic. Pull this away from the body and discard.

3 | Using a sharp chef's knife, cut the tentacles from the head, just below the eye, then discard the head.

4 | Turn the tentacles inside out, at the top you should be able to see a small round beak—this is the mouth. Use your fingers to pull it away from the tentacles and discard.

5 | Hold the body of the squid in one hand and use your thumb to prize away and free the "ears" (these are the fins of the squid that hang off the main body), gently pulling away any membrane with them. Trim and discard the membrane and set aside the rest.

6 | Depending on how you intend to cook the squid, it can be prepared in different ways: cut the body into rings for calamari or butterfly it by making a cut down one side of the body with a sharp chef's knife, then opening it out like a book.

7 | Cut the butterflied squid in half lengthwise, then slice each half into three pieces.

8 | Using the sharp knife, carefully and gently score the squid in a diagonal crosshatch pattern, being careful not to cut all the way through the flesh. The squid is now ready for cooking (see p.140).

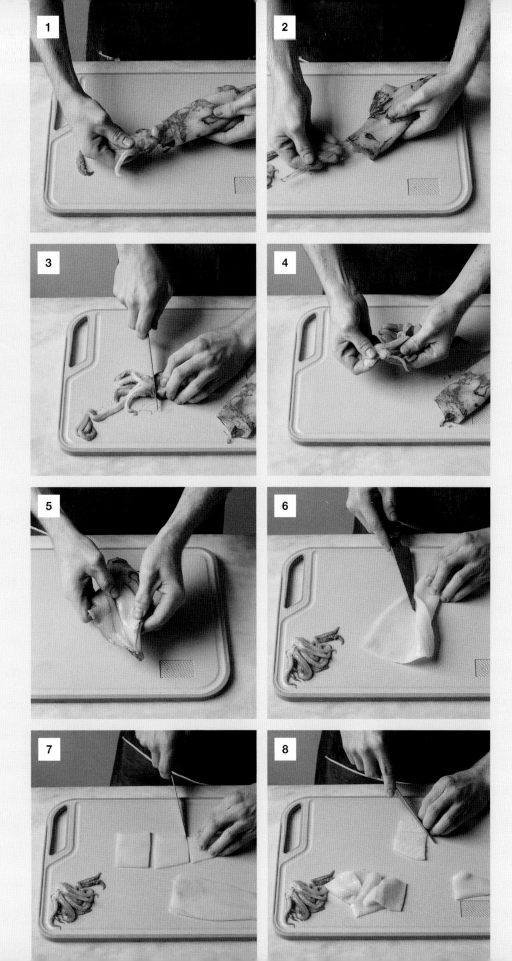

Grilled squid with nuoc cham

Prep 20 minutes

Cook 5 minutes

Serves 4

Successful squid cooking is all about extremes; it needs to be either very fast and hot or slow and low to avoid it becoming tough and chewy. The fierce heat of the grill pan (or outdoor grill) cooks the squid quickly, turning it soft and tender, while giving it a kiss of smoke and char.

4 whole squid, about ½lb (200g) each
2 tsp vegetable oil
salt and freshly ground black pepper
Thai basil, leaves picked
Nuoc Cham dipping sauce (see p.427), to serve

1 | Follow steps 1–8 from Preparing Squid (see p.138) for all four squid. Put the prepared squid into a large bowl, pour in the oil, season well with salt and pepper, then toss to coat.

2 | Heat a grill pan over high heat until smoking hot. Cook the squid pieces for 1–1½ minutes on each side, pressing them down with a spatula so they become nicely golden and charred.

3 | Place the grilled squid on a serving platter or plate, sprinkle over the Thai basil and serve with the nuoc cham spooned over with extra on the side for dipping.

TIP

To barbecue the squid, heat the coals until white hot, then spread them out in an even layer. Put the rack on top, roughly 8 in (20 cm) from the coals. Toss the squid in the oil, season, and cook for 1–1½ minutes on each side as above. Use tongs to turn and flip the squid pieces, then move them onto a plate, sprinkle with Thai basil and serve with the nuoc cham dipping sauce.

Broiled sardines with warm nduja-honey dressing

Prep 5 minutes

Cook 15 minutes

Serves 4

Part of the oily fish family, sardines have darker, fattier flesh than more delicate types of white fish, which makes them perfect for cooking under the dry, hot heat of a broiler without falling apart.

8 sardines, gutted (see p.129)

For the nduja-honey dressing
¼lb (90g) nduja
2 tbsp extra-virgin olive oil, divided
3 garlic cloves, thinly sliced

2 tbsp honey
juice and finely grated zest of 1 unwaxed lemon
salt and freshly ground black pepper

To serve
flatbread
plain yogurt
Pink Pickled Onions (see p.459)

1 | Preheat the broiler to high.

2 | While the broiler is heating, make the dressing. Warm the nduja in 1 tablespoon of the olive oil in a small saucepan over medium-high heat for 2–3 minutes, breaking it up with the side of a spoon. Add the garlic and cook for 2 minutes, then remove the pan from the heat. Stir in the honey, lemon zest and juice, and season lightly with salt (the nduja is already quite salty), and pepper.

3 | Put the sardines onto a baking sheet and drizzle with the remaining olive oil and season with salt. Put the tray under the hot broiler on the middle shelf for 3–4 minutes on each side, until the skin of the sardines browns and starts to bubble and blister.

4 | Place the sardines on a serving plate. Warm the dressing, if needed, then spoon it over the sardines and serve with flatbread, yogurt, and pickled onions.

TIP

If you can't get sardines, use 4 small prepared mackerel instead. Make 2 diagonal cuts, about ½ in (1 cm) deep, on each side of the fish. Broil the mackerel for 10–16 minutes, turning once, depending on the size of the fish, until the skin is golden and the flesh is cooked through—it should readily flake into large pieces once cooked.

STEAMING & POACHING SEAFOOD

Fish and shellfish are some of the most delicate types of food and respond well to sensitive handling and cooking. Steaming and poaching are two classic methods that are particularly good for seafood since both are gentle and produce tender and moist results. Suitable for both whole fish and fillets, try steaming or poaching as ways to cook milder-tasting fish, such as sea bass, haddock, cod, red snapper, skate, and sea bream, rather than stronger-tasting oily fish, including mackerel and sardines.

Steaming, unlike poaching, doesn't come into direct contact with the cooking liquid. Instead, the fish or shellfish is cooked on a rack above the steaming liquid or in a parchment paper or foil parcel, which seals in the juices, keeping it tender.

Poaching uses liquid, such as a sauce, stock, wine, water with flavorings, or milk (particularly good for smoked fish, see p.44), to cook the seafood. The poaching liquid can be reduced and thickened after cooking the seafood to serve as a sauce.

WHOLE SEA BASS WITH GINGER & GREEN ONIONS

Prep 15 minutes

Cook 25 minutes

Serves 4

This recipe encompasses two techniques—steaming and baking. The fish is cooked in a sealed parcel so it steams in its own juices in the oven, giving perfectly soft flesh that remains moist as well as a ready-made soy-infused sauce. If you have a large steamer pan or basket, you could try cooking the fish parcel in that too. Scale and gut the fish yourself (see pp.128–129) or ask your fishmonger to do it for you.

1 whole prepared sea bass, about 1¾lb (800g)
salt and freshly ground black pepper
2-in piece of fresh ginger, peeled,
  ½ thinly sliced, ½ cut into matchsticks (see p.163)
2 garlic cloves, peeled and thinly sliced
1 cup (30g) cilantro, stalks separated from
  the leaves
3 green onions, finely sliced on the diagonal, divided
5 tbsp dark soy sauce
1½ tbsp light brown sugar
½ tbsp toasted sesame oil
juice of 1 lime
rice and steamed Broccolini (see p.172),
  to serve

1 | Preheat the oven to 350°F (180°C). Lay a large sheet of foil on a large baking sheet, about 14 x 16 in (40 x 35cm), letting the edges overhang the sides. Cut a large sheet of parchment paper (roughly the same size as the foil) and place it on top of the foil. Place the sea bass on the parchment paper and season lightly with salt and pepper over both sides of the fish and inside the cavity.

2 | Open the cavity of the fish and stuff in the ginger slices, garlic, cilantro stalks and 1 of the sliced green onions.

3 | Mix together the soy sauce, brown sugar, and sesame oil in a small bowl, then spoon it over the fish.

4 | Gather up the parchment paper to encase the fish in a parcel, scrunching the edges together to seal, then repeat with the foil to make a completely sealed parcel, with no gaps for the steam or sauce to escape. Put the tray in the oven for 20–25 minutes, until the fish flesh is pearly white. To check the fish is ready, open up the parcel and use a fork to see if it easily flakes away from the bone.

5 | Transfer the fish to a serving platter, spooning over the juices from the parcel. Sprinkle over the shredded ginger, remaining green onions, and cilantro leaves. Squeeze over the lime juice to finish and serve with rice and steamed broccolini.

TIP

*An alternative way to tell
if the fish is cooked is by
looking at the eyes — the
fish is ready once they
have turned opaque white.*

PREPARING MUSSELS

Prep 20 minutes
───────────
No cook
───────────
Serves 2

Mussels are economical to buy and easy to prepare. Start by simply giving them a good wash to get rid of any sand in the shells, then remove barnacles and the stringy "beard," which attaches the mussel to the ropes or rocks in the sea. Mussels are extremely perishable, so make sure you buy them close to cooking. Once prepared, these shiny black shellfish make a winning quick-cooking, nutritious flavor bomb.

2¼lb (1kg) mussels

1 | Rinse the mussels under cold running water in the sink. Using a small brush, scrub each mussel to remove any sand or grit and place in a bowl of water.

2 | Discard mussels that have a broken shell. If any mussel shells are partly open, give them a gentle tap on the work surface, if alive they will close. Discard if the shells don't shut.

3 | Using a small, sharp knife, carefully scrape any barnacles or white marks off the shells. Don't worry if you can't get every single bit off.

4 | Take the "beard," protruding from the side of the shell, firmly between your thumb and forefinger and slowly and confidently pull it away from the shell, then discard. Drain and rinse the mussels again, ensuring there is no sand or grit in the bottom of the bowl.

Moules marinière

Prep 30 minutes

Cook 15 minutes

Serves 2

This classic French dish of mussels steamed in white wine in a covered pan is simple to prepare. First clean the mussels following the method (left). Make sure you've got plenty of fresh crusty bread to soak up the wine-infused juices.

2¼lb (1kg) mussels
4 tbsp (50g) salted butter
1 onion, finely chopped
4 fat garlic cloves, thinly sliced
salt and freshly ground black pepper
½ cup (100ml) dry white wine
½ cup (100ml) heavy cream
1 handful of flat-leaf parsley, finely chopped
crusty bread, to serve

1 | Follow steps 1–4 from Preparing Mussels (left). Set aside briefly until needed.

2 | Heat the butter in a large saucepan over medium heat. Once foaming, add the onion and garlic, season with salt and pepper, and cook for 8–10 minutes, stirring, until softened.

3 | Turn the heat up to high and pour in the wine. Once bubbling, carefully add the mussels, cover with the lid and cook for 2–3 minutes, shaking the pan every now and again, until the shells open. If the shells remain closed, put the lid back on and cook for another 1–2 minutes before checking again.

4 | Remove the pan from the heat, pour in the cream and sprinkle in the parsley. At this stage, any mussels that remain closed should be discarded. Ladle the mussels into two bowls with the sauce and serve with crusty bread for dipping.

SHELLING & DEVEINING SHRIMP

Prep 30 minutes

No cook

Serves 4–6

Shrimp are delicious cooked both in the shell and without, especially if garlic butter is involved! However, some recipes call for removing the shell and the black vein or digestive tract that runs down the length of the back before cooking. Of course, you can buy them ready prepared but this is a useful technique to have under your belt. Peeling shrimp can be a messy business, so feel free to wear gloves.

2¼lb (1kg) raw shell-on large shrimp

1 | Holding a shrimp upright with the head in one hand and the body firmly in the other, use a twisting and pulling motion to pull off the head.

2 | Turn the body of the shrimp so the legs are upright, then use both thumbs to prize open the shell and peel away the shell and legs. Repeat with the remaining shrimp. (You can save the head and shells to use in a Shellfish Stock, see p.414).

3 | Once all the shrimp are peeled, make a long, shallow incision with a sharp chef's knife down the curved back of the shrimp down to the tail end. Inside you will see a black vein. Using the tip of the knife or a cocktail stick, start from the tail end to pull it out, then discard.

4 | The shrimp are now ready to use or will keep covered in the fridge for up to 24 hours.

Shrimp saganaki

Prep 40 minutes

Cook 20 minutes

Serves 4–6

The taste of these shrimp, poached in a garlicky tomato sauce and finished with a sprinkling of feta under the broiler, will transport you to a Greek beach taverna on a hot sunny day. It is a great way to use peeled and deveined shrimp (left) because their juices infuse the sauce as they cook. And there's no need to get your hands messy picking them out of the sauce to remove the shell.

2¼lb (1kg) raw shell-on large shrimp, or use
   ready-prepared peeled ones
4 tbsp olive oil, plus extra for serving
1 red onion, peeled and finely chopped
4 fat garlic cloves, peeled and finely chopped
1 red chile, finely chopped
large pinch of salt, plus extra to season
1 (8oz/225g) can crushed tomatoes
¼ cup (85g) tomato paste
⅔ cup (150ml) dry white wine
1 cup (30g) flat-leaf parsley, leaves and stalks,
   chopped
freshly ground black pepper
8oz (200g) feta cheese
1 lemon, cut into 4 wedges
warm crusty bread (ciabatta works well here),
   to serve

1 | Follow steps 1–4 from Shelling & Deveining Shrimp (left). Set aside briefly until needed.

2 | Heat the oil in a large ovenproof skillet over medium heat. Add the red onion, garlic and chile with a large pinch of salt and cook, stirring regularly, for 6–8 minutes, until the onion softens.

3 | Preheat the broiler to high.

4 | Add the crushed tomatoes, tomato paste, wine, and most of the parsley to the pan, stir and bring the sauce to a simmer.

5 | Season the prepared shrimp with salt and pepper, then stir them into the sauce, spreading them out with a wooden spoon so they are roughly in a single layer. Cook for a couple of minutes until the shrimp just begin to turn pink.

6 | Crumble the feta over the top and drizzle with a little more olive oil. Slide the pan under the broiler for about 3 minutes, until the shrimp turn completely pink and the feta starts to melt and turn golden on top.

7 | Serve with the remaining parsley sprinkled over the top, lemon wedges for squeezing, and, most importantly, crusty bread to soak up the sauce.

FRYING
SEAFOOD

Pan-frying (or shallow-frying) is arguably the most classic and simple way to cook fish and shellfish. Like frying a steak or lamb chops, you're looking to build a crisp, browned exterior, where applicable, while still keeping the seafood moist and tender within. This method suits both whole fish and fillets and requires just enough oil or butter to cover the base of the skillet on medium-high heat. A dusting of seasoned flour gives fish, especially thin white fish fillets, a crisp, golden coating, while shellfish, such as shrimp and squid, cook in a matter of minutes when pan-fried.

Deep-frying fish and shellfish, usually in batter or breadcrumbs, is one of the most popular ways to cook seafood—and justifiably so. The coating protects the more delicate seafood from the heat of the oil, while giving an appetizing golden color and a wonderful crunch. First off, a large saucepan or deep skillet is half-filled with oil and heated to a recommended 365°F (180°C). Keep an eye on the temperature—you want it to be hot enough to cook the coating without it turning soggy, but not too hot so it over-darkens before the seafood inside has had a chance to cook.

SIMPLE
PAN-FRIED HAKE

Prep 5 minutes
+ resting

Cook 10 minutes

Serves 4

Hake is perfect for pan-frying—its thick skin crisps up in the hot oil in the pan, while the meaty flesh flakes easily when cooked without falling apart. Try to find thick fillets, which will allow you to achieve the combination of super-crisp skin without overcooking the flesh. The technique below works with all fish fillets, whether they have skin or not—simply reduce the cooking time slightly if the fish fillets are thinner and smaller. Serve the hake with the herby, piquant Salsa Verde (see p.443) spooned over.

4 thick hake fillets, bones removed, skin on
1 tbsp neutral oil, such as vegetable or sunflower
salt and freshly ground black pepper
Salsa Verde (see p.443), to serve

1 | Pat the hake fillets dry with paper towel, then place on a plate and drizzle with the oil, ensuring the fillets are evenly coated. Season each fillet on both sides with salt and pepper. Leave at room temperature for 15 minutes to take the chill off the fish.

2 | Add to a large, heavy skillet just enough oil to cover the bottom and place over medium-high heat. Add the fillets, skin-side down, and gently press with a spatula to ensure they make even contact with the bottom of the pan. Cook the fillets for 3–4 minutes, until the skin is crisp and golden.

3 | Using the spatula, carefully turn the fish over and cook for a further 3 minutes, until golden in places and the fish flesh has turned white and opaque. Move the pan off the heat and leave the fish to rest and finish cooking for 2 minutes in the hot pan. Serve with the salsa verde spooned over.

TIPS

If preferred, you can remove the skin from the hake before cooking, see p.150 for the how-to guide.

The hake is fried in a neutral-flavored oil but for a richer flavor you could add a pat of butter as well. Using a mixture of the two types of fat ensures the butter doesn't burn.

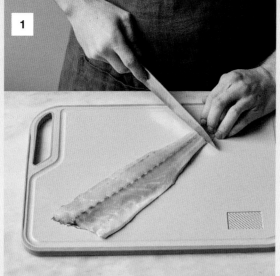

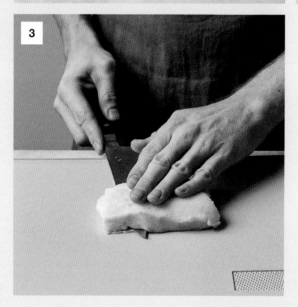

SKINNING
A FISH FILLET

Prep 5 minutes

No cook

Makes 1 fish fillet

If you prefer your fish fillet without skin, removing it is easy following these simple steps.

1 | Pat the fish fillet dry with paper towel—this will help you grip it better and prevent slipping. Put the fillet, skin-side down, on a large cutting board. Holding the tail in one hand, use a sharp fish knife (this has a slight bend in it, making it much easier to make a flat cut along the skin of the fish) to cut down into the fish an inch or so from the tail.

2 | Turn the knife so it is slightly angled between the skin and the flesh of the fillet. Gently pull the skin of the fish toward you while cutting along the fillet, as close to the skin as possible (but without cutting through it), to cleanly remove the skin.

3 | To remove the skin from a thick fish fillet, align the knife horizontally just above the skin. Put your hand on top of the fish to secure it, then carefully cut between the fillet and the skin to remove it.

Thai fishcakes

Prep 15 minutes

Cook 20 minutes

Serves 4

A popular appetizer in Thai restaurants, these fishcakes are herbaceous and citrusy with a hint of spice. The white fish is pulsed briefly in a food processor with the curry paste, which gives the fishcakes a pleasing, slightly "bouncy" texture when cooked. Pan-frying works best for fishcakes because you want to get them nice and caramelized on the outside as they cook, without becoming too dry in the middle.

1lb (500g) thick white fish fillets, such as cod, coley, haddock, or hake, cut into chunks
2 tbsp Thai red curry paste
salt and freshly ground black pepper
1 tbsp cornstarch
1 red bird's eye chile, seeded and finely chopped
3 green onions, finely chopped
1 handful of cilantro, leaves and stalks, finely chopped
1 tsp light brown sugar
2 tsp fish sauce
juice of ½ lime
2–3 tbsp neutral oil, such as vegetable or sunflower
Thai sweet chili sauce, for dipping

1 | Follow step 3 from Skinning a Fish Fillet (left) and carefully pick out any bones.

2 | Put the white fish in a food processor with the curry paste and some salt and pepper, then pulse briefly together to a chunky paste.

3 | Scrape the mixture into a mixing bowl, then add the cornstarch, chile, green onions, cilantro (reserving a few leaves to serve if you like), brown sugar, fish sauce, and lime juice and mix well until evenly combined.

4 | Fill a small bowl or ramekin with cold water. Lightly wet your clean hands, then divide the fish mixture into 12 even portions. Shape each portion into a round patty, about 1 in (2.5 cm) thick, placing them one at a time on a baking sheet—keep your hands damp as you shape them to stop the mixture from sticking. Repeat to make 12 patties in total.

5 | Heat a large, nonstick skillet over medium-high heat and pour in half of the oil. Cook the fishcakes for 2–3 minutes on each side until golden brown and firm in the middle. You will have to do this in batches, depending on the size of your pan, adding more oil as needed. Serve the fishcakes sprinkled with a few reserved cilantro leaves, if you like, and sweet chili sauce on the side for dipping.

CRISPY FISH SANDWICHES

Prep 15 minutes

Cook 20 minutes

Serves 4

If you haven't tried deep-frying before this is a great recipe to start with because the fish takes no time to cook and you're not using as much oil as other similar recipes. It's a good idea to invest in an inexpensive digital cooking thermometer, if possible, because one of the secrets to successful deep-fried fish is getting the oil at just the right temperature—you want it to be hot enough to crisp the batter and turn it golden as well as cook the fish perfectly inside; too hot and the batter will start to burn before the fish gets a chance to cook, but too cold and the batter will be soggy and the fish undercooked. If you don't have a thermometer, no worries, there is an alternative easy option (below)!

4 boneless, skinless cod, haddock, or pollock fillets,
    about 1lb (500g) total weight
vegetable oil, for deep-frying

For the batter
1½ cups (200g) all-purpose flour
2 tsp baking powder
1 tsp fine sea salt, plus extra to season
1¼ cups (330ml) ice-cold lager or IPA

For the tartar sauce
½ cup (125g) Mayonnaise (see p.420) or store-bought
1 tbsp capers, drained and finely chopped
12 cornichons, 4 finely chopped, and 8 sliced
    lengthwise, to serve
1 handful of flat-leaf parsley, leaves and stalks,
    finely chopped
juice of ½ lemon
freshly ground black pepper

To serve
2 heads butter lettuce, leaves separated
8 thick slices of white bread, toasted (optional)
½ lemon, cut into 4 wedges

1 | Start by making the tartar sauce. Mix the mayonnaise, capers, cornichons, and parsley together in a small bowl. Add enough lemon juice to taste and season with salt and pepper. (Squeeze any remaining lemon juice over the lettuce.) Set aside until needed.

2 | Cut the fish fillets into pieces about 4 in (10 cm) long x 1 in (2.5 cm) wide—they don't need to be perfect. Season the fish with salt and pepper.

3 | Line a plate with paper towel. Fill a large, deep skillet or wok one-third full with oil and heat over medium-high heat to 365°F (180°C) or, if you don't have a cooking thermometer, until a cube of bread browns in 20 seconds. If the oil becomes too hot, simply turn off the heat and leave it to cool for a few minutes before testing the temperature again.

4 | While the oil is heating (keep an eye on it), make the batter. Using a balloon whisk, whisk the flour, baking powder, and salt together in a large bowl. Pour in the ice-cold lager, continuously whisking, to make a smooth batter.

5 | The oil should now be up to temperature. Working one piece at a time, dip the fish pieces into the batter until coated, then carefully place them in the hot oil. The best way to do this is to hold the fish close to the surface of the oil and carefully lay it into the oil away from you. You will need to cook them in two batches.

6 | Fry the fish pieces for 2–3 minutes, turning once, until the batter puffs up, becoming lightly golden and crisp, and the fish is flaky and tender inside. Using a slotted spoon, transfer the fish to the paper-towel-lined plate and sprinkle with salt. Repeat with the rest of the fish and batter.

7 | If you like crispy scraps, use the slotted spoon to drizzle any remaining batter into the oil through the holes in the spoon, frying them for a minute or so until golden and crunchy. Once fried, transfer them to a separate paper-towel-lined plate and turn off the oil.

8 | Spread the tartar sauce on 4 slices of bread. Place the fish on top, followed by the lettuce leaves, the sliced cornichons, and any crispy scraps, then sandwich together with the remaining bread. Serve with the lemon wedges for squeezing over.

TIP

Cooking oil can be reused up to three times for deep-frying but should be discarded after that. To dispose of your leftover oil, leave it to cool completely, then pour it into an empty sealable plastic container. Check your local recycling program rather than throwing it away.

CANNED & SMOKED SEAFOOD

Canned fish is having something of a revival and there are plenty of reasons why—it makes an affordable and convenient source of protein, it's incredibly versatile, and is a great pantry standby.

Canned sardines in tomato sauce, for instance, make an easy ready-made pasta sauce. Mix them with some garlic and chile fried in olive oil and serve with spaghetti topped with toasted pine nuts. Canned tuna can be combined with mayonnaise and used to fill baked potatoes or mixed into a Béchamel Sauce (see p.41) for a pie filling, while canned salmon is great in fishcakes or can be flaked into the Lemony Pesto Potato Salad (see p.170) for a more substantial meal.

Also look for canned mackerel, which works with Asian flavors, including noodle dishes.

Smoked fish, such as salmon and mackerel, have a longer fridge life than fresh and are equally versatile. They're good paired with rich, creamy ingredients to balance out their stronger flavor. Try smoked salmon with the classic Scrambled Eggs (see p.27), in the Ultimate Fish Pie (see p.44), or as a sandwich or bagel filling with cream cheese and chives, while smoked mackerel makes a quick pâté (below).

Check out canned/jarred and smoked shellfish, including smoked oysters, mussels, or octopus, which make a great alternative to clams in a pasta dish.

Smoked mackerel pâté

Prep 10 minutes

No cook

Serves 4

Unlike most meat or vegetable pâtés, this smoked mackerel one requires very little preparation and no cooking—you basically mix all the ingredients in a bowl. This recipe uses plain smoked mackerel fillets but if you are a fan of pepper, use one with a crust of crushed peppercorns instead. Just note that the texture will be less smooth and the smoky pâté will come with a fiery hit from the topping.

9oz (250g) smoked mackerel fillets, skin removed
5oz (150g) full-fat cream cheese
juice and finely grated zest of 1 unwaxed lemon
1 handful of chives, finely chopped
1–1½ tbsp creamed horseradish, to taste
large pinch of cayenne pepper
salt and freshly ground black pepper

To serve
slices of brioche or sourdough, toasted
ready-cooked beets, sliced (optional)

1 | Using clean hands or two forks, flake the fillets of mackerel into large pieces in a mixing bowl. Add the cream cheese, lemon juice and zest, chives, and 1 tablespoon of the creamed horseradish. Beat well with a wooden spoon until combined, then season with salt (you may not need much—the fish is quite salty) and pepper.

2 | Taste the pâté and add the extra horseradish, if you like. Eat right away, or cover the bowl and chill until ready to use. You can spoon the pâté into individual ramekins or a serving bowl and bring it out of the fridge 15 minutes before serving.

3 | When ready to serve, sprinkle the top of the pâté with cayenne pepper and serve with brioche or sourdough toast and slices of cooked beet, if you like.

TIPS

This pâté is great to make in advance because it lasts for up to 5 days stored in an airtight container in the fridge. It also freezes well for up to 3 months; defrost it in the fridge overnight before serving.

If you're more of a smoked salmon fan, you can use that instead, swapping the same weight of mackerel for the hot smoked variety.

VEGETABLES

VEGETABLES

This truly diverse group of foods offers the cook an infinite number of culinary possibilities. Broadly divided into "families" (see guide below), vegetable types vary from sprightly leafy greens and golden winter squashes to bold-tasting brassicas and prized asparagus. The ways to cook them are equally varied, from roasting and steaming to grilling and frying, with each creating a different result, depending on the type of vegetable you cook with—just consider the difference in texture and flavor between a sliced raw onion to one that is briefly stir-fried or roasted until tender and sweet.

Vegetables are not only an essential part of a diet from a culinary point of view, they also benefit our health, providing impressive amounts of fiber, vitamins, minerals, and antioxidants.

Storage
Most vegetables will keep well stored in a cool, dry place with ventilation, while leafy greens and delicate veggies are best kept in the fridge. Tomatoes should be kept separate and are best stored at room temperature—the cold affects their flavor and texture.

VEGETABLE	TYPE	COOKING METHOD	PERFECT FOR ...
Leafy greens	Spinach, chard, spring greens, kale, salad leaves	Steam, boil, bake, raw	Creamy casseroles, salads, stir-fries, sauces.
Brassicas	Broccoli, cabbage, cauliflower, Brussels sprouts	Steam, bake, boil, roast, raw	Slaws, cheesy casseroles, spice-coated and roasted, stir-fries.
Onion family	Onions, leeks, garlic	Bake, fry, sauté, roast	Stir-fries, toppings, sauces, roasts, soups, stews.
Roots & tubers	Carrots, beets, celery root, parsnips, turnips, rutabaga, potatoes, sweet potatoes	Steam, boil, roast, bake	Soups, stews, fries, creamy casseroles, spicy roasts, mashed, curries, sauces.
Winter & summer squashes	Zucchini, cucumber, pumpkin, butternut squash	Bake, steam, roast, stir-fry, raw	Soups, roasts, stuffing, fritters, pies, salads, sauces.
Shoots & stalks	Asparagus, fennel, celery, endive	Steam, boil, raw, roast, grill	Tart fillings, soups, salads, stir-fries, casseroles.
Pods & seeds	Green beans, peas, fava beans, sugar snap peas, corn	Steam, boil, raw, grill	Fritters, sauces, stir-fries, dips, soups, salads, sauces.
Fungi	Button and field mushrooms, portobello, shiitake, oyster, porcini	Fry, sauté, stir-fry, bake	Sauces, stir-fries, soups, stews, burgers, stuffed.
Vegetable fruits	Eggplants, tomatoes, fresh chiles, peppers, avocados	Roast, bake, fry, sauté, grill, raw	Sauces, stir-fries, bakes, dips, salsas, curries, stews, salads.

Clockwise, from top, sweetheart cabbage, garlic, zucchini, green beans, beets, shiitake mushrooms, rainbow chard, tomatoes, and red endive.

PREPARING VEGETABLES

Many recipes in this book start with slicing or chopping an onion. This fundamental skill isn't difficult, but a knowledge of the technique makes it so much easier to achieve the perfect slice, dice, or wedge. This skill applies to all vegetables, not just onions, and a good starting point, whether eating them raw or using in your cooking, is to master the basics of preparation. The way you cut a vegetable can affect the texture, appearance, and timing of a dish—and even its taste to a certain extent. A finely diced red onion works well in a salad, for instance, adding pops of fresh spiciness, yet if you chopped that same onion into large chunks it would completely overpower the same salad, rather than enhance it.

It's always best to prepare vegetables just before you plan to use/eat them because they lose their flavor and nutrient value with time and can also become soggy or limp. If the vegetable is prone to discoloration and browning, you can put it in water with a little lemon juice or vinegar, but try not to leave it for too long. A large or medium-size, sharp chef's knife is invaluable. It may sound a little intimidating, but in reality you are more likely to cut yourself with a knife that is dull because it makes chopping all the more cumbersome. A sharp knife allows for precision and will make you a better cook from the get-go, saving you time and building your confidence in the kitchen. Remember practice makes perfect!

SLICING AN ONION

Being able to finely slice an onion correctly is a game changer as it is frequently used in many recipes—both raw and cooked—but don't fret, you'll soon be slicing it as fast as a professional.

1 | Using a large, sharp chef's knife, on a cutting board, trim and discard both ends of the onion, then cut it in half vertically. Peel off the skin.

2 | Turn the onion so one of the cut ends is facing you. Put one hand on the onion to secure it firmly on the cutting board, then thinly slice until you reach halfway along the onion.

3 | Turn the onion over so it is more secure on the cutting board, then continue to slice it in the same way. Repeat with the second half of onion.

CHOPPING
AN ONION

Whether sautéed or used as part of a sauce or stew, a chopped onion is probably the most useful technique you'll learn in the kitchen and is at the heart of so many recipes in this book.

1 | Using a large, sharp chef's knife, cut the onion vertically in half, from the tip to the root end. Trim the tip, then peel the onion, leaving the root end intact.

2 | Put the onion, cut-side down, with the root end facing away from you, then cut the onion into vertical slices, but do not slice through the root end because this helps hold the onion together.

3 | Turn the onion 90 degrees and with your knife make two horizontal cuts, one-third and two-thirds the way up the onion, again not cutting through the root end.

4 | Turn your knife vertical again, starting from the end opposite the root, cut across the vertical slices into small dice. Discard the root end.

SHREDDING CABBAGE

This slicing technique works with all types of cabbage, whether red, white, Savoy, or pointed. It is especially good for when you are making a slaw (see p.165) because you want fine slices that are easy to eat and can be coated in a dressing.

1 | Peel away any tough or damaged outside leaves from the cabbage. Using a large, sharp chef's knife, cut the cabbage vertically in half through the root end, while securing it with your other hand.

2 | Place one half of the cabbage cut-side down on your cutting board and cut it in half through the root. Repeat with the other half so you now have four pieces.

3 | Take one of the quarters and place it on its side. Starting from the end opposite the root, very thinly slice the cabbage, holding it securely with your other hand, all the way down to the woody root end, which you can discard. Repeat with all four pieces.

TIPS

Instead of shredding the cabbage with a knife, use a box grater to coarsely grate it or a vegetable peeler to cut it into long, thin shreds.

Prepare cabbage just before eating raw or cooking to avoid it turning soft and limp. Alternatively, store prepared in an airtight container in the fridge for up to 1 day.

JULIENNE A CARROT

Julienne is a fancy term for cutting a vegetable, such as a carrot, beet, or celery root, into long, matchstick-shaped pieces. It is a useful technique to learn for presentation purposes if a vegetable is going to be used as a garnish, for instance, or in a salad, such as the slaw (see p.165). You can also use this technique to cut fresh ginger into thin matchsticks.

1 | Trim the root end from the carrot and peel with a vegetable peeler. Cut the carrot horizontally into 2 or 3 pieces, depending on its size—this will make it more manageable to julienne.

2 | Take one of the carrot pieces, turn it vertically, then carefully cut into ⅛-in (3-mm) thick slices using a large, sharp chef's knife. Cut the remaining carrot into ⅛ in (3 mm) slices, making stacks of 2 or 3 slices.

3 | Take one stack of carrot slices, place vertically on the board, then cut it into thin matchsticks, securing the stack with the other hand. Repeat until all the carrot has been cut into julienne strips.

SLICING
A PEPPER

When preparing a pepper you want to minimize waste, yet also ensure you remove all the bitter white pith and seeds before slicing or chopping into pieces.

1 | Lay the pepper horizontally on a cutting board. Using a large, sharp chef's knife, slice off the top ½ in (1 cm) of the pepper at the stalk end, then flip it over and slice off the bottom ½ in (1 cm).

2 | Cut away the central white core, then remove it with any small white seeds from the top and bottom.

3 | Put the pepper, cut-side down, then cut it in half vertically. Place one pepper half, flat-side facing up, then turn the knife horizontally and carefully remove any white pith and stray seeds, and discard. Repeat with the other half.

4 | Place a pepper half, skin-side down, on the cutting board, and cut into ¼-in (5-mm) thick slices, then repeat with the other pepper half.

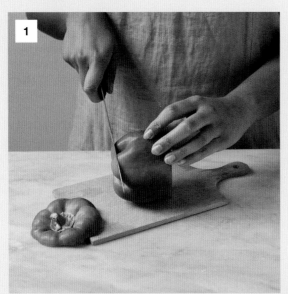

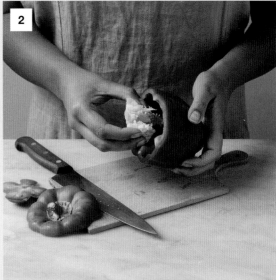

Alabama white sauce slaw

Prep 20 minutes

No cook

Serves 4 as a side

This crunchy slaw uses the valuable vegetable preparation skills detailed on the previous pages. This is a twist on a classic slaw and comes with a Southern American–style dressing, which is usually served with smoked chicken or turkey. It has a creamy piquant kick and works just as well as a dressing for this crisp raw vegetable salad.

½ small red or white cabbage
1 carrot
1 red onion

1 red bell pepper
1 handful of chives, finely chopped, to serve

For the dressing
¼ cup (75g) Mayonnaise (see p.420) or store-bought
3 tbsp apple cider vinegar
juice and finely grated zest of ½ unwaxed lemon
1 tbsp Dijon mustard
1 tbsp honey
1 tbsp horseradish sauce
1 tsp garlic powder
1 tsp ground paprika
salt and freshly ground black pepper

1 | First make the dressing. Spoon the mayonnaise into a large serving bowl, then add the rest of the ingredients. Season well with salt and pepper, then use a balloon whisk to mix everything together.

2 | Prepare the cabbage, carrot, onion, and red pepper following the instructions on pp.160–164.

3 | Add the prepared vegetables to the bowl and toss until they are coated in the dressing. Sprinkle over the chives, to serve. This salad can be stored in an airtight container in the fridge for up to 3 days.

TIP

The flavor of this slaw improves when made a few hours ahead of serving. Time allows the flavors of the dressing to mingle, while the vegetables soften in the dressing.

Watermelon
Greek salad

*Prep 15 minutes
+ pickling*

No cook

Serves 4

A Greek salad on a hot day is a thing of beauty. For an added twist, this version features lightly pickled red onion for zing and watermelon for sweetness. For the best flavor, make sure you buy watermelon and tomatoes at the peak of ripeness. The cucumber should also be crisp and crunchy with no sign of softness.

1 red onion, thinly sliced
1 tsp dried oregano
3 tbsp red wine vinegar
salt and freshly ground black pepper
8oz (200g) ripe cherry tomatoes, halved
1 cucumber, quartered lengthwise and cut into
    1½ in (4 cm) pieces
¼ small ripe watermelon, about 2¼lb (1kg), rind
    removed and cut into 1½ in (4 cm) pieces
⅓ cup (100g) pitted Kalamata olives, drained
4 tbsp extra-virgin olive oil
6oz (150g) feta cheese, crumbled
1 handful of mint leaves

1 | Put the red onion into a large bowl and add the oregano and vinegar. Season with salt and pepper, toss well, and leave to pickle for 10 minutes.

2 | Add the cherry tomatoes, cucumber, watermelon, and olives to the bowl containing the pickled onion. Pour in the olive oil and toss well to combine.

3 | Divide the salad between four plates, spooning over any dressing left in the bowl. Crumble over the feta and sprinkle with mint leaves. This is best served immediately at room temperature.

TIP

To enhance and retain the flavor and texture of your tomatoes, store them out of the fridge at room temperature. They will also continue to ripen.

Gujarati carrot salad

Prep 5 minutes

Cook 5 minutes

Serves 3–4

A version of this crunchy, raw carrot salad is served across India. It is fragrant from whole toasted spices, refreshing from the citrus, and comes with pops of green chile, making it the ideal accompaniment to richly flavored meat dishes, such as Curried Lamb Koftas (see p.118). It's equally good as a standalone dish, providing a speedy taste explosion, or served with crispy fried paneer for a vegetarian meal.

⅔lb (300g) carrots, peeled
½–1 green or red chile, halved, seeded if preferred, and finely sliced into half moons
1 tbsp vegetable oil
1 tbsp black mustard seeds
1 tsp cumin seeds
juice of 1 lemon
salt and freshly ground black pepper

1 | Follow steps 1–3 from Julienne a Carrot (see p.163). Alternatively, coarsely grate the carrot using the large holes of a box grater or a food processor. Put the prepared carrots in a medium serving bowl with the chile.

2 | Heat the vegetable oil in a small saucepan over medium heat. Add the mustard and cumin seeds. Cook, stirring with a wooden spoon, until the seeds start to pop and smell fragrant, about 1 minute, then remove the pan from the heat.

3 | Immediately spoon the seeds and hot oil over the carrot salad. Squeeze in the lemon juice and give everything a good stir. Season with salt and pepper to taste.

TIP

Eating this salad soon after making ensures the carrot retains its crunchy texture. Any leftovers will keep stored in an airtight container in the fridge for up to 3 days. For the best flavor, bring the salad back to room temperature before serving.

BOILING & BLANCHING VEGETABLES

Boiling, or cooking in water, is one of the simplest methods to prepare vegetables and is particularly good for firm, starchy root types, such as potatoes, turnips, and beets. Ensure you adjust the boiling time according to how you plan to use the vegetable. For example, in the Lemony Pesto Potato Salad (see p.170) you want the potatoes to be tender but still hold their shape, whereas for mashed you are aiming to cook them to the point of almost falling apart.

When preparing root vegetables, it's important to cut them to the same size pieces so they cook evenly, then cover with cold water in a pan, put on the lid, and bring to a boil. Conversely, green vegetables should be added to boiling water, then simmered slowly to retain their color and slight crunch. Avoid covering the pan when cooking green vegetables because they lose their vibrant color, in contrast to vegetables, such as carrots and beets, which should be cooked in a covered pan to retain their brightness.

Blanching is the opposite of boiling—you want to briefly immerse vegetables in boiling water until softened but not cooked—this way they retain their flavor, color, and crunch. After blanching, drain and place the vegetables under cold running water or in a bowl of ice-cold water to stop them cooking any further. Use this method for removing the skin from tomatoes or in the green bean salad (below).

Parboiling, as the name suggests, is when a vegetable is part-cooked before it is used as part of another dish, for instance, the Brown Butter & Caper Asparagus (see p.51), where the green stalks are softened slightly in boiling water before sautéing.

SESAME GREEN BEAN & SUGAR SNAP SALAD

Prep 10 minutes

Cook 10 minutes

Serves 3–4 as a side

Here, green beans and sugar snap peas are briefly blanched in lightly salted boiling water until sweet and still crisp. They are then refreshed in ice-cold water, a simple technique that preserves their vibrant green color and stops them from overcooking and losing their crunch. Serve the salad with the Pork Chops & Miso-Lime Shallots (see p.116) or over fluffy basmati rice with a perfectly Fried Egg (see p.25) for a winning veggie dinner.

large pinch of salt, plus extra to season
½lb (200g) green beans, ends trimmed
½lb (200g) sugar snap peas
2 tbsp toasted sesame seeds
1 tbsp sesame oil
2 tbsp rice wine vinegar
1 tbsp soy sauce or tamari, plus an
   extra splash, if liked

1 tsp honey
1 handful of mint, leaves picked
freshly ground black pepper
juice of ½ lime

1 | Bring a medium saucepan of water to a boil and add a large pinch of salt—this is a great way to gently season the beans from the start of cooking. Add the green beans, return the water to a boil and cook for 2 minutes, until slightly softened.

2 | Meanwhile, fill a medium bowl with ice-cold water. Using a slotted spoon, lift the blanched green beans out of the pan into the bowl (this will stop them from cooking any further and preserve their color), then leave for 1–2 minutes to cool completely.

3 | Repeat this process with the sugar snap peas, cooking them for just 30 seconds before refreshing in the iced water. Drain the vegetables and put them in a serving bowl.

4 | Using a fork, whisk together the sesame seeds, sesame oil, vinegar, soy or tamari, and honey in a small bowl until combined. Spoon the dressing over the green vegetables, then add the mint leaves, a little salt and pepper, and toss to combine. Check the seasoning, then squeeze over the lime juice before serving.

TIP

This salad can be made the day before serving. Keep it in the fridge in an airtight container, then bring it up to room temperature for 30 minutes before serving.

LEMONY PESTO POTATO SALAD

Prep 10 minutes

Cook 30 minutes

Serves 4

This zingy potato salad is packed full of flavor, the perfect accompaniment to barbecue or Whole Roasted Sea Bream (see p.130). The trick here is to cook the potatoes in well-salted water until tender but not falling apart. Waxy new potatoes, such as Yukon Gold, are best for this because they soften but retain their shape—plus they don't need to be peeled.

1⅔lb (750g) waxy new or baby potatoes, such
   as Yukon Gold, cut in half
salt and freshly ground black pepper
1 cup (200g) Fresh Basil Pesto (see p.442)
2 shallots, peeled and finely chopped
juice and finely grated zest of ½ unwaxed lemon
1 tbsp Dijon mustard
1 handful of basil leaves

1 | Put the potatoes in a large saucepan and pour in enough cold water to completely cover. Add salt, cover with a lid, and bring the water to a boil over medium-high heat. Once the water is boiling, take off the lid and reduce the heat. Simmer the potatoes for 20 minutes, until the point of a knife easily slides into the middle of the potato.

2 | Put a colander in the sink, then drain the potatoes, leaving them to steam-dry for a few minutes.

3 | Put the potatoes into a large serving bowl. Stir in the pesto, shallots, lemon juice and zest, and mustard. Season with salt and pepper and mix well until combined. Sprinkle with basil leaves and serve.

TIP

This is a great salad to make in advance, even the day before. Bring it up to room temperature 1 hour before serving.

Mashed potatoes

Prep 10 minutes

Cook 20 minutes

Serves 4

The workhorse of the potato world and an unsung hero, creamy, buttery mashed potatoes are wonderfully comforting and make an excellent side dish or topping to a pie. They're particularly good with the Chicken, Leek & Mustard Pie (see p.74) or Beef Bourguignon (see p.120), or anything with gravy! Use starchy potatoes, such as Russet, which make for a fluffy, creamy texture, and cook them fully, almost to the point of falling apart, before mashing to avoid any lumps. When cooked, drain them well, add lots of butter, and season generously with salt and pepper—no one likes bland mashed potatoes.

1⅔lb (750g) starchy potatoes (such as Russet),
    peeled and quartered
salt and freshly ground black pepper
½ cup (100ml) whole milk
6 tbsp (75g) salted butter, cubed

1 | Put the potatoes in a large saucepan and pour over enough cold water to completely cover. Season well with salt and put the pan over medium-high heat with the lid on.

2 | Once the water is boiling, take off the lid and reduce the heat. Simmer the potatoes for 20 minutes, until completely soft—a table knife should slide into the center with no resistance.

3 | Drain the potatoes in a colander in the sink, then put them back into the saucepan and leave to steam-dry for a few minutes. Pour in the milk and add the butter.

4 | Using a potato masher, mash the potatoes until completely smooth. Season with salt and pepper to taste before serving.

TIP

If making mashed potatoes a few hours in advance, follow steps 1–3 until the potatoes are cooked, then drain and put them back into the pan. Leave to one side at room temperature. Once ready to mash, reheat the potatoes over low heat with the milk and butter, then mash until smooth and creamy.

STEAMING
VEGETABLES

This is a pure and simple way to cook vegetables, allowing them to retain their natural flavor, nutrients, and crunch, without becoming water-logged or soggy. Vegetables are steamed over a covered pan of boiling water in a basket—although a colander or strainer will suffice—and most importantly they don't touch the water, but cook in the rising steam. To ensure the vegetables cook evenly, cut them into uniform pieces and try not to overcrowd the steamer basket—you ideally want them to be in a single layer. A tiered steamer is useful for cooking multiple types of vegetable—especially those with differing flavors.

STEAMING
BROCCOLINI

Prep 5 minutes

Cook 5 minutes

Serves 4

This method works for many different types of vegetable—in fact any vegetable that can be boiled can be steamed—so it's a simple yet useful one to have under your belt. Green vegetables are particularly good steamed because it concentrates their vibrant color and flavor—with broccolini, the stalks soften while the tips avoid becoming water-logged. Serve this with the Asian-Style Crispy Shallot & Peanut Dressing (see p.433) to take it to another level.

⅔lb (300g) broccolini, woody ends trimmed
Crispy Shallot & Peanut Dressing (p.433), to serve
   (optional)

1 | Pour water into the bottom of a saucepan and bring it to a boil or use just-boiled water from the kettle. Turn the heat to medium-low so the water is simmering. Place the broccolini in the steamer basket, spreading it out in a single layer. Sit the steamer basket above the pan—it shouldn't touch the water below. Cover the pan with the lid.

2 | Steam the broccolini for 3–4 minutes, depending on the size of the florets, until tender. Test the stalk with the point of a knife to check that it is ready. Remove the broccolini from the steamer and serve right away with the dressing, if you like.

Hunan-style steamed eggplant with chiles

Prep 10 minutes

Cook 10 minutes

Serves 2

This popular dish, originating from the Hunan province of central China, is a healthy and delicious way to serve eggplant. Rather than frying the eggplant, which uses a lot of oil, it is steamed until soft and tender. It also takes on the flavor of the sauce as it cooks. The eggplant can be steamed on the stove or cooked in a microwave.

1 large globe eggplant or 2 medium Chinese
  eggplants, cut into 3-in (7.5-cm) long slices

For the seasoning
1 tbsp finely chopped red chile
1 handful of green onions, chopped
1 tbsp soy sauce
1 tbsp Chinese black vinegar
1 tsp toasted sesame oil
1 tsp sugar
1 tsp minced garlic

1 tsp minced fresh ginger
½ tbsp oyster sauce
½ tsp salt

To finish
sesame seeds
fresh cilantro leaves
chili oil (optional)
Cooked Rice (see p.202), to serve

1 | Place the eggplant in a steamer basket set over a pan of simmering water and cook for 5–7 minutes, until tender. Alternatively, place the eggplant in a microwaveable shallow bowl, pour over 1 tablespoon of water, cover tightly with plastic wrap, and microwave on high for 3–4 minutes.

2 | While the eggplant is cooking, combine the seasoning ingredients in a bowl to make a sauce.

3 | If steaming the eggplant, heat the sauce in a small pan for 2–3 minutes, until warmed through, then pour it over the eggplant when tender. If microwaving the eggplant, remove the bowl and pour the uncooked sauce over to evenly coat. Cover tightly, return the eggplant to the microwave, and cook on high for another 2–3 minutes.

4 | Transfer the eggplant to a serving bowl, sprinkle over the sesame seeds and cilantro. Drizzle with chili oil, if you like, and serve with rice.

TIP

To finely chop a chile, use a sharp chef's knife to cut the chile in half lengthwise, discarding the stalk. Leave the seeds in for heat or remove if preferred, then cut each half into thin strips. Turn the strips horizontally, then finely chop into small dice.

BAKING & ROASTING VEGETABLES

Roasting or baking (the terms are largely interchangeable) is a game changer when it comes to cooking vegetables. The dry heat of the oven enhances their flavor, concentrating the starches so they become sweeter and take on a delicious, slightly caramelized, and often crisp exterior. Firm root vegetables, such as carrots, parsnips, beets, and squash, are excellent roasted, while the flavor and texture of cauliflower, tomatoes, eggplants, peppers, and onions also benefit from roasting. Simply add a splash of olive oil and maybe lift the flavor with the addition of herbs and spices. Then, of course, there are potatoes. Nothing beats the flavor and texture of the crispy skin and soft, creamy inside of a baked potato, or the roast potato with its golden crunch and fluffy center. Pure comfort food!

ULTIMATE ROAST POTATOES

Prep 5 minutes + cooling

Cook 1 hour 15 minutes

Serves 6–8

These roast potatoes have a deeply golden, crisp exterior with the fluffiest, creamiest center. Great eaten on their own, or even as a comforting snack dipped into Vegan Gravy (see p.419), these roast potatoes are a great side dish for Chicken Cacciatore (see p.92) or most anything else. For the best roast potatoes, use a large, starchy variety, such as Russet. These will give you the best ratio of super crisp shell with fluffy potato center.

4½lb (2kg) starchy potatoes (such as Russet), peeled
salt and freshly ground black pepper
⅓ cup (100g) duck or goose fat, or ⅓ cup (100ml) vegetable oil
1 handful of rosemary sprigs

1 | Cut the smaller potatoes in half and any large potatoes into quarters—you want them all to be roughly the same size, with a few slightly smaller ones if you like extra crispy bits.

2 | Put the potatoes in your largest saucepan that has a lid and pour in enough cold water to just cover them. Salt the water generously. Put the saucepan over high heat, cover with a lid, and bring to a boil. Once boiling, turn the heat down to medium-high and cook, part-covered with a lid, for 7 minutes, until a small, sharp knife slides easily into the center and the edges crumble slightly when touched.

3 | Preheat the oven to 425°F (220°C). Drain the potatoes well in a colander, then immediately put them back into the hot pan. Put the lid on the pan, then with one hand holding the lid and the other the pan handle, shake it a few times to fluff up the outside of the potatoes—this ensures they become crisp during roasting. Put the potatoes on a baking sheet to steam-dry and cool for 10 minutes.

4 | Meanwhile, measure the fat or oil into a large, heavy-bottomed roasting pan, about 10 x 14 in (34 x 28 cm), and heat in the oven for 10 minutes—you want it to be super hot. Carefully remove the roasting pan from the oven and, using a large metal spoon, lower the potatoes into the hot fat, rolling them around so they are coated on all sides and seasoning with salt and pepper as you go.

5 | Once all the potatoes are on the baking sheet and evenly spaced out, roast in the oven for 20 minutes. Reduce the heat to 400°F (200°C) and cook for a further 20 minutes, until starting to crisp on the bottom. Carefully remove the baking sheet from the oven and use a metal spatula to turn the potatoes so the crispy bits are now on top. Roast the potatoes for a further 20 minutes, turn them again, and add the rosemary sprigs. Cook for a further 10–15 minutes, until golden and crisp all over and the insides are soft and creamy.

HONEY & THYME
ROASTED ROOT VEGETABLES

Prep 10 minutes

Cook 35 minutes

Serves 4

Root vegetables, such as carrots and parsnips, are particularly good roasted and are a world away from the overcooked boiled alternative—just make sure to cut them into similar-size pieces so they cook evenly. The sweet glaze gives the vegetables a lovely glossy coating and complements their flavor. Serve as a side to any roasted meat (see pp.100–107) or a nut roast (see p.290).

1lb (500g) each of carrots and parsnips,
    peeled
2 tbsp olive oil
salt and freshly ground black pepper
2 tbsp honey or maple syrup
1 handful of thyme sprigs, leaves stripped

1 | Heat the oven to 425°F (220°C). Cut the carrots and parsnips in 2-in (5-cm) long sticks.

2 | Put the carrots and parsnips in a large roasting pan, pour over the olive oil, then season with plenty of salt and pepper and toss until combined. Spread the vegetables into a single layer, so they cook evenly, and roast for 20–25 minutes, tossing with a spatula halfway, until tender and starting to color.

3 | Drizzle the honey or maple syrup over the carrots and parsnips, then sprinkle with the thyme leaves. Return the tray to the oven for 5–8 minutes, until the vegetables are sticky and caramelized.

Shawarma-spiced whole baked cauliflower

Prep 20 minutes

Cook 1 hour 15 minutes

Serves 4

Roasting is a perfect way to cook cauliflower, especially when it's coated in an aromatic Middle Eastern spice blend. The dry heat of the oven caramelizes the outside of the cauliflower as it roasts, giving it a slight sweetness and softening the center—there's none of the sogginess, pungency, or bitterness you get from over-boiled cauliflower! The herby condiment Zhoug (see p.445) and Tabbouleh (see p.213) are both perfect accompaniments.

1 recipe quantity of Shawarma Spice Mix (see p.448) or store-bought
4 tbsp extra-virgin olive oil
1 whole cauliflower
1 cup (250g) plain or Greek yogurt
1 small garlic clove, peeled and finely grated
juice and finely grated zest of ½ unwaxed lemon
salt and freshly ground black pepper
1 handful of cilantro leaves
½ cup (30g) pomegranate seeds
Tabbouleh (see p.213) and Zhoug (see p.445), to serve

1 | Preheat the oven to 400°F (200°C). Line a roasting pan with parchment paper.

2 | Add the shawarma spice mix into a large bowl and pour in the olive oil, mixing to make a thin paste.

3 | Carefully trim the cauliflower, removing the bottom of the stalk and any large, thick leaves. Add the cauliflower to the bowl and toss well to coat it evenly in the spice oil.

4 | Place the cauliflower in the lined roasting pan, scraping the bowl to spoon any remaining spice oil over, and roast for 1 hour 15 minutes, until a knife easily pierces the center of the stem.

5 | Meanwhile, mix together the yogurt, garlic, and lemon juice and zest in a bowl. Season with salt and pepper to taste.

6 | Spread the yogurt mix onto a large serving plate and place the roasted cauliflower on top, scraping any spices left in the tray. Finish with a sprinkling of cilantro leaves and pomegranate seeds, then serve with tabbouleh and zhoug on the side.

Veggie lasagna

Prep 20 minutes

Cook 1½ hours

Serves 4–6

Having a great lasagna recipe in your cooking repertoire is a must, and while the meat version is classic, vegetables really come into their own in this veggie baked dish, and also make it more economical. The zucchini and eggplant are grilled before assembling, which gives them a lovely smoky flavor and depth of color. The lasagna is then baked until the vegetables become meltingly soft and meld with the layers of pasta and tomato and béchamel sauces. It can be prepared up to 2 days in advance (see Tip, right) and freezes well, making it perfect for batch cooking.

3 tbsp olive oil, plus extra for drizzling
1 red onion, peeled and finely chopped
pinch of salt, plus extra for seasoning
4 fat garlic cloves, peeled and finely chopped
½–1 tsp dried chili flakes, depending on taste
1 cup (30g) basil, leaves picked and stalks
    finely chopped
2 (14.5oz/400g) cans diced tomatoes
1 (15oz/400g) can lentils, drained and rinsed
3½oz (100g) sun-dried tomatoes, chopped
2 tbsp balsamic vinegar
freshly ground black pepper
1 eggplant, sliced into ½-in (1-cm) thick rounds
2 zucchini, sliced into ½-in (1-cm) thick rounds
1 recipe quantity of Béchamel Sauce (see p.41) or
    16fl oz (500ml) store-bought
¾lb (300g) dried no-cook lasagna sheets, depending
    on the shape of your dish
5oz (125g) mozzarella cheese, drained and
    torn into chunks
crisp green salad, to serve

1 | Heat 1 tablespoon of the olive oil in a medium saucepan over medium heat. Add the onion along with a pinch of salt and cook, stirring occasionally, for 8–10 minutes, until softened.

2 | Add the garlic, chili flakes, and basil stalks and cook, stirring, for 1 minute, then add in the diced tomatoes, lentils, and sun-dried tomatoes with the balsamic vinegar. Give everything a good stir and leave it to simmer for 15 minutes, stirring occasionally. Season with salt and pepper.

3 | Meanwhile, toss the eggplant and zucchini slices in the remaining olive oil in a large bowl with your hands until evenly coated. Season with salt and pepper. Heat a large, grill pan or nonstick skillet over high heat. Once hot, add the vegetable slices in a single layer and cook for 2–3 minutes on each side until slightly blackened in places and softened. Remove to a plate and repeat until all the vegetables are cooked.

4 | Follow steps 1–4 from How to Make a White Sauce using the béchamel variation. Preheat the oven to 400°F (200°C).

5 | To assemble the lasagna, spread one-third of the tomato lentil sauce into a medium baking dish, about 9 x 13in (30 x 20cm), then top with an even layer of lasagna sheets.

6 | Spoon one-third of the béchamel sauce on top, followed by one-third of the grilled vegetables and half the basil leaves.

7 | Spoon over another third of the tomato-lentil sauce, then top with a second layer of lasagna sheets and another third of the béchamel sauce, vegetables, and rest of the basil leaves. Repeat with a final layer of tomato sauce, then finish with a third layer of pasta and the rest of the béchamel sauce. Top with the torn chunks of mozzarella and drizzle with a little extra olive oil.

8 | Bake the lasagna for 30–35 minutes, until a small, sharp knife slides into the middle with no resistance and the top is bubbling and golden. Leave to stand for 5 minutes before serving with a crisp green salad.

TIPS

The individual components for this lasagna can be made up to 2 days in advance, including the tomato sauce, béchamel, and grilled vegetables. Simply assemble and bake on the day when ready to serve.

Alternatively, prepare the lasagna up to the end of step 7, then chill, covered, in the fridge overnight before baking.

To freeze, leave the lasagna to cool and divide into individual containers. Freeze for up to 3 months. When ready to serve, defrost thoroughly before reheating at 350°F (180°C) for 15–20 minutes.

For a meat alternative, swap the vegetable filling for the Bolognese Sauce (see p.122). It may not be completely traditional but it is still delicious.

BLENDING VEGETABLES

Many different types of vegetable, from leeks, peas, and green beans to carrots and cauliflower, can be blended and it is a quick and easy way to transform them into a velvety sauce or soup. The vegetables need to be cooked first until tender, whether that be boiled, steamed, or roasted, before blending.

A blender, immersion blender, or food processor are the most efficient tools for blending (also known as puréeing), but a ricer, fine-mesh strainer, or food mill are also effective. You may also need to press the purée through a fine-mesh strainer to remove any stubborn bits of skin to make it super smooth.

BUTTERNUT SQUASH SAUCE

Prep 10 minutes

Cook 40 minutes

Serves 3–4

Roasting the butternut squash before puréeing concentrates its sweet flavor by drawing out moisture and caramelizing the starches in the vegetable. Here, the squash is spiked with roasted garlic, chili flakes, and lemon zest, while the soft goat cheese adds depth and richness to the blended sauce. The purée can be tossed with freshly cooked pasta for a quick meal, stirred into a risotto base (see p.204), or added to the gnocchi recipe (see p.182). However, if you want to make a soup rather than a sauce, simply leave out the goat cheese and add ⅔ cup (150ml) of water or stock instead to thin the purée.

1 small butternut squash, about 1lb 10oz (750g)
1 tbsp olive oil, divided
salt and freshly ground black pepper
1 garlic bulb
½ tsp dried chili flakes
finely grated zest of 1 unwaxed lemon
5oz (125g) soft, rindless goat cheese, roughly chopped

1 | Preheat the oven to 425°F (220°C). Line a roasting pan with parchment paper. Cut the squash in half lengthwise, leaving the skin and seeds. Drizzle 1 teaspoon of the olive oil over the flesh and season with salt and pepper. Place cut-side down in the lined roasting pan and drizzle another teaspoon of olive oil over the skin.

2 | Slicing horizontally, cut off the top of the garlic bulb to expose the cloves inside and discard the top. Place the garlic in a piece of foil large enough to make a parcel, drizzle with the remaining oil, then gather the edges of the foil together to seal. Place it next to the squash in the roasting pan.

3 | Roast the squash and garlic for 35–40 minutes, until both are tender. A small, sharp knife should slide into the center of the squash easily, and if you gently squeeze the garlic bulb, the cloves should give. Leave both to cool for 5 minutes.

4 | Turn the squash over and use a spoon to scoop out the seeds and discard. Scoop out the flesh into a blender, and discard the skin.

5 | Unwrap the garlic bulb and squeeze the cloves into the blender. Add the chili flakes, lemon zest, goat cheese, and ⅓ cup (100ml) of water.

6 | Purée the squash to a smooth sauce, the consistency of heavy cream, adding a splash more water, if needed. Season with salt and pepper to taste. The sauce will keep covered for up to 3 days in the fridge.

TIP

This butternut sauce freezes well. Portion it into lidded containers and freeze for up to 3 months. It can be reheated from frozen or left to defrost.

Butternut squash & sage gnocchi

Prep 15 minutes

Cook 50 minutes

Serves 3–4

This may be a simple gnocchi dish, but it feels really special with its creamy, indulgent sauce made from roasted and puréed butternut squash. Most of the cooking time is taken up with roasting the squash in the oven. If you make the sauce in advance, the meal comes together in a matter of minutes and makes the perfect veggie dish for impressing your friends.

1 recipe quantity of Butternut Squash
   Sauce (see p.180)
2 tbsp olive oil, plus extra for drizzling
1 large handful of sage, leaves picked
salt and freshly ground black pepper
1lb (500g) package of fresh gnocchi
juice of ½ lemon, to taste (use the zest in the
   squash sauce)
large pinch of dried chili flakes
⅓ cup (50g) pumpkin seeds, toasted (see step 4, right)

1 | Follow steps 1–6 to make the Butternut Squash Sauce (see p.180).

2 | Heat the olive oil in a large, high-sided skillet over medium-high heat. Once sizzling, add the sage leaves and fry for 1 minute, until darkened slightly in color, then use a slotted spoon to transfer them to a plate lined with paper towel. Leave the sage to cool and crisp up.

3 | Turn the heat to low, pour the butternut sauce into the pan, and reheat gently, stirring occasionally.

4 | Meanwhile, fill a medium saucepan with water, generously salt, and bring to a boil. Add the gnocchi and cook for 1 minute less than instructed on the package—they are ready when they float to the surface of the water.

5 | Using a slotted spoon, lift out the gnocchi from the saucepan and place directly into the skillet of sauce. Mix gently to coat the gnocchi in the sauce. If the sauce has thickened too much for your liking, add a splash of the gnocchi cooking water to loosen. Season with extra salt and pepper to taste and stir in the lemon juice.

6 | Divide the gnocchi between three or four bowls, depending on everyone's appetite. Top with the chili flakes, crisp sage leaves, pumpkin seeds, and a drizzle of olive oil, to serve.

Cauliflower soup
with chili pumpkin seeds

Prep 15 minutes

Cook 30 minutes

Serves 4

This soup makes the most of two cooking techniques (roasting and blending) and is a great one to make in advance and reheat when needed. The majority of the work is done in the oven, which softens and enhances the flavor of the cauliflower, then it is blended with stock until smooth. The spicy pumpkin seeds add a crunchy kick, which is in contrast to the creaminess of the soup, but do reduce the quantity of chili oil if you prefer things less hot.

1 medium head cauliflower, cut into medium florets
4 unpeeled garlic cloves
1 onion, peeled and cut into 8 wedges
2-in piece of fresh ginger, peeled
    and cut into ¾-in (2-cm) thick slices
2 tbsp olive oil
4 tsp cumin seeds, divided
4 tsp mustard seeds, divided
salt and freshly ground black pepper

4¼ cups (1 liter) Chicken or Vegetable Stock
    (see p.414) or store-bought
⅓ cup (100ml) heavy cream
⅓ cup (50g) pumpkin seeds
1 tsp chili oil, plus extra to serve
1 handful of mint leaves (optional)

1 | Preheat the oven to 425°F (220°C).

2 | Toss the cauliflower, whole garlic cloves, onion, and ginger with the olive oil and 3 teaspoons each of cumin and mustard seeds in a large roasting pan. Season with plenty of salt and pepper, then spread into an even layer. Roast for 25 minutes, stirring halfway, until the cauliflower is tender.

3 | Remove the garlic cloves and squeeze them out of their papery casing into a large saucepan. Using a spatula, scrape everything else in the roasting pan into the saucepan, making sure to get all the bits from the bottom. Add the stock and heavy cream and bring to a simmer over medium-high heat. Remove the pan from the heat and use an immersion blender to blend everything to a velvety, smooth purée, adding a splash of water if it is too thick. Taste and add extra salt and pepper if needed.

4 | Meanwhile, toast the pumpkin seeds in a small, dry skillet over medium heat, stirring occasionally, until they begin to turn golden and pop. Turn off the heat, add the remaining 1 teaspoon each of cumin and mustard seeds and let them toast in the residual heat of the pan. Stir in the chili oil and season with salt.

5 | Reheat the soup, if needed, then ladle it into four bowls. Top with the chili pumpkin seeds, extra chili oil, and mint leaves, if using, to serve. Any leftovers will keep in the fridge for up to 3 days or freeze for up to 3 months in individual containers.

BRAISING & STEWING VEGETABLES

Both braising and stewing are widely used in vegetable cooking around the world, and for good reason. These methods of low, slow cooking can transform a hard, slightly bitter vegetable into one that is meltingly tender and full of flavor—this really is the magic of cooking. These methods simultaneously unlock the inner sweetness of vegetables as well as allow them to take on the flavors of other ingredients. While the methods for braising and stewing are similar, one key difference is that the former uses much less liquid and the pan is covered with a lid, see the delicious braised cabbage (below). For a stewed vegetable dish, check out the Sweet Potato, Spinach & Peanut Quinoa Stew (see p.214).

FIVE-SPICE BRAISED CABBAGE

Prep 10 minutes

Cook 35 minutes

Serves 4

This braised cabbage is gently simmered until tender and comes with a hint of warmth from the five-spice and a fruity tang from the pomegranate molasses. Serve it as a side dish to any roasted meat.

2 tbsp olive oil
1 onion, finely chopped
pinch of salt, plus extra to season
1 tbsp five-spice powder
1 red cabbage, shredded (see p.162)
1½-in piece of fresh ginger, peeled and
    cut into matchsticks (see p.163)
3 tbsp pomegranate molasses
1 tbsp light brown sugar
freshly ground black pepper

1 | Heat the olive oil in a large saucepan or Dutch oven over medium heat. Add the chopped onion and a pinch of salt and cook for 8–10 minutes, stirring regularly, until softened and translucent. Sprinkle in the five-spice powder and cook for 30 seconds, stirring well. Add the shredded cabbage with the ginger, ¾ cup (200ml) of water, the pomegranate molasses, and brown sugar.

2 | Bring to a simmer, cover, and cook gently for 15 minutes, stirring occasionally. Remove the lid and cook for a further 5 minutes, until the cabbage is tender and glossy. Season with salt and pepper.

TIP

For a fancy finish, sprinkle over fresh parsley leaves, a handful of pomegranate seeds, and another drizzle of pomegranate molasses.

Fennel, chile & garlic braised lima beans

Prep 10 minutes

Cook 25 minutes

Serves 2 as a main, 4 as a side

The fennel is first browned in oil, then braised in a small amount of wine until it becomes slightly caramelized, sweet in flavor, and tender—a winning combination with the lima beans, crème fraîche and garlic. Serve as side to the Grilled Lamb Chops (see p.112), or enjoy as a complete meal with chunks of crusty bread for soaking up the creamy sauce. The green fronds from the top of the fennel bulb add a pop of color sprinkled over the dish before serving.

4 tbsp olive oil, divided
1 large fennel bulb, green fronds picked and saved, root trimmed, sliced lengthwise into 8 wedges
salt and freshly ground black pepper
4 fat garlic cloves, peeled and finely sliced
1 red chile, finely sliced
2 tsp fennel seeds
⅔ cup (150ml) dry white wine
1 (15.5oz/400g) can lima beans, liquid reserved

3 tbsp full-fat crème fraîche
1 handful of parsley, leaves and stalks, roughly chopped
crusty bread, to serve

1 | Heat 3 tablespoons of the olive oil in a medium, deep skillet with a lid over medium-high heat.

2 | Season the fennel with salt and pepper, then lay the wedges in an even layer in the pan. They should all fit snugly—arrange them so the wedges slot together well. Cook for 4 minutes, undisturbed, on each side until deeply golden and caramelized.

3 | Create a space in one part of the pan (this should be easier as the fennel will have collapsed slightly). Turn the heat to medium.

4 | Pour the remaining olive oil into the gap. Add the garlic and chile and cook, stirring for 1 minute, until lightly golden. Add the fennel seeds and cook for 30 seconds more, then stir to combine the fennel with the flavorings.

5 | Pour in the white wine and let it bubble away until reduced by half, then add the lima beans with the liquid from the can. Cover the pan with the lid and cook for 12 minutes, stirring occasionally, then remove the lid and cook for a further 3 minutes, stirring, until the fennel is completely tender.

6 | Stir through the crème fraîche and parsley, season with salt and pepper to taste, then sprinkle over the reserved fennel fronds. Serve with crusty bread to soak up the sauce.

GRILLING & BROILING VEGETABLES

A fantastic way to cook vegetables, these methods turn the ordinary into something special. By cooking under or over intense, dry heat, you turn up the flavor dial and vegetables become sweeter with an added hint of smoke. As the exterior caramelizes, the texture of the inside becomes soft and unctuous. Whether broiling or grilling outdoors or in a grill pan on the stove top, both result in a slightly blackened appearance, adding to the flavor. Make sure you heat the grill or pan on high before you start to cook, to ensure a hit of dry heat. Marinating vegetables prior to cooking, or basting them during cooking, will keep them moist and also add a glossy glaze. Some vegetables may need to be blanched before grilling, like the corn in the Miso Corn-on-the-Cob (see p.190). This ensures the vegetable is cooked inside before adding a layer of smoky charred flavor on the outside.

ROASTING PEPPERS

Prep 15 minutes + cooling

Cook 20 minutes

Serves 4

You can buy roasted red peppers in a jar but broiling them yourself is super easy and the peppers become tender with a slight bite, smoky, and oh so sweet.

6 mixed bell peppers, a combination of red, yellow, and orange works well

1 | Preheat the broiler to high with the rack on the upper shelf. Put the peppers on a baking sheet and prick them all over with a sharp knife. Broil the peppers for 15–20 minutes, turning every 5 minutes, until the outsides are very charred and they start to collapse and soften.

2 | Transfer the peppers to a large bowl, cover with a clean kitchen towel (this will encourage the peppers to soften further as they steam and make them easier to peel), and leave for 15–20 minutes.

3 | Put the whole peppers on a cutting board, then peel away the skin (it should come away easily now they have cooled) and discard. Once peeled, cut the peppers in half lengthwise, pull away the stalk, then use a teaspoon to scoop out and discard the seeds.

Baba ganoush

Prep 15 minutes + cooling

Cook 40 minutes

Serves 4

This Middle Eastern dip is as popular as its sister, hummus. Made from charred, softened eggplants with tahini (a sesame seed paste that adds a velvety richness), the dip is the perfect balance of smoky and creamy. Here are three different ways to cook the eggplant—over a gas stove top, under the broiler, or on a barbecue grill. Choose the method that works best for you, but remember to make sure the heat is high, whichever one you go for.

3 eggplants
juice and finely grated zest of ½–1 unwaxed lemon
3 tbsp tahini
1 garlic clove, peeled and finely grated
1 tsp ground cumin
½ tsp sumac (optional)
2 tbsp extra-virgin olive oil, for drizzling
salt and freshly ground black pepper
crudités of your choice, such as carrot, cucumber, and
    bell pepper strips, and toasted pita bread, to serve

1 | First, prick the eggplants all over with a sharp knife. Using tongs, place one of the eggplants directly over the gas flame of your stove top (you may want to protect it with foil) and cook for around 12 minutes, turning occasionally, until the outside has completely charred, softened, and started to collapse. Repeat with the remaining eggplants.

2 | Transfer the charred eggplants to a large bowl, cover with a clean kitchen towel (this will encourage them to soften further and make them easier to peel) and leave for 20 minutes or until cool enough to handle.

3 | Once cool, use your fingers to peel away the blackened skin, transferring the flesh to a cutting board. Don't worry about removing all the blackened bits, a little leftover skin adds a nice smoky flavor. Discard the liquid in the bowl.

4 | If you prefer a textured baba ganoush, use a knife to finely chop the flesh, then transfer it to a bowl. Add the remaining ingredients, using the smaller quantity of lemon at first, then mash with a fork until combined. Season with salt and pepper. Taste and add more seasoning and the rest of the lemon juice, if you like.

5 | If you prefer a smoother dip, put the eggplant flesh into a blender with all the other ingredients and blend until smooth, seasoning with salt and pepper. Start with half the lemon juice and add more to taste.

Cooking variations

To cook the eggplants on the grill: place them directly on the rack over the hottest part of the coals, or gas equivalent. Grill for around 12 minutes, turning with tongs, until the outside of each eggplant has charred, softened, and collapsed.

To broil the eggplants: place them on a baking sheet under a preheated high broiler and cook for 5 minutes on each side, until the outside of each eggplant has charred, softened, and collapsed—this will take 15–20 minutes.

Roasted & marinated pepper fattoush

Prep 30 minutes + standing and marinating

Cook 30 minutes

Serves 4

Here, the peppers are roasted until softened and charred, then peeled, allowing them to take on the flavor of the lightly spiced marinade. This Middle Eastern–inspired salad is then topped with crispy, golden pita chips for a bit of crunch.

1 recipe quantity of Roasted Peppers (see p.186) or jarred roasted red peppers
6 tbsp extra-virgin olive oil, plus extra to taste
3 tbsp sherry vinegar, plus extra to taste
4 tsp Za'atar (see p.449) or store-bought, divided
½ tsp dried chili flakes
1 small garlic clove, peeled and finely grated
salt and freshly ground black pepper
2 pita breads
1 head Romaine lettuce, sliced
1 cucumber, halved lengthwise and sliced into half moons
8oz (200g) radishes, finely sliced
1 small red onion, peeled and finely sliced
1 cup (30g) dill, chopped
8oz (200g) feta cheese

1 | Follow steps 1–3 from Roasting Peppers (see p.186).

2 | Thickly slice the roasted peppers into 1-in (2.5-cm) wide strips, then place in a bowl or a lidded container.

3 | Add 4 tablespoons of the olive oil, the sherry vinegar, 2 teaspoons of the za'atar, the chili flakes, and garlic to the peppers. Season with salt and pepper, then give everything a good stir. Leave to marinate for at least 30 minutes or overnight in the fridge.

4 | When you're ready to serve the salad, preheat the oven to 400°F (200°C). Let the peppers come up to room temperature if they've been in the fridge overnight.

5 | Cut the pita into random-size triangular pieces onto a large baking sheet. Toss with the remaining olive oil and za'atar, then season with salt and pepper. Spread the pita out evenly and bake for 8–10 minutes, turning with a spatula halfway through, until golden and crisp. Leave to cool.

6 | Put the peppers with their marinade in a large serving bowl with the lettuce, cucumber, radishes, red onion, and dill. Add the pita chips with any spices left on the tray, then crumble over the feta in large chunks. Toss to combine, check the seasoning and add a splash more vinegar and/or olive oil if needed.

TIPS

You can char the peppers on a gas stove top instead of under the broiler. Hold the peppers with tongs directly over the flame, turning until blackened all over.

The marinated peppers will keep for up to 3 days in the fridge. Make sure you bring them up to room temperature before eating for the best flavor.

The peppers are delicious on toast or in a simple salad with torn mozzarella and basil leaves, or in a pasta salad.

Vegetables   189

Grilled miso corn-on-the-cob

Prep 15 minutes

Cook 15 minutes

Serves 4

Slightly charred corn is one of the best side dishes—super sweet with a hint of smokiness. It's best to parboil the corn first to soften the kernels before hitting them with the heat of the grill pan to char the outside. The corn is also basted with lots of butter infused with miso, ginger, and lime to keep it moist and take it to another level of flavor.

½ recipe quantity of Miso-Ginger Butter (see p.48), softened
4 ears corn on the cob, husks and silk removed, each cut in half to make 8 pieces
1 tbsp sesame seeds
1 tsp dried chili flakes
2 tsp vegetable or olive oil
salt and freshly ground black pepper

1 | Follow the instructions to make the Miso-Ginger Butter (see p.48).

2 | Carefully lower the corn into a medium saucepan of boiling salted water and simmer for 4 minutes, until slightly softened and the kernels turn bright yellow. Drain the corn in a colander in the sink, then put it into a bowl. (At this point, you can leave the corn to cool completely and keep it covered in the fridge for up to 2 days before using.)

3 | Mix together the sesame seeds and chili flakes in a small bowl and set aside.

4 | To grill the corn, heat a large grill pan over medium-high heat. Drizzle the corn with oil, season with salt and pepper and toss well to coat. Place the corn in the pan and grill for 6 minutes, turning regularly, until blackened in places and the outside is caramelized.

5 | Remove the pan from the heat and spoon the miso butter over the corn, turning and basting it for a few minutes until evenly coated. Take care—it will spit.

6 | Return the pan to the heat, sprinkle the sesame seeds and chili flakes over the corn and cook for another minute before serving with the butter from the pan spooned over the top.

Cooking variation

To cook the corn on the grill: toss the parboiled corn in a bowl with the oil and plenty of salt and pepper. Grill for 3–4 minutes, depending on the level of heat, turning regularly until lightly charred in places. Smear each piece with some of the butter, sprinkle with the sesame seeds and chili flakes, then cook for another 1–2 minutes, until golden and glossy. Serve with the remaining butter spooned over.

FRYING VEGETABLES

Most types of vegetable benefit from this fast, efficient method of cooking to maximize their flavor and retain a crisp texture, while maintaining precious nutrients. Whether sautéed, shallow-fried or stir-fried in a splash of oil, it's essential to use high direct heat. This allows the vegetables to brown and caramelize on the outside, concentrating their flavor, while simultaneously cooking them on the inside.

GINGER & SOY STIR-FRIED GREENS

Prep 10 minutes

Cook 10 minutes

Serves 2 or 4 as a side

Stir-frying is a great method of cooking vegetables in a short amount of time to retain nutrients and texture. Be sure to cut them into similar-size pieces so they cook evenly, and measure other ingredients before you start to cook. Serve with Cooked Rice (see p.202).

3 tbsp soy sauce
1 tbsp vegetable oil
⅔lb (300g) green vegetables of choice, cut into
    similar-size pieces
pinch each of salt and freshly ground black pepper
3 garlic cloves, finely chopped
2-in piece of fresh ginger, peeled and cut into
    matchsticks (see p.163)
2 tsp cumin seeds
splash of toasted sesame oil (optional)

1 | In a small bowl, mix together the soy sauce with 2 tablespoons of water and set aside. Heat a wok or large high-sided skillet over high heat. When it starts to smoke, add the oil. Swirl the oil in the pan, then add your choice of greens with a pinch of salt and pepper. Stir-fry for 2–3 minutes, tossing regularly, until the vegetables soften slightly.

2 | Add the garlic, ginger, and cumin seeds and stir-fry for 2 minutes, until aromatic. Carefully pour the soy sauce mixture into the pan, add a splash of sesame oil, if using, and toss together for 30 seconds, until the greens are coated in a luscious sauce. Spoon into a serving dish or serve over rice. A fried egg and Crispy Chili Oil (see p.452) also make great accompaniments.

EASY HOMEMADE
FRENCH FRIES

*Prep 10 minutes
+ steam-drying*

Cook 30 minutes

Serves 4

There's nothing quite like perfectly cooked homemade fries. For ease and simplicity, this recipe doesn't go down the triple-cooked route, but the results are still impressive. Don't be put off by deep-frying, it's the best method to ensure your fries have a crisp, golden exterior with fluffy insides. It's also important to select the right type of potato for deep-frying—Russet works well because it crisps up nicely and has a fluffy interior when cooked.

2¾lb (1.25kg) white potatoes, such as Russet, peeled
vegetable oil, for deep-frying
salt

1 | Cut each potato into ¾-in (2-cm) thick slices, then turn and cut them into ¾-in (2-cm) wide fries.

2 | Put the potatoes into a large bowl of cold water and gently turn to remove some of their starch—this helps them crisp up once they're fried. Drain well in a colander.

3 | Bring a large pan of salted water to a boil. Carefully add the potatoes and cook for 9 minutes, until they cook through, softening at the edges but not falling apart. Drain the potatoes well in a colander.

4 | Leave the potatoes to drain for a minute, then put them into a large roasting pan, spread out in an even layer and allow to steam-dry for 15 minutes—this will ensure they become crispy when fried.

5 | Half fill a large, deep saucepan with vegetable oil and heat to 340°F (170°C) or until a cube of bread browns in 30 seconds. Carefully lower one-third of the potatoes into the hot oil and fry for 4–5 minutes, until crisp and golden, turning the fries carefully now and again so they cook evenly. Using a slotted spoon, lift the fries out of the hot oil onto a baking sheet lined with parchment paper to drain.

6 | Meanwhile, preheat the oven to 325°F (160°C). Keep the fries warm in the oven while you cook the two remaining batches. Season the chips well with salt before serving.

TIP

If you prefer to bake your fries, follow steps 1–4, spreading them out on a large baking sheet, rather than a roasting pan, to steam-dry. Preheat the oven to 400°F (200°C). Toss the potatoes in vegetable oil until lightly coated, then spread out again on the baking sheet and cook in the oven, turning once, for 40–45 minutes, until golden and crisp. You can also cook them in an air fryer in the same way, reducing the cooking time to 25–30 minutes.

CARAMELIZED ONIONS

Prep 5 minutes

Cook 50 minutes

Serves 4–6

These caramelized onions utilize several cooking techniques for perfect results. First, you simmer the onions in water to soften, then sauté them in oil until golden—the first step means you need much less oil for sautéing. In contrast to stir-fried vegetables, which are cooked quickly over high heat, patience is key. You want to sauté the onions slowly over a lower heat so they become sweet and golden, rather than scorch. Use the onions in the Pissaladière (right), in macaroni and cheese for a caramelized onion twist (see p.42) or on burgers as a barbecue favorite.

6 onions, peeled and finely sliced
large pinch of salt
1 tbsp olive oil
2 tbsp (30g) salted butter

1 | Put the onions into a large, deep skillet, pour in 1¾ cups (400ml) of cold water and add a large pinch of salt.

2 | Place the pan over high heat, bring the water to a boil and cook the onions for 30 minutes, stirring every now and again, until the water evaporates. The noise in the pan will change from watery and spluttery to a sizzling frying sound.

3 | Once the water has evaporated, add the oil and butter to the pan and reduce the heat to medium-low. Sauté, stirring regularly, for 20 minutes, until the onions are really soft, golden, and caramelized. Serve as a topping for a Pissaladière tart (right) or as preferred.

TIPS

For a dairy-free alternative, simply double the quantity of oil and omit the butter.

Once caramelized, the onions will keep in an airtight container in the fridge for up to 5 days.

Pissaladière tart

Prep 15 minutes

Cook 1 hour 20 minutes

Serves 4–6

This Provençal baked classic makes use of sweet, sautéed, caramelized onions as a topping. While it's more traditional for the tart to have a crisp bread dough base, this version uses puff pastry, which makes it much easier and quicker to make, and it's just as delicious. Briny black olives and salty anchovies add balance to the sweetness of the slow-cooked, golden onions.

1 recipe quantity of Caramelized Onions (left)
1 sheet pre-rolled puff pastry
2 (2oz/55g) cans anchovies in oil, drained
1 handful of pitted black olives
6 thyme sprigs, leaves stripped
2 tbsp milk
crisp green salad with French Dressing (see p.429), to serve

1 | Follow steps 1–3 to make the Caramelized Onions (left). This can be done up to 5 days in advance, see the Tip (left).

2 | Preheat the oven to 400°F (200°C).

3 | Unroll the pastry and place it, parchment-paper-backing side down, onto a baking sheet.

4 | Spoon the onions on top, then spread them out in an even layer, leaving a ¾-in (2-cm) border all the way around. Lay the anchovies diagonally across the top of the onions in a criss-cross pattern. Dot over the olives and sprinkle with the thyme leaves.

5 | Brush the edges of the pastry with milk and bake for 25–30 minutes, until the pastry is crisp and golden, checking the underneath to make sure the base is cooked properly. Serve with a dressed crisp salad.

Corn fritters
with smashed avocado

Prep 20 minutes

Cook 10 minutes

Serves 2

A savory take on pancakes, these lightly spiced fritters make a winning brunch. They are shallow fried until crisp and golden on the outside and light and fluffy on the inside. Serve topped with creamy, smashed avocado and crisp halloumi.

1 tsp ground cumin
½ tsp dried chili flakes
¼ cup (30g) all-purpose flour
½ tsp baking powder
1 large egg
1–2 tbsp milk, plus extra if needed
salt and freshly ground black pepper
1 (8oz/200g) can corn, drained (or frozen, defrosted, see below)
1 handful of cilantro leaves, finely chopped
2 green onions, thinly sliced
4 tsp olive oil

To serve
1 avocado, skin and stone removed and chopped
juice of 1 lime
8oz (225g) block of halloumi cheese, patted dry and cut into ¾-in (2-cm) thick slices

1 | In a large bowl, add the cumin, chili flakes, flour, baking powder, egg, and 1 tablespoon of the milk. Using a balloon whisk, mix until smooth. The batter should be a thick consistency that drops off a spoon. If it is too thick, whisk in the remaining milk. Season the batter well with salt and pepper, then stir in the corn and three-quarters of the cilantro and green onions. Add a splash more milk if needed. Set aside briefly.

2 | Put the avocado into a small bowl and add the lime juice and a little salt and pepper. Use a fork to mash until mostly smooth.

3 | Preheat the oven to 325°F (160°C).

4 | Heat 3 teaspoons of the olive oil in a large nonstick skillet over medium-high heat. Place 3–4 large spoonfuls of the batter into the pan, each fritter should be roughly 4 in (10 cm) in diameter, making sure you leave plenty of room between each one so they have space to cook. Fry for 1–2 minutes on each side, until golden and crisp on the outside.

5 | Using a spatula, remove the fritters from the skillet onto a baking sheet and keep warm in the oven, while you fry the rest of the fritters—the batter makes 6–8 in total.

6 | Keep the fritters warm in the oven, then return the skillet to medium-high heat. Pour in the remaining olive oil, then add the halloumi slices and fry for 2 minutes on each side until evenly golden—at first some water will leak out of the halloumi, then they will turn crisp and golden.

7 | Serve the corn fritters in a pile with the smashed avocado and halloumi on top. Sprinkle with the remaining cilantro and green onions.

Using frozen vegetables

Frozen vegetables make a convenient and useful alternative to fresh, and it's well worth keeping a supply in the freezer. You can use straight from frozen in fried and stir-fried dishes because the additional water helps them cook evenly, part-steaming as they fry.

Corn: either leave to defrost in a bowl or pour over enough hot water to cover. Leave for a minute, then drain well through a strainer. Add to fritters, sauces, and soups.

Spinach: also good in fritters or added to soups, sauces, and curries—defrost or use straight from frozen. You can buy frozen spinach either chopped or whole leaf—both are good.

Peas: these are often much tastier than fresh because they're frozen when freshly picked and tender. Add a handful to soups, curries, purées, and sauces.

Mixed vegetables: they're economical and ready prepared, so there's no need for time-consuming peeling and chopping. Perfect for stir-fries, soups, and stews.

RICE

&

GRAINS

RICE

A staple food for more than half of the world's population, the expression "rice is life" goes to show how important this grain is to so many people. Basmati, jasmine, carnaroli, red, arborio, and black rice are just a handful of familiar names, yet the number of rice varieties stretches impressively into the thousands. The gluten-free grain is hugely versatile and most regions have a repertoire of rice dishes, from paella in Spain and biryani in India to risotto in Italy and pilafs in the Middle East—each celebrates the grain and is a perfect example of its adaptability.

Storage
Keep in an airtight container or jar with a lid in a cool, dry place and avoid contact with moisture and strongly flavored ingredients.

PREPARING RICE

If making a risotto, rice pudding, paella, or other similar short-grain rice dish, it's important to avoid rinsing the rice before cooking, which reduces the starch. It is this high level of starch, released during cooking, that you are looking to retain to give the dish the desired slightly creamy, soft consistency. Long-grain rice, such as basmati or jasmine, on the other hand, needs to be rinsed well before cooking to get rid of this excess starch and ensure separate fluffy grains when cooked. You can prepare long-grain rice in a variety of ways:

Rinse: put the rice in a metal strainer and rinse it well under cold running water, moving the grains around with one hand until the water runs clear.

Wash: put the rice in a bowl, pour over enough cold water to cover, then use your hands to agitate the grains in the water—this will encourage the starches to release from the rice, turning the water from clear to cloudy white. Drain the rice through a metal strainer, put it back into the bowl, and repeat until the water remains clear—this usually takes about five washes.

Soak: soak the rice in a bowl of cold water for 30 minutes before draining and using. This plumps up the grains and also stops them from sticking together when cooked.

Your rice is now ready to cook (see the guide, below, and on the next page) for the best methods.

TYPE OF RICE	COOKING METHOD	COOKING TIME
Basmati/jasmine/long-grain	Absorption and boiling	10 minutes + steaming
Black rice	Boiling	25 minutes
Brown rice (wholegrain basmati/jasmine/long-grain)	Absorption and boiling	30–40 minutes
Wild rice	Boiling	35–40 minutes
Red (Camargue) rice	Boiling	30 minutes
Short-grain (risotto/paella/pudding rice)	Absorption	20 minutes–1 hour

From left, black rice, risotto rice (front), basmati,
brown rice, wild rice, and red rice.

COOKING RICE USING
ABSORPTION METHOD

Prep 10 minutes

Cook 15 minutes

Serves 4

The classic way to cook rice is by the absorption method, which involves cooking the grain in liquid, usually water, until it is absorbed and the rice is tender and fluffy. This method particularly suits white rice varieties, such as long-grain basmati, which demands a gentle style of cooking for light, separate grains. The key to success is using a pan with a tight-fitting lid and following the ratio of about 1 part rice to 2 parts liquid. It's also possible to cook brown rice using this method, although it requires slightly more water to compensate for the longer cooking time.

1¼ cups (240g) basmati, jasmine, or other long-grain rice
large pinch of salt

1 | Prepare the rice by choosing one of the options on page 200. Drain the rice well, then put it into a small saucepan with a tight-fitting lid. Add a large pinch of salt and pour over 2 cups (500ml) cold water.

2 | Put the pan over medium heat and bring the water to a boil. Turn the heat down to the lowest setting, put the lid on and cook gently, undisturbed, for 10 minutes, or until the water is absorbed and the rice is tender.

3 | Remove the pan from the heat and leave the rice to sit, covered, for 5 minutes. Remove the lid and gently fluff up the grains with a fork.

Boiling method variation

Most varieties of long-grain rice can also be cooked using the boiling method, but it particularly suits sturdier varieties, such as brown, black, wild, and red rice. It is unsuitable for short-grain rice because the grains tend to become soggy in the excess amount of water. To follow this method, put the prepared rice (see p.200) in a small saucepan and cover with plenty of lightly salted cold water. Bring the water to a boil, then turn the heat down slightly and simmer until the rice is tender, leaving the pan uncovered. (Take care when using this method for white basmati and other long-grain varieties as they can become mushy if boiled too vigorously.) Drain the rice in a strainer and allow it to stand for a couple of minutes to steam-dry.

Using a rice cooker

Rice cookers are extremely popular in Asia and are becoming more so in Europe and the US. They come with a host of useful functions, for example, many allow you to set the time for when you want to start cooking the rice, and they're also able to keep it warm safely for long periods. Their real selling point is in cooking perfect rice every time, simply with the press of a button and with no effort. Different brands of rice cooker can vary, so follow the instructions that come with your machine for the best results.

Jollof rice

Prep 15 minutes

Cook 45 minutes

Serves 6

This spicy vegetarian rice dish is popular in many West African countries. It comes with numerous local variations but is principally a combination of long-grain rice, tomatoes, chiles, onions, and spices. Serve it as a side to stews and curries or with grilled or fried meat, chicken, or fish.

2¾ cups (500g) long grain or basmati rice
1 (14.5oz/400g) can diced tomatoes
1 large onion, peeled and roughly chopped
2 red chiles, such as Scotch bonnet or bird's eye, seeded if preferred
1 red bell pepper, seeded and roughly chopped
⅓ cup (100ml) vegetable oil
4 tbsp tomato paste
3 garlic cloves, crushed, or 1 tsp garlic powder
1½-in piece of fresh ginger, peeled and minced

2 cups (500ml) hot Chicken Stock or Vegetable Stock (see p.414) or good-quality store-bought
1 bay leaf
1 tsp curry powder
1 tsp dried thyme
salt, to taste

1 | Rinse the rice well in a strainer under cold running water until the water runs clear and set aside.

2 | Blend the tomatoes, onion, chiles, and bell pepper in a food processor or blender until smooth.

3 | Heat the oil in a large saucepan over medium heat, add the tomato paste and cook, stirring, for 2 minutes. Add the blended tomato mixture, garlic, and ginger and cook over medium-low heat, stirring often, for 10 minutes, until reduced and thickened.

4 | Add the rice to the pan, then add the stock and stir to coat the rice in the sauce. Add the bay leaf, curry powder, and thyme. Bring to a boil and cover the pot tightly with a lid. If the lid isn't a tight fit, cover the top of the pan with foil and then place the lid on top.

5 | Reduce the heat to low and simmer for 10 minutes. Remove the lid and check the amount of liquid, adding an extra ¾ cup (200ml) of water if it looks too dry. Replace the lid, cook for another 10 minutes, then check the liquid again, adding more water if needed. Cook the rice for about 35 minutes in total until soft and the liquid has been absorbed. Season with salt to taste and leave the rice to sit for 5 minutes, then stir and serve.

Simple risotto

Prep 10 minutes

Cook 30 minutes

Serves 4

This classic risotto is a one-pan dish of beauty. Made using short-grain rice, typically arborio or carnaroli, it is cooked using the absorption method (see p.202). Risotto requires constant stirring, so a little patience is needed, but the process can be meditative, watching the grains of rice swell as they absorb the stock to create a creamy texture. Using a good-quality stock makes all the difference to the flavor of the finished risotto, so it is a great recipe to try the homemade Chicken or Vegetable Stock (see p.414).

2 tbsp olive oil
1 onion, peeled and finely chopped
pinch of salt, plus extra to season
4 garlic cloves, peeled and finely chopped
1⅔ cups (300g) risotto rice, such as arborio or carnaroli
1 cup (250ml) dry white wine
6 cups (1.4 liters) hot Chicken Stock or Vegetable Stock (see p.414) or good-quality store-bought
3 tbsp (50g) salted butter, cut into cubes
½ cup (50g) finely grated Parmesan cheese or vegetarian alternative
freshly ground black pepper

1 | Heat the olive oil in a large, high-sided skillet over medium heat. Add the onion and a pinch of salt. Cook, stirring occasionally, for 6–8 minutes, until softened and very lightly colored. Add the garlic and cook for 1–2 minutes more, then stir in the risotto rice.

2 | Toast the rice in the pan, stirring, for 1 minute to coat it in the oil mixture, then pour in the white wine. Once the wine has bubbled away and there is no smell of alcohol, add 2 ladlefuls of hot stock. Cook, stirring constantly, until the stock is absorbed by the rice, then add 2 more ladlefuls. Continue to add the stock, 2 ladlefuls at a time, and cook, stirring for around 20 minutes, until the rice is creamy and tender with a slight bite (you should have about ¾ cup (175ml) of the hot stock remaining at this point).

3 | Remove the pan from the heat and stir in the butter and cheese until melted. Season the risotto with salt and pepper to taste, adding the remaining stock if you prefer a wetter, looser consistency. Spoon the risotto into four bowls and enjoy.

Flavor variations

Chorizo & corn: peel away the papery skin and cut ½lb (225g) of chorizo into small cubes. Add the chorizo with 1 tablespoon of olive oil and the onion in step 1. Increase the heat to medium-high and cook for 6–8 minutes, until the chorizo is crisp and has released its oils and the onion is lightly golden. Follow steps 2–3, adding 1½ cups (320g) canned or thawed corn with the butter and Parmesan and heat through.

Shrimp & saffron: stir in 3 large pinches of saffron to the hot stock and leave for 5 minutes for the flavor to infuse. Follow steps 1–2 using the saffron-infused stock. Before adding the butter and cheese, stir in ⅔lb (300g) raw, peeled large shrimp. Cook, stirring for 2–3 minutes, until the shrimp turn pink, then add the butter and cheese. Sprinkle over a handful of chopped flat-leaf parsley, to serve.

Asparagus, pea & lemon: follow steps 1–2, then stir in ½lb (200g) asparagus tips, cut into ¾-in (2-cm) pieces, and ⅔ cup (150g) frozen peas. Stir, cooking for 2–3 minutes, until tender. Next, add the butter and cheese until melted. Finish the risotto with the finely grated zest of 1 unwaxed lemon, adding a good squeeze of juice to taste.

TIP

Any leftover cold risotto will keep for up to 2 days in an airtight container in the fridge. When reheating, add a splash of water to the rice to loosen, then make sure you heat it well and the rice is piping hot before serving.

BAKING RICE

Prep 5 minutes

Cook 20 minutes

Serves 4

This hands-off method of cooking rice frees up space on your stove and is perfect for when you want to get on with other things in the kitchen. Cooking rice in the oven follows the principle of the absorption method (see p.200), but is arguably better because the pan is evenly surrounded by heat, rather than it coming from just underneath. For this reason, you need slightly less water: 1 part rice to roughly 1.75 of water should suffice.

1¼ cups (240g) basmati, jasmine, or other long-grain rice
pinch of salt

1 | Preheat the oven to 200°C (400°F). Prepare the rice by choosing one of the options on p.200. Drain the rice well in a strainer, then put it into a small, deep roasting pan, about 12 x 8 in (30 x 20 cm). Sprinkle with the salt, then pour over 1¾ cups (400ml) of cold water—the rice should be just covered.

2 | Cover the pan tightly with foil and bake in the center of the oven for 20 minutes, until the water has been absorbed and the rice is fluffy and cooked. Fluff up the grains with a fork to serve.

TIPS

Baking rice is handy when feeding a crowd because it doesn't require any attention during cooking, leaving you time to prepare the rest of the meal.

To lend extra flavor to the rice, add aromatics such as bay leaves, whole spices, or saffron. A pat of butter, stirred in at the end of cooking, adds richness and flavor.

Coconut & lime-baked chicken rice

Prep 15 minutes

Cook 50 minutes

Serves 4

The flavors of coconut, lime, and Thai curry spices infuse the basmati rice as it bakes, while the chicken and eggplant turn this dish into a hearty meal. It's best to brown the chicken thighs first to add color and caramelize and crisp up the skin.

8 skin-on, bone-in chicken thighs
salt and freshly ground black pepper
3 tbsp vegetable oil, divided
generous 1 cup (225g) basmati rice, prepared (see p.200)
4 green onions, green and white parts, cut into 1-in (2.5-cm) long pieces
3 garlic cloves, peeled and finely grated
2-in piece of fresh ginger, peeled and finely grated
1 eggplant, chopped into ¾-oz (2-cm) pieces
3 tbsp Thai green curry paste
juice and finely grated zest of 1 lime
6 lime leaves (optional)
1 (13.5oz/400g) can coconut milk

To serve
2 green onions, finely sliced
1 handful of cilantro leaves
1 lime, cut into 4 wedges

1 | Preheat the oven to 400°F (200°C).

2 | Season the chicken thighs all over with salt and pepper. Place a large skillet over medium-high heat. Add 1 tablespoon of the vegetable oil, then the chicken thighs, skin-side down, in a single layer. Cook the thighs for 5–8 minutes, until the skin is browned. Take the pan off the heat and set aside briefly.

3 | Put the rice in a large roasting pan, about 14 x 12 in (40 x 30 cm). Add the green onions with the garlic, ginger, eggplant, Thai green curry paste, lime juice and zest, and lime leaves, if using. Pour in the coconut milk, then half-fill the can with water and pour this into the pan. Give everything a good stir, season with salt and pepper, then spread into a single layer.

4 | Nestle the chicken thighs into the rice mixture, skin-side up, then drizzle over the remaining vegetable oil. Bake, uncovered, for 35–40 minutes, until the chicken and rice are cooked through and the liquid is absorbed. Serve with the green onions and cilantro leaves sprinkled over and wedges of lime for squeezing.

TIP

This is a great meal for freezing. Leave it to cool, then freeze in individual containers. Defrost thoroughly before reheating in a saucepan with a lid and a splash of water. Once boiling, cook for 10 minutes to ensure both the chicken and the rice are piping hot all the way through.

USING UP COOKED RICE

Leftover cooked rice makes an excellent second meal or side dish and can be chilled or even frozen to use at a later date. For food safety reasons, leave the rice to cool as quickly as possible, then transfer it as soon as it is cold to an airtight container to store in the fridge for up to 3 days. It can be frozen at this point too.

To reheat rice, place it in a tightly covered bowl in the microwave on high or in a covered saucepan with a splash of water and heat until piping hot throughout, then fluff up the rice with a fork. If the rice is frozen, defrost it thoroughly in the fridge before reheating in the same way.

Serve reheated rice as a side or even for breakfast topped with a fried egg (see p.25) and Crispy Chili Oil (see p.452). Leftover cold rice is also perfect for stir-frying, such as in the popular Indonesian dish, *nasi goreng*, or egg-fried rice (below). Since the grains contain less water, they remain separate when fried.

VEGETABLE EGG-FRIED RICE

Prep 10 minutes

Cook 10 minutes

Serves 2

This leftover rice dish makes a really quick and easy meal. Ensure your rice is completely cold before stir-frying so the grains remain separate when reheated. This will also enable you to reheat it fully and safely (cooked cold rice should be reheated until piping hot throughout), as well as give nice crunchy bits when fried.

2 tbsp vegetable oil
½ recipe quantity of cooked basmati rice, chilled (see p.200 for the Absorption Method)
½lb (250g) mixed vegetables, such as carrot, red bell pepper, onion, baby corn, and snow peas, evenly sliced, chopped, or halved
½ cup (75g) frozen peas
1¼-in piece of fresh ginger, peeled and cut into matchsticks (see p.163)
3 garlic cloves, peeled and chopped
2 large eggs, at room temperature, lightly beaten
3 tbsp soy sauce
salt and freshly ground black pepper

1 | Pour the vegetable oil into a large wok or high-sided skillet over high heat. Once the oil is smoking hot, carefully add the cooked rice. Using a spatula or wooden spoon, break up any clumps of rice and stir-fry for 3–4 minutes, until the rice starts to crisp up in places.

2 | Add the mixed vegetables, frozen peas, ginger, and garlic and stir-fry for 3 minutes—you want the vegetables to be just cooked, but still crunchy.

3 | Make a well in the center of the wok or pan. Pour in the beaten eggs and leave it to cook for 30 seconds, until set on the bottom but still runny on top.

4 | Fold the eggs into the rice, stirring everything together and breaking up any large pieces. Stir until the eggs are cooked, forming small flecks evenly spread throughout the rice.

5 | Pour in the soy sauce and season with salt and pepper, then stir through the rice mixture.

6 | Give everything one last stir to make sure the rice is heated until piping hot, then serve.

OTHER GRAINS

Rice is covered earlier in this chapter, but in most cuisines around the world, a much wider spectrum of grains have been a staple food for many hundreds of years, and still play a major part in diets today. The edible seed of plants from the grass family, grains are a primary source of carbohydrates as well as in some cases a good source of protein. Many types come under the term grain, including barley, corn, bulgur wheat, couscous, quinoa, spelt, and wheat, each with its own characteristics, cooking method, and uses.

Perfect as a side dish, grains can also be used as an ingredient in bread, oatmeal, pasta, salads, pilafs, stews, burgers, fritters, and even beer. In the recipes that follow, there is a selection of a few of the most popular types of grains for you to try.

Storage
Keep in an airtight container or jar with a lid in a cool, dry place and avoid contact with moisture and strongly flavored ingredients.

COOKING GRAINS

As with rice, there are primarily two methods of cooking grains: boiling and absorption. In both cases, rinse the grains well in a strainer under cold running water before cooking. If cooking grains by the boiling method, cover them generously in lightly salted water, then bring to a boil. Turn the heat down slightly and simmer until tender, then drain well. When cooking grains by the absorption method, you need to use the correct ratio of grain to liquid (below). During cooking, the grain absorbs the liquid until tender, then it is allowed to steam-dry briefly in the heat of the pan so no excess water remains. The method for cooking couscous is slightly different in that the grains are steeped in hot liquid until tender (see p.215).

TYPE OF GRAIN	COOKING METHOD	COOKING TIME
Pearl barley	Boiling	20–30 minutes
Bulgur wheat	Absorption: use 1.25x the amount of liquid to grain	12–15 minutes
Couscous (instant)	Absorption: use 1.25x the amount of just-boiled liquid to grain, poured over in a bowl and covered	Leave to steep for 5–10 minutes
Buckwheat	Boiling	10–15 minutes
Quinoa	Boiling	15–20 minutes
Amaranth	Boiling	10–15 minutes
Freekeh	Boiling	30 minutes
Spelt	Boiling	30 minutes

Clockwise, from top, amaranth, bulgur wheat, buckwheat,
couscous, freekeh, quinoa, pearl barley, and spelt (center).

COOKING BULGUR WHEAT

Prep 5 minutes

Cook 15 minutes

Serves 4

Bulgur is a whole grain made from cracked wheat. Rich in fiber, vitamins, and minerals, bulgur is known for its distinctive nutty flavor and slightly chewy texture, making it a great option for salads, such as the classic Tabbouleh (right). It is also good in pilafs, combined with ground meat to make koftas, and works as a replacement for rice and couscous. When cooking bulgur, use 1.25x the amount of water to grain. The grain absorbs all the water as it cooks to become soft with a slight bite and shouldn't require any draining.

1 cup (150g) bulgur wheat
pinch of salt

1 | Rinse the bulgur wheat in a metal strainer under cold running water. Put it into a medium saucepan and cover with 1¼ cups (300ml) of cold water and a pinch of salt.

2 | Put the pan over medium-high heat, bring the water to a boil, then reduce the heat to low. Cover with a lid and simmer very gently for 12–15 minutes, until the water is absorbed.

3 | Remove the pan from the heat and leave to steam-dry for 5 minutes, then fluff up the grains with a fork before serving.

TIP

You can cook the bulgur wheat in vegetable or chicken stock in place of the water, and to add extra flavor, stir in a pat of butter just before serving.

Tabbouleh

Prep 15 minutes

Cook 15 minutes

Serves 4

Bulgur wheat is the main ingredient in this popular Middle Eastern salad. Fresh and zingy from the lemon juice, this tabbouleh features plentiful amounts of fresh herbs, cherry tomatoes, and finely sliced red onion as well as toasted hazelnuts for added crunch. Serve with the Shawarma-Spiced Whole Baked Cauliflower (see p.177).

1 recipe quantity of cooked Bulgur Wheat (left)
1 red onion, peeled and very finely sliced
3½oz (100g) cherry tomatoes, quartered
1 tsp ground coriander
1 large bunch of mixed herbs, such as cilantro, mint, and parsley, leaves picked and finely chopped
¼ cup (30g) hazelnuts, toasted (see p.288), roughly chopped, divided
juice of 1 lemon
6 tbsp extra-virgin olive oil
salt and freshly ground black pepper

1 | Follow steps 1–3 from Cooking Bulgur Wheat (left).

2 | Meanwhile, put the red onion and tomatoes in a large serving bowl and sprinkle in the ground coriander. Add the herbs and three-quarters of the hazelnuts, the lemon juice, and olive oil.

3 | Add the warm, cooked bulgur to the bowl and season with salt and pepper to taste. Mix well, then top with the remaining chopped hazelnuts to serve.

TIP

The salad will keep stored in an airtight container in the fridge for up to 3 days.

Sweet potato, spinach & peanut quinoa stew

Prep 5 minutes

Cook 40 minutes

Serves 2

Quinoa is an ancient South American grain, and its global popularity has risen in part due to its high nutrient content. The tiny grain is a good source of protein and fiber and is also popular with those following a gluten-free diet. It can be served as a side dish, in fritters, or added to soups and stews to make them more substantial. In this vegan one-pan dish, the quinoa cooks and expands in the vegetable stock, acting as a thickener. Make sure you rinse the quinoa well before cooking to remove any bitterness found in the grain.

1 tbsp olive, canola, or sunflower oil
1 red onion, peeled and finely sliced
pinch of salt, plus extra to season
2 fat garlic cloves, peeled and finely sliced
3 tbsp tomato paste
1 tsp dried oregano
1½ tsp ground cumin
½ tsp cayenne pepper

1 large sweet potato, about ½lb (250g), peeled and cut into ¾-in (2-cm) pieces
3 cups (750ml) Vegetable Stock (see p.414) or store-bought
scant ½ cup (70g) quinoa, rinsed well
3½oz (100g) baby spinach leaves
2 tbsp peanut butter (crunchy or smooth)
juice and finely grated zest of ½ unwaxed lemon
freshly ground black pepper

1 | Pour the oil into a large saucepan over medium heat. Add the red onion and a pinch of salt. Cook, stirring occasionally, for 8–10 minutes, until softened. Add the garlic and cook, stirring, for 2 minutes more. Add the tomato paste, oregano, cumin, and cayenne pepper. Give everything a good stir and cook for 1 minute, then add the sweet potato.

2 | Pour in the vegetable stock and bring to a simmer, then stir in the quinoa and let the stew simmer, stirring occasionally, for 15–20 minutes, until the sweet potato is tender and just holding its shape and the quinoa is cooked through. The quinoa should have doubled in size and will be tender with a slight bite.

3 | Stir in the spinach and peanut butter. Once the spinach has wilted, add the lemon juice and zest and season with salt and pepper to taste. Divide between two bowls to serve.

TIPS

This stew is great for batch cooking. Double the quantity and divide into individual portions, then keep in the fridge for up to 5 days or freeze for up to 3 months. Defrost in a small saucepan over low heat, then simmer for 10 minutes to heat through.

You can up the number of vegetables or swap them, depending on what you need to use up in the fridge. Try using a handful of sugar snap peas, snow peas, or kale instead of the spinach.

COOKING COUSCOUS

Prep 5 minutes

Cook 10 minutes

Serves 4

A staple in North African cooking, couscous is made from tiny balls of semolina, similar to pasta. Most of what we find in stores is "instant" couscous, which means the grains are precooked so they simply need rehydrating in just-boiled water or stock. While it's one of the easiest grains to prepare, make sure to use the correct ratio of couscous to liquid—too much makes for soggy grains. A classic accompaniment to tagines, couscous also adds texture to salads and stuffings, taking on the flavor of stronger ingredients.

1 cup (200g) couscous
1¼ cups (300ml) just-boiled Chicken Stock or
   Vegetable Stock (see p.414) or store-bought
2 tbsp (30g) salted butter, cut into small dice
salt and freshly ground black pepper

1 | Put the couscous into a medium heatproof bowl and pour over the hot stock. Cover tightly with plastic wrap.

2 | Leave the couscous to cook/rehydrate for 5–10 minutes, until the stock is absorbed and the grains are plump, then fluff up with a fork and dot over the butter. Season with salt and pepper to taste and fold gently to combine.

Couscous royale

Prep 20 minutes

*Cook 3 hours
20 minutes*

Serves 4

This lavish, celebratory North African dish features three different types of meat—a luxury that would only have been afforded to nobility and royalty in the past, hence its name. For the uninitiated, it's a rich lamb and chickpea stew with roasted harissa chicken thighs and spicy merguez sausages, all piled onto fluffy, buttery couscous.

3 tbsp extra-virgin olive oil, plus extra for drizzling
1¼lb (500g) boneless lamb shoulder, cut into
   1½-oz (4-cm) chunks
salt and freshly ground black pepper
1 onion, peeled and finely chopped
1 tbsp tomato paste
1½ tbsp ras el hanout
2 tsp ground cumin

pinch of saffron
1 cinnamon stick
½ tsp cayenne pepper
1 (14.5oz/400g) can diced tomatoes
1 carrot, peeled and cut into 2-in (5-cm) long pieces
1 zucchini, cut into 2-in (5-cm) long pieces
1 turnip, peeled and cut into 2-in (5-cm) long pieces
1 (15.5oz/400g) can chickpeas, drained
4 bone-in, skin-on chicken thighs
4 merguez sausages
2 tbsp harissa
½ cup (100g) plain yogurt
1 recipe quantity of cooked Couscous (above)
1 handful of flat-leaf parsley, chopped
(Continued overleaf.)

1 | Heat a large Dutch oven or heavy-based saucepan over medium-high heat with 1 tablespoon of the olive oil. Season the diced lamb with salt and pepper, then add half to the pan and cook for 2 minutes on each side, until browned all over. Using a slotted spoon, remove the lamb from the pan into a bowl. Add another 1 tablespoon of oil to the pan and repeat with the second batch of lamb until browned.

2 | Turn the heat to medium-low, add the remaining oil to the pan with the onion and a pinch of salt and cook for 6–8 minutes, until softened. Add the tomato paste and all the dried spices and cook for a minute, stirring.

3 | Pour in the diced tomatoes along with a full can of water. Add the carrot, then return the lamb and any juices from the bowl. Bring to a simmer, cover with the lid, then turn the heat to low and simmer gently for 1½ hours, stirring occasionally.

4 | Add the zucchini to the pan with the turnip and chickpeas. Simmer for another 1½ hours, with the lid off, until the sauce has thickened and the lamb is meltingly tender. Stir the sauce now and again to stop it burning on the bottom and add a splash of water, if needed. Season with salt and pepper to taste.

5 | When the lamb has 1 hour left to cook, preheat the oven to 400°F (200°C). Put the chicken thighs into a roasting pan, drizzle with a little oil, season well with salt and pepper, and roast for 30 minutes.

6 | Remove the tray from the oven, add the merguez sausages and spoon in 1 tablespoon of the harissa, then toss together until combined and evenly coated. Roast for another 20 minutes, until the chicken is caramelized and cooked through.

7 | Meanwhile, mix the remaining harissa with the yogurt.

8 | To serve, spoon the couscous onto four serving plates and top with the lamb stew, a chicken thigh, and a sausage. Sprinkle with parsley leaves and serve with a spoonful of the harissa yogurt.

Saffron butter couscous with almonds & pomegranate

Prep 10 minutes

Cook 15 minutes

Serves 4–6 as a side

This couscous recipe is heady with golden saffron, which comes from the stamen of a crocus flower and is said to be the most expensive spice in the world. The saffron infuses the buttery dressing, which lifts the blank canvas of couscous, while the toasted almonds and pops of fruity pomegranate seeds add crunch. This side dish would be great served with the grilled Lamb Chops (see p.112), replacing the Sauce Vierge (see p.426) with the tangy Zhoug (see p.445).

1 cup (200g) couscous
1¼ cups (300ml) just-boiled Vegetable Stock (see p.414) or store-bought
2 large pinches of saffron, divided
6 tbsp (100g) salted butter
3 garlic cloves, finely chopped
½ tsp ground cumin
½ tsp ground coriander
juice of 1 lemon
1 large handful of cilantro leaves, finely chopped

½ cup (50g) flaked almonds, toasted (see p.288)
½ cup (50g) pomegranate seeds
salt and freshly ground black pepper

1 | Put the couscous into a large heatproof bowl. Mix the vegetable stock with one pinch of the saffron and pour it over the couscous, stir, and cover with plastic wrap. Leave for 5–10 minutes, until the stock has been absorbed, then fluff up the grains with a fork.

2 | Meanwhile, make the dressing. Put the butter and garlic in a small saucepan over medium-low heat and cook, stirring, for 3–4 minutes, until the garlic smells aromatic. Remove the pan from the heat, then stir in the remaining saffron, the ground cumin, and ground coriander. Leave to cool for 5 minutes, then squeeze in the lemon juice.

3 | Add the cilantro to the couscous with most of the almonds and pomegranate seeds, reserving a few to serve. Mix well, then pour over three-quarters of the dressing and season with salt and pepper to taste, then mix again to combine.

4 | Spoon the couscous onto a serving plate, pour over the remaining dressing, and sprinkle with the rest of the almonds and pomegranate seeds.

TIPS

The couscous will keep, covered, for up to 3 days in the fridge.

To make a more substantial dish, add a handful of chopped cherry tomatoes, ¼ chopped cucumber, and ½ diced red bell pepper.

MAKING SOFT POLENTA

Prep 5 minutes

Cook 20 minutes

Serves 4

Made from dried ground white or yellow corn (cornmeal), polenta is a staple ingredient in Northern Italy. Most polenta sold is the instant variety, which is precooked and much quicker to prepare than traditional polenta, which can take up to 50 minutes. Soft polenta is a classic Italian side to hearty stews, often in place of mashed potatoes and, similarly, it's a great place to hide plenty of butter and cheese.

5 cups (1.25 liters) Vegetable Stock or Chicken
 Stock (see p.414) or store-bought
1⅔ cups (200g) instant polenta
½ cup (125g) salted butter, diced
3½oz (100g) Parmesan or Cheddar cheese,
 finely grated
salt and freshly ground black pepper

1 | Bring the stock to a boil in a large saucepan over medium-high heat. Add the polenta in a steady stream, whisking continuously and vigorously with a balloon whisk to make sure there are no lumps.

2 | Return the polenta to a boil, then reduce the heat to low and gently simmer for 15–20 minutes, stirring regularly until soft, smooth, and creamy.

3 | Remove the pan from the heat, add the butter and cheese and leave to stand for 2–3 minutes, occasionally stirring with a wooden spoon, until combined. Season with salt and pepper to taste.

Polenta variation

Polenta fries and wedges: you can use polenta to make fries (and wedges) but reduce the quantity of stock to 2½ cups (1 liter)—you can also make these using any leftover polenta. Put the cooked polenta into a greased baking dish, layered about ¾–1½-in (2–4-cm) thick. Cover the surface with plastic wrap and leave to cool and set. The polenta can be chilled at this point to firm up further to cook another day.

Once set, remove the plastic wrap and upend the slab of polenta onto a cutting board. Cut into 1¼-in (3-cm) wide strips or triangular wedges. To cook, place on a parchment-paper-lined baking sheet, drizzle generously with olive oil, and bake for 25 minutes, turning halfway, until crisp and starting to color. Alternatively, heat 2–3 tablespoons of olive oil in a skillet and fry until golden and crisp, about 3–4 minutes on each side.

TIP

To flavor the polenta, you can add finely chopped rosemary, chipotle paste, or hot/sweet smoked paprika.

Mushroom ragu
with soft polenta

Prep 20 minutes

Cook 2 hours

Serves 4

This flavor-packed mushroom ragu is paired with cheesy soft polenta (left) and topped with a sprinkling of zesty, herby Gremolata (see p.443) for a comforting, hearty meal. Since the mushroom ragu is vegan, you could swap the butter and cheese in the polenta for plant-based alternatives, if you like. To save time, make the mushroom ragu up to 2 days in advance, then reheat while making the polenta before serving.

¾oz (20g) dried porcini mushrooms
3 tbsp olive oil, divided
1lb (500g) button mushrooms, quartered
3 portobello mushrooms, sliced
1 onion, peeled and finely chopped
2 celery stalks, finely chopped
1 medium carrot, peeled and finely chopped
pinch of salt, plus extra for seasoning
4 garlic cloves, chopped
1 tbsp fennel seeds

1 tsp dried chili flakes
1 tbsp tomato paste
1 cup (250ml) dry red wine
1 (15oz/400g) can crushed tomatoes
2 cups (500ml) Vegetable Stock or Chicken Stock (see p.414) or store-bought
freshly ground black pepper
1 recipe quantity of Soft Polenta (left) and Gremolata (see p.443), optional, to serve

1 | Put the dried porcini mushrooms into a small bowl and pour over 1 cup (250ml) of hot water.

2 | Meanwhile, heat 2 tablespoons of the olive oil in a large saucepan or Dutch oven over high heat. Add the button and portobello mushrooms and cook for 10–15 minutes, stirring regularly, until softened and beginning to caramelize—most of the moisture should have evaporated. Using a slotted spoon, scoop the mushrooms into a bowl.

3 | Turn the heat to medium and add the remaining oil with the onion, celery, carrot, and a pinch of salt. Cover with the lid and cook for 8–10 minutes, stirring often, until softened. Add the garlic, fennel seeds, and chili flakes and cook for 2 minutes, then stir in the tomato paste and cook for a further minute.

4 | Scoop out the porcini mushrooms from the soaking liquid and roughly chop. Add to the pan with three-quarters of the soaking liquid, leaving any grit from the mushrooms in the bottom of the bowl. Pour in the red wine and bring to a gentle boil for 1 minute before adding the crushed tomatoes, stock, and returning the cooked mushrooms to the pan.

5 | Bring the ragu to a boil, then reduce the heat and simmer gently, part-covered with a lid, for 1 hour, until thickened. Season with salt and pepper to taste.

6 | Meanwhile, follow steps 1–3 from Making Soft Polenta (left).

7 | Spoon the soft polenta into four bowls, top with the mushroom ragu, and serve sprinkled with the gremolata, if you like.

MAKING OATMEAL

Prep 5 minutes

Cook 5 minutes

Serves 1

The genius of oatmeal is that it requires just two ingredients—oats and milk or water—to create a nutritious and affordable breakfast. Old fashioned rolled oats work best here for quick oatmeal. You can also try steel-cut oats which are processed differently; take longer to cook; and yield a nutty, hearty texture. Likewise, choose between water or milk, depending on how rich and creamy you like your oatmeal, or opt for half and half instead. This makes a classic thick oatmeal, but if you prefer a looser consistency increase the quantity of liquid to 1½ cups (350ml). Finish the oatmeal with your favorite toppings (right).

⅓ cup (50g) old fashioned rolled oats
1¼ cups (300ml) water or milk of your choice
pinch of salt (optional)
milk of your choice, to serve

1 | Put the oats into a small saucepan and pour in the water or milk of choice. Add a pinch of salt, if using.

2 | Put the pan over medium heat and cook, stirring regularly with a wooden spoon, for 4–5 minutes, until thick and creamy.

3 | Spoon the oatmeal into a serving bowl, pour over a little milk, and finish with the topping of your choice.

Topping ideas

1 tbsp raspberry jam + 1 tbsp peanut or almond butter or tahini

1 handful of Granola (see p.300) + sliced fruit of your choice (pear, plum, and banana work well) + a drizzle of honey

1–2 tbsp demerara sugar + a splash of cream

⅓ cup (50g) frozen berries of your choice + ½ tsp ground cinnamon + 1 tbsp maple syrup. To make a quick compote, put all the ingredients in a heatproof bowl and microwave in 30-second bursts, stirring after each one. Alternatively, heat the berry mixture in a small saucepan over medium heat.

TIP

Cook the oatmeal in a microwave instead of a pan. Add the oats, water or milk, and salt, if using, to a microwave-safe bowl. Cook in 30-second bursts, stirring after each, until the oats have absorbed most of the liquid and the oatmeal has thickened to your liking.

Berry overnight oats

Prep 5 minutes
+ overnight
soaking

No cook

Serves 2

This creamy, filling breakfast doesn't require any cooking since the oats are simply soaked overnight until soft and plump. At the same time, the frozen berries defrost in the oat mixture, turning the grain a vibrant pink. You can use water or milk for the oats, or a combination of half and half, depending on how rich and creamy you like it.

1 cup (150g) frozen mixed berries
⅔ cup (100g) old fashioned rolled oats
1¼ cups (300ml) water or milk of your choice
pinch of salt (optional)

To serve
2 tbsp Greek, plain, or dairy-free yogurt
2 tsp honey or maple syrup
2 tbsp mixed seeds, toasted (see p.288), optional

1 | The night before serving, mix together the frozen berries, oats, water or milk, and a pinch of salt, if using, in a medium serving bowl—at this point it will look quite liquid but the oats will absorb much of this as they soak.

2 | Cover the bowl and leave the oats to soak in the fridge overnight.

3 | The next day, divide the soaked oats between two serving bowls. Top with the yogurt, honey or maple syrup, and toasted seeds, if you like, to serve.

PASTA,

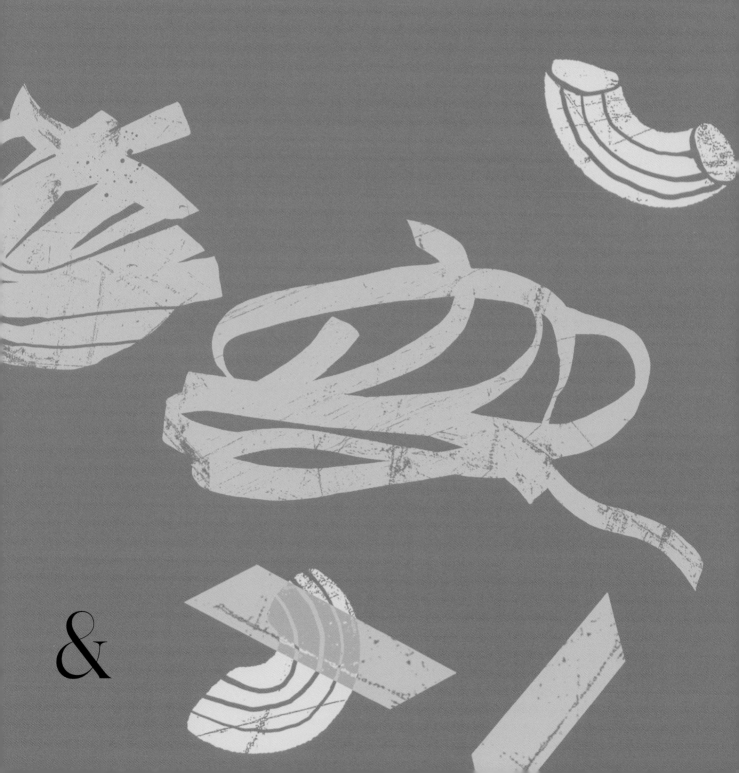

&

NOODLES

DUMPLINGS

DRIED PASTA

This chapter starts with dried pasta, an absolute must-have staple in many kitchens and for good reason—it has a long shelf life and takes less than 15 minutes to cook, making it a perfect pantry standby when you're looking to rustle up a speedy meal. Dried pasta comes in a multitude of different shapes, sizes, and types. Pasta made with wheat, more specifically hard durum wheat, is the most popular type and comes with or without the inclusion of egg. The egg gives the pasta a more golden color and, some say, a slightly richer flavor.

Look also for dried pasta prepared with other types of grain, such as buckwheat or brown rice, and even pulses, including red lentils, soy beans, or chickpeas. Along with being nutritious, these are usually gluten-free (double check the package), which is essential if you are serving it to those with an intolerance or allergy to wheat.

A typical serving of dried pasta is around 2½–3½oz (75–100g) per person, depending on the type of sauce you are accompanying it with—and how large your appetite is.

Storage
Keep dried pasta in a cool, dry cupboard in a sealed package or container.

MATCHING PASTA WITH SAUCES

Pairing a dried (and fresh) pasta shape with the right type of sauce can make all the difference to the success of your dish, since they work to complement each other, rather than one dominating. This useful guide (below) gives you a few pointers to get you started and you'll also find some more suggestions for sauce and pasta pairings later in the book (see pp.235–238) with a few recipes for sauces.

PASTA TYPE	SHAPE	PERFECT WITH ...
Thick, short tubes	Penne, rigatoni, macaroni	Heavy, creamy sauces; vegetable sauces; pesto; cheese sauces; Bolognese; baked dishes.
Long, thin strands	Spaghetti, linguine, capellini	Light, garlicky, oil-based sauces; seafood; tomato sauce; light, creamy sauces; pesto.
Wide, long ribbons	Pappardelle, tagliatelle	Robust, meaty ragus; tomato sauces.
Shells/twists	Conchiglie, farfalle, trofie	Heavy, creamy sauces; meat sauces; tomato sauces; pesto.
Pasta sheets and tubes	Lasagna, cannelloni	Meat or tomato sauces; creamy cheese and spinach sauces; baked dishes.
Small shapes	Stellini, orzo, fregola	Pesto; soups; broths; salads.
Filled pasta	Ravioli, tortellini, tortelloni	Oil-based and creamy sauces; seafood sauces; light tomato sauces; broths.

Clockwise, from top, macaroni, tagliatelle, linguine,
penne, pappardelle, rigatoni, and orzo (center).

COOKING
DRIED PASTA

Prep 5 minutes

Cook 15 minutes

Serves 2

There are a few must-dos when cooking dried pasta. Firstly, make sure you have a plentiful amount of boiling salted water in the saucepan and the water remains boiling rapidly when cooking the pasta. The water should be generously salted, about 2 tablespoons of salt per gallon (4 liters) of water—the saying goes that it should be as salty as the sea! Stir the pasta in the first few minutes to prevent it from clumping together, then cook it for the length of time given on the package. When cooked, pasta should be tender with a slight resistance, otherwise known as "al dente."

½lb (200g) dried pasta of your choice
salt

1 | Fill a deep saucepan with water and season well with salt. When the water comes to a rapid boil over medium-high heat, carefully drop in the pasta; it should be completely submerged in a generous amount of water.

2 | Return the water to a rolling boil and set a timer. During the first few minutes of cooking, stir now and again to ensure the pasta doesn't clump or stick.

3 | Toward the end of the cooking time, scoop out a cupful of the water to add to the sauce later—this will help thin and loosen it. Put a large colander in the sink and drain the cooked pasta, then use as liked.

Roasted cherry tomato & mascarpone rigatoni

Prep 15 minutes

Cook 1 hour

Serves 4

This is a terrific pasta recipe for when you're cooking for others and want to do most of the work in advance. Simply roast the cherry tomato sauce a day in advance, cook the pasta before you want to serve it, and then toss everything together. Rigatoni is the perfect pasta shape here, because the sauce coats both the outside and the inside, meaning each bite is packed with saucy flavor.

1 garlic bulb, separated into cloves
6 tbsp olive oil, divided
1¾lb (800g) vine-ripened cherry tomatoes
½–1 tsp dried chili flakes, plus extra to serve (optional)
1lb (400g) dried rigatoni pasta
8oz (250g) mascarpone
1 cup (30g) basil, leaves picked
juice and finely grated zest of ½ unwaxed lemon
salt and freshly ground black pepper
⅓ cup (50g) pine nuts, toasted (see p.288)
garlic bread, to serve (optional, but delicious)

1 | Preheat the oven to 350°F (180°C).

2 | Put the whole garlic cloves in a 8 x 12 in (30 x 20 cm) roasting pan, pour over 1 tablespoon of the olive oil, then cover the tray tightly with foil. Roast for 15 minutes—you start roasting the garlic before the tomatoes so the cloves have time to soften.

3 | Add the cherry tomatoes, chili flakes, and the remaining olive oil to the roasting pan (everything should fit snugly in a single layer). Re-cover tightly with foil and roast for 30 minutes, until the tomatoes start to burst and the garlic is very soft.

4 | Squeeze the garlic cloves from their skins onto a cutting board, then use the back of a kitchen knife to mash into a rough purée. Return the garlic to the tomatoes in the pan.

5 | Follow steps 1–3 from Cooking Dried Pasta (left), using 1lb (400g) rigatoni for four people.

6 | Once the pasta is cooked, drain, reserving a cupful of the cooking water. Return the pasta to the saucepan over medium heat. Add the mascarpone with the pasta cooking water and stir well until combined into a sauce. Gently fold in the roasted garlicky tomatoes and most of the basil, saving some to serve.

7 | Add the lemon juice and zest, then season with salt and pepper to taste.

8 | Divide the pasta between four bowls. Top with the remaining basil leaves, pine nuts, and a sprinkling of extra chili flakes, if you like. Serve with garlic bread, if using.

Sausage, cream & mustard orzotto

Prep 10 minutes

Cook 25 minutes

Serves 2

This is a great way to cook orzo pasta, treating it in the same way you would short-grain arborio rice in a risotto, so rather than being boiled separately and added to the sauce, everything is cooked together in one pan. It has a much silkier finish than rice, which is perfect when matched with this creamy mustard and sausage sauce.

1 tbsp extra-virgin olive oil
6 sweet Italian, Toulouse, or garlic pork sausages
1 onion, peeled and finely sliced

3 garlic cloves, peeled and finely sliced
½lb (200g) dried orzo pasta
⅔ cup (150ml) dry white wine
3 cups (750ml) hot Chicken Stock (see p.414)
   or store-bought
1½ tbsp wholegrain mustard
⅓ cup (100ml) heavy cream
1 large handful of flat-leaf parsley leaves,
   finely chopped
salt and freshly ground black pepper
½ cup (40g) finely grated Parmesan cheese, to serve

1 | Heat the olive oil in a medium, high-sided skillet over medium-high heat. Using a small, sharp chef's knife, split the skin of each sausage, then tear the meat into small nuggets straight into the pan, discarding the skin. Add the onion and sauté, stirring often, for 4–5 minutes, until the sausages and onion are golden and caramelized.

2 | Add the garlic and cook for another minute, before adding the orzo. Stir well to coat the orzo in the oil mixture. Pour in the wine and bring to a gentle boil for 2 minutes, stirring. Don't worry if the orzo sticks a little to the bottom of the pan at this point, it will free itself during cooking.

3 | Pour in half of the hot stock and bring to a simmer. Cook, stirring occasionally, for 6–7 minutes, until the stock has almost been absorbed. Continue to spoon in more stock, a ladleful at a time, adding more once the last batch has been absorbed, and cook for a further 5–6 minutes, until the orzo is *al dente*.

4 | Stir in the mustard, cream, and parsley, then simmer for 2–3 minutes, until slightly thickened and reduced. Season with salt and lots of black pepper. Divide into four bowls, then sprinkle the Parmesan over the top to serve.

Spaghetti
alla puttanesca

Prep 5 minutes

Cook 30 minutes

Serves 2

Originating in Naples, this classic pasta dish varies in its use of fresh or canned tomatoes, but since this is primarily a pantry recipe, canned seems more fitting here. What is always a given is the salty hit from the capers, anchovies, and olives. Spaghetti is the perfect shape for the light, oily tomato sauce.

1 (2oz/50g) can of anchovies in olive oil
1 small red onion, peeled and finely chopped
small pinch of salt, plus extra to season
2 fat garlic cloves, peeled and finely sliced
¼–½ tsp dried chili flakes
1 tbsp tomato paste
1 (15oz/400g) can crushed tomatoes
½lb (200g) dried spaghetti
1 tbsp capers, drained
1 handful of pitted black olives, drained and sliced
freshly ground black pepper
1 large handful of flat-leaf parsley, leaves and stalks, roughly chopped

1 | Pour the oil from the anchovies into a medium skillet over medium heat. Add the onion with a small pinch of salt. Cook, stirring regularly, for about 8 minutes, until softened.

2 | Add the anchovies, garlic, and chili flakes and cook, stirring, for 2 minutes, until the anchovies break down in the oil and the garlic is lightly golden, then add the tomato paste. Cook, stirring for another minute.

3 | Add the crushed tomatoes to the pan, then use the back of a wooden spoon or a potato masher to break them into smaller pieces. Bring the sauce to a simmer, then turn down the heat to low and let it bubble gently for 15 minutes, stirring occasionally.

4 | Stir the capers and black olives into the sauce to heat through, then season to taste. It is unlikely to need any salt, just plenty of black pepper.

5 | Meanwhile, once the sauce has been cooking for 5 minutes, follow steps 1–3 from Cooking Dried Pasta (see p.226), but rather than draining the pasta through a colander, use tongs to transfer it straight to the sauce in the skillet. Save a cupful of the cooking water.

6 | Add the parsley to the sauce, then toss together adding enough of the reserved pasta cooking water to loosen. Divide between two bowls and enjoy.

FRESH PASTA

If you're looking to elevate your pasta game, making your own fresh pasta is beyond satisfying and, most importantly, very achievable. The dough is made with just a few ingredients—00 flour, eggs, and a little salt (some prefer to leave the latter out)—and by following the instructions, below, you can transform these into a smooth, silky ball of dough ready for kneading, rolling, and shaping. It is important to use the right type of flour—00 is a finely milled strong white wheat flour and results in a smooth-textured dough, but it is possible to use bread flour or all-purpose flour, if more convenient, although the result will be slightly different.

The first decision when making your fresh pasta is to choose whether the dough is made entirely by hand or with the help of a food processor—the choice is entirely yours and there are instructions for both methods (below). Both result in fresh pasta with a slightly different texture but it's all down to personal preference. The machine method is obviously quicker, but by making it by hand you get a real feel for the texture of the dough.

Storage
Fresh pasta will keep wrapped in the fridge for up to 1 day. It can also be frozen for up to 3 months.

MAKING FRESH PASTA DOUGH

Prep 20 minutes + resting

No cook

Serves 2

There are many options and recipes for fresh pasta dough, some recommend using semolina with the 00 flour, while others opt for all egg yolks or just whole egg. After many tests, this is the one that works best for both simplicity and taste—the egg yolks add richness and flavor, while the whole egg acts as a binder. Most importantly, seek out 00 flour, the Italian fine white wheat flour has the perfect level of gluten for delicious fresh pasta.

1¼ cups (150g) 00 flour
1 large egg
2 egg yolks (see Separating Eggs p.32)
pinch of salt

1 | On a large, clean work surface, sift the flour into a mound, then make a 6-in (15-cm) well in the center. Crack the whole egg into the well, followed by the egg yolks. Add a pinch of salt, then use a fork to beat the eggs lightly until combined. Gradually draw in a little of the flour from the wall of the well and mix until you have a thick paste in the center.

2 | Keep mixing in more flour, a little at a time, to incorporate it into the eggs until you have a stiff, shaggy dough. It will look very rough and dry at this point—it is supposed to; don't panic.

3 | Using a dough scraper or clean hands, start to bring the dough together into a ball. Knead the dough with a firm steady motion, giving it a quarter turn with one hand, while pressing downward and forward with the heel of your other hand until the dough feels smooth and elastic. This will take about 10 minutes. (If the dough is too dry when kneading, wet your hands, rather than the dough to add moisture, or if it is too wet, add a little extra flour.)

4 | Wrap the ball of dough in plastic wrap and leave it to rest for at least 1 hour to allow it to relax before rolling and stretching.

TIPS

To make the dough by machine, add the flour, egg, yolks, and salt to the bowl of a food processor and pulse until it forms a smooth dough. Place the dough onto a work surface and knead as instructed (left).

The pasta dough can be made the day before use and kept wrapped in the fridge overnight.

Reserve the whites when separating the eggs to make the Black Forest Gateau Pavlova (see p.400).

  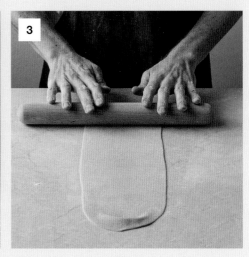

ROLLING PASTA
DOUGH BY HAND

Prep 40 minutes
+ resting

No cook

Serves 2

With a bit of elbow grease, patience, and a rolling pin, it is more than achievable to roll and stretch fresh pasta by hand, instead of through a machine. It is not a difficult technique to master, but it does require you to work quickly so the dough doesn't dry out.

1 recipe quantity of Fresh Pasta Dough (see p.230)
00 flour, for dusting worktop

1 | Follow steps 1–4 for Making Fresh Pasta Dough (see p.230). Remove the dough from the fridge, unwrap, and cut it in half. Take one piece of dough and place it on a lightly floured work surface, then flatten it slightly with your fingers into a disk. Wrap the other piece of dough to stop it from drying out, but leave it at room temperature.

2 | Lightly flour the disk of dough and press it into a neat rectangle ready for rolling out.

3 | Lightly flour a rolling pin, then gently and evenly roll the pasta into a long rectangle, regularly turning the dough until it is roughly 6 in (15 cm) wide and $^1/_8$ in (3 mm) thick. Dust the top with flour if it sticks. Repeat with the remaining dough piece.

4 | If making filled pasta, like Ravioli (see p.236), you can use it right away but for other shapes, such as Pappardelle (see p.234), leave the pasta to dry slightly, draping the long strands over a clean, parchment-paper-lined clothes hanger for 1 hour. For smaller pasta shapes, put them in a tray dusted with polenta or semolina at room temperature for 1 hour to dry.

ROLLING PASTA DOUGH WITH A MACHINE

Prep 30 minutes + resting

No cook

Serves 2

Pasta machines come in two types, hand-cranked and electric, and are readily available and relatively economical to buy. They can be a real asset if you intend to make fresh pasta regularly and result in the smoothest, silkiest dough.

1 recipe quantity of Fresh Pasta Dough (see p.230)
00 flour, for dusting worktop

1 | Follow steps 1–4 for Making Fresh Pasta Dough (see p.230). Remove the dough from the fridge, unwrap, and cut it in half. Take one piece of dough and press it into a rectangle with the palm of your hand on a lightly floured work surface, until about ½ in (1 cm) thick. Dust it all over with flour. Wrap the other piece of dough to stop it from drying out, but leave it at room temperature. Firmly attach the pasta machine to the work surface, then flour the rollers and the work surface in front of the machine. Set the pasta roller to its widest setting (read the manufacturer's instructions for your machine—they can differ), then feed the pasta through.

2 | Fold the pasta in half, then roll it through again. Rolling the pasta through the machine twice at this point makes for the silkiest dough.

3 | Reduce the setting by one notch to make the rollers slightly closer together, then roll the pasta through this setting. Repeat, reducing the setting by one notch each time, until you have rolled the pasta from the widest setting on the machine to the penultimate one. As the pasta becomes longer and thinner, ensure it is well-floured and handle the dough lightly. Flour the pasta well and set it to one side. Repeat with the remaining dough piece. You should now have two long, thin, oblong sheets of pasta, about 6 in (15 cm) wide and ⅛ in (3 mm) thick. You can trim the pasta strips to neaten the edges.

4 | If making filled pasta, like Ravioli (see p.236), you can use it right away but for other shapes, including Pappardelle (see p.234), leave it to dry slightly, draping the long strands over a clean, parchment-paper-lined clothes hanger for 1 hour. For smaller pasta shapes, put them in a tray dusted with polenta or semolina at room temperature for 1 hour to dry.

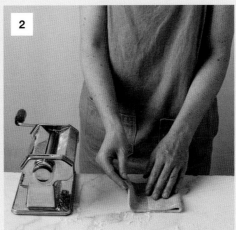
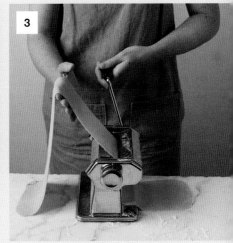

CUTTING
FRESH PASTA

*Prep 50 minutes
+ resting*

No cook

Serves 2

You can, of course, choose to make any shape of pasta with your rolled-out fresh dough, but this recipe is for pappardelle, which is the ideal shape for cutting by hand. It doesn't matter if the long, wide strips of pasta are a little bit uneven because this just adds to their homemade appeal. Make sure you dust the work surface with flour to stop the pasta from sticking.

1 recipe quantity of Fresh Pasta Dough (see p.230)
⅔ cup (100g) semolina or polenta
00 flour, for dusting worktop

1 | Follow steps 1–4 from Making Fresh Pasta Dough (see p.230). Follow steps 1–4 from Rolling Pasta Dough by Hand (see p.232) or Machine (see p.233), depending on preference. Sprinkle the semolina or polenta into a 9 x 13 in (30 x 20 cm) deep baking dish. The semolina prevents the strands of pasta from sticking together. Take the rolled-out sheets of fresh pasta and cut each one in half, so you have 4 rectangular pieces, about 6 x 12 in (30 x 15 cm) each.

2 | Take one rectangle of dough and place it on a floured work surface with one of the shorter sides facing you. Dust the top with a little more flour, then roll it away from you into a neat spiral.

3 | Place the rolled-up dough on a cutting board and cut it into 1¼-in (3-cm) wide strips. Unroll, then place the long strands of pasta in the baking dish and toss well in the semolina or polenta. Repeat with the remaining pasta dough. Cover with a clean kitchen towel.

TIP

To cook fresh pasta, bring a large saucepan of water to a boil and add plenty of salt. Add the fresh pasta to the pan, stir, and cook for 1–2 minutes, depending on its thickness and shape, until tender and light in color. It should still retain a little firmness. If in doubt, try a piece!

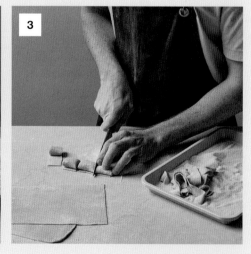

Pasta alla norma pappardelle

Prep 1 hour 5 minutes + resting

Cook 35 minutes

Serves 2

This sauce is made from slow-cooked tomatoes, garlic, and eggplant and works wonderfully with the long, wide strands of fresh pappardelle because its texture and shape mean the sauce clings to and coats the homemade pasta.

1 recipe quantity of Fresh Pasta Dough (see p.230) or ½lb (200g) store-bought fresh pappardelle
1 handful of basil leaves
⅓ cup (30g) finely grated Parmesan cheese or vegetarian alternative

For the sauce
1 eggplant, cut into 1¼-in (3-cm) chunks
3 tbsp extra-virgin olive oil, divided
good pinch each of salt and freshly ground black pepper, plus extra to season
3 garlic cloves, thinly sliced
½ tsp dried chili flakes
1 (15oz/400g) can crushed tomatoes

1 | Follow steps 1–4 from Making Fresh Pasta Dough (see p.230). Follow steps 1–4 from Rolling Pasta Dough by Hand (see p.232) or Machine (see p.233), depending on preference.

2 | Follow steps 1–5 from Cutting Fresh Pasta (left). Cover the pappardelle and leave it to dry at room temperature while you make the pasta sauce.

3 | Place the eggplant chunks into a medium bowl with 1 tablespoon of the olive oil and a good pinch of salt and pepper, then toss well until combined.

4 | Heat a large, deep skillet over medium-high heat. Add the eggplant and sauté for 4–5 minutes, tossing it now and again, until softened and starting to color.

5 | Turn the heat to medium-low and move the eggplant to one side of the pan. Pour the remaining oil into the gap, add the garlic and cook for 2 minutes, then add the chili flakes and crushed tomatoes with half a can of warm water. Use the side of a wooden spoon to break up the tomatoes slightly, then season with salt and pepper.

6 | Mix the eggplant into the tomatoes and bring the sauce almost to a boil. Reduce the heat to low and simmer for 30 minutes, until the sauce has reduced and thickened and the eggplant is very soft.

7 | To cook the pasta, follow the instructions in the Tip (left). Using tongs, carefully lift the pasta from the saucepan straight into the skillet. Toss the pasta in the sauce, adding a ladleful of the pasta cooking water if the sauce is too thick. Divide between two plates and top with the basil leaves and grated cheese, to serve.

LEMONY RICOTTA & SPINACH RAVIOLI

Prep 55 minutes + resting

Serves 2 as a starter

Fresh pasta can be stuffed with all sorts of fillings from meat and seafood to this vegetarian version, a lemony twist on the classic ricotta and spinach. Ravioli is perhaps the best-known filled pasta shape, but once you've mastered it, try experimenting with different ones—there are amazing online tutorials to help you. You will need a small piping bag for this recipe.

1 recipe quantity of Fresh Pasta Dough (see p.230)
5½oz (150g) ricotta cheese
6oz (170g) frozen chopped spinach, drained, and squeezed dry
1 small garlic clove, peeled and crushed
good grating of fresh nutmeg
juice and finely grated zest of ½ unwaxed lemon
salt and freshly ground black pepper
⅔ cup (75g) semolina or polenta

1 | Follow steps 1–4 from Making Fresh Pasta Dough (see p.230). While the dough rests, make the filling. In a small bowl, beat together the ricotta, spinach, garlic, nutmeg, and lemon zest. Season with plenty of salt and pepper. Spoon the filling into a small piping bag.

2 | Follow steps 1–4 from Rolling Pasta Dough by Hand (see p.232) or Machine (see p.233), depending on preference. Sprinkle the semolina or polenta into a large baking sheet in an even layer. Lightly flour the work surface and put the two rolled-out sheets of pasta horizontally in front of you, placing them one in front of the other. Snip off the end of the piping bag and pipe 6 large blobs, each about 1 large tablespoon in size, onto the pasta sheet nearest you, ensuring there is a 2½–3½-in (6–8-cm) gap between each mound.

3 | Have a bowl of cold water ready to one side. Dip a finger into the bowl of cold water, then dampen the pasta around each of the ricotta mounds.

4 | Lift the second sheet of pasta on top, then using the sides of your hands, gently mold the upper layer of pasta around the mounds of filling, removing as much air as possible and pressing together the two sheets of pasta until they stick firmly.

5 | At this stage, you can either use a 4-in (10-cm) circular cutter, as here, to stamp out round parcels or a knife or pasta wheel cutter to cut the ravioli into 6 squares.

6 | Move the cut ravioli onto the semolina-dusted baking sheet, leaving plenty of room around each one. Sprinkle a little more semolina on top, then leave for 30 minutes, until slightly dry and firmer.

7 | After drying, you are ready to cook and serve your filled ravioli, see Ravioli with Brown Butter & Hazelnut Sauce (p.238), or the filled pasta will keep covered in the fridge for up to a day. (You can also freeze it for up to 3 months.)

TIPS

If serving the ravioli as a main course, double the quantity of pasta dough as well as the filling.

Save any fresh pasta off-cuts to serve with the Simple Tomato Sauce (see p.422). They will keep for up to 3 days stored in an airtight container with lots of polenta or semolina to prevent them sticking together.

Ravioli with brown butter & hazelnut sauce

*Prep 1 hour
+ resting*

Cook 15 minutes

*Serves 2 as
a starter*

This is the ideal starter recipe when making ravioli from scratch. The parcels of fresh pasta have a creamy ricotta and spinach filling with a hint of lemon and are served tossed in a simple brown butter sauce with crunchy chopped hazelnuts. This is a dish that will make you feel like a genius in the kitchen!

1 recipe quantity of Lemony Ricotta & Spinach
    Ravioli (see p.236)
4 tbsp (50g) salted butter
¼ cup (30g) hazelnuts, chopped
squeeze of lemon juice, taste
1 handful of basil leaves
salt and freshly ground black pepper
⅓ cup (30g) finely grated Parmesan cheese,
    to serve

1 | Follow steps 1–6 from making Lemony Ricotta & Spinach Ravioli (see p.236).

2 | Melt the butter in a small saucepan over medium-high heat. Cook for 4–5 minutes, stirring regularly, until the butter turns a deep brown color and smells nutty (see p.51). Remove the pan from the heat and stir in the chopped hazelnuts.

3 | To cook the ravioli, bring water to a boil in a medium, deep saucepan. Season generously with salt. Line a baking sheet with parchment paper.

4 | Once the water is boiling, carefully add the ravioli and cook for 1–2 minutes, they should float to the surface when cooked. Using a slotted spoon, scoop them out onto a parchment-paper-lined tray—this will stop the ravioli from being waterlogged, then divide them between two serving plates.

5 | Add a squeeze of lemon juice to the brown butter, whisk to combine, and reheat briefly, if needed. Spoon the sauce over the ravioli, and top with basil leaves and grated Parmesan, to serve.

TIP

This rich, buttery sauce will also work with long pasta, such as linguine and spaghetti, either fresh or dried. Instead of the hazelnuts, you can sprinkle over toasted chopped walnuts (see p.288) and fresh parsley.

DRIED NOODLES

There is a wide range of dried noodles to choose from, all of which can be transformed into simple, tasty meals in a matter of minutes. We often associate noodles with China, but you'll find other types in many parts of the world, from Eastern Europe to Japan. They are produced using a variety of base ingredients, usually influenced by their origin, and in a multitude of thicknesses. In Vietnamese cuisine, for instance, you will find soft-textured, silky rice noodles, while in China, there are firmer wheat noodles or those made with egg. In Japan, soba noodles made from buckwheat flour and thick, slippery, wheat udon are popular, yet this list barely scratches the surface. Similarly, there is a multitude of ways to prepare and serve noodles, such as cold, hot, in a broth or sauce, fried until crisp, stir-fried, and more ...

Storage
Keep dried noodles in a cool, dry cupboard in a sealed package or container. Check the use-by date.

NOODLE TYPE	SHAPE	PERFECT IN ...
Wheat noodles	Thin, medium, thick, round, flat, knife-cut, udon, somen, ramen, chow mein	Broths, stir-fries, hot-pots, Japanese ramen, hot-oil dressings, braises, curries.
Egg noodles	Thin, medium, thick, round, flat	Stir-fries, hot-pots, deep-fried until crisp, dressed in a sauce, salads.
Rice noodles	Vermicelli, thin, medium, thick ribbon, round, flat, ho fun	Thai salads, *pad Thai*, Vietnamese *pho*, soups, stir-fries, summer rolls, deep-fried until crisp.
Buckwheat (soba) noodles	Thin, medium, round, flat	Japanese-style soups, broths, stir-fries, hot or cold with a dipping sauce.
Glass (cellophane) noodles (made from mung beans, sweet potato, or potato starch)	Vermicelli, thin, medium, thick, round, flat, mung bean sheets	Soups, broths, stir-fries, hot-pots, spring rolls, salads, deep-fried until crisp.

Clockwise, from top, vermicelli rice noodles, buckwheat (soba) noodles, thin egg noodles, thick round udon, flat udon, flat wheat noodles, medium egg noodles, and flat rice noodles (center).

COOKING DRIED NOODLES

Prep 5 minutes

Cook 5 minutes

Serves 4

Preparing and cooking dried noodles is much the same as dried pasta—you need a pan containing plenty of boiling salted water to allow the noodles space to unravel and expand. A brief stir after adding the noodles to the pan helps separate the strands and ensure they don't stick together. Cooking times can vary depending on the type and thickness of the noodle, so please check the instructions on the package. Here, the recipe uses dried wheat noodles, which form the foundation of the ramen dish on the following page. Dried rice vermicelli are perhaps the quickest type to cook. More accurately, they are immersed in just-boiled water, rather than cooked, for 2–3 minutes, before draining and serving.

½lb (250g) dried wheat noodles

1 | Bring a large saucepan of lightly salted water to a boil. Remove the noodles from their package and drop into the boiling water.

2 | Stir well in the first minute to stop the noodles from sticking to each other. Check the package instructions for the cooking time—it's usually around 3–5 minutes.

3 | When just tender, drain the noodles well in a metal strainer and either serve right away or save for later, refreshing the noodles under cold running water until cool and to prevent them from sticking together.

Miso chicken & corn ramen

Prep 15 minutes

Cook 10 minutes

Serves 4

This is a simplified version of the popular Japanese noodle broth but still uses the foundation flavors of miso and soy sauce to add richness and depth. Dried wheat noodles provide substance to the dish, which also utilizes leftover roast chicken (see p.70) as a topping. If you don't have cooked chicken on hand, use store-bought instead but make sure the meat has the skin on. Re-frying the chicken crisps up the skin and turns it golden and crunchy (see Tip, below), which is in contrast to the soft texture of the noodles, herbs, and vegetables. Experiment with your own toppings, particularly if you don't eat chicken; a soft-boiled egg (see p.18) and extra vegetables, such as leafy greens, broccoli, and asparagus are also delicious. You can use Vegetable Stock (see p.414) instead of chicken.

2 tbsp vegetable oil
⅔lb (300g) leftover cooked chicken (see p.70) or store-bought, shredded into bite-size pieces
2 garlic cloves, peeled and finely chopped
1½-in piece of fresh ginger, peeled and finely chopped
4 tbsp white miso paste
4 tbsp soy sauce
2 tbsp rice wine vinegar
½lb (250g) dried wheat noodles
6½ cups (1.5 liters) Chicken Stock (see p.414) or store-bought, just-boiled
4 green onions, thinly sliced
2½ cups (340g) corn, thawed if frozen
½lb (200g) bean sprouts
1 handful of cilantro leaves
Crispy Chili Oil (see p.452) or store-bought, to serve

1 | Heat the vegetable oil in a large, deep skillet or wok over medium-high heat. Warm the chicken for 5–6 minutes, tossing regularly, until crisp and caramelized. Add the garlic and ginger and cook for another 2 minutes. Remove from the heat and mix in the miso, soy sauce, and rice wine vinegar.

2 | Cook the dried wheat noodles following steps 1-3 (left), then divide between four deep bowls.

3 | Divide the hot stock between the bowls and stir gently to loosen the noodles. Top each bowl with a little pile of green onions, corn, and bean sprouts.

4 | Top each bowl with a pile of the crispy chicken and its sauce, then sprinkle with cilantro leaves and a drizzle of crispy chili oil, if you like.

TIP

If you have leftover skin from the cooked chicken meat, place in an even layer on a baking sheet and roast in the oven at 400°F (200°C) for 15–20 minutes, until really crisp. Break into shards and pile on top of the ramen just before serving.

FRESH NOODLES

It's a long-fought tug-of-war between the Chinese and the Italians about who invented noodles, but both have likely been eating some version made from wheat flour and water for many hundreds of years. Like their dried equivalent, fresh noodles come in a variety of types (wheat, egg, rice, buckwheat) and thicknesses from super fine to thick ribbons, ready to use in broths, braises, stir-fries, or as a side dish. Satisfyingly silky and chewy, with a pleasing bounce, fresh noodles are not as difficult to make as you may think (see below) so it's well worth giving them a try—and as an added bonus they only take a few minutes to cook.

Storage
Fresh noodles will keep wrapped in the fridge for up to 1 day. They can also be frozen for up to 3 months.

HAND-PULLED NOODLES

*Prep 20 minutes
+ resting*

Cook 5 minutes

Serves 4

Widely popular across China, these wide, "belt-like," hand-pulled fresh noodles are also known as biang biang. Thick and chewy in texture, the wheat noodles get their name from the satisfying sound the dough makes when it is slapped on the work surface as it is stretched and pulled into noodles. Once pulled, the noodles are immediately dunked into boiling water to cook for a speedy 2 minutes, before serving with a flavorful topping and fresh aromatics. The noodles may look intimidating to make but once you've got the hang of the technique they really are quite simple—and the good news is they don't require any special tools, apart from a chopstick. The main requirement is time to knead and rest the dough. Patience is definitely a virtue here as the dough benefits from at least 2 hours resting until soft and pliable, ready for pulling action.

4 cups (500g) all-purpose flour, plus extra for dusting
pinch of salt
2 tbsp vegetable oil, for coating

1 | Mix the flour and salt together in a large mixing bowl. Gradually, pour in 1 cup (250ml) of water to make a rough dough. Knead the dough on a lightly floured work surface for 2–3 minutes, until soft. Cover the bowl and leave to rest for 30 minutes.

2 | After resting, knead the dough again until smooth, then divide into 4 balls. Cover and leave to rest for another 1 hour. Roll out the dough balls into ½-in (1-cm) thick, palm-size ovals. Cover each one liberally with oil, then cover and leave to rest on a lined baking sheet for another hour.

3 | To form the noodles, place a chopstick horizontally across the center of one of the oval-shaped pieces of dough to make an indent.

4 | Holding either end of the dough, stretch and pull it, working from the middle to make it longer, slapping the dough against the work surface to help elongate it.

5 | When the dough is about 3 ft (1 m) long, use your hands to split it along the indent running down the center to form it into a loop.

6 | Using your hands, continue to separate the dough in half into a long noodle loop.

7 | When the noodle loop is about ¾ in (2 cm) wide, place it on a floured work surface or a drying rack and repeat with the rest of the dough. (You can cut the noodles into shorter, more manageable lengths at this point.)

8 | The noodles are ready for cooking right away. Bring a large saucepan of salted water to a boil. Add the noodles (you may need to cook them in batches) and cook for 3–5 minutes, depending on how thick they are, until tender. Using tongs, lift the noodles out of the pan once cooked and place in a serving bowl. They are now ready to serve (see p.246).

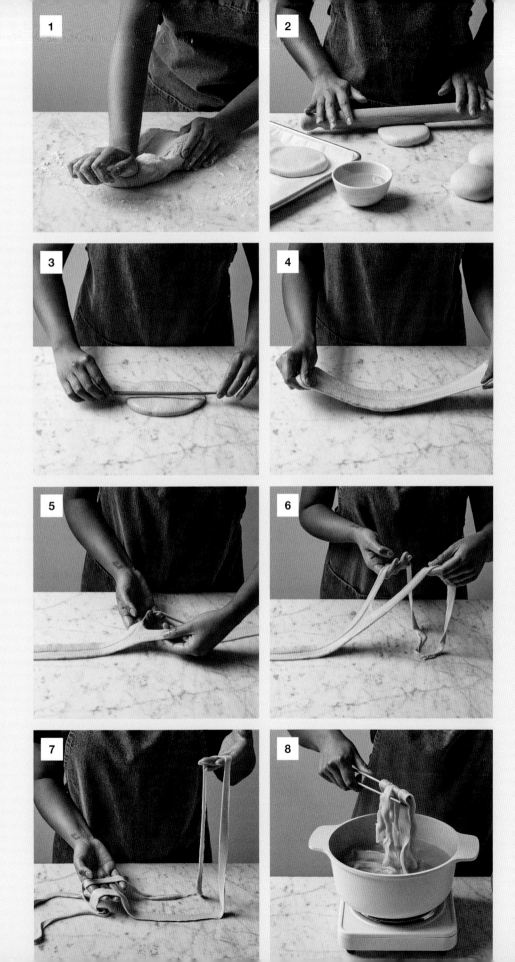

Hand-pulled noodles with aromatics & cumin lamb

Prep 30 minutes + resting

Cook 10 minutes

Serves 4

Thick and chewy, these fresh, hand-pulled noodles are satisfying to eat. Once made, they are best cooked right away and can either be served with just the aromatic sauce or, for a more substantial dish, topped with the cumin-infused lamb stir-fry.
If serving with the lamb topping, it would be worth preparing this first, then reheating briefly if needed.

1 recipe quantity of Hand-Pulled Noodles (see p.244)

For the sauce
4 garlic cloves, minced
4 handfuls of chopped green onions
4 tbsp soy sauce
2–3 tbsp dried chili flakes (depending on how spicy you like it)
2 tbsp rice vinegar
½ cup (120ml) vegetable oil
2 tbsp chili oil (optional)

1 | Follow steps 1–8 to make and cook the Hand-Pulled Noodles (see p.244).

2 | While the noodles are cooking, prepare the ingredients for the sauce.

3 | Drain the cooked noodles and divide them equally into four serving bowls. Top each serving with the garlic, green onions, soy sauce, dried chili flakes and rice vinegar.

4 | Heat the vegetable oil in a small saucepan until smoking, then carefully pour it into the bowls over the noodles and aromatics/seasonings. This will make the aromatics sizzle and cook them (as well as make your kitchen smell delicious). Mix everything together and serve right away, or for a more substantial dish top with the cumin lamb (right).

Cumin lamb topping (optional)
This aromatic lamb stir-fry can be spooned on top of the dressed noodles (left) to make a more substantial noodle dish.

2 tbsp vegetable oil, divided
1 tbsp cumin seeds
3 garlic cloves, minced
2-in piece of fresh ginger, peeled and thinly sliced
1 small red chile, finely chopped (optional)
½lb (250g) lamb shoulder or leg, thinly sliced (you can buy this ready-sliced in Asian grocery stores)
½ onion, thinly sliced
1 tbsp ground cumin
1 tbsp + 1 tsp soy sauce
½ tbsp Chinese cooking wine (optional)
1 tsp Chinese black vinegar
1 tsp sugar
pinch of salt
1 large handful of cilantro leaves (optional)

1 | To make the lamb topping, heat 1 tablespoon of the vegetable oil in a large wok or skillet over medium-high heat. Add the cumin seeds, garlic, ginger, and chile and sauté for 1 minute, until aromatic. Add the sliced lamb and cook for 3–4 minutes, turning regularly, until it is no longer pink. Remove from the wok and set aside.

2 | In the same wok or pan, add the remaining oil with the onion and cook for 3–4 minutes, until softened.

3 | Return the cooked lamb to the wok/pan and add the rest of the seasoning ingredients. Toss and mix thoroughly and cook for another 1–2 minutes. Serve the lamb over the cooked dressed noodles, with a sprinkling of cilantro, if using.

Hot oil udon

Prep 10 minutes

Cook 5 minutes

Serves 2

This speedy, flavor-packed vegan dish uses straight-to-wok noodles in a new way—blanching them in boiling water until slightly softened, while retaining their chewy bite. The various flavor components are then divided between two serving bowls with sizzling hot oil being the magic ingredient to bring everything together, lightly cooking the vegetables at the same time.

1 tsp Sichuan peppercorns
1 tsp cumin seeds

3 tbsp soy sauce
1–2 tsp dried chili flakes (depending on how spicy you like it)
10oz (300g) package cooked thick udon noodles
1 cup (50g) sugar snap peas, finely sliced lengthwise
2 green onions, green and white part, finely chopped
1 garlic clove, peeled and minced
1 handful of salted roasted peanuts, roughly chopped
4 tbsp vegetable oil

1 | Add the peppercorns and cumin seeds to a small, dry saucepan. Toast over medium heat for 1 minute or until they smell fragrant, then put them into a pestle and mortar and roughly grind.

2 | Put the toasted spices into a small bowl and stir in the soy sauce and chili flakes, adding the smaller quantity if you don't like too much heat.

3 | Fill a medium saucepan with water and place over high heat. Bring it to a rapid boil. Loosen the noodles with your fingers into individual strands and put them into the boiling water. Cook for 1 minute, then drain through a colander.

4 | Divide the noodles between two serving bowls. Spoon the soy dressing equally over each, then sprinkle with the sugar snap peas, green onions, garlic, and roasted peanuts.

5 | Pour the vegetable oil into the small saucepan you used earlier (no need to wash it). Bring the oil to a rapid sizzle over high heat, then immediately pour it evenly over the noodles. Serve immediately.

TIP

Instead of sugar snap peas, you could try snow peas, canned corn, or thinly sliced radishes.

Späetzle

Prep 20 minutes + resting

Cook 10 minutes

Serves 4

Originating in central Europe, but most synonymous with German Swabian cuisine, späetzle is described variously as a type of pasta or noodle or dumpling. There's a variety of ways to prepare it, including the use of a specially made späetzle press, or using a colander or cheese grater. Serve the späetzle in a creamy cheese sauce with crispy onions as a main dish or toss simply in butter and enjoy as a side dish.

4 large eggs, at room temperature
2¼ cups (300g) all-purpose flour
¾ cup (100g) fine semolina
1 tsp salt
¾ cup (175ml) sparkling water

For the sauce
1 tbsp olive oil
2 onions, peeled and finely sliced
pinch of salt, plus extra to season

2 garlic cloves, peeled and finely chopped
⅔ cup (150g) crème fraîche
3½oz (100g) Gruyère cheese, grated
salt and freshly ground black pepper
½ cup (25g) chives, snipped

1 | To make the späetzle batter, crack the eggs into a large mixing bowl and whisk with a balloon whisk for around 3 minutes, until light and frothy. Mix in the flour, semolina, and salt with a wooden spoon until combined. Gradually, pour in the sparkling water, mixing continuously, until you have a stiff, smooth batter, similar in consistency to thick melted cheese. Leave to stand for 15 minutes.

2 | Bring a large saucepan of salted water to a boil.

3 | If you don't have a späetzle press, which is similar to a potato ricer, the easiest and perhaps most convenient alternative method is to use a box grater. Once the water is boiling, hold the grater above the pan of water and press some of the batter through the large holes with the help of a spatula, moving it back and forth to make small, thin, stubby dumplings. Take care not to burn yourself on the steam rising from the water. Cook the späetzle for 1 minute, or until they rise to the surface, then lift out with a slotted spoon into a colander and rinse under cold running water to stop them cooking any further. Place in a bowl while you cook the remaining batches of batter. Once all the batter has been used up, take the pan off the heat and save the cooking water because you will need some of it for the sauce.

4 | To make the sauce, heat the oil in a large pan over medium-low heat. Add the onion with a pinch of salt and cook gently, stirring often, for around 10 minutes, until golden. Add the garlic and cook for another 2 minutes, until fragrant. Add the späetzle to the pan and cook for a minute or so, then take the pan off the heat. Add the crème fraîche and Gruyère, mixing until the cheese melts, then pour in a ladle of the reserved cooking water. Mix vigorously until the sauce has emulsified and clings to the dumplings, adding more cooking water if needed to make a sauce. Taste and season with salt and pepper, then sprinkle over the chives and serve.

DUMPLINGS

The ultimate comfort food, dumplings come in numerous forms in many cuisines. There are filled dumplings, such as Japanese gyoza (below) or Chinese wonton, Turkish manti, Polish pierogi, and Italian ravioli (see p.236), and what they all have in common is they are a way of wrapping meat, poultry, seafood, or chopped vegetables in a thin layer of dough. Historically, they were made as a convenient and practical way to make the expensive protein element, such as meat or seafood, go a bit further, as well as create a delicious complete meal.

Whether boiled, steamed, or fried, the secret to a good-tasting dumpling is to achieve the right balance of filling to wrapper—crucially, you want to be able to taste both. The flavor of the dumpling is further enhanced by the way it is served: simply with a dipping sauce or immersed in a flavorful broth or stew.

Not all dumplings are filled—there are numerous versions made with balls of dough, normally bread-, flour-, or suet-based, that expand when cooked in a stew, water, stock ,or sauce, such as the classic Italian Gnocchi (see p.253).

PORK & CHIVE GYOZA

Prep 1 hour + resting

Cook 20 minutes

Serves 4 (makes 32)

You may have shied away from the challenge of making dumplings before, especially producing the dough wrapper from scratch, but it can be a satisfying and rewarding skill to learn. What better way to start than with these Japanese gyoza, which are called jiaozi in China. The pork-filled dumplings are pan-fried for a crispy, golden bottom, before being steamed until the filling and wrapper become transparent and cooked through. Perfection!

1½ cups (200g) all-purpose flour, plus extra for dusting
pinch of salt
⅓ cup (100ml) warm water
about 3 tbsp vegetable oil, for frying
Soy & Ginger Dipping Sauce (see p.427), to serve

For the filling
½lb (250g) ground pork
2 garlic cloves, peeled and finely grated
1½in piece of fresh ginger, peeled and
   finely grated
1 handful of chives, finely snipped
1 tbsp cornstarch
1 tbsp soy sauce
pinch each of salt and freshly ground
   black pepper

1 | First, make the dumpling wrappers. Add the flour with a pinch of salt to a mixing bowl. Pour in the warm water and mix well with a table knife until it starts to clump together. Bring everything together with your hands into a dough, then put it onto a lightly floured work surface and knead for about 5 minutes, until smooth and even. Wrap and leave the dough at room temperature for 30 minutes to rest.

2 | While the dough rests, mix all the filling ingredients in a bowl and add a good pinch of salt and pepper. Cover and chill the filling in the fridge while you roll out the dough.

3 | Lightly flour the work surface, unwrap the dough and cut it in half. Rewrap one of the pieces, then roll the other into a long, ¾-in (2-cm) thick log. Repeat with the other piece of dough. Cut the dough into ¾-in (2-cm) wide pieces. You should have around 32 pieces of dough with a few spare in case of tearing.

4 | Flatten one piece of dough with the palm of your hand on a lightly floured work surface, then use a rolling pin to roll the dough into a 3½-in (9-cm) diameter, thin circle. To do this, roll the dough out in one direction, then turn it 90 degrees, roll again, and repeat until you have a thin, even circle. Repeat with the remaining dough pieces, flouring each one well before stacking them on top of each other in groups of five to prevent sticking. (Continued overleaf.)

TIPS

Instead of pan searing (see p.251), cook the dumplings in a large pan of boiling salted water for 5–6 minutes (you may need to cook them in batches), until cooked through and silky. Alternatively, steam in batches for 8 minutes.

To freeze the dumplings, place them uncooked in a single layer on a parchment-paper-lined tray and, once frozen, transfer to a sealable freezer bag. Cook the dumplings from frozen, pan searing them (see p.251), then steam in a covered pan for 5–6 minutes. Alternatively, boil for 7–8 minutes, until cooked through.

Instead of making your own wrappers, buy premade gyoza wrappers in Asian supermarkets. You can find them in the freezer section.

5 | Fill a small bowl with cold water. To shape, take one dough wrapper in the palm of your hand and place a teaspoon of the filling in the center. Dip a finger into the water and run it around the edge of the wrapper. Gently bring the two sides of the wrapper together to meet in the middle, but do not seal.

6 | Starting from one end of the gyoza, make small pleats between your thumb and index finger, roughly ½ in (1 cm) apart, folding the dough back on itself and pressing the edges together to seal. Keep folding until you reach the opposite end—the gyoza will bend into a slight crescent shape. Place the gyoza on a lightly floured baking sheet and, holding the folded side, press it down to flatten the base slightly. Repeat to make about 32 dumplings in total.

7 | To cook, put a large, lidded skillet over medium-high heat and add 1 tablespoon of the oil. Put a third of the dumplings in the pan with their pleats facing upward, leaving a gap between each one (you will need to cook them in batches, depending on the size of your pan). Sear the dumplings for 2 minutes, until the bottoms are crisp and golden.

8 | Carefully pour ⅓ cup (100ml) of water into the pan and cover with the lid. Turn the heat to low and steam the gyoza for 3–4 minutes, until cooked through and the water evaporates. Remove the gyoza from the pan to a plate and cover with an upturned bowl to keep them warm. Wipe the pan clean with paper towel and repeat as above with the remaining oil and gyoza. Serve them with the dipping sauce.

MAKING GNOCCHI

Prep 40 minutes

Cook 1 hour 10 minutes

Serves 2, or 4 as an appetizer (makes 1lb/500g)

The trick to making homemade gnocchi (potato dumplings) is to cook the potatoes until perfectly soft and dry, which is why you bake them whole in their skins, rather than boil in water. This gives the dough a much-needed firm texture, making it easier to handle, shape, and cook. Once cooked, the gnocchi should be light and fluffy, but still have the perfect chew. A potato ricer is recommended because it ensures even, finely mashed potato that is dry and not sticky. Don't waste the potato skins, they can be baked in the oven with a splash of oil until crispy.

1lb (500g) Russet potatoes, left whole
1 egg yolk (see p.32 on Separating Eggs)
½ cup (75g) 00 flour
salt and freshly ground black pepper

1 | Preheat the oven to 190°C (375°F). Put the whole potatoes onto a baking sheet and bake for 1 hour, until cooked all the way through when pierced with the point of a knife. You're looking to cook the potatoes thoroughly without browning them too much. Leave to steam and cool on the tray for 15 minutes. Slice the potatoes in half, then use a spoon to scoop out the flesh, discarding the skins (see above).

2 | Press the potato flesh through a potato ricer into a mound on a clean work surface. Alternatively, press the cooked potato flesh through a metal strainer.

3 | Make a well in the center of the mashed potato and add the egg yolk, flour, and a good pinch of salt and black pepper. Using a fork, start to gently fold the egg yolk mixture into the potato. (Continued overleaf.)

4 | Once the potato mixture starts to come together, use your hands to fold and knead it into a smooth and uniform dough. If it is a little sticky, knead in another sprinkling of flour. Cover and leave to rest at room temperature for 15 minutes.

5 | Cut the dough into 4 pieces. Lightly flour the work surface and use your hands to gently roll one of the pieces into a 12-in (30-cm) long cylinder or log, about ¾ in (2 cm) in diameter. Cut the cylinder into 15 pieces, each about ¾ in (2 cm) long. Repeat with the remaining gnocchi dough.

6 | Lightly flour a fork and gently roll the gnocchi over the top of the tines, making indented lines. Alternatively, using a pasta or gnocchi board, gently roll each piece with your thumb down the board, making similar indentations.

7 | Fill a large saucepan with water, season well with salt and bring to a boil over medium-high heat. Add the gnocchi and cook (in batches) for about 2 minutes—they are cooked when they float to the surface, then drain well.

TIP

To freeze the gnocchi, dust a large baking sheet with flour and arrange the uncooked gnocchi in a single layer. Once frozen, transfer the gnocchi to a sealable freezer bag and store for up to 3 months. Cook the gnocchi straight from frozen.

Potato gnocchetti with chicken broth & Parmesan

Prep 20 minutes

Cook 20 minutes

Serves 2 or 4 as a starter

Gnocchetti literally translates to "small gnocchi," although these little bites have more chew, less fluffiness, and are similar to pasta in texture. "*En brodo*" or "in broth" is a classic Italian way to serve gnocchetti, and the quality of your stock will make all the difference to the taste of the final dish. If you're looking to be extra fancy, serve topped with a drizzle of Herb Oil (see p.440).

1 recipe quantity of Gnocchi (see p.253)
4½ cups (1 liter) Chicken Stock or Vegetable Stock (see p.414) or good-quality store-bought
freshly ground black pepper
2 tbsp extra-virgin olive oil, plus extra for drizzling
4 tbsp (50g) salted butter
¾ cup (75g) finely grated Parmesan cheese or vegetarian equivalent
finely grated zest of 1 unwaxed lemon, plus a squeeze of juice
8 tbsp Herb Oil (see p.440), to serve (optional)

1 | Follow steps 1–7 from Making Gnocchi (see p.253). Cut the ball of gnocchi dough into 8 pieces.

2 | Lightly flour the work surface and use your hands to gently roll out one piece of the dough into a thin, 12-in (30-cm) long cylinder or log, about ½ in (1 cm) in diameter. Cut the cylinder into 15 small pieces, each about ¾ in (2 cm) long. Repeat with the remaining gnocchi dough.

3 | Fill a large saucepan with water, season well with salt, and bring to a boil over medium-high heat. Add the gnocchi and cook for about 1 minute—they are cooked when they float to the surface, then drain well. Leave them to steam-dry for 2–3 minutes.

4 | Meanwhile, pour the chicken or vegetable stock into a pan and bring to a boil, then season to taste. Cover with the lid and keep the stock warm.

5 | Heat the olive oil in a large, nonstick skillet over medium-high heat. Carefully add the gnocchetti and cook for 1–2 minutes, until starting to turn crisp and golden. Melt in the butter and toss for another minute until each piece is coated.

6 | To serve, spoon the gnocchetti into four bowls. Ladle over the warm stock and top with grated cheese, lemon zest, and a squeeze of juice. Season with pepper and spoon over the herb oil, if using, or add a drizzle of olive oil.

TIP

Instead of the herb oil, sprinkle over chopped flat-leaf parsley or torn basil leaves.

BEANS

&

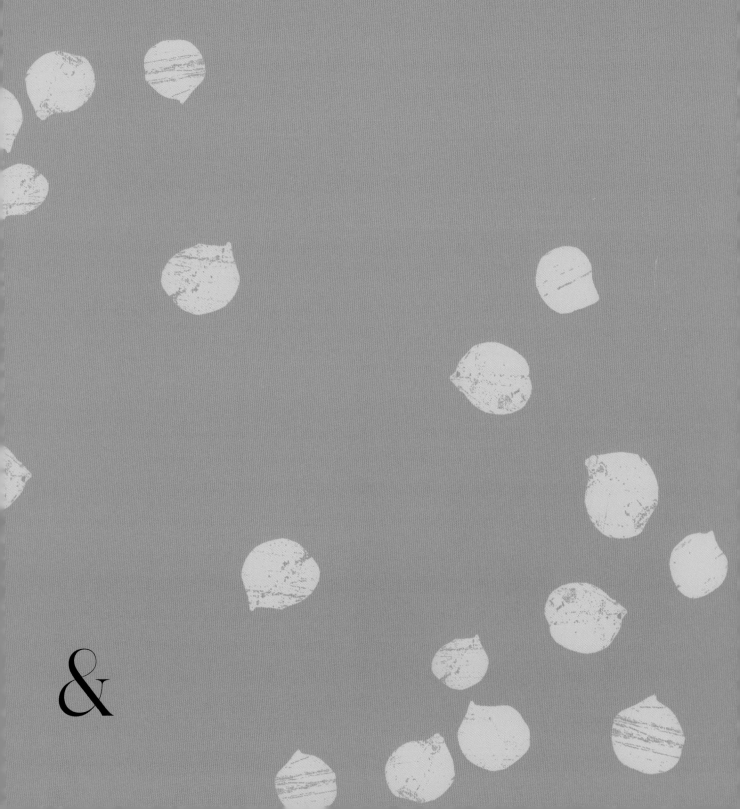

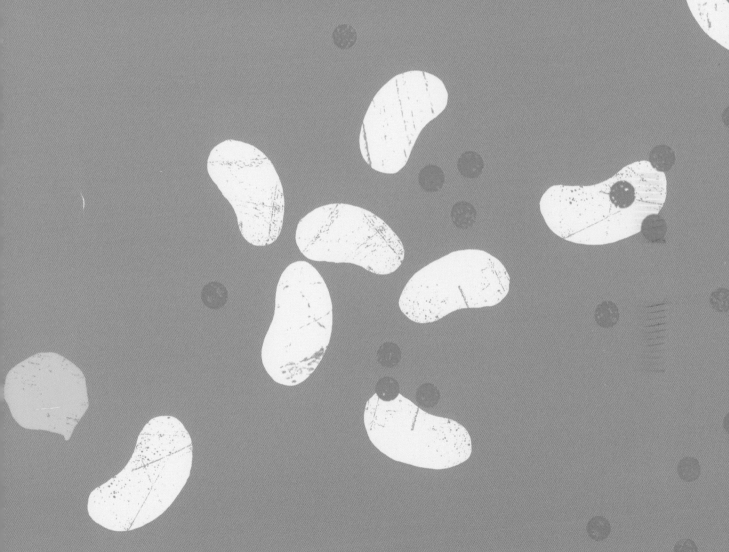

PULSES

BEANS & PULSES

Beans, peas, and lentils come under the umbrella term pulses—a large group of foods that has for many hundreds of years been an economical and nutritious source of sustenance around the world. In the past, discovering that fresh beans and legumes could be dried and stored for months meant people could secure a much-needed source of food for the times of the year when fresh produce was scarce.

Treat dried beans and pulses like a blank canvas. While they slowly cook, you can add aromatics to the simmering water—sturdy herbs like bay leaves, thyme and rosemary, or spices including cloves, cardamom, star anise, or fennel seeds all work well. Like dried beans, canned ones also benefit from the addition of herbs and spices, but unlike dried, take mere minutes to cook or heat through so are perfect for quick meals.

Storage
When buying dried beans and pulses, purchase them from somewhere that has a regular turnover and look for ones that are plump, smooth, and unwrinkled. Pulses that are old or past their best take much longer to cook and can remain tough after cooking. Store beans in an airtight container in a dark cupboard.

PREPARING BEANS

Canned beans make a convenient and easy pantry staple, but if you regularly cook with beans then dried ones are more cost effective. Bear in mind that dried beans double their weight when cooked, so halve the quantity in a recipe if it uses canned. Aside from lentils and split peas, most beans require presoaking to soften them and speed up the cooking time. For easy reference, there's a guide below to soaking and cooking times. For dried beans, rinse to remove any dirt, and pick through to find any beans that have gone bad or small stones. Put beans into a metal strainer and rinse well under cold running water, swishing them with your hand until the water runs clear. Then place them into a large bowl and pour over plenty of cold water, enough to generously cover. Put a plate on top and leave to soak for 6–8 hours or overnight.

TYPE OF PULSE	SOAKING TIME	COOKING TIME	PERFECT IN ...
Black beans/black-eyed peas/borlotti beans/pinto beans	Overnight	1–1½ hours	Caribbean-style curries and stews, burgers, refried, burrito bowls, chili (alternative to kidney beans), soup.
Red kidney beans	See p.260	1½ hours	Chili, burgers, stews, refried beans.
Lima beans	Overnight	1½–2 hours	Salads, dips, casseroles.
Cannellini beans/flageolet beans/navy beans	Overnight	1–1½ hours	Soups, stews, baked beans, salads.
Chickpeas	Overnight	1–1½ hours	Dips, curries, falafel, casseroles.
Adzuki beans	No soak or 3 hours	35 minutes–1 hour	Soups, salads, fritters, pastes.
Split lentils	No soak	15–20 minutes	Dals, soups, pâtés.
Whole lentils/mung beans	No soak	30–40 minutes	Salads, casseroles, soups, dals.
Split peas	No soak	1½ hours	Dals, burgers, soups.

Clockwise, from top, red kidney beans, peas, lima beans, black beans, chickpeas, borlotti beans, navy beans, red split lentils, green lentils, and yellow split peas (center).

COOKING
BEANS & PULSES

Although soaking reduces their cooking time, dried beans and pulses still take a while to cook until tender. Put your choice of bean into a large saucepan and cover with plenty of cold water. Bring to a boil, skimming off any foam that rises to the surface. Turn down the heat, part-cover with a lid, and simmer until tender (see cooking table on page 258 for timings). Drain well and use in the same way as canned beans. Toward the end of cooking, watch carefully; there is a fine line between the beans being tender and becoming mushy. Avoid adding salt during cooking because this can toughen the skins.

Kidney beans need to be cooked in a slightly different way because they contain toxins that must be removed through an additional period of boiling. After soaking, put the beans into a large pan, cover with plenty of cold water, bring to a boil, and boil for 10 minutes. Drain and discard the cooking water (this will include the toxins). Cover with more cold water, bring back to a boil, and simmer until tender.

BOILING LENTILS

Prep 5 minutes

Cook 35 minutes

Makes 1lb (500g) cooked lentils

The beauty of lentils is that they don't require presoaking before cooking. They come in many different varieties from red, green, and brown to these Puy lentils with their pretty, green-speckled skin. Puy keep their shape when cooked and add substance to stews, sauces, and salads, like the goat cheese one on the next page.

½lb (250g) Puy lentils
salt

1 | Rinse the lentils well in a metal strainer under cold running water until the water runs clear. Put them into a large saucepan and cover with 4½ cups (1 liter) of cold water.

2 | Bring the water to a boil, then turn the heat down to a simmer. Part-cover the pan with a lid and cook the lentils for 30–35 minutes, until tender. Season with salt toward the end of the cooking time. Drain well through a metal strainer, then use as required.

Goat cheese, celery root, lentil & balsamic salad

Prep 15 minutes

Cook 50 minutes

Serves 4–6

Puy lentils have a slightly nutty taste and firm texture that works well with stronger flavors, such as this robust slow-roasted garlic and balsamic dressing. Use the best balsamic vinegar you can afford because it will bring out the depth and sweetness of the lentils and celery root.

1 medium celery root, peeled and cut into small chunks
5 tbsp extra-virgin olive oil, divided
salt and freshly ground black pepper
10 thyme sprigs, leaves stripped
6 whole garlic cloves, unpeeled
1 recipe quantity of cooked Puy Lentils (left)
1 tbsp honey
1 tbsp Dijon mustard
4 tbsp balsamic vinegar
3 tbsp red wine vinegar
4oz (125g) arugula
½ cup (50g) hazelnuts, toasted and chopped
6oz (150g) goat cheese

1 | Preheat the oven to 375°F (190°C). Put the celery root into a large roasting pan. Pour over 2 tablespoons of the olive oil, season well with salt and pepper, then sprinkle over the thyme and whole garlic cloves. Toss until combined and roast for 40–45 minutes, until the celery root and garlic are tender.

2 | Meanwhile, follow steps 1–2 from Boiling Lentils, (see left).

3 | Remove the garlic from the tray and leave it to cool slightly. Discard the thyme. Drizzle the honey over the celery root and return it to the oven for a final 5 minutes to caramelize.

4 | To make the dressing, squeeze the garlic cloves out of their papery skins into a small bowl. Spoon in the mustard and mash together with the back of a fork. Pour in both types of vinegar and the remaining olive oil. Season with salt and pepper to taste and mix until smooth and combined.

5 | Drain the lentils and put them into the roasting tray, add the arugula, and toss with the celery root until combined. Pour over three-quarters of the dressing and toss again.

6 | Place the salad onto a large serving plate or divide it between four plates. Sprinkle over the hazelnuts and spoon over the remaining dressing. To finish, crumble or cut the goat cheese into pieces and sprinkle it over the top.

TIP

Swap the dried lentils for canned green lentils, about 2 (15.5oz/400g) cans, or you could try a pouch of ready-cooked beans or mixed grains.

Ewa riro
(beans cooked in sauce)

Prep 15 minutes + soaking

Cook 2½ hours

Serves 6

This is a delicious and versatile dish from the Yoruba-speaking part of Nigeria. The richly flavored bean stew can be eaten on its own, served with bread or plain Boiled Rice (see p.202), or with a side of boiled or fried plantain. Carotino oil contains palm and canola oil and has a slightly reddish color, use pure canola oil instead if you can't find it.

1lb (500g) dried black-eyed peas
salt, to taste
4 tomatoes, roughly chopped or 7oz (200g) canned diced tomatoes
2 medium onions, peeled, 1 roughly chopped and 1 finely chopped
3 garlic cloves, peeled
2-in piece of fresh ginger, peeled and roughly chopped
2 red chiles, such as Scotch bonnet or bird's eye
⅓ cup (200ml) carotino or canola oil
4 tbsp tomato paste

1 | Rinse the beans in a strainer under cold running water, then place in a large bowl. Pour in enough cold water to generously cover the beans and leave to soak for 6–8 hours or overnight

2 | Drain and rinse the beans and add to a large saucepan of water, about 12 cups (3 liters). Bring the water to a boil, then turn the heat down to medium-low, part-cover the pan with a lid, and cook for about 2 hours, until the beans are very soft. Season with salt just before the beans are ready, then drain and return the beans to the pan.

3 | Meanwhile, blend the tomatoes with the roughly chopped onion, the garlic, ginger, and chiles in a food processor or blender until a rough purée—you don't want it too smooth.

4 | Heat the oil in a separate medium saucepan over medium heat. Add the finely chopped onion and sauté for 2 minutes, until slightly softened. Stir in the tomato paste and cook for another 2 minutes.

5 | Add the blended tomato mixture, season with salt to taste, and cook for about 20 minutes, stirring regularly, until the liquid has reduced and thickened.

6 | Stir the tomato sauce into the cooked beans and heat through for 5 minutes, stirring regularly. Serve with boiled rice or bread for soaking up the sauce, and with a side of boiled or fried plantain, if you like.

TIP

Instead of boiling, cook the beans in a pressure cooker for 1 hour, using 6½ cups (1.5 liters) of water.

Trinidad-style curry chana

Prep 10 minutes

Cook 30 minutes

Serves 6

In the eastern reaches of the Caribbean, places like Guyana and Trinidad and Tobago, typical dishes feature a heavy Indian influence, a remnant of the indentured Indo-Caribbeans who traversed oceans to escape poverty and work in a new land. One type of dish stands out in particular and that is curry, eaten daily by many. Almost any food can, and is, made into a curry, but the prevalence of chickpeas (natively known as chana) makes them a popular choice. Chickpea curry comes into its own in the famed street-food dish doubles, when it is served between two pieces of flatbread with various condiments. Give it a try or serve this with cooked white rice (see p.202).

1½ tbsp mild curry powder
1 tbsp ground cumin
1 tbsp garam masala
6 tbsp cooking oil of choice

1 medium onion, peeled and finely chopped
2 (15.5oz/400g) cans chickpeas, drained
Cooked Rice (see p.202), to serve

For the green seasoning
2 tbsp roughly chopped cilantro
3 garlic cloves, peeled and chopped
½ Scotch bonnet chile, seeded and chopped
1 tsp lemon or lime juice (optional)
pinch of salt, plus extra to season

1 | In a small bowl, mix together the curry powder, ground cumin and garam masala. Set aside briefly.

2 | Using a pestle and mortar or small blender, grind all the ingredients for the green seasoning with the citrus juice, if using, and 1 tablespoon of water to make a paste. Mix in a pinch of salt and set aside.

3 | Heat the oil in a large, heavy-bottomed saucepan on medium-high heat. Add the onion and sauté for 3 minutes, until slightly softened and translucent. Add the spice mix, stir to combine with the onions, and cook for another minute.

4 | Stir in the prepared green seasoning, then add the chickpeas. Cook, stirring for 1–2 minutes, until everything is combined.

5 | Pour in 2 cups (500ml) of water, bring almost to a boil, then turn the heat down to low, cover with the lid, and simmer for 15 minutes. Remove the lid and cook for another 10 minutes, until the liquid has almost evaporated, leaving a thick sauce, and some of the chickpeas are starting to break down. Serve the curry with rice.

Tarka, coconut & spinach dal

Prep 10 minutes

Cook 35 minutes

Serves 4–6

Learning how to make this dal couldn't be simpler. The red split lentils make for a nutritious, plant-based, and economical meal that's just perfect for batch cooking. The dal is finished with a traditional tarka topping, a blend of aromatic whole spices cooked briefly in oil, which adds another level of flavor. Before you start cooking, it is important to rinse the lentils well in a strainer under cold running water to get rid of any dust and debris—they are ready when the water runs clear.

¾lb (350g) red split lentils, rinsed well
2-in piece of fresh ginger, finely grated
2 fat garlic cloves, peeled
2 tsp turmeric powder
2 tsp ground cumin
large pinch of salt, plus extra to season
1 (13.5oz/400g) can coconut milk
8oz (200g) baby spinach leaves
freshly ground black pepper

For the tarka
2½ tbsp coconut oil or vegetable or sunflower oil
1 tbsp cumin seeds
1 tbsp black mustard seeds
12 fresh curry leaves
4 small whole dried red chiles (optional)

To serve
1 lime, cut into 4 wedges
warmed chapatti or naan

1 | Put the lentils into a large saucepan. Add the ginger, garlic, turmeric, cumin, and a large pinch of salt. Pour in the coconut milk and 4½ cups (1 liter) of cold water and bring to a boil over medium-high heat. Turn the heat down and simmer, stirring occasionally, for 25–30 minutes, scooping out any white froth that rises to the surface, until the lentils are tender and start to break down—the dal should be the consistency of thin porridge.

2 | Remove the pan from the heat, add the spinach, stir, and let the leaves wilt off the heat. Season the dal with salt and pepper to taste, then cover the pan with a lid to keep warm.

3 | To make the tarka, heat the oil in a small skillet over medium-high heat. Add a small pinch of the cumin seeds to check the temperature—if they begin to pop the oil is ready. Add the rest of the cumin and the mustard seeds and cook, stirring, for 30 seconds. Next, add the curry leaves and dried chiles, if using. Keep stirring for another 30 seconds, until the curry leaves curl and sizzle.

4 | Ladle the dal into serving bowls and, as soon as the tarka is ready, spoon it over the dal along with the oil in the pan. Serve with lime wedges for squeezing over and warmed chapatti or naan for scooping. The dal will keep in the fridge for up to a week and is perfect for weekday meals.

SLOW-COOKING BEANS

When slow-cooked, beans become soft and unctuous in texture, their starches thickening and enriching the accompanying sauce. It is a perfect method for cooking dried peas and whole lentils too, and you'll discover many traditional dishes from around the world, including Boston Baked Beans (below) and Cassoulet (see p.268), that use this technique. During cooking, partly cover the pan to prevent the sauce from evaporating too much—the slight gap ensures the cooking liquid doesn't boil over.

BOSTON BAKED BEANS

Prep 10 minutes + overnight soaking

Cook 4 hours 50 minutes

Serves 4

These beans are super comforting and will knock anything you get in a can out of the park. Don't be put off by the long cooking time—it's mostly hands-off, and you'll be richly rewarded. Using dried beans makes for the softest and richest dish once baked. The starches slowly seep out of the beans and into the sauce, making it thick, rich, and glossy.

½lb (250g) dried navy or cannellini beans, rinsed well
2 bay leaves
2 tbsp extra-virgin olive oil
8 slices of bacon, cut into 1¼-in (3-cm) long pieces
2 onions, peeled and finely chopped
3 celery stalks, finely chopped
2 green bell peppers, seeded and finely chopped
6 whole garlic cloves, unpeeled
large pinch of salt, plus extra to season
2 tbsp molasses
2 tbsp light brown sugar
1 tbsp brown or spicy mustard
2 tbsp tomato paste
1 (15oz/400g) can crushed tomatoes
freshly ground black pepper
2–3 tbsp apple cider vinegar
1 handful flat-leaf parsley leaves, roughly chopped

1 | Soak the beans for 6–8 hours or overnight (see p.258). The next day, drain the beans well, then put them into a large saucepan and add the bay leaves. Pour in enough cold water to cover generously and bring to a boil over medium-high heat, skimming any white foam from the surface. Turn the heat down to medium-low and simmer for 1–1½ hours, until the beans are tender, then drain well.

2 | Heat a large oven safe casserole dish or Dutch oven over medium-high heat. Pour in the olive oil and add the bacon. Cook, stirring regularly, for 4–5 minutes, until the fat on the bacon has crisped slightly.

3 | Add the onions, celery, green peppers, garlic cloves, and a large pinch of salt. Cover with the lid and cook for 6–8 minutes, stirring occasionally, until softened slightly.

4 | Spoon in the molasses, brown sugar, mustard, and tomato paste, then add the canned tomatoes, breaking them up lightly with the back of the wooden spoon. Refill the can with water and add that too. Stir in the cooked beans and season with salt and pepper.

5 | Preheat the oven to 325°F (160°C). Cover the pot with foil, then top with the lid to give a tight seal and place in the oven for 3 hours—checking after 2 hours to make sure the pan hasn't dried out, and adding more water if needed. The baked beans will be thick, saucy, and tender. Pick out the garlic cloves and squeeze them out of their skins, discard the skins, and roughly mash. Return the garlic to the beans, season well with salt and pepper and vinegar, to taste, then sprinkle over the parsley.

6 | Serve with your favorite roast chicken or barbecue ribs. The stew will keep, covered, in the fridge for up to 3 days.

TIPS

*Swap the dried beans for
2 (15.5oz/400g) cans of navy
or cannellini beans. Add the drained
beans in step 4.*

*To freeze, divide into individual
containers and store for up to
3 months. Defrost thoroughly,
then reheat in a small pan for
10 minutes before serving.*

Classic cassoulet

*Prep 20 minutes
+ overnight
soaking*

*Cook 4 hours
45 minutes*

Serves 4

The recipe for this hearty, slow-cooked bean and meat stew comes from southern France and is classic country fare. Traditionally cooked in an earthenware pot, the beans, usually navy, are an important part along with various types of meat, including confit duck, sausage, and pork belly. This dish is a celebration of those ingredients.

¾lb (300g) dried navy beans (or you could
    use flageolet or cannellini)
4 bay leaves
3 tbsp duck fat, divided
⅓lb (150g) pork belly or thickly cut pancetta, cut
    into 1¼-in (3-cm) dice
4 duck legs or confit duck legs
salt and freshly ground black pepper
1lb (400g) sweet Italian, Toulouse, or garlic pork
    sausages, each cut into 3–4 pieces
1 onion, peeled and finely chopped
2 carrots, peeled and finely chopped
2 celery stalks, finely chopped
1 bulb garlic, halved horizontally
1 handful of thyme sprigs
5 cups (1.2 liters) Chicken Stock (see p.414) or
    store-bought
1 cup (100g) breadcrumbs
1 handful of flat-leaf parsley, roughly chopped
baguette or crusty bread, to serve

1 | Soak the beans for 6–8 hours or overnight (see p.258). The next day, drain the beans well, then put them into a large saucepan and add the bay leaves. Pour in enough cold water to cover generously and bring to a boil over medium-high heat, skimming any white foam from the surface. Turn the heat to medium-low, part-cover with the lid, and simmer for 1 hour, until the beans are tender, then drain well.

2 | Heat 1 tablespoon of the duck fat in a large oven safe casserole dish or Dutch oven over medium-high heat. Add the pork belly or pancetta and cook for 3–4 minutes, turning occasionally, until the fat renders into the pan and the meat is crisp. Using a slotted spoon, scoop it into a bowl.

3 | Add the remaining duck fat to the pan. If using fresh duck legs, season them well with salt and pepper (if you're using confit duck there's no need for

seasoning because they are salt-cured). Cook the duck legs or confit duck for 3–4 minutes on each side until deep golden and the skin is crisp. Scoop into the bowl with the slotted spoon.

4 | Add the sausage pieces to the pan and cook for 4–5 minutes, until browned all over, then place in the bowl. Add the onion, carrots, celery, garlic, and thyme with a pinch of salt, reduce the heat to medium and cook for 8–10 minutes, until the vegetables soften.

5 | Preheat the oven to 325°F (160°C). Add the cooked beans, stock, pork belly, fresh duck legs (but not the confit, if using), and sausages. Turn the heat up, bring to a boil, then cover with a lid and transfer to the oven for 1½ hours. If the pan is very full, put a roasting pan in the oven below the casserole dish to catch any drips.

6 | Remove the casserole dish from the oven and stir. Bring the duck legs to the surface, so the skin can crisp a little. If using confit duck legs, add these now, placing them on top. Return to the oven, and cook, uncovered, for 1 hour, until cooked through.

7 | Sprinkle the breadcrumbs over the top of the cassoulet, then return the pan to the oven for a final 30 minutes, until golden and bubbling. Sprinkle with parsley and serve with slices of baguette or crusty bread.

TIPS

Cassoulet is great to make in advance. It will keep in the fridge for up to 3 days or freeze in individual portions for up to 3 months. To serve, defrost thoroughly before reheating in a pan over medium heat. Bring to a boil, then simmer for at least 10 minutes to heat through.

You can use 3 (15.5oz/400g) cans of drained navy beans instead of the dried ones, adding them in step 5.

BLENDING &
MASHING PULSES

Blending and mashing may sound like basic skills but they are useful and simple techniques to have on hand when looking to expand your repertoire of bean, lentil, and pea dishes. With the help of a food processor or blender, it is easy to transform cooked pulses into a creamy, silky dip, such as the Hummus (below) or a pâté, sauce, stuffing, or fritter. A potato masher also makes easy work of smashing cooked pulses, breaking the skins to expose their soft, comforting, center for a nutritious alternative to mashed potatoes or used to make Black Beans (see p.272) or Chipotle Black Bean Burgers (see p.276).

HUMMUS

Prep 10 minutes

No cook

Serves 2–4

This creamy dip is made with canned chickpeas for both convenience and speed but you can, of course, use dried ones. Just follow the instructions for soaking and cooking (see p.258) , using about ½ cup (115g) dried chickpeas—some also recommend the addition of a teaspoon of baking soda to the cooking water to soften the beans and reduce the cooking time slightly. The secret ingredient in this smooth, velvety hummus is the chickpea water, or aquafaba, from the can. (If using cooked dried beans, substitute the liquid from the can with water.)

1 (15oz/400g) can chickpeas in water, saving the liquid
  from the can
4 tbsp tahini
1 small garlic clove, peeled
juice and finely grated zest of ½ unwaxed lemon
salt and freshly ground black pepper
extra-virgin olive oil, to finish

1 | Drain the canned chickpeas over a bowl through a metal strainer, saving the liquid from the can.

2 | Add the tahini, garlic, and lemon juice and zest to a high-powered blender or food processor. Add in the drained chickpeas with half of the reserved liquid.

3 | Blend the chickpea mixture until completely smooth, this will take around 2–3 minutes, adding a splash more liquid from the can, depending on how you like your hummus and how soft the chickpeas are. Season with salt and pepper to taste.

4 | Spoon the hummus into a serving bowl and drizzle with olive oil. Check the seasoning, adding more salt and pepper if needed. The hummus will keep in the fridge in an airtight container for up to 5 days.

TIPS

Try flavoring your hummus with spices, including ground cumin, ground coriander, or Za'atar (see p.449), or blend with roasted red peppers.

Use the hummus in place of butter in sandwiches, as an accompaniment to Falafel (see p.274) in pita bread, or as a base for a roasted vegetable and lentil salad.

Black beans

Prep 5 minutes

Cook 15 minutes

Serves 4

The beauty of this recipe is that you take a plain staple ingredient like a can of beans and transform it into a spiced, savory side that adds interest and substance to any meal. Serve these beans as part of Huevos Rancheros (right) or as a side to any spiced chicken dish or roasted vegetables. The final texture of the dish is all down to personal preference, you can leave the beans lightly mashed or go for a smoother-textured mixture.

1 (15oz/400g) can black beans, drained
2 tbsp vegetable oil
1 onion, finely chopped
pinch of salt, plus extra to season
3 garlic cloves, finely chopped
1 green chile, finely chopped
1 tsp ground cumin
½ tsp smoked sweet paprika
freshly ground black pepper
juice of ½ lime
1 handful of cilantro leaves, finely chopped
warmed flatbread, to serve

1 | Put the drained beans into a mixing bowl, then use a potato masher to crush the beans, leaving them almost whole, roughly mashed, or smooth as preferred.

2 | Heat the vegetable oil in a medium skillet over medium-high heat. Add the onion and a pinch of salt. Cook for 6–8 minutes, stirring regularly, until the onions are soft and translucent.

3 | Add the garlic and chile and cook, stirring regularly, for another minute, before adding the ground cumin and smoked paprika.

4 | Add the mashed beans into the pan along with half a can of water and cook for 5 minutes, until piping hot. Season the beans with salt and pepper and squeeze in the lime juice. Stir through the cilantro and serve on its own with warm flatbread or as part of the huevos rancheros (right).

TIP

These black beans will keep in the fridge, covered, for up to 3 days. Alternatively, freeze for up to 3 months. Any leftover beans are great reheated with tortilla chips.

Huevos Rancheros

Prep 20 minutes

Cook 20 minutes

Serves 4

This classic Mexican breakfast usually comes with a warm, cooked tomato salsa, but this has been swapped for a quick and easy *pico de gallo*—a fresh, zingy, raw salsa made with tomato, onion, chile, and lime juice. Once you've mastered this salsa, you'll be making it on repeat, if only as a dip for your tortilla chips. The crispy fried egg (see p.25) sets everything off, the yolk mixed with the spiced beans is pure comfort and joy.

1 recipe quantity of Black Beans (see left)
½ tbsp vegetable oil
6oz (150g) chorizo, casings removed
4 large eggs, at room temperature
3½oz (100g) tortilla chips
2 avocados, peeled, stone removed, and sliced
3½oz (100g) feta cheese, crumbled
hot sauce, to serve (optional)

For the *pico de gallo*
8oz (200g) cherry tomatoes, finely chopped
1 small onion, finely chopped
½–1 green chile, finely chopped (depending on how spicy you like it)
1 handful of cilantro leaves, finely chopped
juice of 2 limes
salt and freshly ground black pepper

1 | Follow steps 1–4 to make the Black Beans (left) and keep warm.

2 | Meanwhile, mix all the ingredients for the *pico de gallo* together in a small bowl, then season with salt and pepper to taste.

3 | Heat the vegetable oil in a large skillet over medium-high heat. Crumble small chunks of chorizo into the pan and cook for 2–3 minutes, stirring regularly, until crisp.

4 | Follow steps 1–3 from Frying Eggs (see p.25), using 2 tablespoons of vegetable oil and following the method for nduja eggs.

5 | To assemble, divide the tortilla chips, beans, chorizo, and avocado between four serving plates. Top each serving with a fried egg and a good spoonful of the salsa. Crumble over the feta and serve with hot sauce, if you like.

FRYING
BEANS & PULSES

This method of cooking may not immediately spring to mind when thinking of pulse dishes, but beans, peas, and lentils lend themselves perfectly to frying for added flavor, color, and texture. Pulse-based croquettes, patties, burgers, pancakes, and fritters work wonderfully fried, becoming golden and crisp on the outside while remaining soft in the middle. In Middle Eastern cuisines, they've perfected this method with Falafel (below), made with either dried fava beans or chickpeas.

MAKING FALAFEL

*Prep 20 minutes
+ soaking and
chilling*

Cook 20 minutes

Serves 4

This homemade version of the popular street food couldn't be further away from the supermarket ones you reheat in the oven. The key is to use soaked dried chickpeas, rather than cooked ones, which give the falafel texture and bite, as well as adding plenty of herbs and spices for flavor. The chickpea flour makes these gluten-free, but if it's difficult to find, use all-purpose flour instead.

½lb (200g) dried chickpeas, rinsed well
1 small red onion, peeled and roughly chopped
1 green chile, roughly chopped
3 garlic cloves, peeled
juice and finely grated zest of 1 unwaxed lemon
2 tsp ground cumin
2 tsp ground coriander
1 tsp ground sumac, plus extra to serve
½ tsp salt, plus extra to season
1 cup (30g) cilantro, leaves and stalks, roughly chopped
1 cup (30g) flat-leaf parsley, leaves and stalks, chopped
4 tsp toasted sesame seeds (optional)
2–3 tbsp chickpea flour or all-purpose flour
½ tsp baking powder (gluten-free, if preferred)
vegetable oil, for frying

To serve
8oz (200g) Hummus (see p.270) or store-bought
4 vine-ripened tomatoes, chopped
1 cucumber, chopped
Pink Pickled Onions (see p.459)
Turkish Chili Sauce (see p.453)
warmed flatbread or pita bread

1 | Soak the chickpeas overnight (see p.258). The next day, drain the chickpeas through a strainer and rinse under cold running water, shaking off any excess. Put the soaked chickpeas into the bowl of a food processor or blender. Add the onion, chile, garlic, lemon zest, cumin, coriander, sumac, salt, and three-quarters of the cilantro and parsley.

2 | Blend the chickpea mixture until very finely chopped and it resembles a coarse paste. Add a splash of water, if needed.

3 | Spoon the mixture into a large mixing bowl, then stir in the sesame seeds, if using, 2 tablespoons of the flour, and the baking powder. Cover the bowl and chill in the fridge for 30 minutes to firm up.

4 | Line a baking sheet with parchment paper. Using clean hands or an ice cream scoop, shape the falafel into 18 walnut-size balls and place them on the lined pan. If the mixture is too wet to handle, add the remaining flour. If it is too dry and crumbly, stir in a splash of water. Line a separate baking sheet with paper towel.

5 | Pour enough vegetable oil into a deep skillet or wok to fill by one-third and place over medium-high heat. Heat the oil to 350°F (180°C), or until a cube of bread browns in 20 seconds. If the oil becomes too hot, turn off the heat and leave it to cool for a few minutes before testing the temperature again. Once the oil is up to temperature, working in batches, carefully lower the falafel into the oil. Fry for 4 minutes, turning halfway, until the outside is deeply golden brown and crisp.

6 | Place the cooked falafel on the paper-towel-lined pan to drain and season with salt. To assemble, spread the hummus onto a large plate and top with the falafel, tomatoes, cucumber, and remaining herbs. Squeeze over the lemon juice and sprinkle with extra sumac. Serve with the pickled onions, chili sauce, and warm flatbread or pita bread. Enjoy!

Chipotle black
bean burgers

Prep 25 minutes

Cook 5 minutes

Serves 4

These spicy vegan burgers make use of canned black beans for simplicity and convenience, but if you have dried ones on hand, you'll need about ½lb (240g) for the rough equivalent of two cans, then follow the soaking and cooking instructions (see p.258). You want the bean mixture to be fairly dry so the burgers hold together when fried, becoming crisp and golden on the outside.

1 tbsp milled flaxseeds
2 (15oz/400g) cans black beans, drained and rinsed
4 green onions, green and white parts, finely chopped
1 tsp garlic powder
1 tsp ground cumin
4 tsp chipotle paste
½ cup (45g) panko breadcrumbs
salt and freshly ground black pepper
2 tbsp olive oil, divided

To serve
4 vegan burger buns, cut in half
2 ripe avocados, halved and stone removed
juice of 2 limes
1 head butter lettuce, sliced
Charred Tomato & Orange Salsa (see p.425)

1 | In a small bowl, mix the milled flaxseeds with 2 tablespoons of water and leave to sit for 5 minutes, until the water is absorbed and it becomes a thick paste—this is your egg replacement, which will help bind the burgers.

2 | Put the drained black beans into a large mixing bowl. Add the green onions, garlic powder, ground cumin, chipotle paste, breadcrumbs, and soaked flaxseeds. Season with plenty of salt and pepper, then use a potato masher to crush the beans into ` a chunky-textured burger mix that holds together but isn't sticky or paste-like.

3 | Using damp, clean hands, divide the mixture into four portions and shape each one into a round burger, roughly 1½in (4cm) thick and 4in (10cm) in diameter. Place the burgers on a plate.

4 | Heat the oven to 350°F (180°C).

5 | Heat a large skillet or grill pan over high heat. Drizzle half of the olive oil evenly over the burgers, then place them, oiled-side down, in the pan. Cook for 2 minutes, until deeply golden brown, then drizzle the remaining oil over the top of the burgers and flip onto the other side. Cook for another 2 minutes, until golden brown and crisp. Transfer the burgers to a baking sheet and keep warm in the oven until ready to serve.

6 | Meanwhile, toast the halved buns, cut-side down, in two batches in the hot pan for around 30 seconds, then turn off the heat.

7 | Using a teaspoon, scoop the avocados into a medium bowl, add the lime juice, then mash with the back of a fork until well smashed. Season with salt and pepper to taste.

8 | To assemble the burgers, spread the mashed avocado across the base of each burger bun. Top with the lettuce and then the burgers. Spoon over the charred tomato salsa and sandwich together with the other half of the bun to serve.

TIPS

To make the burgers a day ahead, follow the method up to step 3, then cover and chill until ready to cook.

Feel free to swap the flaxseed for 1 large egg, lightly beaten.

Brioche buns would also work well here, and you could add some crumbled feta on top of the burgers before serving.

TOFU & TEMPEH

Tofu, also known as bean curd, is made from soy beans in much the same way as soft cheese (the coagulated fresh soy milk is formed into curds and then pressed into a solid block). This plant-based protein comes in varying levels of firmness, ranging from silken to extra firm. The beauty of tofu is that it is a blank canvas—being mild in taste, it readily takes on the flavors of stronger ingredients, such as sauces, spices, garlic, and ginger.

Although silken tofu doesn't usually require pressing, firmer alternatives will benefit from this so they retain their shape and absorb added flavors. To drain, remove the block of tofu from its liquid in the package, then press it between multiple sheets of paper towel or in a clean kitchen towel until almost dry.

Originating from Indonesia, tempeh is also made from soy beans, which are cooked and fermented for a firm, almost nutty texture. It doesn't need much in the way of preparation, simply slice or cut into cubes, but like tofu benefits from marinating before cooking. It is also high in protein and low in fat.

Storage
Some brands of silken tofu don't require storing in the fridge and will keep unopened at an ambient temperature. However, for the most part, tofu and tempeh need to be kept chilled. Store in their packaging or covered so they don't absorb flavor. You can also freeze them, resulting in a slightly firmer, "meatier" texture once defrosted.

TYPE OF TOFU/TEMPEH	HOW TO PREPARE	COOKING METHOD	PERFECT IN ...
Silken tofu	Add raw to smoothies or blend into sauces and desserts as a cream replacement or use as an egg replacement	Eat uncooked or heat gently and handle with care to avoid it breaking up. If blending into sauces, avoid boiling to prevent curdling	Cut into cubes and add to spicy broths or blend into a tomato pasta sauce, or use as a base for a chocolate mousse or Indian Scrambled Tofu (see p.37)
Firm/extra firm tofu	Drain well and pat dry with paper towel, then slice or cut into cubes	Bake or fry. For an extra crisp coating, dust in seasoned cornstarch or flour before cooking	Marinate in strongly flavored sauces with spices. Add a spoonful of honey or maple syrup to lend a sticky glaze.
Smoked/seasoned tofu	Same as firm/extra firm (above)	Bake, fry, or scramble (crumble the tofu first)	Use in stir-fries, rice, and noodle dishes.
Tempeh	Pat dry with paper towel, then slice or cut into cubes	Steaming tempeh removes any bitterness, or bake and fry like tofu	Can withstand bold flavors, such as Asian and Middle Eastern spices, pastes, and sauces.

Clockwise, from top, smoked tempeh, silken tofu,
smoked tofu, firm tofu, and tempeh.

TERIYAKI TOFU

Prep 10 minutes

Cook 15 minutes

Serves 2–4

This recipe showcases the versatility of tofu and its ability to take on stronger flavors, in this instance, teriyaki sauce. The secret to getting a crispy coating on tofu is to drain it well and then dust in cornstarch, which helps dry it further, before frying. Serve the tofu over steamed jasmine rice and with Ginger & Soy Stir-Fried Greens (see p.191) for a hearty vegan meal.

10oz (280g) extra-firm tofu, drained well
3 tbsp cornstarch
salt and freshly ground black pepper
2 tbsp vegetable or sunflower oil
2 green onions, green and white parts, finely sliced
1 red chile, finely sliced, seeded if preferred

For the teriyaki sauce
3 tbsp soy sauce or tamari
1 fat garlic clove, peeled and finely grated
2-in piece of fresh ginger, peeled and finely grated
2 tbsp light brown sugar
1 tbsp rice wine vinegar
1 tsp cornstarch

1 | Pat dry the tofu with paper towel, pressing it gently to get rid of any excess liquid. Cut the tofu into roughly 1¼ x ¾-in (3 x 2-cm) pieces.

2 | Put the cornstarch into a shallow bowl and season with salt and pepper. Toss the tofu in the seasoned cornstarch, ensuring it is lightly and evenly coated, then transfer to a plate.

3 | Heat the oil in a wok or large, high-sided skillet over high heat. Add the tofu to the pan, making sure there is enough space between each piece, and cook for 5–6 minutes, turning often, until the tofu is golden and crisp on all sides. (You may need to cook the tofu in two batches, adding 1 tbsp more oil to the pan.) Turn the heat off and leave the tofu in the pan.

4 | To make the teriyaki sauce, add the soy sauce or tamari, garlic, ginger, brown sugar, vinegar, cornstarch and 3 tablespoons of water to a small pan. Place the pan over medium-high heat and let the sauce bubble away for a couple of minutes, stirring, until the sugar dissolves and the sauce is thick and glossy.

5 | Pour the teriyaki sauce over the tofu in the wok or pan, toss to coat, and warm through until the tofu is glossy and golden. Serve topped with the green onions and sliced chile for a pop of freshness with rice and stir-fried greens on the side.

Flavor variations

Sriracha & lime: mix 2 tablespoons of sriracha sauce, 1 tablespoon of maple syrup or honey, and the juice and finely grated zest of 1 lime in a small bowl. Cook the tofu following the method in step 3, then pour over the glaze, tossing for a couple of minutes before serving topped with toasted sesame seeds.

Garam masala & mango chutney: mix 1 tablespoon of Garam Masala (see p.448) into the cornstarch in a shallow bowl, then add the tofu and mix until lightly coated all over. Cook the tofu following the method in step 3, then glaze with 2 tablespoons of mango chutney, tossing for a couple of minutes. Serve the tofu topped with chopped Bombay mix and fresh cilantro.

TIPS

If you prefer to bake, rather than fry, the tofu, preheat the oven to 400°F (200°C). Toss the tofu in the cornstarch and spread it out in a single layer on a baking sheet lined with parchment paper, drizzle with some oil, and cook for 20–25 minutes, turning halfway, until crisp and golden.

Swap the teriyaki tofu for the chicken in the Sesame Chicken Salad (see p.75) or serve as a filling for the Bao Buns (see p.318).

Chili tempeh naan

Prep 15 minutes

Cook 10 minutes

Serves 2

The chili-spiced cornstarch gives the cubes of tempeh a crisp coating when fried. The tempeh is then tossed with stir-fried vegetables coated in a rich chili gravy and served atop naan for the ultimate vegan comfort food. You could use tofu or paneer as alternatives to the tempeh, if preferred.

2 tbsp soy sauce
3 tbsp ketchup
2 tbsp hot chili sauce
2 tsp rice wine vinegar

2 tbsp cornstarch
½ tsp chili powder
salt and freshly ground black pepper
8oz (200g) tempeh, drained and patted dry with paper towel, then cut into ¾-in (2-cm) cubes
5 tbsp vegetable oil, divided
1 red onion, peeled and roughly chopped
1 red bell pepper, seeded and roughly chopped
1 green bell pepper, seeded and roughly chopped
3 fat garlic cloves, peeled and finely chopped

To serve
2 large naan, warmed (garlic and cilantro work well)
2 green onions, green and white part, finely sliced

1 | Mix the soy sauce, ketchup, chili sauce, and vinegar with 3 tablespoons of water in a small bowl. Set aside.

2 | Using a fork, mix the cornstarch with the chili powder and a generous pinch of salt and pepper in a wide, shallow bowl.

3 | Add the tempeh to the spiced cornstarch mixture and toss until evenly coated.

4 | Heat a wok or large, high-sided skillet over high heat. Once hot, pour in 3 tablespoons of the oil and add the tempeh, leaving space between each piece so that they cook evenly. Cook the tempeh for about 5 minutes, turning regularly with tongs, until golden on all sides. Remove onto a plate lined with paper towel to drain.

5 | Pour the remaining 2 tablespoons of oil into the pan and add the red onion, both peppers, and garlic. Stir fry for 2–3 minutes, until the vegetables begin to soften but still have a bit of crunch.

6 | Turn the heat down to medium. Pour in the chili sauce mix, return the tempeh to the pan, and give everything a good stir. Let the sauce bubble away for a couple of minutes until thickened to a rich gravy.

7 | Spoon the chili tempeh and vegetables onto the warmed naan and top with the green onions, to serve.

Mapo tofu

Prep 10 minutes

Cook 25 minutes

Serves 2

Mapo tofu is a popular Sichuan dish. The region is known for its spicy food, particularly the use of Sichuan pepper. This dish certainly packs in the flavor—cubes of tofu (both silken and medium-firm tofu work here) are braised in a rich Sichuan pepper sauce with ground pork or beef and green onions. If you prefer a milder-tasting dish, you can leave the Sichuan peppercorns whole and then pick them out before serving. Alternatively, for a more traditional, spicy dish, grind after roasting and sprinkle them over at the end of cooking so they infuse the whole dish. This recipe can easily be made vegan without detracting from its flavor, simply by swapping the ground meat for a plant-based alternative.

1 tbsp vegetable oil
1 tbsp Sichuan peppercorns
⅓lb (150g) ground beef or pork, or plant-based alternative

3 garlic cloves, minced
1 tsp sugar
1 heaped tbsp Chinese spicy bean paste (*doubanjiang*)
1 cup (250ml) Vegetable Stock (see p.414) or store-bought
10oz (300g) tofu (silken or medium-firm), drained and cut into bite-size cubes
salt, to taste
½ tbsp cornstarch (optional)
1 handful of finely chopped green onions
Cooked Rice (see p.202), to serve

1 | Heat the oil in a wok or large, deep-sided skillet with a lid over medium heat. Gently fry the Sichuan peppercorns for 2–3 minutes, tossing the pan occasionally, until fragrant and slightly darker in color. For a milder-tasting dish, leave the peppercorns whole in the pan. Alternatively, pick them out of the oil with a slotted spoon, leave to cool, then grind in a mortar and pestle to sprinkle over at the end of cooking.

2 | To the same pan, add the ground meat and cook for 4–5 minutes, until browned and the fat has rendered out. Add the garlic and stir-fry for 30 seconds, until fragrant. Next, stir in the sugar, spicy bean paste, and stock until combined. The sauce should be glossy and red with a good sheen on top.

3 | Place the tofu on top and gently move it around so it's partially submerged in the liquid. Turn the heat down to low, cover with the lid, and simmer for 5–10 minutes, until the sauce has slightly reduced. Taste and adjust the seasoning, adding salt, if needed, or if it's too spicy, add a little extra sugar to balance out the flavor. If the sauce needs thickening, turn the heat up and simmer, without the lid, for a few more minutes until reduced. Alternatively, mix the cornstarch with 2 tablespoons of water, add to the pan, and simmer, stirring, for a few minutes until thickened.

4 | Toss in the green onions and stir gently a final time until just wilted in the sauce. Depending on your taste, either remove the whole Sichuan peppercorns or sprinkle the ground ones over and serve the mapo tofu over cooked rice.

NUTS

&

SEEDS

NUTS

With the exception of peanuts, which are actually legumes, nuts are the fruit of trees and come with a hard, protective shell and edible kernel. They make a valuable and versatile asset in cooking, adding flavor and texture as well as nutritional value to both sweet and savory dishes. You can buy nuts whole in their shells, although shelled nuts are undoubtedly more convenient and ready to use. Shelled nuts come in many forms: whole, halved, toasted, untoasted, blanched, ground, flaked, chopped, or even blended into a richly flavored oil, such as walnut or hazelnut.

Nuts make a great base for a meat-free roast, burger, stuffing, croquette, granola, or simply a nutritious energy-boosting snack. Sprinkled over oatmeal, cereal, ice cream, soup, or a salad, they not only add a welcome crunch but also give a flavor boost, especially if toasted first (see p.288). They come into their own as a deliciously creamy dairy-free milk (see p.64), yogurt, cream, and cheese (see p.65).

Some people avoid nuts due to their high fat content, but these are largely beneficial monounsaturated or polyunsaturated fats. In fact, nuts are described as being "nutritionally dense," because not only are they an impressive source of protein, which makes them particularly useful if you follow a plant-based diet, they also provide a range of minerals, including calcium, potassium, and magnesium, as well as vitamin E and plenty of fiber. Some people suggest soaking nuts before eating and cooking to increase their digestibility, but this is not essential.

Storage
Always buy nuts in small quantities, especially if you don't intend to use them on a regular basis, since they are prone to turn rancid. Store in an airtight container in the fridge or a cool, dark cupboard for up to 3 months. You can also keep them in a lidded container in the freezer; there is no need to defrost them before use.

NUT	HOW TO BUY	PERFECT IN ...
Almonds	Whole, blanched, flaked, slivered, ground	Plant-based milk, cream, almond paste, baking, sauces, nut butter, as a decoration.
Cashews	Whole, halved, roasted	Plant-based milk, cream, cheese, sauces, curries, stir-fries, nut butter.
Coconut	Whole, chopped, flaked, dried, cream, milk	Plant-based milk, curries, desserts, stews, soups, curries, baking.
Hazelnuts	Whole, blanched, ground, oil	Plant-based milk, baking, granola, nut loaves.
Peanuts	Whole, roasted, oil	Nut butters, baking, satay sauce, stir-fries, curries, stews, as a garnish.
Pecans	Halved	Plant-based milk, baking, granola, as a decoration.
Pine nuts	Whole	Pesto, salads, sauces.
Pistachios	Whole, chopped, oil	Plant-based milk, stuffings, nut crusts, baking.
Walnuts	Whole, halved, oil	Stuffing, baking, salads, granola.

Clockwise, from top, pine nuts, Brazil nuts, unroasted peanuts,
hazelnuts, walnuts, pistachios, cashews, and almonds.

TOASTING NUTS
(IN THE OVEN)

Prep 5 minutes

Cook 10 minutes

Makes 3½oz
(100g)

This is the best and easiest way to toast nuts, especially if you have a large quantity. The oven ensures an even heat, giving the nuts a golden color all over—just remember to shake the pan occasionally to stop them from burning. If toasting almonds in their skin or dark-colored nuts, there won't be a distinct change in color so check they're ready by cutting one in half and they should be golden throughout—they'll also smell wonderfully toasty when ready. Nuts can be bought pre-toasted, but their shelf life tends to be shorter and the roasted flavor less pronounced.

3½oz (100g) nuts of your choice

1 | Preheat the oven to 350°F (180°C). Put the nuts in a small roasting pan and spread out in a single layer so they toast evenly. Put in the oven for 6–8 minutes, checking every few minutes, until light golden and they smell nutty and toasted. Leave to cool before using, or store in an airtight container at room temperature for up to 1 month.

TOASTING NUTS
(ON THE STOVE TOP)

Prep 5 minutes

Cook 5 minutes

Makes 1¾oz
(50g)

Nuts that benefit the most from toasting in a skillet are smaller types, such as pine nuts, because their kernels can be tossed like seeds while they cook to ensure even browning. This method is also suitable if you're toasting a small amount of nuts and don't want to heat the oven up; for larger quantities, the oven method is preferable and much easier to control. Remember to keep the heat low to ensure the nuts don't burn.

⅓ cup (50g) pine nuts

1 | Put the pine nuts in a small skillet over medium-low heat. Cook, tossing regularly, for 4–5 minutes, until the nuts have turned an even golden brown color. At first they won't look like they are doing anything, but suddenly start to turn so it's wise to keep an eye on them.

BLANCHING NUTS

Prep 15 minutes

No cook

Makes 3½oz (100g)

You can buy ready-blanched nuts (without their papery skin), but it is easy to do it yourself if you can find the type with their brown skin on.

1 cup (100g) skin-on hazelnuts or almonds

1 | Put the nuts in a medium heatproof bowl and pour over boiling water to cover. Leave to soak for 4–5 minutes, then drain well through a colander in the sink.

2 | Put the soaked nuts onto a paper-towel-lined baking sheet to dry and cool for a few minutes. Use your fingers to peel or rub the skins away from the nuts. Alternatively, rub the nuts between 2 sheets of paper towel.

GRINDING NUTS

Prep 5 minutes

No cook

Makes 3½oz (100g)

Some recipes call for ground nuts, specifically in baking. You can buy pre-ground nuts, but freshly ground ones definitely have the best flavor. Just make sure you stop when the nuts are finely chopped and still dry—go too far and you could end up with a nut butter (see p.297). You can also toast them before grinding for a deeper, nuttier flavor.

¾ cup (100g) pistachios

1 | Put the nuts into a small food processor or blender. Using the pulse function, grind the nuts in very short bursts until evenly and very finely chopped—you are looking for a fine, dry breadcrumb texture.

Nut-stuffed butternut squash

Prep 30 minutes

Cook 2 hours 15 minutes

Serves 4

This nutty squash is perfect for entertaining. The harissa-spiked nut mixture is encased in butternut squash and slow-roasted until super soft inside with a crisp, golden skin. Serve it with Vegan Gravy (see p.419) for an impressive meat-free main dish.

1¾oz (50g) unsalted mixed nuts
1 large butternut squash, cut in half lengthwise, seeds scooped out with a spoon
2 tbsp olive oil, divided
1 tbsp harissa
1 onion, peeled and finely chopped
pinch of salt, plus extra to season
3 garlic cloves, peeled and finely chopped
1 handful of thyme sprigs, leaves stripped
½ cup (50g) breadcrumbs
1 cup (125g) cooked Puy lentils
¼ cup (30g) dried cranberries
1 large handful of flat-leaf parsley, finely chopped
freshly ground black pepper

1 | Preheat the oven to 350°F (180°C). Follow step 1 from Toasting Nuts in the oven (see p.288).

2 | Using a teaspoon, scoop out the flesh from each half of the butternut squash to leave a ¾-in (2-cm) thick shell. Finely chop the scooped-out squash and set aside briefly.

3 | Heat half of the olive oil and all the harissa in a large skillet over medium heat, stirring until combined. Add the onion and chopped squash with a pinch of salt and cook, stirring often, for 12–14 minutes, until the squash is almost soft. Add the garlic and thyme and cook for another 2 minutes.

4 | Turn the oven to 375°F (190°C).

5 | Scrape the squash mixture into the bowl of a food processor with the toasted nuts, breadcrumbs, and lentils, then pulse until the nuts are roughly chopped and the mixture becomes a coarse purée. Stir in the cranberries and parsley.

6 | Put the squash halves onto a baking sheet, cut-side up and season well with salt and pepper. Divide the stuffing between each hollowed-out squash half, pressing it down until compact. Carefully and swiftly, sandwich the two halves of squash together, placing them on top of one another, to create a "whole" squash. Using kitchen twine, tie the two halves together at intervals.

7 | Drizzle the remaining olive oil over the squash and season with salt and pepper. Roast in the oven for about 1¾ hours, until the skin is crisp and golden and the inside is completely tender when prodded with the point of a knife. Carve into slices and serve.

TIP

You can make and stuff the butternut squash ahead of time, then keep it covered in the fridge for up to 2 days before roasting.

Chicken & cashew Kung Pao

Prep 20 minutes

Cook 30 minutes

Serves 4

A version of the classic spicy Sichuan stir-fry, this is packed with flavor and ready in minutes. Cashews are used instead of the more usual peanuts and fried until golden, adding a savory, nutty depth to the dish as well as a welcome crunch.

2 tbsp vegetable oil, divided
½ cup (75g) unsalted, unroasted cashew nuts
4 boneless, skinless chicken thighs, cut into
   bite-size pieces
salt and freshly ground black pepper
1 onion, chopped
2 celery stalks, finely sliced diagonally
1 green bell pepper, seeded and cut into
   1½-in (4-cm) pieces
1 red bell pepper, seeded and cut into
   1½-in (4-cm) pieces
4 garlic cloves, peeled and finely chopped
2-in piece of fresh ginger, peeled and
   finely chopped

2 tsp Sichuan peppercorns, lightly crushed
6 dried red chiles or 2 fresh red chiles,
   seeded and thinly sliced
2 tsp cornstarch
2 tbsp soy sauce
1 tsp sugar
Cooked Rice (see p.202), such as jasmine, to serve

1 | Heat half of the vegetable oil in a wok or large, deep-sided skillet over medium-high heat. Add the cashews and toast for 1–2 minutes, until golden brown, then use a slotted spoon to scoop them out into a bowl. Set aside.

2 | Season the chicken pieces with salt and pepper. Turn the heat to high and add the remaining oil to the wok or pan. Add the chicken and cook for 5–6 minutes, stirring now and again, until browned all over.

3 | Add the onion, celery, and bell peppers to the pan and stir-fry for 3–4 minutes, until beginning to caramelize and soften.

4 | Turn the heat to medium-low. Add the garlic, ginger, Sichuan peppercorns, and dried or fresh chiles and stir-fry for another 2–3 minutes, until softened.

5 | Mix the cornstarch with 1 teaspoon of water in a bowl to make a paste, then top up with ⅔ cup (150ml) of cold water. Pour the cornstarch water into the wok or pan with the soy sauce and sugar. Stir and simmer for 10 minutes, until the sauce reduces and thickens and the chicken is cooked.

6 | Stir in the toasted cashews and season with salt and pepper to taste, adding a splash more soy sauce, if you like. Serve with cooked rice.

Pistachio & coriander-crusted rack of lamb

Prep 20 minutes

Cook 35 minutes + resting

Serves 2

If you're looking for a great summer alternative to a traditional roast dinner, this lamb dish is it. The spiced pistachio crust toasts as the lamb roasts, becoming crisp and golden in places as well as helping to absorb some of the lamb juices as the meat rests. The rack of lamb should be French-trimmed—this is where the meat and sinew are removed from each rib bone, making for a neat, professional finish. All supermarket-bought lamb racks usually come prepared, or ask your butcher to do it for you. Serve the lamb with a fresh tomato salad and the Olive Tapenade (see p.424) for a date-night win.

1 French-trimmed rack of lamb, with 4–6 ribs, about ¾lb (350–400g) total weight
2 tsp coriander seeds
½ cup (50g) shelled unsalted pistachios
1 handful of flat-leaf parsley
2 tsp vegetable oil
salt and freshly ground black pepper
1 tbsp Dijon mustard
½ recipe quantity of Olive Tapenade (see p.424), to serve

For the salad
3 large ripe tomatoes, sliced into rounds
½ red onion, peeled and finely sliced
1 small handful of mint leaves
2 tbsp extra-virgin olive oil
1 tbsp red wine vinegar

1 | Remove the rack of lamb from the fridge 1 hour before cooking, place on a plate and keep it covered at room temperature.

2 | Meanwhile, toast the coriander seeds in a dry skillet over medium heat for 1–2 minutes, tossing regularly, until lightly toasted. Put the coriander seeds into a small food processor. Add the pistachios and parsley leaves and pulse together until finely chopped, then transfer to a shallow bowl.

3 | Preheat the oven to 375°F (190°C). Using a small, sharp chef's knife, lightly score the fat on the lamb in a diamond pattern—this will help it render down during roasting. Drizzle over the oil and season well with salt and pepper.

4 | Return the skillet to high heat. Put the lamb in the hot pan, fat-side down, and cook for 3–4 minutes, until golden and crisp. Using tongs to hold it in place, brown each end of the lamb rack for 30 seconds, then place it in a small roasting pan.

5 | Brush the lamb all over with an even coating of mustard, then put it into the shallow bowl and sprinkle over the pistachio crumb, pressing to make the coating sticks and piling it onto the fat-cap side until completely covered. Put the rack back into the roasting pan, with the fat cap facing upward, piling more of the crumb on top. Roast for 20–25 minutes (20 minutes for rare and 25 for medium blushing pink meat). Move the lamb onto a warm plate, cover loosely with foil, and let rest for 15 minutes.

6 | While the lamb rests, make the salad. Put the tomato slices on a serving plate and sprinkle over the onion and mint. Drizzle with the olive oil and vinegar, then season with salt and pepper to taste.

7 | To serve, slice the lamb between each rib into chops and serve with the salad and olive tapenade on the side.

USING NUTS
IN SAUCES

Nuts make surprisingly good sauces and can also be used as a thickener. Their creamy, dense texture and slightly buttery flavor enhances the richness and mouthfeel of a sauce, as well as boosting its nutritional value. This versatility is demonstrated in many cuisines around the world, for instance, cashews form the base of the Indian curry sauce, korma, or there's the Spanish red pepper and almond sauce, Romesco (below), or the Middle Eastern walnut dip, Muhammara (see p.296). When blended until smooth, nuts take on other flavors beautifully, especially dried spices, while adding their own creamy consistency.

ROMESCO SAUCE

Prep 5 minutes

Cook 10 minutes

Serves 4–6

This smoky Spanish sauce/dip sometimes contains tomatoes in addition to the toasted almonds and roasted red peppers. This version omits tomatoes so the flavor of the smoked paprika shines through, however, feel free to reduce the quantity of red pepper by ¼ cup (50g) and replace it with the same amount of sun-dried tomatoes in oil, drained. Serve the sauce spooned over Pan-Fried Hake (see p.148).

¾ cup (100g) blanched almonds
1 (16oz/450g) jar of roasted red peppers, drained
1½ tsp sweet smoked paprika
1 small garlic clove, peeled
1–1½ tbsp sherry or red wine vinegar
2 tbsp extra-virgin olive oil
salt and freshly ground black pepper

1 | Preheat the oven to 350°F (180°C). Follow step 1 from Toasting Nuts in the oven (see p.288), then set aside the almonds to cool. Once cool, put the toasted almonds, roasted peppers, smoked paprika, garlic, 1 tablespoon of the vinegar, and the olive oil into a blender.

2 | Blend to a smooth sauce, the consistency of thick Greek yogurt. Season with salt and pepper to taste, adding the extra ½ tablespoon of vinegar, if needed. Blend again to evenly distribute the seasonings in the sauce. Use right away or store in an airtight container in the fridge for up to 3 days.

Honey-glazed chorizo
sausages with romesco

Prep 5 minutes

Cook 20 minutes

Serves 2–4

The spicy smokiness of the fresh chorizo sausages complements the flavor of the nutty, smoky roasted red pepper sauce perfectly. Just make sure you buy chorizo sausages in casings instead of dry-cured chorizo. This makes the perfect light lunch or snack, or serve as part of a sharing meal.

½lb (200g) chorizo sausages
½ recipe quantity of Romesco Sauce (left)
1 tbsp honey
1 handful of flat-leaf parsley, leaves picked
crusty bread or toast, to serve

1 | Preheat the oven to 400°F (200°C). Line a small roasting pan with parchment paper.

2 | Cut the chorizo into bite-size pieces, then place in the pan in the oven for 15 minutes, until cooked and lightly colored on the outside.

3 | Meanwhile, follow steps 1–2 from Romesco Sauce (left)—you will only need half for this recipe and the rest will keep in an airtight container for up to 3 days.

4 | Drizzle the honey over the cooked chorizo and return the tray to the oven for a further 3–5 minutes, until sticky and caramelized.

5 | Spread the romesco over the base of a serving plate, then pile the honey chorizo sausages on top and sprinkle over the parsley leaves. Serve with crusty bread or toast

Muhammara

Prep 5 minutes

Cook 10 minutes

Serves 4–6

This popular Syrian dip is often served as part of a mezze spread with warmed bread. It is similar to romesco in that it uses roasted red peppers, but the choice of nuts and spicing is different. Breadcrumbs are often included as a thickener but here walnuts alone do the same job. Serve with the simple Yogurt Flatbread (see p.308) or as an accompaniment to the Shawarma-Spiced Whole Baked Cauliflower (see p.177) as a vegan alternative to the plain yogurt.

¾ cup (100g) walnut halves
1 (16oz/450g) jar of roasted red peppers, drained
1 tsp ground cumin
½–1 tsp dried Aleppo pepper (depending on how spicy you like it)
1 small garlic clove, peeled
2 tbsp pomegranate molasses
2 tbsp extra-virgin olive oil
salt and freshly ground black pepper

1 | Preheat the oven to 350°F (180°C).

2 | Follow step 1 from Toasting Nuts in the oven (see p.288), then set aside the walnuts to cool.

3 | Once cool, put the walnuts, red peppers, cumin, Aleppo pepper, garlic, pomegranate molasses, and olive oil into a blender.

4 | Blend the mixture to a smooth sauce, the consistency of thick Greek yogurt. Season with salt and pepper to taste. Blend again to evenly distribute the seasonings in the sauce. Use right away or store in an airtight container in the fridge for up to 3 days.

TIP

If you prefer a chunkier dip, use a food processor instead of a blender, then pulse to your desired consistency.

MAKING
NUT BUTTER

Prep 15 minutes

Cook 10 minutes

Makes 10oz
(300g)

As well as being rich in protein, nuts contain a high percentage of beneficial fats, making them ideal for turning into a rich and creamy nut butter, without the unwanted additives often found in store-bought alternatives. Using a high-powered food processor or blender and a little patience, grind the nuts to release the oils and eventually break them down into a thick, paste-like consistency. Toasting the nuts beforehand is optional, but it does bring an added depth of flavor to the nut butter, plus the heat helps extract the oils, making them easier to grind. This is a recipe for cashew butter, although you could use the same method to make peanut, almond, hazelnut, macadamia and, if you're feeling fancy, pistachio butter—or go for a combination.

2¼ cups (300g) untoasted unsalted cashews
large pinch of salt

Flavorings (optional)
1 tsp vanilla paste
½ tbsp cocoa powder, sifted
1 tbsp maple syrup

1 | Preheat the oven to 180°C (350°F). Follow step 1 from Toasting Nuts in the oven (see p.288), then set aside the cashews to cool. Transfer the nuts to a small food processor and blend, occasionally scraping down the sides, until the nuts change from dry and finely chopped to the consistency of wet sand.

2 | At this point, add a large pinch of salt and any optional additional flavorings, then continue to blend until the oils have separated from the nuts.

3 | Scrape down the inside of the bowl once more and keep blending to a creamy nut butter—it can be completely smooth or slightly crunchy, it's up to your personal preference. Spoon the nut butter into a sterilized jar (see p.456) and store in the fridge for up to 1 month.

TIP

If making pistachio butter, you can skip step 1 because pistachios don't benefit from toasting, and this will also help preserve their vibrant green color when blended.

SEEDS

Seeds may be tiny, but they pack a punch health-wise, and make a welcome flavorful addition to sweet or savory dishes. Nutritionally, seeds are a powerhouse providing impressive amounts of good fats, protein, vitamins—particularly vitamin E—and minerals, including iron, as well as fiber.

They can be used in multiple ways, including dips and pastes, breads, cakes, pastries, cookies, burgers, fritters, pasta dishes, pilafs, and Granola (see p.300) or as a crunchy topping for salads, soups, stir-fries, ice cream, or yogurt.

Like nuts, seeds benefit from toasting before use to enhance their flavor and crunch. Ideally, toast them in a dry skillet so you can keep a keen eye on them because they can easily burn. If toasting large quantities or when combining them with nuts, you can also opt for the oven method (see p.288). In addition to changing color and turning golden, larger seeds, such as pumpkin and sunflower, will begin to pop when ready, so be careful. If using flaxseeds and chia seeds in baking as a plant-based alternative to eggs, you will need to soak them first in a small amount of water (see p.36). This will soften them and turn them into a jellylike mixture, ready to use.

Storage

Like nuts, seeds are prone to turning rancid due to their high fat content so it's a good idea to buy them in small, usable quantities, especially if you don't intend to use them regularly. After opening the package, transfer to an airtight container and store in the fridge or a cool, dark cupboard. It is better to buy whole seeds, rather than ground, because they are less likely to spoil and will retain their nutritional value. You can also keep them in the freezer—there is no need to defrost them before use.

SEED	HOW TO BUY	PERFECT IN ...
Chia	Whole, ground	Egg alternative, breakfast cereals, baking, smoothies.
Flaxseeds	Whole, ground, oil	Egg alternative, baking, granola, salads.
Pumpkin	Whole, shelled, oil	Baking, breads, salads, dips, dressings, granola.
Poppy	Whole	Bread, baking.
Sesame	Whole, oil	Tahini, dukkah, baking, bread, stir-fries, Asian dishes, granola.
Sunflower	Whole, oil	Baking, salads, granola, breads.

Clockwise, from top, ground flaxseeds, poppy seeds, sunflower seeds, chia seeds, sesame seeds, and pumpkin seeds (center).

MIXED SEED & HONEY GRANOLA

Prep 10 minutes

Cook 30 minutes

Makes 2¼lb (1kg)

Making your own granola couldn't be simpler and gives you the option to use your own favorite mix of nuts and seeds. It is also sure to contain less sugar and fewer additives than store-bought alternatives. This granola just uses seeds but you can introduce nuts too, as well as swapping the spice for just cinnamon—the beauty of this recipe is that it is truly adaptable. You can also try roasting the seeds with the oats first to give the granola a deeper toasted flavor.

3¼ cups (500g) old fashioned rolled oats
1lb 2oz (500g) mixed untoasted seeds (pumpkin, sunflower, sesame, and poppy seeds work well)
2 tbsp ground cinnamon
1 tbsp ground ginger
1 tbsp ground nutmeg
large pinch of salt
1 tbsp vanilla extract
⅔ cup (150g) coconut oil, melted
½ cup (150g) honey or maple syrup

1 | Preheat the oven to 350°F (180°C). Line a large baking sheet with parchment paper. In a large mixing bowl, stir together the oats with the seeds, cinnamon, ginger, nutmeg, and a large pinch of salt until combined.

2 | Pour in the vanilla extract, melted coconut oil, and honey or maple syrup, then mix well with a wooden spoon to combine the wet ingredients with the dry.

3 | Scrape the mixture onto the lined baking sheet and spread it out into a single layer so everything cooks evenly. Bake for 25–30 minutes, stirring every 10 minutes to bring the browned outside edges into the middle, until golden and crunchy.

4 | Leave the granola to cool, then break up any large pieces and store in a lidded container at room temperature for up to 1 month.

Shrimp, ginger, edamame & seeded quinoa

Prep 10 minutes

Cook 20 minutes

Serves 2

The mixed seeds in this entrée salad add an unexpected toasty crunch, which complements the nuttiness of the quinoa. This is a great dish to make a day ahead, simply keep in the fridge, then bring it up to room temperature 20 minutes before serving. To make the salad completely gluten-free, swap the soy sauce for tamari.

½ cup (100g) quinoa, rinsed well
large pinch of salt
2oz (60g) mixed seeds
large pinch of dried chili flakes
⅔ cup (100g) frozen shelled edamame beans
6oz (150g) cooked large shrimp
½ cucumber, seeded and diced
¼ cup (100g) chopped radishes
1 large handful of cilantro, leaves and stalks,
   roughly chopped

For the dressing
1 tbsp toasted sesame oil
3 tbsp soy sauce or tamari
juice and finely grated zest of 1 lime
2 tsp honey
2-in piece of fresh ginger, peeled
   and finely grated

1 | Cook the quinoa in a medium saucepan of salted boiling water, stirring occasionally, for 15–20 minutes, until the grains have doubled in size and are tender with a slight bite.

2 | Meanwhile, put the seeds in a small skillet over medium-low heat and toast for 4–5 minutes, stirring regularly, until golden and the larger ones have started to pop. Remove from the heat, put into a bowl, then mix in the chili flakes and leave to cool.

3 | To make the dressing, mix all the ingredients with a balloon whisk in a large serving bowl until combined. Set aside.

4 | Put the frozen edamame into a small heatproof bowl, add boiling water, and leave for 2–3 minutes to defrost, then drain through a metal strainer, shake off any excess water, and transfer to the bowl containing the dressing.

5 | Once the quinoa is cooked, drain through a fine mesh strainer, then rinse under cold running water to cool. Leave the strainer over the sink for a few minutes to drain off any excess water.

6 | Add the cooked cooled quinoa into the serving bowl. Add the shrimp, cucumber, radishes, cilantro, and toasted seeds and coat everything with the dressing. Give it a good stir, then divide the salad between two plates to serve.

HOMEMADE TAHINI

Prep 10 minutes

Cook 5 minutes

Makes 7oz (200g)

This traditional creamy Middle Eastern condiment is made from toasted and ground sesame seeds and is surprisingly easy to prepare. It features white sesame seeds, although it is possible to use black ones for a twist on the classic. A fundamental part of the chickpea dip hummus, tahini can also be used as a creamy addition to dressings, as a spread, sauce (see p.432), or in baking.

⅓ cup (200g) white sesame seeds
3 tbsp vegetable or sunflower oil
large pinch of salt

1 | Toast the sesame seeds in a small, dry frying pan over medium-low heat for 3–4 minutes, stirring often, until golden. Make sure you stir the seeds regularly because some will brown faster than others. Put the seeds into a bowl and leave to cool.

2 | Put the cooled toasted seeds into a small food processor and blend until the consistency of wet, crumbly sand.

3 | Add the oil and a large pinch of salt and blend again until completely smooth and creamy. Spoon into a sterilized jar (see p.456) and store for up to 1 month in the fridge.

TIPS

Tahini makes a great base for a rich and creamy dressing when mixed with olive oil and lemon juice. There is also the option to add other flavorings, such as crushed garlic or chopped herbs.

Mix tahini with miso paste and soy sauce or tamari to add a deep, umami flavor to Asian broths or noodle soups.

DUKKAH

Prep 5 minutes

Cook 5 minutes

Makes about 3oz
(85g)

In Arabic dukkah means "to pound"—the spices, nuts, and seeds are traditionally pounded in a pestle and mortar. The condiment makes the ultimate savory spiced topper and pretty much improves the taste of everything! Try sprinkling it over the Charred Cabbage Wedges with Whipped Tahini (see p.304), over soft Boiled Eggs (see p.18), or spooned into extra-virgin olive oil for the ultimate dip to serve with flatbread.

1 tbsp cumin seeds
1 tbsp coriander seeds
2 tsp pink peppercorns (optional)
2 tbsp sesame seeds
½ cup (50g) almonds, toasted (see p.288), chopped
large pinch of salt

1 | Toast the cumin and coriander seeds in a small, dry skillet over medium heat, tossing them occasionally, for about 1 minute, until aromatic. Add the pink peppercorns, if using, and toast for 30 seconds.

2 | Put the toasted spices into a pestle and mortar or spice grinder and leave to cool slightly. Using the pestle, roughly grind the toasted spices (or pulse them in the grinder for 20 seconds).

3 | Put the skillet back on medium-low heat and sprinkle in the sesame seeds. Toast for 3–4 minutes, stirring regularly, until golden. Leave to cool.

4 | Add the toasted cooled sesame seeds and the toasted almonds to the spices. Season with a large pinch of salt and give everything a good stir to evenly combine. Store in an airtight container in the fridge or at a cool room temperature for up to 3 weeks.

TIP

Any nuts would work well here. Instead of the almonds, try peanuts, hazelnuts, and macadamia, or opt for toasted pumpkin seeds instead.

Charred cabbage with whipped tahini & dukkah

Prep 20 minutes

Cook 30 minutes

Serves 4 as a side

This veggie side dish uses creamy Tahini (see p.302) as a base for charred cabbage wedges—their smoky flavor complements the richness of the sauce perfectly. You can use store-bought tahini or make your own following our simple recipe. This makes a wonderful side to The Perfect Steak (see p.114) or pair it with the Marinated Pepper Fattoush (see p.188) for a veggie feast.

4 tbsp Tahini (see p.302) or store-bought
3 tbsp Dukkah (see p.303) or store-bought
1 large sweetheart cabbage (or small head of white cabbage), cut into 4 wedges lengthwise
salt and freshly ground black pepper
2 tbsp olive oil
juice of ½–1 lemon
1 tsp maple syrup (optional)
1 handful of dill, leaves picked

1 | Follow steps 1–3 from Homemade Tahini (see p.302), then follow steps 1–4 from Dukkah (see p.303); alternatively use store-bought for both.

2 | Preheat the oven to 400°F (200°C). Line a baking sheet with parchment paper.

3 | Put a large, nonstick skillet over high heat. Season the cut sides of the cabbage wedges with salt and pepper, then pour the olive oil into the hot pan.

4 | Lay the cabbage wedges in the pan, one of the cut-sides down and cook for 2 minutes, until nicely charred. Using tongs, turn the cabbage onto the other cut side and cook for another 2 minutes. Transfer the charred cabbage, cut-sides up, onto the lined baking sheet and roast in the oven for 15 minutes, until tender. A small, sharp knife should readily pierce the stalk of the cabbage once cooked.

5 | Meanwhile, spoon the tahini into a small bowl. Add the juice of ½ lemon and 4 tablespoons of water, then whisk together with a fork. The tahini will immediately seize and look like it has split but this is normal, the water and whisking will bring it back together into a smooth sauce.

6 | Season the tahini mixture with salt and pepper to taste, adding the remaining lemon juice if you like things sharper and/or the maple syrup, if you prefer a little sweetness. If the tahini is still a little thick, whisk in a little extra water—you want it to be the consistency of plain yogurt.

7 | Spread the whipped tahini across the base of a serving plate. Lay the charred cabbage wedges on top, then sprinkle with the dukkah and dill, to serve.

TIP

Instead of the Dukkah, sprinkle 2 tablespoons of toasted almonds, hazelnuts, or walnuts (see p.288) over the cabbage.

BREAD &

ENRICHED

DOUGHS

BREAD

Bread-making, for the most part, is something that requires a dose of patience and a little care, but you will be greatly rewarded for your efforts with homemade crusty loaves, fluffy buns, and any number of wonderful baked dough products. Making bread is as much a science as it is a craft and once you are familiar with the various stages—mixing, kneading, rising, shaping, proving, and baking—you'll be able to turn your hand to any type of loaf. Similarly, it pays to get to know your ingredients, principally flour, yeast, salt ,and water.

Wheat flour is the main ingredient in most bread and you'll need "strong" or "bread" flour, which has a higher protein gluten content than most other types of flour and works best with yeasted loaves (see p.312). When the yeast is activated it gives off carbon dioxide gas, which develops the gluten, helping to give the finished baked loaf a risen, open texture. If you have never baked before, be reassured—it's more than possible to create a loaf to be proud of. With that in mind, this chapter starts with the most simple of breads—ones made without yeast.

Storage
Dry ingredients, such as flour and dried forms of yeast, react with moisture and should be stored in a cool, dry cupboard. Keep an eye on the use-by date, which is especially important with yeast since out-of-date packets will hamper the rise of your loaf.

YEAST-FREE YOGURT FLATBREAD

Prep 15 minutes + resting

Cook 10 minutes

Makes 4

Bread made without yeast uses other raising agents, such as baking powder and baking soda. When these leavening agents are mixed with flour and a wet ingredient it creates an instant reaction. The main advantage is that they don't require prolonged kneading and rising—it's perfectly possible to make a delicious meal accompaniment in under an hour.

You'll be amazed at just how simple and easy these light, fluffy flatbreads are to make. The combination of all-purpose flour and baking powder with yogurt creates a rise in next to no time and without the need of yeast. Cooked in a skillet, rather than baked, the heat of the pan causes pockets of air in the flatbreads to expand making them puff up as they cook. Serve them with everything from Baba Ganoush (see p.187) and Slow-Roasted Anchovy & Rosemary Lamb Shoulder (see p.106) to Gilled Sardines with Warm Nduja-Honey Dressing (see p.141).

1½ cups (200g) all-purpose flour, plus extra for dusting
2¼ tsp baking powder
½ cup (150g) plain yogurt
½ tsp salt

1 | Using a wooden spoon, mix the flour, baking powder, yogurt, and salt in a mixing bowl, then bring the dough together with your hands into a ball.

2 | Transfer the dough to a lightly floured work surface and gently and briefly knead for 1–2 minutes, using the palm of your hand to press and push the dough away from you, taking care not to tear it—you're looking for a smoothish ball. The dough should be quite wet, but add a little extra flour if it feels too sticky.

3 | Put the dough back into the cleaned bowl, cover with a kitchen towel, and let rest for 10 minutes. Using a sharp chef's knife, cut the dough into four equal pieces. Put three back into the bowl and re-cover.

4 | Using a rolling pin, roll out one piece of the dough on a lightly floured work surface into a rough, circular-shaped flatbread, about 7 in (18 cm) in diameter and ¼ in (5 mm) thick. Transfer the flatbread to a baking tray, sprinkle with flour, and repeat with the remaining dough pieces.

5 | Heat a heavy-bottomed skillet, large enough to accommodate the flatbread, over high heat for 2 minutes. Place a flatbread into the hot pan and cook for about 1 minute on each side until there are noticeable air bubbles and it is cooked through with some charring in places. Remove from the pan, cover with a kitchen towel to keep it warm, and repeat to make the remaining flatbreads.

TIP

These flatbreads are best eaten as soon as they are cooked. If you do have any leftover breads, wrap them in foil with a splash of water and reheat in an oven preheated to 350°F (180°C) for 10 minutes.

Green onion & Cheddar soda bread

Prep 10 minutes

Cook 40 minutes

Makes 1 loaf

Soda bread is aptly named since baking soda is used as the main raising agent. When combined with moisture and an acidic ingredient, like buttermilk, it creates a chemical reaction that causes the bread to rise when baked. This means it is super quick to make because kneading and a long rising time are not needed. It's best served on the day of making when still warm and slathered with butter. It can also be sliced, put in the freezer, then toasted direct from frozen.

¾ cup (100g) all-purpose flour, plus extra for dusting
2 cups (275g) whole wheat flour
1 tsp salt
1 tsp baking soda
¾ cup (100g) finely grated extra sharp
    Cheddar cheese
3 green onions, green and white part, finely chopped
1¼ cups (300ml) Buttermilk (see p.45) or store-bought

1 | Preheat the oven to 400°F (200°C). Lightly flour a cookie sheet with all-purpose flour.

2 | Mix together both types of flour, the salt, and baking soda in a large mixing bowl with a wooden spoon. Add three-quarters of the cheese and the green onions, stir to combine, then pour in the buttermilk.

3 | Start mixing with the wooden spoon, then once the mixture forms large, shaggy flakes, use clean hands to bring it together into a soft, slightly sticky, but not wet dough. Shape the dough into a round ball (you may need to lightly flour your hands), then place it in the center of the floured cookie sheet.

4 | Using a serrated knife, cut a cross in the center of the loaf, about a third deep—this will help control the rise of the bread and ensure it cooks in the middle.

5 | Sprinkle over the remaining cheese and bake in the center of the oven for 30–40 minutes, until risen and it sounds hollow when the underside is tapped. Leave to cool on a wire rack before serving.

Flavor variations

Oat loaf: for a plain loaf, leave out the green onions and cheese and sprinkle a handful of old fashioned rolled oats over the top of the uncooked loaf before baking.

Sweet currant loaf: replace the green onions and cheese with ½ cup (50g) of currants or golden raisins mixed into the dough, then sprinkle 1 tablespoon of demerara sugar over the top of the loaf before baking.

Making use of leftover bread

It may be preempting things to include tips on using up leftover bread here, but it's worth a reminder that bread is one of our most commonly wasted foods. Yet, there really is no need to throw it away—it freezes well (sliced or whole), and when slightly stale makes fantastic croutons or breadcrumbs (below).

Croutons: preheat the oven to 400°F (200°C). Cut any leftover bread into 1-in (2.5 cm) pieces. Place on a baking sheet and drizzle with olive oil (you want around 1 tablespoon of oil for every 3½oz/100g of bread), season with salt and pepper, toss with your hands, then spread out in a single layer. Bake for 8–10 minutes, turning halfway, until evenly golden and crisp. Croutons are perfect sprinkled over soups and salads, such as the classic Caesar Salad (see p.431) for added crunch.

Breadcrumbs: pulse the slightly stale bread in a food processor to fine or coarse crumbs, depending on preference and the recipe. Use right away or keep in an airtight container in the fridge for up to 3 days or freeze for up to 3 months. The breadcrumbs can be used straight from the fridge or freezer for coating fish, instead of panko in the Crispy Fish Sandwiches (see p.152), as a binder in the Chipotle Black Bean Burgers (see p.276), or fried until crisp and golden (below).

Pangrattato (pictured above): referred to as "poor man's Parmesan" in Italy, these breadcrumbs are fried in olive oil until crisp and golden. They make a delicious crunchy topping for cooked pasta, including spaghetti with Simple Tomato Sauce (see p.422). This version includes fragrant garlic, lemon for freshness, and parsley for a pop of color.

Pulse 3½oz (100g) of slightly stale bread (crusts removed if very hard) in a mini food processor to coarse crumbs. Heat 2 tablespoons of olive oil in a small skillet over medium heat. Add in the breadcrumbs and cook, stirring, for 4–5 minutes, until evenly golden in color.

Move the breadcrumbs to one half of the pan, pour another tablespoon of olive oil into the space left in the pan and add 1 large crushed garlic clove. Cook, stirring, for 30 seconds, then mix the garlic through the breadcrumbs. Turn the heat off under the pan, and stir through 1 bunch of finely chopped flat-leaf parsley and the finely grated zest of 1 unwaxed lemon. Season with salt and pepper to taste and serve right away sprinkled over the top of pasta.

MAKING
YEASTED BREAD

One step on from making flatbread, or non-yeasted bread, is yeasted bread. There are various types of yeast you can use, from natural or wild yeasts found present in the environment, such as those used in the popular sourdough, to commercially made yeast. If you're relying on natural yeasts, then a period of fermentation is needed to create what is called a "starter." It is this process that with time ultimately results in a light, open-textured loaf when baked. However, commercially made yeast, both fresh and dried, is the most controllable type to use in baking.

Fresh yeast comes in a creamy-colored block and gives a more pronounced "yeasty" flavor to breads and pastries (it's prized in croissant-making for this reason), but it's not readily available and has a shorter shelf life than dried. (If a recipe calls for fresh yeast and you want to use dried, simply halve the quantity.) Some types of dried yeast need to be activated in lukewarm water before use, but perhaps the easiest type to use is "instant" dry yeast, which doesn't need rehydrating beforehand—you simply sprinkle it into the dry ingredients and you're good to go.

SIMPLE WHITE
BÂTARD

Prep 20 minutes
+ rising and
proving

Cook 35 minutes

Makes 1 large
loaf

This simple white loaf is a great starting point for baking your first yeasted bread. "Bâtard" refers to the shape of the loaf, which is more oval than the classic round. The same dough can also be used to make the Rosemary & Olive Focaccia (see p.315) and the Skillet Pizzas (see p.316), showing just how versatile it is. It's key to follow the instructions for kneading because this will develop the gluten in the flour and distribute the yeast evenly, resulting in a good rise. Make sure your water is not too hot—you don't want to kill the yeast— it should be lukewarm or tepid, about 72°F (22°C).

3¾ cups (500g) bread flour, plus
    extra for dusting
2 tsp salt
1 tsp instant dry yeast
1½ cups (350ml) lukewarm water
splash of neutral oil, for greasing

1 | **Mixing the dough:** Put the flour, salt, and yeast into a large mixing bowl, stir until combined, then make a well in the center. Pour the lukewarm water into the well. Using clean hands, mix until you have a rough, shaggy dough.

2 | **Kneading the dough:** turn the dough out onto a lightly floured work surface and dust the top with more flour. Using clean hands, bring the dough together into a ball. Knead with a firm steady motion, firmly pressing downward and away from you with the heel of one

hand to stretch it, then lift, fold, and give the dough a quarter turn. Repeat this process of kneading, stretching, folding, and turning for about 5 minutes, until the dough becomes smooth, silky, and elastic. You'll know the dough is ready when it springs back when pressed with a finger.

3 | **Let rise:** put the dough in a clean, lightly oiled bowl; cover with a kitchen towel; and let rise in a warm, draft-free place for 2 hours, until doubled in size and is well-risen and puffy.

4 | **Shaping the dough:** turn the dough out onto a lightly floured work surface. Starting from one side, pinch the dough between your fingers, stretching it out slightly, then fold it back on itself to the center of the ball. Repeat working your way around the dough, turning it 90 degrees each time, and continuing until the dough forms a tight ball.

5 | Flip the dough over so the seam is underneath, then use your hands to gently roll the dough into an oval shape, roughly 8–10 in (20–25 cm) long, with slightly tapered ends.

6 | **Proving the dough:** line a baking sheet with parchment paper, then carefully move the shaped loaf onto it, with the seam underneath. Cover and let prove (final rise) for 1 hour, until risen by half. (Continued overleaf.)

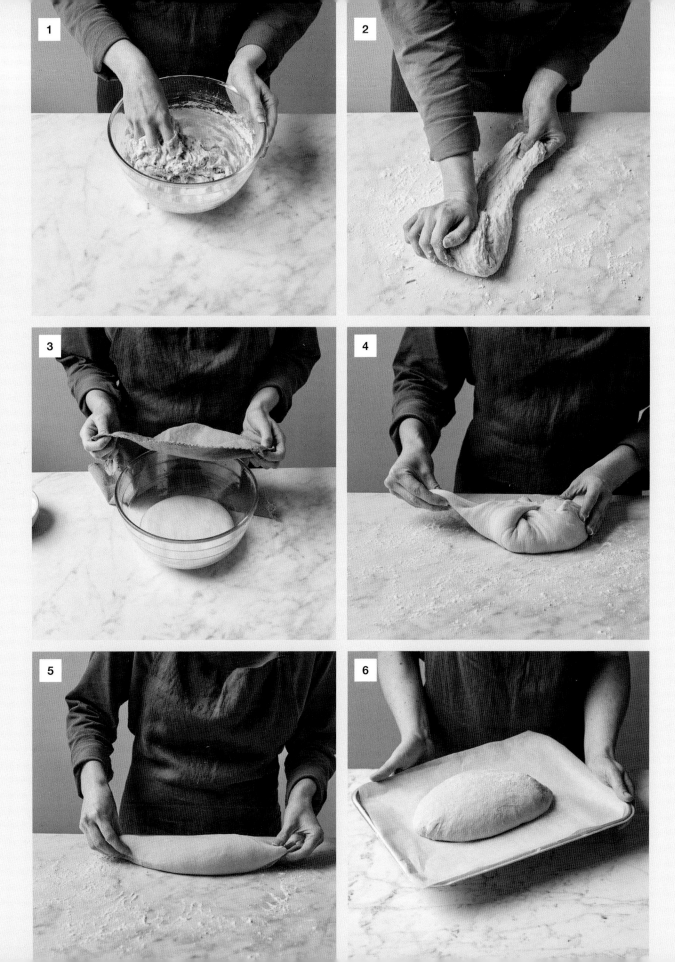

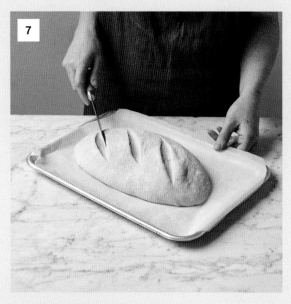

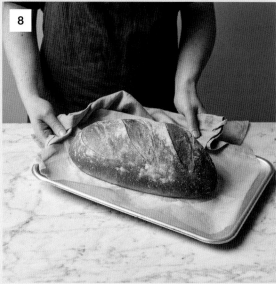

7 | Finishing the dough: Thirty minutes before the dough has finished proving, preheat the oven to 425°F (220°C) and place a thick baking sheet on a rack in the middle of the oven, with nothing above it. Using a small, sharp chef's knife, make three 1¼-in (3-cm) deep diagonal cuts or slashes down the length of the dough.

8 | Baking the bread: Carefully slide the loaf, on its parchment paper, onto the preheated baking sheet in the oven. Bake for 20 minutes, then reduce the oven to 375°F (190°C) and bake for another 15 minutes, until risen, crusty, and golden brown. To tell if your loaf is ready, using a kitchen towel or oven gloves, hold it in one hand and gently tap the underside, it should sound hollow when cooked. If it doesn't, bake the bread for another 5 minutes and check again.

9 | Move the bread to a wire rack and let cool completely before slicing.

TIPS

For a round loaf with a crusty finish, bake the shaped dough in a heavy cast-iron casserole dish or Dutch oven, which mimics a baker's oven. Preheat the dish in the hot oven, then score a cross in the top of the loaf and use the parchment paper to carefully lift it into the hot pan. Cover with the lid and bake for 20 minutes, then remove the lid, turn down the heat, and continue to bake for a further 15 minutes, until golden brown.

Freshly made bread will keep for a few days stored in an airtight bag or container. For the best toast, slice the loaf and put it into a freezer bag, then freeze. Toast the slices straight from frozen.

Try adding different flavors to the bread dough: grated cheese and chives, sesame seeds, poppy seeds—make it your own!

Rosemary
& olive focaccia

*Prep 2 hours +
rising, overnight
proving and
resting*

Cook 35 minutes

Makes 1 loaf

This classic Italian bread is pressed into a shallow pan before baking, resulting in an open-textured, light bread with a crisp, caramelized crust. The amount of water added is slightly higher than the Simple White Bâtard because the dough doesn't need to support itself during baking, thanks to the baking dish, and a wetter dough results in a lighter crumb. Additionally, the dough is stretched and folded in the bowl to build up the gluten, then proved overnight in the fridge. This slows the activity of the yeast, but gives the flavor of the dough more time to develop, making for an incredibly delicious loaf.

1 recipe quantity of Simple White Bâtard dough
  (see p.312)
5 tbsp extra-virgin olive oil, plus extra to grease/finish
2 tsp salt
¾ cup (100g) pitted green olives
4 sprigs of fresh rosemary, leaves stripped
sea salt flakes, for sprinkling

1 | Follow step 1 from Simple White Bâtard (see p.312), increasing the lukewarm water to 1¾ cups (400ml) and adding 2 tablespoons of the olive oil to the yeast mixture. When you have a rough, shaggy dough and the flour has been mixed in, cover the bowl with a kitchen towel and leave at room temperature for 15 minutes.

2 | Lightly dampen your hands with water. With the dough in the bowl, pick up one side of the dough and stretch it vertically, about 6 in (15 cm), taking care not to tear it, then fold the dough over on itself. Turn the bowl 90 degrees and repeat three more times. You'll notice the dough becomes smoother and more uniform as you do this. Cover the bowl and leave for 30 minutes.

3 | Repeat the stretching and folding as above, leaving the dough for 30 minutes, then repeat for a third time. The dough should be smooth and stretchy by this stage. Cover and let rise in a warm place for 2 hours, until doubled in size and bubbly.

4 | Line a 10 x 12 in (30 x 25 cm) shallow baking dish with parchment paper and lightly oil all over. Turn the dough out into the dish and gently press it out to roughly fill the tin in an even layer. Cover tightly with plastic wrap and let prove in the fridge overnight.

5 | The next day, remove the dish from the fridge 2½ hours before baking to let the dough come to room temperature. Preheat the oven to 425°F (220°C). Spoon 2 tablespoons of olive oil over the top of the dough. Using your fingertips, press to make dimples all over the surface of the dough, sprinkle over the olives and rosemary, then drizzle with the remaining 1 tablespoon of oil. Sprinkle over salt and bake for 30–35 minutes, until risen and golden on top. Carefully slide onto a cooling rack to cool.

TIP

If you want to make the focaccia without the overnight prove, once it is in the dish, let it prove in a warm place for 2 hours, until doubled in size, then bake.

Skillet pizzas

Prep 45 minutes
+ rising and
proving

Cook 30 minutes

Makes 4

The crust of these pizzas is made with the same dough as the Simple White Bâtard. However, the method differs in that you initially cook the pizzas in a skillet—the high heat of the stove causes the base to rise and fluff up—then finish them off under a hot broiler to give a bubbling, golden top. Use the largest burner on your stove to ensure an even temperature and crispy crust. With this method, you cook the pizzas one at a time, but it's a great recipe to make with friends—everyone can share the finished pizza while the next one cooks.

1 recipe quantity of Simple White Bâtard dough
   (see p.312)
all-purpose flour, for dusting
1 (14.5oz/400g) can diced tomatoes
2 tsp Italian seasoning
1 (8oz/250g) ball buffalo mozzarella, drained
   and shredded
salt and freshly ground black pepper
1 handful of basil leaves, to finish

Pizza topping of your choice, choose from:
pepperoni
cooked Italian sausage
salami
Roasted Peppers (see p.186) or store-bought
thinly sliced garlic cloves
finely grated Parmesan cheese

1 | Follow steps 1–4 for mixing, kneading, and rising the dough from Simple White Bâtard (see p.312).

2 | Lightly flour the work surface and divide the dough into 4 equal pieces. Placing your hand over one piece of dough, roll it in a circle on the spot until it forms a tight ball. Repeat with the remaining pieces of dough.

3 | Lightly flour a baking sheet, then put the dough balls onto it, leaving about 2½ in (6 cm) between each one to allow for them to rise. Cover with a kitchen towel and let prove in a warm draft-free place for 2 hours, until doubled in size and puffy.

4 | To make the sauce, put the diced tomatoes and Italian seasoning into a small bowl, then season well with salt and pepper.

5 | Put one piece of dough on a lightly floured work surface and use your flattened fingers to press the dough out to an even round. Pick the dough up, then turn, stretch, and press it into a circle about 10 in (25 cm) in diameter. Repeat with the remaining pieces of dough.

6 | Heat a large, ovenproof skillet over high heat. Preheat the broiler to high with the rack at the top of the oven.

7 | Once the skillet is really hot, carefully place one of the pizza bases into the pan, then spoon over 4–5 dessert spoons of the tomato sauce, spreading it out evenly, leaving a 1¼-in (3-cm) border around the edge. Sprinkle the mozzarella and your choice of fillings over the sauce. Cook for 2 minutes on the stove, until the dough has puffed up and the underside is golden and cooked.

8 | Put the skillet under the broiler for 4–5 minutes, until the top is golden and bubbling. Slide the pizza out onto a cutting board, sprinkle with basil and cut into slices. Carefully wipe the skillet clean with paper towel and repeat with the remaining dough and toppings.

TIPS

You can make the dough up to 2 days in advance, follow the method up to the end of step 3, then chill until ready to use. Alternatively, freeze the uncooked dough for up to 3 months.

To use from frozen, simply defrost in the fridge overnight, then bring the dough back up to room temperature and follow from step 4 onward.

HOMEMADE BAO BUNS

*Prep 30 minutes
+ rising and
proving*

Cook 30 minutes

Makes 12–14

These light, fluffy buns originate from Taiwan and are steamed rather than baked to give them a soft, almost marshmallowy, texture. After steaming, the bao can be filled with anything from slow-cooked, savory meat or vegetables to shredded hoisin chicken and Quick Pickled Cucumbers (see p.459).

¼ cup (50ml) whole milk, heated until lukewarm
1 tsp sugar
½ cup (125ml) lukewarm water
1 tbsp vegetable oil
½ tbsp rice vinegar
2¼ cups (300g) all-purpose flour, plus extra for dusting
½ tsp salt
½ tsp instant dry yeast
½ tsp baking powder
cooking oil spray

1 | Pour the lukewarm milk into a bowl with the sugar, lukewarm water, vegetable oil, and rice vinegar, and whisk with a fork until combined. Add the flour, salt, and yeast into a large mixing bowl, stir until combined, then make a well in the center. Pour the milk mixture into the well. Using clean hands, mix until you have a rough, shaggy dough. Knead and let the dough rise following steps 2–4 from Simple White Bâtard (see p.312). Turn the risen dough out onto a lightly floured work surface. Dust the dough with flour and roll it out evenly until about ¾ in (2 cm) thick. Sprinkle the surface of the dough with the baking powder.

2 | Using a 3½-in (8-cm) round cutter (a wine glass also works well), stamp out 8 disks of dough.

3 | Spray the surface of each disk evenly with the cooking oil (or lightly brush the surface using an oiled pastry brush).

4 | Cut eight 4-in (10-cm) squares out of parchment paper. Carefully fold each dough circle in half into a half-moon shape, then move onto a parchment paper square and let prove for 30 minutes, until risen and puffy.

5 | Set a steamer basket over a pan or wok of gently simmering water. Lift the bao buns, still on their paper squares, into the steamer basket, leaving enough space between each one to expand—you will need to cook them in batches. Cover with the lid and steam for 8–10 minutes, until puffed up and risen. Repeat until all the bao are cooked.

6 | Remove each bao from the steamer and carefully prize the bun open slightly in the middle. They are now ready for filling (below).

Hoisin chicken bao filling

2 tbsp vegetable oil
10oz (300g) leftover roast chicken, shredded
  (see p.85) or store-bought
3 tbsp hoisin sauce
salt and freshly ground black pepper

To serve

4 tbsp Mayonnaise (see p.420) or store-bought
Quick Pickled Cucumbers (see p.459), sliced
1 handful of cilantro leaves
½ cup (50g) salted peanuts, roughly chopped

1 | Heat the vegetable oil in a large skillet over medium-high heat. Add the chicken and stir-fry for 5 minutes, until starting to crisp up and piping hot.

2 | Remove the pan from the heat and add the hoisin along with 3 tablespoons of water to make a sauce. Season with salt and pepper to taste.

3 | To fill the bao, squeeze a little mayonnaise into each opened steamed bun and add a spoonful of the chicken filling, some cucumber, and a few cilantro leaves. Finish with a sprinkling of chopped peanuts.

TIPS

The Teriyaki Tofu (see p.280) makes a great filling for the bao buns.

The bao buns will keep covered in an airtight container for up to 2 days; simply reheat in a microwave to serve.

BAGELS

Prep 40 minutes
+ rising and
proving

Cook 25 minutes

Makes 8

Bagels are traditionally poached before baking, which gives them their characteristic dense, chewy texture and thin, caramel-colored crust. The ring-shaped rolls are perfect for spreading with cream cheese and filling with Beet & Orange Cured Salmon (see p.134).

1 recipe quantity of Simple White Bâtard dough
  (see p.312), using 2 tsp instant dry yeast
1 tbsp honey
all-purpose flour, for dusting
1½ cups (350ml) lukewarm water
1 tbsp baking soda
1 large egg, at room temperature, lightly
  beaten
4 tbsp sesame or poppy seeds

1 | Follow steps 1–4 from Simple White Bâtard (see p.312), increasing the instant dry yeast to 2 teaspoons and adding the honey to the lukewarm water, and then mix, knead, and let the dough rise until doubled in size. Turn the dough out onto a lightly floured work surface and cut into 8 equal pieces. Using one hand, take a piece of dough and roll it in a circle on the same spot until it forms a tight ball. Repeat with the remaining pieces of dough.

2 | Lightly flour the handle of a wooden spoon, then poke it through the center of the dough ball to make a hole. Flour 2 large baking sheets.

3 | Flour your hands and gently pick up one piece of dough. Put your index fingers from both hands through the hole, then gently turn them round to stretch the hole until it is about 1¼–1½ in (3–4 cm) wide. Place it gently on the floured sheet and repeat with the remaining pieces of dough.

4 | Preheat the oven to 425°F (220°C). Bring a large, wide saucepan of water to a boil and add the baking soda. Turn the heat down to a simmer, carefully add 4 bagels and cook for 1 minute on each side, until puffed up slightly. Meanwhile, line 2 baking sheets with parchment paper. Using a slotted spoon, carefully remove the bagels from the pan and place them on the lined baking sheets. Repeat with the remaining 4 bagels, then leave for 10 minutes to steam dry.

5 | Brush the top of each bagel with beaten egg, then sprinkle over the seeds.

6 | Bake the bagels for 15–18 minutes, until light golden brown, then place on a wire rack to cool before serving.

TIP

The bagels will keep fresh for a day or so, any spare can be frozen. If they are going to be toasted once defrosted, slice them in half before freezing. Defrost the bagels for 30 minutes at room temperature.

ENRICHED DOUGH

This type of yeast-based bread dough is "enriched" through the addition of milk, cream, or eggs, giving the finished product a more luxurious, richer taste and softer, finer, almost cake-like crumb. This type of dough particularly suits sweeter breads, such as Brioche (below) and Cinnamon Buns (see p.324).

For all enriched dough recipes, a kitchen stand mixer is recommended, because the added fat or eggs make them stickier and more difficult to handle than regular bread dough. They may also need a longer kneading and rising time because the fat can slow down the gluten in the flour needed for a good rise.

BRAIDED BRIOCHE LOAF

Prep 45 minutes + rising and proving

Cook 30 minutes

Makes 1 loaf

The pinnacle of enriched doughs, made with generous amounts of butter and eggs, the classic French brioche should be deep golden on the outside and have a light, tender, cake-like crumb when baked. Instant dry yeast is used here for convenience. You'll need a large loaf pan, about 8–10 in (20–25 cm) in length.

¼ cup (50ml) whole milk
2 cups (250g) bread flour, plus extra for dusting
2 tbsp sugar
1 tsp salt
2 tsp instant dry yeast
3 large eggs, at room temperature
10 tbsp (150g) salted butter, cut into cubes and softened, plus extra, melted, for greasing the pan
splash of neutral oil

1 | Gently warm the milk in a small saucepan or microwave until lukewarm—you want it to be about body temperature.

2 | Put the flour, sugar, salt, and yeast into the bowl of a stand mixer fitted with a dough hook and mix briefly. Pour in the lukewarm milk and crack in 2 of the eggs. Crack the remaining egg into a small bowl and lightly beat with a fork. Pour half of the beaten egg into the stand mixer. (Cover the rest with plastic wrap and keep at room temperature for brushing on top of the loaf before baking.)

3 | Mix on a low speed for 2 minutes, then increase the speed to medium and mix for 10 minutes, until a smooth dough forms. With the mixer running, add the butter, a cube at a time, and mix well until incorporated before adding the next cube. It should take 3–4 minutes to add all of the butter, then mix again for 5 minutes, until a shiny, smooth dough forms.

4 | Turn the dough out into a clean, lightly oiled bowl, cover with a kitchen towel, and let rise in a warm, draft-free place for 2 hours, until doubled in size and puffy.

5 | When risen, turn the dough out onto a lightly floured work surface and cut into 3 equal pieces. Roll each piece into a log the same length as your loaf pan, about 8–10 in (20–25 cm).

6 | To braid the dough, place the 3 rolled-out pieces vertically on a lightly floured work surface and press them together at the top to join. Cross the right-hand strand over the strand in the middle, then cross the left-hand strand over the middle strand. Repeat, braiding the dough until you reach the end, then press the strands together to join at the bottom.

7 | Lightly brush the inside of a large loaf pan with melted butter. Carefully but confidently lift the braided dough into the loaf pan, cover loosely with a kitchen towel and let prove in a warm place until doubled in size and puffy, about 1½ hours.

8 | Preheat the oven to 400°F (200°C). When ready to bake, lightly brush the top of the brioche with the reserved beaten egg and bake for 10 minutes. Turn the oven down to 350°F (180°C) and bake for another 20 minutes, until risen and deeply golden. Remove from the oven and turn out of the pan onto a wire rack to cool.

Burger bun variation

To make burger buns, follow steps 1–4 (left), then turn the dough out onto a lightly floured work surface and divide into 10 pieces. Roll each piece into a tight ball following step 2 from Skillet Pizzas (see p.316). Place on parchment-paper-lined baking sheets and let prove for 2 hours, until well-risen and puffy. Brush the top of each bun with beaten egg and sprinkle over sesame or poppy seeds, if you like. Bake at 400°F (200°C) for 15–18 minutes, until risen, golden, and cooked through. Leave to cool on a wire rack.

CINNAMON/ CARDAMOM BUNS

Prep 45 minutes + rising and proving

Cook 20 minutes

Makes 12

A classic Nordic bake, these fragrant, soft buns are slightly gooey and soft in the middle thanks to a layer of spice-infused, sweet butter. The dough is enriched with butter, milk, and eggs, which gives a soft, fine-textured crumb. The trick is in the shaping: the dough is twisted to expose some of the spiced butter so the sugar caramelizes slightly and the spices infuse the dough. Demerara sugar with its large crystals makes a nice topping if you have it. Turbinado—or raw sugar—works well too.

1 cup (250ml) whole milk
4 tbsp (50g) salted butter, cut into cubes
3¾ cups (500g) bread flour, plus extra for dusting
2 tbsp sugar
1 tsp salt, plus a pinch for the filling
1 tsp instant dry yeast
2 large eggs, at room temperature, plus
  1 yolk for glazing
¼ cup (50g) demerara or turbinado sugar

For the spiced-butter filling
6 tbsp (75g) salted butter, softened
⅓ cup (75g) packed light brown sugar
1½ tbsp ground cinnamon or ground cardamom

1 | Gently heat the milk and butter in a small saucepan, until the butter just melts. It should feel lukewarm to the touch, but not hot. Put the flour, sugar, salt, and yeast into the bowl of a stand mixer fitted with a dough hook and mix briefly. Pour in the lukewarm milk mixture and crack in 2 eggs. Mix on a low speed for 2 minutes, then increase the speed to medium and mix for a further 6–8 minutes, until a smooth, shiny dough forms.

2 | Scrape down the sides of the bowl, cover with a kitchen towel and let rise in a warm, draft-free place for 2 hours, until doubled in size and puffy. While the dough is rising, make the spiced-butter filling. Put the softened butter into a medium mixing bowl and beat well with a wooden spoon. Add the sugar and your choice of spice with a pinch of salt and beat until smooth and creamy.

3 | Once the dough has risen, gently turn it out onto a lightly floured work surface, making sure you have enough space to roll it out into a large rectangle. Dust the top of the dough with flour, then use a rolling pin to roll the dough out to a rectangle, about 14x 22 in (55 x 35 cm) with one of the longer sides facing you.

4 | Spoon the softened spiced butter on top of the dough and use a spatula to spread it into an even layer. Starting from the left-hand side, fold a third of the dough over itself, then repeat on the right-hand side, folding it on top, like a letter, so you have a rectangle of dough with 3 layers.

5 | Turn the dough around so one of the long sides is facing you and use the rolling pin to gently roll and seal the edges of the dough, then cut it vertically into 12 (1¼-in/3-cm) wide strips.

6 | Line 2–3 large baking sheets with parchment paper. Take one strip of dough and, holding both ends, gently stretch until almost doubled in length, then twist it 3–4 times so you have a loose spiral.

7 | Holding one end of the strip, coil it tightly into a spiral to create a round bun, then tuck the far end underneath, pressing it to stick. Place it on one of the lined baking sheets and repeat with the rest of the strips of dough, leaving a 1½-in (4-cm) gap between each bun to allow for spreading. Cover the trays with kitchen towels and let prove for 1 hour, until well-risen and puffy.

8 | Preheat the oven to 375°F (190°C). Lightly beat the remaining egg yolk in a small bowl and use a pastry brush to glaze the top of the buns, then sprinkle with the sugar. Bake for 18–20 minutes, until risen and evenly golden.

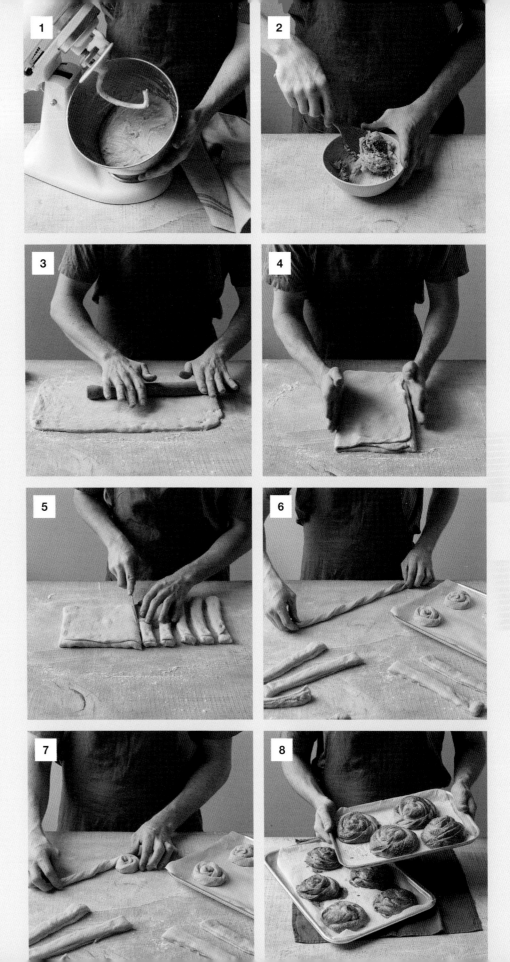

PASTRY

&

BATTERS

PASTRY

Homemade pastry is hard to beat when well made; its crisp, buttery texture crumbles, flakes, and melts in the mouth and is pretty irresistible. This is all the more remarkable considering basic pastry dough is made from just three simple ingredients: flour, fat, and water. While pastry-making may appear daunting, by following a few simple rules and with a little attention to detail, you'll find it a satisfying and rewarding technique to master.

Before you start, try to buy the best-quality ingredients you can afford and make sure you measure them accurately. One of the most important things to remember, relevant to all types of pastry, from sweet and savory pie crust to the more elaborate puff pastry, is to not overwork the dough, which can make it tough. Ideally, handle the dough gently, working quickly and lightly. Equally crucial is to allow the pastry adequate time for chilling and resting because these make the dough easier to handle and will help avoid shrinkage during baking. Heat is the enemy when making pastry, so ideally work in a cool kitchen using ice-cold water, chilled butter, and with cold hands!

Storage
Homemade pastry will keep wrapped in the fridge for 1–2 days, or freeze for up to 6 months.

MAKING SHORTCRUST PASTRY

Prep 15 minutes by hand or 5 minutes in a processor + chilling

No cook

Makes about 14oz (400g)

The term "shortcrust" refers to the texture of the pastry, which is slightly crumbly, rather than flaky. Shortcrust is the perfect base for savory tarts, quiches, and flans and, if you are someone who doesn't like things too sugary, you can also use it for sweet tarts—it works really well with a chocolate filling for a salty-sweet combo. Although, there is also a recipe for sweet shortcrust (below). The methods for both are similar and they can be prepared by hand or in a food processor—either way they make great beginning recipes if you've never made pastry before.

2 cups (250g) all-purpose flour, plus extra for dusting
pinch of salt
9 tbsp (140g) cold salted butter, cut into small cubes
2–4 tbsp ice-cold water

1 | If making the pastry by hand, sift the flour and salt into a large bowl and add the butter. Rub the cubes of butter between the tips of your fingers and thumbs into the flour. Pull the flour up as you work in the butter to aerate it and continue until the mixture resembles coarse sand or breadcrumbs.

2 | Sprinkle 2 tablespoons of the ice-cold water over the top of the flour mixture and stir it in with a table knife to bring the pastry together into a rough, scraggy ball. If the dough looks a little dry, add a splash more of the ice-cold water and mix again. It is important to add just enough water to bring the dough together but not make it too wet.

3 | Turn the dough out onto a work surface and use your hands to bring it together into a smoothish ball, working it gently.

4 | Flatten the dough slightly into a disk, wrap in plastic wrap, and let it rest in the fridge for 30 minutes before using.

Sweet shortcrust variation
Follow steps 1–4 from Making Shortcrust Pastry, choosing either the hand or food processor method (right), adding 2 tablespoons of sifted powdered sugar with the all-purpose flour, salt, and butter. Reduce the quantity of ice-cold water to 1 teaspoon and add to the rubbed-in butter mixture 1 large egg yolk, at room temperature. If the pastry looks a little dry, add a splash more water until the dough comes together into a ball.

TIPS

Once made, the pastry will keep, covered, in the fridge for up to 2 days or freeze for up to 3 months, defrosting it in the fridge before use. The pastry will require a light kneading with your hands to soften before being rolled out.

You can also make the pastry in a food processor. Add the flour, salt, and butter to the food processor and pulse until the mixture resembles coarse breadcrumbs. Add 2 tablespoons of the ice-cold water and pulse again until the pastry just comes together (you probably won't need the rest of the water). Shape the dough into a ball, then flatten it into a disk, wrap, and chill for 30 minutes before using.

LINING A TART PAN
& BAKING BLIND

*Prep 30 minutes
+ chilling*

Cook 35 minutes

*Makes 10 in
(25 cm) lined
tart pan*

The recipe for Shortcrust Pastry (see p.328) makes the right amount to line a 10-in (25-cm) loose-bottomed fluted tart pan, although you can use this method for any size of pie or tart pan—simply roll the correct amount of dough out to a circle 2 in (5 cm) larger than the pan. You'll need a few other kitchen essentials, including a rolling pin, parchment paper, and pie weights or dried rice/beans. Before rolling, it is important to chill the pastry first to make it easier to handle as well as chilling it after lining the pan to let it rest. The crust is blind-baked, which means it is completely cooked before the filling is added to ensure the crust is baked through.

1 recipe quantity of Shortcrust Pastry (sweet
   or savory), chilled (see p.328)
all-purpose flour, for dusting
pie weights or dried rice/beans

1 | Follow steps 1–4 from Making Shortcrust Pastry (see p.328). After the pastry has chilled for 30 minutes, lightly dust the work surface and your rolling pin with flour. Roll the pastry into a large circle using gentle pressure until it is about ¼ in (5 mm) thick and 12 in (30 cm) in diameter. Occasionally, give the pastry a quarter turn to shape it into an even round and dust the work surface with a little more flour to stop it sticking.

2 | To lift the pastry into the 10 in (25 cm) loose-bottomed fluted tart pan, lightly fold the sides of the circle into the middle so you have a rough rectangle shape. Place the folded pastry into the base of the pan, using the rolling pin to help if needed, then carefully unfold the sides, one at a time.

3 | Press the pastry evenly into the base and up the sides of the pan, leaving a 1¼–2-in (3–5-cm) overhang.

4 | Trim the overhang slightly with scissors, leaving ½–¾ in (1–2 cm) to allow for any shrinkage during blind baking—you can remove the excess before adding the filling. Use any surplus pastry to patch up any little tears, or keep it in the fridge to repair any holes after blind baking. Prick the base of the pastry all over with a fork and chill in the fridge for 20 minutes.

5 | Meanwhile, preheat the oven to 400°F (200°C). Cut a round of parchment paper slightly larger than the diameter of the tart pan and crumple it into a ball. Unravel the ball and place it in the chilled crust so it lines the base and goes up the sides. Fill the lined crust three-quarters full with pie weights or dried rice/beans.

6 | Put the tart pan onto a baking sheet in the center of the oven and bake for 20 minutes, until the overhanging pastry is pale golden.

7 | Lift out the parchment paper and weights. Patch up any little holes, if there are any, with the reserved pastry, then return the pastry crust to the oven for 10–12 minutes, until the base is golden brown and the crust is cooked.

8 | Using a large chef's knife, cut away any remaining overhanging pastry—your crust is now ready for filling and baking or can be left to cool.

TIPS

Ceramic pie weights last for years. Let them cool and store in an airtight container. If you can't find pie weights, uncooked rice or dried beans work just as well.

If the weather is hot, you may need to extend the chilling time by 10 minutes before baking, or place the crust in the freezer instead.

You can bake the crust the day before filling. Leave the baked crust to cool, and wrap in plastic wrap until ready to use.

Broccoli, hazelnut & Cheddar quiche

Prep 45 minutes + chilling and baking blind

Cook 35 minutes

Serves 8

This tart has a shortcrust pastry crust and a savory custard filling, which is baked at a low temperature until just set. The filling is a play on the classic broccoli and cheese soup but you could also try Caramelized Onions (see p.194) or smoky bacon and Gruyère for a take on the classic quiche Lorraine.

1 recipe quantity of Shortcrust Pastry (see p.328)
1 small broccoli head, cut into medium florets and stalk roughly chopped
1½ tbsp olive oil
salt and freshly ground black pepper
3 large eggs, at room temperature
⅔ cup (150ml) whole milk
⅔ cup (150ml) heavy cream
good grating of fresh nutmeg
¼ cup (30g) hazelnuts, toasted (see p.288) and roughly chopped
5½oz (150g) Cheddar cheese, shredded
crisp salad leaves, to serve (optional)

1 | Follow steps 1–4 from Making Shortcrust Pastry (see p.328).

2 | Follow steps 1–8 from Lining a Tart Pan & Baking Blind (see p.330).

3 | While the crust is blind-baking, put the broccoli florets in a roasting tray, toss with the olive oil, and season with salt and pepper. Spread the broccoli out in a single layer so it roasts evenly. Once you remove the blind-baked pastry from the oven, keep the oven on and roast the broccoli for 20 minutes until tender and a little charred. Let cool.

4 | Once the crust and broccoli are cooked, turn the oven down to 325°F (160°C).

5 | Crack the eggs into a large bowl, add the milk and cream, then whisk well with a fork until fully combined—you want to make sure there are no lumps of egg white left. Season generously with salt and pepper and a good grating of nutmeg.

6 | To fill the cooled crust, add the roasted broccoli, half the hazelnuts, and three-quarters of the cheese, then pour over the egg mixture. Top with the remaining cheese and hazelnuts. Carefully transfer the tart pan, still on the baking sheet, to the oven and bake for 35 minutes, until the filling is just set with a slight wobble in the center.

7 | Transfer the quiche to a wire rack and let cool slightly. You can serve the quiche slightly warm, at room temperature, or cold from the fridge, depending on preference. Cut it into 8 slices and serve with a crisp salad.

TIP

The quiche will keep for up to 5 days in the fridge once cool. If serving warm, reheat in a 350°F (180°C) oven for 10 minutes.

Lemon tart

Prep 40 minutes
+ chilling and
baking blind

Cook 35 minutes

Serves 8–10

The light, tangy filling is the perfect foil to the sweet, buttery crust. It's best to bake the lemon tart low and slow to ensure the filling remains slightly soft and creamy, then remove it from the oven before it is completely set. Enjoy the tart on the day of making with a good spoonful of whipped cream and a dusting of powdered sugar.

1 recipe quantity of Sweet Shortcrust Pastry
  (see p.328)
6 large eggs, at room temperature
3 large egg yolks, at room temperature (see p.32
  on Separating Eggs)
pinch of salt
1 cup (225g) sugar
finely grated zest of 3 unwaxed lemons
juice of 6 lemons (about ½ cup/120ml)
1¼ cups (300ml) heavy cream
1–2 tbsp powdered sugar and whipped cream,
  to serve

1 | Follow the method for making Sweet Shortcrust Pastry (see p.328).

2 | Follow steps 1–8 from Lining a Tart Pan & Baking Blind (see p.330).

3 | While the crust is cooling, turn the oven down to 275°F (140°C).

4 | Crack the whole eggs into a large mixing bowl, add the egg yolks, salt, sugar, lemon zest, juice, and cream. Whisk well with a balloon whisk until thoroughly combined—you want a smooth custard aside from the bits of lemon zest.

5 | Working near the oven, pour the filling into the cooked crust, then carefully put the pan, still on the baking sheet, in the center of the oven. Bake for 35 minutes, until the outer two-thirds of the custard is set but the central part still has a slight wobble.

6 | Let the tart cool completely in the pan on a wire rack. Once cool, remove the sides of the tart tin, if applicable, then dust the top with powdered sugar, sifting it through a fine mesh strainer. Cut the tart into 8–10 slices and serve with a spoonful of whipped cream.

TIP

The lemon tart will keep for up to 5 days in the fridge, although the filling will become firmer once chilled. It is important to cool the tart at room temperature before putting it in the fridge because this will help prevent the top from cracking.

MAKING EASY
PUFF PASTRY

*Prep 40 minutes
+ chilling*

No cook

*Makes about
1lb 2oz (500g)*

*This is the quick-and-easy sister to puff pastry.
With both types of pastry, the butter is layered
throughout the dough so as it bakes the water in
the butter evaporates giving you risen, puffed layers.
When making puff pastry you use large slabs of
butter, while with this easy puff pastry small pieces
are incorporated into the dough through rolling and
folding. This makes the dough much easier to
handle and the margin for success much better.
As with most handmade pastry, temperature is key.
Make sure the butter is frozen before starting, that you
use ice-cold water, and ideally it's not a hot day! The
white wine vinegar in the dough helps with the texture,
making for a delicious flaky pastry that melts in the
mouth once baked.*

2 cups (250g) all-purpose flour, plus extra for dusting
½ tsp salt
½ cup plus 6 tbsp (200g) salted butter, frozen
¼ cup plus 2 tbsp (75ml) ice-cold water
2 tsp white wine vinegar

1 | Sift the flour into a mixing bowl with the salt and
mix briefly to combine. Using a box grater, coarsely
grate the butter into the flour, then toss with a table
knife to coat each piece in the flour.

2 | Pour the ice-cold water into the bowl with the
vinegar. Mix briefly with a table knife to bring it
together into clumps, then turn the dough out onto the
work surface and knead briefly to form into smooth
ball, adding a splash more water if it's too dry.

3 | Lightly dust the work surface and the dough with
flour, then roll it out to a rectangle, about 10 x 14 in
(35 x 25 cm).

4 | With one of the short sides of pastry facing you,
fold the bottom third up over itself, then fold the top
third down, like a letter. Press with the rolling pin to
gently seal the edges, then cover and chill for 1 hour.

5 | Turn the pastry 90 degrees, then roll it out again
into a 10 x 14 in (35 x 25 cm) rectangle. Repeat the
letter fold, folding the right side a third of the way
over the left, then the left over the top, pressing
to gently seal the edges. Cover and chill the pastry
for another hour.

6 | Repeat for a third time, turning the dough
90 degrees and rolling and folding the pastry,
as step 4, then cover and chill for a further hour.
Turn the dough 90 degrees and repeat as step 5.
The pastry should by now be smooth and even,
with no noticeable lumps of butter. (If not, repeat
the folding and chilling step once more.) Wrap the
pastry in plastic wrap and store in the fridge until ready
to use—it will keep for up to 2 days.

TIP

*The pastry can be frozen for up
to 6 months. Defrost in the fridge
overnight before use.*

Pork & chili jam sausage rolls

Prep 1 hour 10 minutes + chilling

Cook 30 minutes

Makes 12

Easy puff pastry is perfect for these lightly spiced, herby, meaty sausage rolls. When baked, the pastry becomes crisp and flaky on the outside while caramelizing with the pork on the bottom. The key to this recipe is to keep the pastry as cold as possible when you work with it, which will make the filling, rolling, and folding so much easier to handle.

1 recipe quantity of Easy Puff Pastry (see p.334)
2½ tbsp fennel seeds
1¼lb (600g) ground pork
4 tbsp chili jam
8 sprigs of fresh thyme, leaves picked
salt and freshly ground black pepper
1 tsp vegetable or olive oil
all-purpose flour, for dusting
2 large eggs, at room temperature, lightly beaten
2 tbsp sesame seeds

1 | Follow steps 1–6 from making Easy Puff Pastry (see p.334).

2 | Heat a small, dry skillet over medium-high heat and toast the fennel seeds for 1–2 minutes, tossing the pan occasionally, until fragrant. Put the seeds into a large mixing bowl and let cool for 2 minutes.

3 | Add the ground pork to the bowl with the chili jam and thyme and season with plenty of salt and pepper. Mix well with your hands until evenly combined.

4 | To check the seasoning, heat the oil in the skillet, add 1 teaspoon of the pork mixture and cook over medium heat for 1 minute on each side until browned. Allow to cool slightly before tasting, then add more salt and pepper to the uncooked pork mixture, if needed.

5 | Cut the puff pastry into two even-size pieces. Wrap and chill one of the pieces while you work with the other.

6 | Lightly flour the work surface and roll one half of the pastry into a rectangle, about 9½ x 12 in (30 x 24 cm). Cut the pastry in half to make 2 long rectangles, measuring 5 x 12 in (30 x 12 cm), with one of the long sides nearest you.

7 | Take a quarter of the ground pork mixture and form it into a long sausage shape down the middle of the pastry rectangle, leaving a border on either side. Brush the top edge of the pastry with a little of the beaten egg.

8 | Starting from the side nearest you, fold the pastry over the pork filling to encase it and roll it over toward the beaten egg side. Gently form it into a long sausage shape with your hands with the pastry seam underneath. Line a baking sheet with parchment paper.

9 | Repeat with the other strip of pastry and another quarter of the pork mixture. Cut each long roll into 3 even-size pieces, so you have 6 sausage rolls in total. Make 3 diagonal cuts on the top of each sausage roll, to allow the steam to escape when baking, then place on the lined baking sheet. Brush the top of each one with egg and sprinkle with the sesame seeds.

10 | Chill in the fridge on the baking sheet and repeat with the other half of pastry and the remaining pork mixture to make 12 sausage rolls in total.

11 | Preheat the oven to 400°F (200°C). Bake the sausage rolls for 25–30 minutes, until the pastry is deeply golden and the filling cooked through. Serve warm or at room temperature.

TIP

You can freeze the unbaked sausage rolls on a baking sheet, then transfer to containers and keep frozen for up to 3 months. Cook them straight from frozen—they will need an extra 10 minutes in the oven.

CHOUX PASTRY

Prep 10 minutes

Cook 5 minutes

Makes enough for 30–32 profiteroles or 16 éclairs

Choux is one of the easiest types of pastry to make because it doesn't need careful handling or chilling since it is not as effected by temperature as other types of pastry dough. This enriched pastry, made with the addition of butter and eggs, is used to make classic French Profiteroles and éclairs (see p.340). Unlike other types of pastry, its high water content helps it puff up as it almost steam/bakes in the oven. You can use all-purpose or bread flour to make the dough—all-purpose gives a softer pastry, whereas bread flour, with its higher gluten content, makes for a crisper shell, perfect for filling with cream and Crème Pâtissière (see p.388).

¾ cup (100g) bread flour
pinch of salt
6 tbsp (75g) salted butter, cut into cubes
3 large eggs, at room temperature, lightly beaten

1 | Sift the flour and salt into a medium mixing bowl.

2 | Heat the butter in a small saucepan with ¾ cup (200ml) of water over medium heat until the butter melts and the water is just boiling, then immediately remove the pan from the heat (you don't want too much of the water to evaporate).

3 | Quickly add the flour to the pan, beating vigorously with a wooden spoon to form a smooth, lump-free dough—it should start to come away from the sides of the pan.

4 | Leave the dough in the pan for 2–3 minutes, until slightly cooled. Gradually, pour a quarter of the eggs into the dough, vigorously beating with a wooden spoon.

5 | Once the first batch of egg has been incorporated, add the next quarter, again beating until mixed in. Continue to add the egg (you may not need all of it), until the dough is a shiny, smooth, soft consistency. It is ready when a spoonful of the dough reluctantly drops off the spoon.

6 | The choux pastry is now ready to use to make Profiteroles (see p.340) or as liked.

TIPS

To avoid the choux pastry cracking during baking, it is important to add the flour quickly and beat vigorously to incorporate.

Make sure you leave the dough to cool slightly before beating in the eggs because you don't want them to scramble. This can also affect the rise of the choux in the oven.

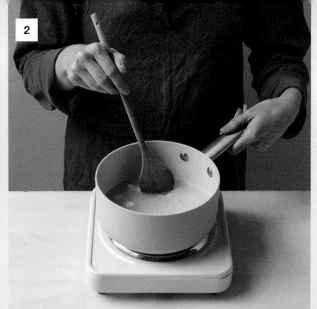

Profiteroles

Prep 40 minutes + cooling

Cook 40 minutes

Makes 30–32

These light, crisp buns of choux pastry are filled with whipped cream or Crème Pâtissière (see p.396) and topped with a rich chocolate ganache for the ultimate decadent mouthful. Don't be intimidated by the number of steps—this recipe is straightforward to make, it just requires a little time and some fun filling. You will need 2 large piping bags.

1 recipe quantity of Choux Pastry (see p.338)
1 recipe quantity of Crème Pâtissière (see p.396) or sweetened cream (see Tip, below)
⅔ cup (140ml) heavy cream
3½oz (100g) plain chocolate (about 70% cocoa solids), chopped into small pieces
pinch of sea salt flakes (optional)

1 | Preheat the oven to 400°F (200°C). Line 2 large baking sheets with parchment paper.

2 | Follow steps 1–5 from Choux Pastry (see p.338).

3 | Spoon the dough into a large piping bag and snip off the end with scissors to create a hole, around ½ in (2 cm) in diameter. Leaving a 1½-in (4-cm) gap between each profiterole to allow for spreading, pipe cherry-tomato-size balls of dough, about 1¼ in/3 cm in diameter, onto the lined baking sheets. The dough should make 30–32 profiteroles in total.

4 | Using a damp finger (it's useful to have a small cup or bowl of cold water on hand), smooth out any dimples on the top of each profiterole, then transfer to the oven and bake for 25–30 minutes, until puffed up, crisp, and deeply golden. A good indicator that they are ready is that they no longer stick to the parchment paper, but do not open the oven door before 25 minutes is up because this can cause them to collapse.

5 | Turn the profiteroles upside down and use a skewer or the handle end of a teaspoon to make a ¼-in (5-mm) hole in the base of each one. Return the choux to the oven, upside down, for a further 3–5 minutes, until the insides have dried out. Transfer the profiteroles to a wire rack, flat-side down, and let cool.

6 | Follow steps 1–5 to make the Crème Pâtissière (see p.396) or use whipping cream (see Tip, below). Spoon it into the second piping bag. Snip the end with scissors (you don't need to have a piping nozzle but may find it easier to use a ½-in/1-cm plain round one). Insert the end of the piping bag into the hole made in one of the profiteroles and fill with your choice of filling, gently squeezing the piping bag as you fill. Place the filled profiterole on the wire rack and repeat.

7 | Once the profiteroles are filled, make the ganache. Warm the heavy cream in a small saucepan over medium heat until just steaming, then pour it over the chopped chocolate in a bowl. Stir with a spatula until combined, let sit for 1 minute, then stir again to make a smooth, thick, glossy ganache. Add a pinch of sea salt flakes, if you like. Carefully dip the rounded top of each profiterole into the chocolate ganache, then place them onto the wire rack, chocolate-side up, to cool and set.

Chocolate éclair variation

Follow the recipe for the Profiteroles but instead of piping the choux pastry into small rounds, use a plain, ½-in (1-cm) diameter piping nozzle to pipe it into 5-in (12-cm) long éclairs on a lined baking sheet. Bake for 35–40 minutes, until puffed up and crisp. Remove from the oven and make a hole in the bottom of each end, as instructed (above). Return to the oven to dry. When cool, fill with your choice of filling.

TIPS

The profiteroles can be made up to the end of step 5 the day before. Once completely cooled, transfer to an airtight container. They are ready for filling the next day.

Instead of crème pâtissière, fill with 2 cups (450ml) whipping cream, whipped with 2 tablespoons of powdered sugar and 1 teaspoon of vanilla extract until it holds its shape.

USING STORE-BOUGHT PASTRY

If you don't have the time to make your own pastry, there are extremely good alternatives you can buy already made and rolled out, especially if you need to accommodate different dietary requirements, such as gluten-free and vegan. Homemade puff and phyllo pastry are technically difficult to master, and with store-bought you'll still get the layers of golden flaky pastry with puff and fine, delicate, crisp layers of phyllo. Premade pie crust is a boon and readily available in the freezer or refrigerator case.

Storage
Store in the fridge or freezer until ready to use and keep an eye on the use-by date.

BAKLAVA

Prep 1 hour

Cook 40 minutes

Makes 24 pieces

Paper-thin layers of phyllo accompany spiced chopped nuts, a honey syrup, and lots of melted butter to make this indulgent treat. This baklava is heavy on the pistachios, but you can use whichever nut you prefer. Don't be put off by the number of steps, baklava is easy to make and is an assembly job, rather than anything complicated, and can be quite meditative.

1½ cups (150g) shelled unsalted pistachios, plus
    ½ cup (50g) finely chopped for the topping
1½ cups (150g) walnut halves
1½ cups (150g) pecan halves
⅓ cup (75g) sugar
½ tsp ground cloves
2 tsp ground cinnamon
pinch of salt
1 cup plus 4 tbsp (300g) salted butter, melted
1 package premade phyllo pastry, about 21 sheets

For the syrup
juice of 1 lemon
2 cinnamon sticks
scant 1 cup (200g) honey
1 cup (175g) sugar

1 | Put the pistachios (setting aside the ones for the topping), walnuts, and pecans into the bowl of a food processor and pulse in 30-second intervals until coarsely chopped. Make sure they are not too fine. Add the sugar, cloves, cinnamon, and a pinch of salt and pulse briefly until combined.

2 | Preheat the oven to 350°F (180°C). Brush a 9 x 13 in (33 x 22 cm) baking dish with some of the melted butter. Dampen 2 clean kitchen towels with water. Unwrap the phyllo pastry and lay it flat between the kitchen towels to stop it from drying out. Place 1 sheet of phyllo pastry in the baking dish. Brush the phyllo all over with melted butter, then layer a second sheet on top. Repeat until you have 7 layers of phyllo pastry in the dish.

3 | Spoon a quarter of the spiced nut mix on top of the pastry and spread into an even layer. Top with another 2 layers of phyllo pastry, brushing each layer with melted butter. Spoon a second layer of the nut mix across the top. Repeat this process twice more until all of the nuts are used up.

4 | Top the last layer of nuts with the final 6 layers of phyllo pastry, brushing with melted butter between each layer until all the pastry has been used, and leaving enough butter to brush the top.

5 | Using a small, sharp knife, cut the baklava into 24 diamonds or rectangles, cutting to the bottom of the pan so that the baklava is easy to remove after baking. Bake in the center of the oven for 35–40 minutes, until the top is evenly golden and the edges are beginning to crisp.

6 | While the baklava is baking, warm the syrup ingredients with 1 cup (250ml) of water in a small pan over medium heat. Simmer for 8–10 minutes, stirring occasionally, until slightly thickened and syrupy. Take the pan off the heat and leave to cool.

7 | Remove the cinnamon sticks from the cooled syrup and pour it over the hot baklava. Sprinkle over the remaining chopped pistachios and leave to cool in the pan before serving.

TIP

The baklava will keep in an airtight lidded container at room temperature for up to 2 weeks.

Caprese galette

*Prep 30 minutes
+ salting*

Cook 45 minutes

Serves 6

This free-form tart doesn't require a pan, instead the premade pie crust is shaped on the baking sheet, so it couldn't be easier. The buttery crust is filled with tomatoes, basil and chili flakes and finished with cooling chunks of mozzarella. Nonessential and purely aesthetic, the galette looks stunning if you use a mixture of different-colored tomatoes.

¾lb (300g) cherry tomatoes, cut in half
1lb (400g) small vine-ripened tomatoes, cut into
  wedges
salt
1 large handful of basil, around 1 cup (15g), leaves
  picked, and stalks finely chopped
1 small red onion, peeled and very finely chopped
½–1 tsp dried chili flakes (depending on how
  spicy you like it)
freshly ground black pepper
1 sheet premade pie crust
all-purpose flour, for dusting
1 large egg, at room temperature, lightly beaten
1 (4oz/125g) ball of buffalo mozzarella, drained
  and torn into pieces
2 tbsp balsamic vinegar or glaze (use the best
  quality you can afford)
1 tbsp extra-virgin olive oil

1 | Put the cut tomatoes into a colander over a large bowl. Season well with salt, tossing so the tomatoes are evenly coated, then leave to drain for 1 hour—the salt will help remove any water from the tomatoes, preventing the pastry from becoming soggy.

2 | After 1 hour, discard the tomato liquid and put the tomatoes into the large bowl. Add the basil stalks, red onion, chili flakes, and a good grinding of black pepper and gently mix. Remove the pastry from the fridge.

3 | Preheat the oven to 400°F (200°C) and line a large baking sheet with parchment paper.
4 | Unroll the circle of pie crust on a floured work surface and carefully transfer it to the parchment-paper-lined baking sheet. Don't worry if some of the pastry hangs over the edge.

5 | Leaving a 2-in (5-cm) border, spoon the tomato filling into the center of the pastry circle in an even layer. Brush the border with the beaten egg, then fold the pastry edge over the tomato filling, overlapping it where necessary to create a roundish tart that is open in the middle. The folded pastry doesn't need to be neat, it looks nice a little rustic and overlapping.

6 | Brush the top of the pastry with beaten egg and bake for 35–40 minutes, until cooked and deeply golden and the tomatoes are soft and jammy.

7 | Transfer the galette to a large serving plate. Leave to cool for 5 minutes, then sprinkle over the mozzarella and basil leaves. Drizzle with balsamic vinegar and olive oil, then season the tart with a good pinch of salt and pepper, to serve.

TIPS

If you want to make the galette in advance, follow the method to the end of step 6, then it leave to cool. To serve, reheat the galette for 10 minutes at 350°F (180°C) before finishing with step 7. Alternatively, leave it to cool to room temperature and tear over the mozzarella just before serving.

For a Middle Eastern twist, crumble 8oz (200g) of feta over the top of the baked galette instead of the mozzarella and finish with 1 tablespoon of Za'atar (see p.449), sprinkled over in place of the balsamic vinegar. You could also drizzle it with 1 tablespoon of pomegranate molasses, if you like.

Mille-feuille

Prep 20 minutes
+ cooling

Cook 20 minutes

Serves 4–6

Meaning literally "one thousand sheets" in French, this version of the classic dessert uses store-bought puff pastry. The golden layers of flaky, crisp pastry come with a filling of vanilla whipped cream and fresh tart raspberries. During baking, top the sheet of puff pastry with a baking sheet to ensure it doesn't puff up and to keep it flat. A large piping bag, fitted with a large ¾–1¼-in (2–3-cm) round or star nozzle, for piping the filling is useful here, but not essential.

1 sheet premade puff pastry
1¾ cups (400ml) whipping cream
2 tbsp powdered sugar, plus extra for dusting
1 tsp vanilla paste or extract
5oz (150g) raspberries

1 | Preheat the oven to 400°F (200°C).

2 | Remove the puff pastry from the fridge and unroll it on a large baking sheet, leaving it on its parchment paper lining. Lightly smooth out the any creases with a floured rolling pin. Take a second sheet of parchment paper the same size, place it on top of the pastry and cover with a second baking sheet. Bake the pastry for 18–20 minutes, until golden and crisp. Carefully lift the pastry onto a wire rack, remove the parchment paper and let cool. Cut the pastry into three 4 x 8-in (20 x 10-cm) pieces using a long, serrated knife.

3 | Whisk the whipping cream with the powdered sugar and the vanilla in a large bowl with a balloon whisk to soft peaks (see p.402)—it should just hold its shape. Spoon the whipped cream into a piping bag fitted with a large round or star nozzle.

4 | To assemble the mille feuille. Put one of the pieces of puff pastry on a flat surface or plate. Pipe the cream in large blobs over the puff pastry (or you can spoon it on top if you don't have a piping bag) and nestle half of the raspberries evenly into the cream. Carefully lay the second piece of puff pastry on top and repeat with the remaining cream and raspberries. Top with the final piece of puff pastry. Carefully cut the mille feuille into 4–6 slices with a sharp, serrated knife. Dust the top of each one with powdered sugar, to serve.

BATTERS

A silky, smooth batter has a higher ratio of liquid to flour than other types of dough, giving it a more pourable consistency, almost like heavy cream. The liquid content ranges from tap and sparkling water to milk and beer, depending on the recipe, while the type of flour used is equally variable. Batters tend to fall into one of four categories: yeasted, non-yeasted, sweet, or savory. Non-yeasted batters get their lightness and rise from a leavening agent, such as baking powder, baking soda, or whisked egg whites. They can be wafer-thin like Crêpes (see p.348) or pillowy and fluffy like Yorkshire Puddings (below) or Perfect Pancakes (see p.349). Yeasted batters, as their name suggests, utilize the bubbly extending nature of yeast for their rise. The batter becomes light and airy and rises during cooking, like the Crumpets on page 350.

YORKSHIRE PUDDINGS

Prep 5 minutes
+ resting

Cook 25 minutes

Makes 8

These crisp, fluffy popovers were traditionally cooked underneath spit-roasting meat, leaving the fat and juices to drip down into the batter as it cooked. The secret to success with these popovers is a high oven and heating the fat before adding the batter so it is given an instant lift as soon as it is poured into the pan.

2 cups (250g) all-purpose flour
½ tsp salt
4 large eggs, at room temperature
¾ cup plus 2 tbsp (200ml) whole milk
2½ tbsp beef dripping, lard, duck or goose fat, or vegetable oil

1 | Mix the flour with the salt in a mixing bowl. Crack in the eggs and pour in the milk with ⅓ cup (100ml) of water. Using a balloon whisk, beat until a smooth batter. Cover and leave to rest for 30 minutes.

2 | Meanwhile, preheat the oven to 450°F (230°C). Put 1 teaspoon of beef dripping or your fat of choice into each hole of 2 x 4-hole popover pan or large muffin tin. Put the pans in the oven for 10 minutes to heat up. After resting, stir the batter, then carefully remove the hot pans from the oven and ladle the batter into the pan dividing between each hole.

3 | Bake in the oven for 20–25 minutes, until well risen and golden brown.

Savory crêpes

Prep 15 minutes + resting

Cook 20 minutes

Serves 2

Eaten widely across Northern France, thin, savory crêpes can be stuffed with almost anything, but the classic is ham and cheese. The key to success with crêpes is to get the pan just hot enough so the top surface sets before the underneath becomes too brown. The first one or two can be tricky to get right because the heat may need adjusting, but persist and you'll be rewarded with thin, light crêpes.

¾ cup (100g) all-purpose flour
large pinch of salt
1 large egg, at room temperature
¾ cup plus 2 tbsp (200ml) whole milk
2 tbsp (25g) salted butter, divided

For the filling
1 tbsp vegetable oil
8oz (250g) button mushrooms, sliced
pinch each of salt and freshly ground black pepper
3 garlic cloves, peeled and chopped

2 tsp Dijon mustard
3½oz (100g) sliced ham, torn into pieces
3½oz (100g) Gruyère cheese, finely grated
2 green onions, finely sliced at an angle
salad with French Dressing (see p.429), to serve

1 | To make the batter, sift the flour into a medium mixing bowl with a large pinch of salt. Whisk in the egg and milk to make a smooth batter. Let rest for 20 minutes.

2 | To make the filling, heat the vegetable oil in a large, heavy-bottomed skillet over medium-high heat. Add the mushrooms and a pinch of salt and pepper. Sauté for 6–7 minutes, stirring occasionally, until beginning to brown. Add the garlic and cook for 2 minutes, until starting to turn golden, then put everything into a bowl.

3 | To cook the crêpes, wipe the pan clean with a paper towel. Put the pan back on medium heat, add 1 tablespoon of the butter and, once melted, tilt the pan so it lightly coats the base, or use a crumpled sheet of paper towel to help spread it.

4 | Pour in a quarter of the batter and immediately tilt and move the pan so the batter coats the base in an even layer. Cook for 1 minute, until the surface of the crêpe sets and the underside is lightly golden. Using a spatula, flip the crêpe.

5 | Dot ½ teaspoon of the mustard over half of the crêpe, then top with a quarter of the ham, cheese and cooked mushrooms. Sprinkle over a few green onions, then fold the crêpe in half, then in half again. Remove the crêpe from the pan and repeat with the rest of the batter and filling, adding more butter to the pan when needed. Serve the crêpes with a dressed salad.

TIP

For a sweet filling, go classic with a squeeze of lemon juice and a sprinkling of sugar. Or fill with hazelnut chocolate spread and a handful of berries or sliced banana.

Perfect
pancakes

Prep 5 minutes

Cook 25 minutes

Serves 4

These classic small, thick pancakes are golden on the outside and soft and fluffy within. The ratio of flour to milk is greater than in the crêpe recipe, resulting in a thicker batter, but since you want them to be light, it includes raising agents like baking powder. Serve them piled high with sweet Spiced Butter (see p.324) and maple syrup or the topping of your choice.

1½ cups (225g) all-purpose flour
2½ tsp baking powder
½ tsp salt
2 tbsp sugar
1 cup (250ml) whole milk
1 large egg, at room temperature
2 tbsp (30g) salted butter, melted, plus 3 tbsp (45g)
   for cooking, divided
Spiced Butter (see p.324) and maple syrup, to serve

1 | Sift the flour, baking powder, salt, and sugar into a medium mixing bowl and stir to combine.

2 | Whisk the milk with the egg in a bowl with a balloon whisk or fork, then pour it over the dry ingredients. Add the melted butter and use a balloon whisk to mix to a smooth pancake batter, the consistency of heavy cream.

3 | Preheat the oven to 325°F (160°C).

4 | Melt 1 tablespoon of the butter in a large, heavy-bottomed skillet over medium heat. Spoon 2 tablespoons of batter per pancake into the skillet. Repeat to cook three pancakes at a time and cook for 2–3 minutes, until bubbles appear on the surface and the underside is lightly golden. Using a spatula, flip the pancakes over and cook for another 2 minutes, until lightly golden. Put on a baking sheet or ovenproof serving platter and keep warm in the oven.

5 | Wipe the pan clean with a paper towel if the butter becomes too brown. Add another tablespoon of butter and repeat with the rest of the batter to make 12 pancakes in total.

6 | To serve, pile 3 pancakes on each plate and top with a pat of spiced butter and a drizzle of maple syrup, or the topping of your choice.

TIP

Try mixed berries and plain yogurt or sliced banana and peanut butter as alternative toppings.

HOMEMADE CRUMPETS

Prep 15 minutes
+ proving

Cook 25–40
minutes

Makes 8–10

Crumpets blur the lines between a batter and dough. The griddle breads start life as a batter but unusually contain yeast, which helps them rise and puff up during cooking—the metal crumpet rings are essential to support the sides as they extend. Once cooked, crumpets are firmer than other non-yeasted alternatives, such as pancakes, and have a light, holey texture and a browned, slightly crisp base— just perfect for soaking up lots of butter.

2 cups (500ml) whole milk
1 tsp sugar
2⅓ cups (300g) all-purpose flour
1 tsp baking powder
½ tsp sea salt
2 tsp instant dry yeast
2 tbsp (30g) salted butter, melted, plus extra
  to serve

1 | Warm the milk with the sugar in a small saucepan over low heat until the milk is just warm to the touch. Take the pan off the heat.

2 | Put the flour into a large mixing bowl with the baking powder, salt, and yeast, then mix until combined. Gradually pour in the milk mixture, while continuously whisking with a balloon whisk, until you have a smooth, thick batter.

3 | Cover the bowl with a clean kitchen towel and prove at room temperature for 45 minutes, until the mixture is bubbly and aerated.

4 | When ready to cook, brush the base of a large skillet with some of the melted butter and place on medium-low heat. Brush the inside of four 4-in (10-cm) metal crumpet rings with some more of the melted butter, then place them in the pan to heat for 1 minute. Ladle in enough of the batter mixture to fill each ring by three-quarters.

5 | Cook for 10 minutes, until the top of each crumpet is covered in set bubbles and the batter is no longer wet. Carefully turn the crumpets in their rings and cook the other side for 2 minutes, until cooked through.

6 | Remove the crumpets from the skillet, carefully lift off the rings, and let cool on a wire rack. Wipe the pan clean with a paper towel and repeat steps 2–4 with the remaining batter to make 8–10 in total. Serve warm, spread with plenty of butter.

TIP

Once cooked, leave the crumpets to cool, then freeze for up to 6 months. To serve, toast straight from frozen.

CAKES,

&

COOKIES

CAKE

You don't need lots of cooking experience or kitchen skills to bake. With a few simple ingredients (go for the best quality you can afford), attention to detail, and by following the techniques guide (below), you'll be able to whip up a cake with confidence and ease. At its simplest, a cake is a combination of flour, fat, egg (or alternative), sugar, and usually a raising agent, yet incredibly, by simply changing the quantity of ingredients you use and adapting how they are combined, it's possible to create an amazing variety of cakes, from individual cupcakes and loaf cakes to bars and impressive multilayered, cream-filled confections.

Storage
Each type of cake varies slightly in its keeping properties but, as a general rule, store cakes in an airtight pan or container in a cool place for up to 5 days. Keep cakes with a cream filling or topping in the fridge for no longer than 2 days.

CAKE-MAKING TECHNIQUES

Cake-making is just as much a science as it is a craft, but it comes with delicious results. Each ingredient has a vital role to play in the process, hence why it's important to measure them accurately before starting. These ingredients, in combination with the method or technique given in the recipe, will give your cake the desired rise, texture, and flavor. The four main methods of cake-making are covered in this chapter and there's a signature cake recipe for each technique for you to try.

Creaming method (see pp.355-359)
Classically used for layer cakes and any flavor derivatives, such as a coffee and walnut cake, vanilla, or lemon-flavored cake, this method starts by creaming or beating the softened butter with the sugar until pale and creamy. This adds a lot of air into the batter, which helps the cake rise. The dry ingredients, such as flour and baking powder, are then gently folded in so as not to lose any precious air.

Whisking method (see pp.360-361)
This method is used to incorporate large amounts of air into the cake batter by whisking together the eggs and sugar until they increase in volume and become pale and creamy. It particularly suits light, delicate cakes that are lower in fat, such as the Pistachio & Raspberry Swiss Roll (see p.360) and is the same technique used to make meringues (see p.400). Some recipes call for the eggs to be separated and the egg whites whisked to stiff peaks, then carefully folded into the cake batter to retain as much air as possible.

Melting method (see pp.362-365)
This is perhaps the most foolproof method since there is no creaming or beating to get air into the batter. Instead, the fat and sugar are simply heated together until melted before adding the eggs, flour, and a raising agent to create a batter. This type of batter tends to be looser than other cake mixtures and results in a denser, more fudgy texture, making it well-suited to Salted Caramel Chocolate Brownies (see p.362) and White Chocolate & Raspberry Blondies (see p.364).

All-in-one method (see pp.366-370)
Arguably the easiest of all cake methods, it simply involves combining all the ingredients in one mixing bowl. That said, to ensure everything is evenly mixed sometimes it is easier, although not essential, if the dry ingredients are combined in one bowl and the wet ingredients in another before whisking them together. Use a handheld mixer, stand mixer, or a wooden spoon to combine the ingredients and aerate the batter, although some recipes call for a food processor to blend everything together for the quickest of all cakes. The texture may be marginally denser than that of whisked or creamed cakes, the Vegan Chocolate Cake (see p.366), for example, but no less delicious.

VICTORIA SPONGE WITH BALSAMIC STRAWBERRIES

*Prep 30 minutes
+ cooling*

Cook 25 minutes

Serves 8–10

This light, airy cake is made by the creaming method (left), whereby the softened butter is whisked with the sugar until light, pale, and creamy. A handheld mixer or stand mixer makes easy work of this, but you could use a wooden spoon to beat the mixture for about 5 minutes instead, although this requires a strong arm and stamina! To avoid the batter splitting, a tablespoon of the flour is folded in with each addition of egg. For this recipe, you will need two 8-in (20-cm) springform cake pans, a wire cooling rack, and an optional metal skewer for testing the cake is cooked through. It is much easier to remove the layers from a springform pan once baked, but you can also use a regular cake pan.

For the cake

1 cup (225g) salted butter, softened, plus extra
  for greasing
2 cups plus 4 tbsp (225g) sugar
4 large eggs, at room temperature
1¾ cups (225g) all-purpose flour
½ tsp salt
2½ tsp baking powder
1 tsp vanilla paste or extract (optional)
1–2 tbsp whole milk
1 recipe quantity of Balsamic Strawberries
  (see p.380), for filling

For the buttercream

½ cup plus 3 tbsp (150g) salted butter, softened
2 tbsp whole milk
2 tsp vanilla paste or extract
2½ cups (300g) powdered sugar, sifted

1 | Preheat the oven to 350°F (180°C). Lightly grease the sides and base of two 8-in (20-cm) springform cake pans with butter, then line the base of each with a round of parchment paper, cut to the same size as the pan.

2 | Using a handheld mixer (or stand mixer), beat the softened butter and sugar together for 3–4 minutes, until pale, light, and creamy, scraping down the sides of the bowl halfway through. (Continued overleaf.)

3 | Add 1 egg and 1 tablespoon of the flour and whisk for about 30 seconds, until well incorporated into the batter, then scrape down the sides of the bowl again. Repeat this process until you have used all the eggs, adding 1 tablespoon of flour each time to ensure the batter doesn't split.

4 | Using a fine mesh strainer or sifter, sift the remaining flour, salt, and baking powder into the bowl. Using a spatula, fold the flour mixture into the cake batter, taking care not to lose too much air. You do this by making a figure-eight motion through the batter with the spatula, folding it confidently but gently to make a smooth batter. Add the vanilla, if using.

5 | Fold in the milk, starting with 1 tablespoon and adding more, if needed, to make a cake batter with a thick dropping consistency.

6 | Divide the cake batter equally between the prepared pans (there should be about 1lb/450g of batter in each one), then smooth the top of each with the back of a spoon. Bake on the middle shelf of the oven for 20–25 minutes, until risen, golden, and a skewer inserted into the middle comes out clean. The cake should spring back when pressed with a finger. Let the cakes cool in their pans for 10 minutes, then remove from the pans to a wire rack to cool completely.

7 | Meanwhile, make the buttercream. Using a handheld mixer (or stand mixer), whisk the softened butter, milk, vanilla, and sifted powdered sugar (reserving 1 tablespoon to decorate) for 3–4 minutes, until light and fluffy. Start on a slow speed before increasing it because you don't want the powdered sugar all over your worktop!

8 | To assemble the cake, follow steps 1–2 from making Balsamic Strawberries (see p.380). Place one of the cakes, domed-side down, on a serving plate. Spoon over any juices from the strawberries, then, using a spatula, spread all of the buttercream over the top in an even layer.

9 | Spoon over the balsamic strawberries and top with the second cake.

10 | Using a fine mesh strainer or sifter, dust the top of the cake with the remaining powdered sugar. The cake will keep in an airtight container in a cool place for up to 2 days.

All-in-one cake variation

Using a handheld mixer or stand mixer, whisk all the ingredients for the cake for 4–5 minutes, until a smooth, light batter, then follow steps 6–10 for baking and filling.

TIPS

For a classic Victoria sponge, replace the buttercream and balsamic strawberry filling with 5½oz (150g) raspberry jam and 1¼ cups (300ml) whipping cream, whisked to soft peaks with 1 tablespoon of powdered sugar and 1 teaspoon vanilla paste or extract (see p.402 for Whipping Cream). Spread the jam over one cake before spooning on the pillowy cream.

If using fresh cream as a filling, enjoy the cake on the day of making or store it in the fridge for up to 2 days and bring back to room temperature before serving.

Spiced carrot cake
with cream cheese frosting

Prep 25 minutes

Cook 30 minutes

Serves 8–10

This carrot cake recipe uses the creaming method (see p.354) to add lightness to the cake, while the addition of oil, carrots, and eggs ensures the crumb is tender and moist. The combination of brown and regular sugar gives the cake a slight caramel flavor that works wonderfully with the grated fresh carrot. Be sure to choose full-fat cream cheese for the frosting to avoid it splitting when whisking with the orange juice.

½ cup plus 3 tbsp (175g) salted butter, softened, plus extra for greasing
2⅓ cups (300g) all-purpose flour
2 tsp baking powder
½ tsp baking soda
2 tsp ground cinnamon
1 tsp ground ginger
½ tsp salt
¼ tsp ground cloves (optional)
¾ cup (150g) packed light brown sugar
¾ cup (150g) sugar
3 large eggs, at room temperature
4 tbsp vegetable oil
¾lb (350g) carrots, coarsely grated
½ cup (50g) pecans or walnuts, toasted (see p.288) and roughly chopped

For the cream cheese frosting
½ cup plus 5 tbsp (200g) salted butter, softened
finely grated zest of 1 and juice of ½ orange
3⅓ cups (400g) powdered sugar
16oz (500g) full-fat cream cheese

1 | Preheat the oven to 350°F (180°C). Lightly grease the sides and base of two 8-in (20-cm) cake pans with butter, then line the base of each with a disk of parchment paper.

2 | Sift the flour, baking powder, baking soda, cinnamon, ginger, salt, and cloves, if using, into a medium mixing bowl. Briefly whisk together to combine and set aside.

3 | Using a handheld mixer (or stand mixer), whisk the softened butter and sugar together for 3–4 minutes, until creamy and a pale caramel color, scraping down the sides of the bowl halfway.

4 | Add the eggs, one at a time, and whisk for 30 seconds between each addition to thoroughly combine, scraping down the sides of the bowl with a spatula after every addition.

5 | Add 3 tablespoons of the spiced flour then, whisking continuously, slowly pour in the oil, until incorporated and smooth. Add the remaining spiced flour and grated carrots and briefly whisk to combine. Divide the cake batter equally between the prepared pans and smooth the top with the back of a spoon.

6 | Bake on the middle shelf of the oven for 25–30 minutes, until risen, golden, and a skewer inserted into the center comes out clean. Let the cakes cool in their pans for 10 minutes, then transfer to a wire rack to cool completely.

7 | Meanwhile, make the frosting. Add the butter, and orange zest and juice to a large mixing bowl. Using a fine mesh strainer or sifter, sift in the powdered sugar, then whisk with a handheld mixer until smooth. Add the cream cheese and briefly whisk to combine into a smooth frosting.

8 | To assemble the cake, place one of the cakes on a serving plate. Spoon over half of the frosting and spread with a spatula into an even layer. Sprinkle over half the nuts. Top with the second cake and spread the remaining frosting over the top of the cake. Finish with the remaining toasted nuts, and serve in slices.

TIP

The added moisture from the carrots and oil keeps the cake moist for up to 5 days. Store in an airtight container in a cool place.

PISTACHIO &
RASPBERRY SWISS ROLL

*Prep 25 minutes
+ cooling*

Cook 15 minutes

Serves 6–8

Originating from central Europe, the Swiss roll (or jelly roll) is a light, rolled-up cake filled with jam and/or cream. It is a whisked cake (see p.354) that gets its airy texture and light crumb from beating the eggs with the sugar until increased in volume. Because this cake features pistachios, which are relatively heavy, the egg yolks and whites are whisked separately to ensure as much air as possible gets into the batter. You will need a 9 x 13 in (32 x 22 cm) Swiss roll pan for this cake.

a little butter, for greasing
¾ cup (75g) unsalted shelled pistachios
4 large eggs, at room temperature
½ cup plus 2 tbsp (125g) sugar
½ cup plus 2 tbsp (75g) all-purpose flour
1 tsp baking powder
½ tsp salt

For the filling and topping
1 tbsp sugar, for sprinkling
1 cup (250ml) whipping cream
1 tbsp powdered sugar, sifted
1 tsp vanilla paste or extract
6 tbsp raspberry jam

1 | Preheat the oven to 350°F (180°C). Lightly grease a Swiss roll pan with butter, then line the base with parchment paper. Cut a second sheet of parchment paper just larger than the pan and set aside for Step 6. Pulse the pistachios in a food processor until very finely chopped—you want them the consistency of ground almonds. Place ¼ cup (50g) in a small bowl and set aside the remainder for later.

2 | Follow steps 1–3 from Separating Eggs (see p.32). Using a handheld mixer, first whisk the egg whites until they form stiff peaks—they should be opaque white and hold their shape in the bowl.

3 | Next (in a separate bowl), whisk the egg yolks and sugar for 3–4 minutes, until the yolks are paler in color, have thickened, and doubled in size.

4 | Add the ¼ cup (50g) of ground pistachios to the egg-yolk mixture, then sift in the flour. Using a spatula, gently fold everything together. Once combined, gently fold in one-third of the egg whites, retaining as much air as possible. Fold in the remaining egg whites until a light, airy batter forms.

5 | Pour the batter into the prepared pan and gently spread it out to cover the base of the pan. Bake on the middle shelf of the oven for 10–12 minutes, until light golden brown and springy to the touch. The cake should start to come away from the sides of the pan.

6 | While the cake bakes, place a clean kitchen towel on the work surface and top with the second piece of parchment paper. Sprinkle 1 tablespoon of sugar and the remaining ground pistachios evenly over the top.

7 | Once baked, while still warm, carefully flip the Swiss roll out of the pan upside down onto the sugary, nutty parchment paper. Peel off the lining paper and use a serrated knife to trim the edges. Score a straight line ¾ in (2 cm) in from the edge down the width of the cake, taking care not to cut it all the way through (this will help you roll the cake). Starting from the scored line, roll up the cake using the kitchen towel and the parchment paper to help you. Let the cake cool, rolled in the kitchen towel.

8 | Meanwhile, make the filling. Using a balloon whisk, whip the cream (see p.402) with the powdered sugar and vanilla in a medium bowl until it just holds its shape. Unroll the cooled Swiss roll, spread over the jam followed by an even layer of the whipped cream, leaving a ½-in (1-cm) border around the edge. Using the same method as before, tightly roll the cake using the paper to help.

9 | Transfer the Swiss roll to an oval plate or board and serve cut into slices. It's best eaten immediately or wrap in plastic wrap and store in the fridge for up to 1 day.

TIP

Omit the pistachios,
if preferred, increasing
the quantity of flour to
1 cup (125g).

SALTED CARAMEL
CHOCOLATE BROWNIES

*Prep 15 minutes
+ cooling*

Cook 30 minutes

Makes 12–16

This failsafe brownie recipe uses the melting method (see p.354), which is perhaps the most straightforward and foolproof cake-making technique. It simply involves mixing the ingredients for the batter together in a saucepan, resulting in cakes and bars with a moist, dense crumb, and particularly suits these brownies with their typical rich, fudgy center.

1 cup (225g) salted butter, cut into cubes, plus
    extra for greasing
7oz (200g) semisweet chocolate, roughly chopped
1½ cups (300g) sugar
3 large eggs, at room temperature
½ cup plus 2 tbsp (75g) all-purpose flour
½ cup (50g) cocoa powder
3½oz (100g) milk chocolate with a caramel filling
    (anything with a melty center is good here),
    roughly chopped
large pinch of sea salt flakes

1 | Preheat the oven to 350°F (180°C). Lightly grease an 8-in (20-cm) square brownie pan with butter, then line the base and sides with parchment paper. Heat the butter, semisweet chocolate, and ¼ cup (75ml) of water in a medium saucepan over low heat, stirring occasionally with a spatula until a rich, smooth, and glossy mixture.

2 | Add the sugar and mix with a balloon whisk until it dissolves, then take the pan off the heat.

3 | Leave the mixture to cool for 2 minutes, then whisk in the eggs until combined. Sift in the flour and cocoa powder through a fine mesh strainer or sifter and mix again to make a smooth batter.

4 | Pour half of the brownie batter into the prepared pan, spreading it out evenly with a spatula.

5 | Sprinkle over half of the caramel milk chocolate. Top with the remaining brownie batter, spreading it out evenly, then sprinkle over the rest of the caramel milk chocolate.

6 | Bake in the middle of the oven for 25–30 minutes, until the edges are set and the center still has a visible wobble. Sprinkle over the sea salt flakes. Let cool in the pan on a wire rack, then cut into 12–16 squares to serve. The brownies will keep in an airtight container for up to 5 days at room temperature.

TIPS

You can make the brownies the day before serving. Let them cool in the pan, then wrap in plastic wrap. As a bonus, they are slightly easier to cut the following day.

To freeze, cut into squares and place slightly spaced out on a baking sheet. Freeze, then move to an airtight container. The brownies can be defrosted individually at room temperature before eating.

These are a great way to use up the odds and ends of chocolate in your pantry—dark, semisweet, milk, or white, you choose.

White chocolate & raspberry blondies

Prep 15 minutes + chilling

Cook 35 minutes

Makes 16

The blondie is a variation of a brownie but without the cocoa powder and semisweet chocolate. Instead, the batter is flavored with vanilla and brown sugar for a caramel flavor and "blonde" color. This version includes fresh raspberries for added tang and white chocolate—just because.

½ cup plus 5 tbsp (200g) salted butter, melted and cooled

1¾ cups (350g) packed light brown sugar

3 large eggs, at room temperature

1 tbsp vanilla paste or extract

2 cups plus 2 tbsp (275g) all-purpose flour

½ tsp salt

5½oz (150g) white chocolate, roughly chopped

3½oz (100g) raspberries

1 | Preheat the oven to 350°F (180°C). Lightly grease an 8-in (20-cm) square brownie pan with a little of the melted butter, then line the base and sides with parchment paper.

2 | Pour the cooled melted butter into a large mixing bowl, then briefly whisk in the brown sugar with a balloon whisk until combined. Whisk in the eggs and vanilla to make a silky smooth mixture.

3 | Sift in the flour and salt and briefly whisk until a smooth, caramel-colored batter forms—you're not looking to incorporate air into the batter, just mixing the ingredients together.

4 | Spread half of the batter into the prepared pan and sprinkle half of the white chocolate and raspberries (you might like to tear some raspberries in half) evenly over the top. Add the remaining blondie batter, spreading it out evenly with a spatula, and finish with the remaining chocolate and raspberries. Bake on the middle shelf of the oven for 30–35 minutes, until the edges crisp and the center still has a slight wobble.

6 | Let cool in the pan on a wire rack, then place in the fridge for at least 30 minutes (this will help the blondies firm up but remain gooey on the inside). The chilling stage is important, so don't skip it, as tempting as it may be! After chilling, cut the blondies into 16 squares to serve. They will keep in an airtight container for up to 5 days at room temperature.

TIP

To freeze, cut into squares and place slightly spaced out on a baking sheet. Freeze, then move to an airtight container. The blondies can be defrosted individually at room temperature before eating.

CARAMEL BANANA CAKE

Prep 15 minutes + cooling

Cook 1 hour

Serves 10–12

This cake couldn't be easier to make, yet it still looks and tastes impressive. It's baked in a tube pan with a distinctive ridged doughnut shape, which is perfect for this banana cake because it remains moist, despite the slightly longer baking time. Delicious plain, the cake is even better with the caramel sauce topping and a sprinkling of chopped salted peanuts.

scant 1 cup (200g) Brown Butter (see p.51)
3 large eggs, at room temperature
1 cup (180g) packed light brown sugar
⅓ cup (100g) sour cream
large pinch of sea salt flakes
1¾ cups (225g) all-purpose flour
1½ tsp baking powder
1 tsp baking soda
4 medium very ripe bananas (around 10oz/300g peeled weight), mashed

To finish
½ cup (125g) Caramel Sauce (see p.407) or store-bought
½ cup (50g) roasted salted peanuts, roughly chopped

1 | Preheat the oven to 350°F (180°C). Follow steps 1–2 from Brown Butter (see p.51) and let cool for 15 minutes. Use 2 teaspoons of the brown butter to grease a 12-cup (2.5 liter) tube pan, about 10½ in (26 cm) in diameter, making sure you brush it into all the crevices.

2 | Pour the rest of the brown butter into a large mixing bowl and whisk in the eggs, brown sugar, sour cream, salt, flour, baking powder, and baking soda for 1–2 minutes with a balloon whisk to make a smooth cake batter. Add the mashed banana and briefly whisk to combine. Pour the batter into the greased tube pan.

3 | Bake on the middle shelf for 50 minutes to 1 hour, until a skewer inserted into the middle of the cake comes out clean. Check the cake after 45 minutes and if it's browning too quickly, cover the top loosely with foil. When ready, let the cake cool in the pan for 15 minutes, then turn out onto a wire rack to cool completely. Drizzle the caramel sauce generously over the cake and sprinkle over the peanuts, to serve. The cake will keep for up to 1 week in an airtight container.

Vegan chocolate cake

*Prep 20 minutes
+ cooling*

Cook 40 minutes

Serves 8–10

This all-in-one (see p.354) vegan chocolate cake doesn't rely on hard-to-find, expensive ingredients. Instead, it uses vegetable oil with nondairy milk and lemon juice to create a type of vegan buttermilk that reacts with the flour and raising agents to create a rise, without the need for eggs. The fudgy cake is then finished with the smoothest tofu frosting, which is almost like a chocolate mousse in texture.

¾ cup (175ml) vegetable oil, plus extra for greasing
1¼ cups (300ml) soy or almond milk
juice of ½ lemon
1¼ cups (250g) packed light brown sugar
⅓ cup (80g) cocoa powder
1¾ cups (220g) all-purpose flour
1½ tsp baking powder
1 tsp baking soda
1 tsp salt
4 tsp just-boiled water
1¾oz (50g) vegan dark chocolate, roughly chopped,
    to decorate

For the frosting
4½oz (125g) vegan dark chocolate, chopped
2 tbsp light brown sugar
10oz (300g) silken tofu, drained
1 tsp vanilla paste or extract
pinch of salt

1 | Preheat the oven to 350°F (180°C). Lightly grease the sides and base of two 8-in (20-cm) cake pans with oil, then line the base of each with a disk of parchment paper.

2 | Using a fork, whisk the soy or almond milk with the lemon juice in a bowl. Leave for 5 minutes to lightly curdle into a type of buttermilk.

3 | In a large mixing bowl, sift in the brown sugar, cocoa powder, flour, baking powder, baking soda, and salt, then mix until combined.

4 | Pour the buttermilk mixture and vegetable oil into the dry ingredients, whisking well to make a smooth cake batter. Finally, whisk in the just-boiled water—this is the secret to a fudgy chocolate cake batter. Divide the batter evenly between the prepared pans.

5 | Bake on the middle shelf of the oven for about 40 minutes, until well risen, springy to the touch, and a metal skewer inserted into the center comes out clean. Let the cakes cool in the pans for 15 minutes, then transfer to a wire rack to cool completely.

6 | To make the frosting, melt the chocolate in a microwave-safe bowl in 30-second intervals or in a heatproof bowl set over a pan of gently simmering water (see p.390). Pour the melted chocolate into a blender with the brown sugar, tofu, vanilla, and a pinch of salt and blend to make a smooth frosting. You may need to scrape down the sides of the blender a couple of times to combine. Chill in the fridge for about 15 minutes, until thickened slightly.

7 | To assemble the cake, place one of the layers, domed-side down, on a serving plate. Spoon half of the chocolate frosting on top and spread with a spatula into an even layer. Top with the second cake and cover with the remaining frosting. Decorate the top with the chopped chocolate and cut into 8–10 slices, to serve. The cake will keep for up to 1 week in an airtight container in a cool place.

TIP

The cake can be baked a day in advance. Once cooled, wrap tightly in plastic wrap, then follow steps 6–7 for icing and filling the next day.

BLUEBERRY
STREUSEL MUFFINS

*Prep 25 minutes
+ cooling*

Cook 25 minutes

Makes 12

The all-in-one method is equally suited to small cakes as it is to large ones. The secret to a good muffin is not to overmix the batter, otherwise it can become dense in texture, while the addition of plain yogurt also helps keep it moist. You can use fresh or frozen blueberries but, if using the latter, be sure to only briefly fold them into the batter to prevent their color from leaching, turning the muffins purple. When baking, the muffins are given a brief blast on high heat to help them rise, then the oven is turned down so the insides cook without becoming over-baked and too brown.

1¾ cups (225g) all-purpose flour
2 tsp baking powder
1 tsp baking soda
½ tsp salt
¾ cup (150g) sugar
2 large eggs, at room temperature
⅔ cup (150g) plain yogurt
finely grated zest of 1 unwaxed lemon
7 tbsp (110g) salted butter, melted and
    cooled slightly
8oz (250g) blueberries, fresh or frozen

For the streusel topping
½ cup (60g) all-purpose flour
¼ cup (50g) packed light brown sugar
½ tsp ground cinnamon
3 tbsp (50g) cold salted butter, cut into cubes

1 | Preheat the oven to 425°F (220°C). Line a muffin pan with 12 paper muffin liners. First, make the streusel topping. Mix all the dry ingredients in a medium mixing bowl, then use your fingertips to rub in the butter until the mixture resembles coarse, damp sand. Set aside in the fridge.

2 | Using a balloon whisk, mix together the flour, baking powder, baking soda, salt, and sugar in a large mixing bowl until well combined.

3 | Crack the eggs into a medium mixing bowl. Add the yogurt and lemon zest, then pour in the melted butter and whisk together to combine—don't worry if it looks a little lumpy or curdled.

4 | Pour the wet ingredients into the dry ingredients, then use a spatula to briefly mix everything until just combined—the thick batter should have no visible pockets of flour. Using the spatula, lightly fold in the blueberries, using a couple figure-eight motions. You don't want to overmix the batter because the fruit will break down and turn it purple.

5 | Spoon the muffin batter into the paper liners with a metal spoon or an ice cream scoop until about three-quarters full.

6 | Spoon 1 tablespoon of the streusel topping over each muffin, patting gently so it sticks. Bake on the middle shelf of the oven for 5 minutes, then turn the heat down to 350°F (180°C) and bake for a further 18–20 minutes, until risen, golden brown, and a skewer inserted into the centers comes out clean. Let cool on a wire rack for about 15 minutes before tucking in.

TIPS

These muffins are wonderful fresh and warm straight out of the oven, but also keep well in an airtight container for up to 3 days. You can reheat the muffins, in the microwave on high for a few seconds or in an oven at 350°F (180°C) for 6–8 minutes.

The muffins can be frozen for up to 3 months, simply defrost and reheat in the same way as above.

Swap the blueberries for the same quantity of raspberries and add 1 teaspoon of vanilla paste or extract to the batter mixture.

Lemon drizzle loaf

Prep 15 minutes + cooling

Cook 40 minutes

Serves 8–10

Everyone needs a good recipe for a loaf cake in their baking repertoire, and this lemon drizzle is an excellent choice. The cake batter is made with the all-in-one method so it's super quick and easy. You will notice two different sugars are used: regular sugar adds lightness to the cake, while large granulated sugar creates the crackly, crunchy top synonymous with a classic lemon drizzle.

½ cup plus 3 tbsp (175g) salted butter, softened, plus extra for greasing

3 large eggs, at room temperature

¾ cup plus 2 tbsp (175g) sugar

1½ cups (175g) all-purpose flour

1½ tsp baking powder

pinch of salt

1 tbsp whole milk

juice (about ⅓ cup) and finely grated zest of 2 unwaxed lemons

½ cup (100g) large granulated sugar like turbinado or demerara

1 | Preheat the oven to 350°F (180°C). Grease a 2lb (900g) loaf pan with butter and line the base and sides with 2 long strips of parchment paper.

2 | Using a handheld mixer (or stand mixer), whisk the butter, eggs, sugar, flour, baking powder, salt, milk, and lemon zest (reserving the juice for the topping) in a large mixing bowl to make a smooth batter. Spoon the batter into the prepared pan and smooth the top with a spatula. Bake on the middle shelf of the oven for 35–40 minutes, until well risen and a metal skewer inserted into the middle of the loaf comes out clean.

3 | To make the drizzle, mix the lemon juice with the turbinado sugar in a small bowl. Prick the top of the warm cake all over with a wooden toothpick, then spoon the drizzle over the cake—the holes will help it soak into the loaf. Let the cake cool completely in the pan before lifting it out onto a serving plate or board. Store in an airtight container for up to 5 days.

TIPS

To freeze, follow the method to the end of step 2, then let the cake cool. Transfer to the freezer for up to 3 months. To serve, prick the top of the cake, as above, and pour the drizzle over once it has defrosted.

Try different citrus fruit—the finely grated zest of 1 grapefruit and the juice of ½ a grapefruit is good too.

COOKIES

If you've never baked before, these recipes are excellent to start with. These are the baked goods for when you're in the mood for something homemade and sweet that doesn't require too much time or effort. That being said, they are also a fantastic way to get to grips with the science behind baking. Learn how fat, gluten in flour, and various types of sugar each play a specific role in your baking, from creating the characteristic contrast of chewy versus crisp in cookies to the melt-in-the-mouth texture of shortbread thanks to its high ratio of butter to flour.

Storage
Keep in an airtight container for up to 3–5 days.

CHOCOLATE CHIP COOKIES

Prep 20 minutes + chilling

Cook 15 minutes

Makes 12

The perfect cookie is a wonderful thing. They have a higher ratio of sugar and fat to flour than other baked goods, which gives them a characteristic caramelized edge with a satisfying chew. Once you've mastered this basic recipe you can change up the flavors in as many ways as you like—there are some ideas (right).

½ cup (100g) packed light brown sugar
½ cup (100g) sugar
½ cup plus 2 tbsp (150g) salted butter, melted and cooled
1 large egg, at room temperature
1 tsp vanilla paste or extract
1½ cups (200g) all-purpose flour
½ tsp baking powder
½ tsp salt
1¼ cups (200g) semisweet chocolate chips
sea salt flakes, to sprinkle (optional)

1 | Add both types of sugar to a medium mixing bowl. Pour in the melted butter and beat together briefly with a wooden spoon until evenly combined. Beat in the egg and vanilla to make a smooth batter.

2 | Add the flour, baking powder, salt, and chocolate chips and mix for a minute or so until there are no lumps of flour and the chocolate chips are evenly distributed throughout the mixture.

3 | Using an ice cream scoop or dessert spoon, divide the cookie dough into 12 equal pieces, about 1¾oz (55g) each, then roll each piece into a ball between the palms of your hands. Chill, uncovered, on a plate for 1 hour.

4 | Preheat the oven to 350°F (180°C) and line two large baking sheets with parchment paper. Place the chilled cookie balls on the lined trays, leaving enough room to allow for spreading as they bake. Bake for 12–15 minutes, until set around the edge and the centers are still slightly soft—they will firm up as they cool. Sprinkle with salt, if you like, then cool on the tray before serving.

TIPS

Once baked, as soon as the trays come out of the oven give them a firm tap on the work surface—this will give the cookies that characteristic wrinkle.

To freeze the uncooked cookies, first chill the shaped balls in the fridge for 1 hour, until firmed up, then freeze for up to 3 months. Bake straight from frozen, adding an extra 2–3 minutes to the cooking time.

Flavor variations

Brown butter, espresso & walnut: follow steps 1–2 for making Brown Butter (see p.51) using ½ cup plus 3 tbsp (175g) of salted butter. Once browned, stir in 2 teaspoons of espresso powder, then let cool. Follow the cookie recipe (left) replacing the chocolate chips with ¾ cup (100g) of toasted chopped walnuts.

Triple chocolate: follow the cookie recipe (left) replacing ½ cup (50g) of the flour with the same quantity of sifted cocoa powder. Replace the 1¼ cups (200g) of semisweet chocolate chips with an equal combination of dark, milk, and white chocolate chips.

Gingerbread spice: follow the cookie recipe (left) replacing the vanilla paste or extract with 2–2½ teaspoons of the Gingerbread Spice Mix (see p.449), depending on how spicy you like them. Halve the amount of chocolate chips and add 3 tbsp finely chopped candied ginger.

Fruit & nut oat bars

*Prep 15 minutes
+ chilling*

Cook 25 minutes

Makes 12

Packed full of oats, dried fruit, and your choice of nuts or seeds, these oat bars make a wonderful on-the-go snack. Like a granola bar, these are made in a similar way to the Cookies (see p.372) in that the butter, sugar, and syrup are melted together before mixing into the dry ingredients. To make the bars easier to cut, let them cool in the pan first.

1 cup (240g) salted butter, cut into cubes, plus extra for greasing
⅓ cup (80g) packed light brown sugar
¼ cup (60ml) light corn syrup
¼ cup (60ml) honey
2 cups (300g) old fashioned rolled oats
¾ cup (100g) dried fruit, such as raisins, golden raisins, dried apricots, or prunes, roughly chopped if large
¾ cup (100g) mixed nuts or seeds, roughly chopped if large
pinch of salt

1 | Preheat the oven to 350°F (180°C). Lightly grease an 8-in (20-cm) square brownie pan with butter, then line the base with parchment paper.

2 | Heat the butter, brown sugar, corn syrup, and honey in a large saucepan over medium heat, stirring occasionally with a wooden spoon, for about 5 minutes, until everything is combined.

3 | Take the pan off the heat, add the oats, dried fruit, mixed nuts or seeds, and a good pinch of salt. Stir everything so the oats are coated in the butter and sugar mixture.

4 | Spoon into the prepared pan and press firmly with the back of a wooden spoon into an even layer. Bake on the middle shelf of the oven for 20–25 minutes, until the top is golden and slightly darker around the edges.

5 | Let the oat bars cool in the pan on a wire rack, then chill for 30 minutes, uncovered, in the fridge—this will help them hold together when cut into 12 pieces in the pan. Store the oat bars in an airtight container for up to 1 week.

TIP

You can freeze the oat bars for up to 3 months. Put them in the freezer on a baking sheet, then transfer to an airtight container once frozen. To serve, defrost at room temperature.

Shortbread

Prep 15 minutes

Cook 20 minutes

Makes 18

This Scottish treat contains in its purest form just three ingredients: flour, butter, and sugar at a ratio of 3:2:1. The high butter content is what makes these cookies so wonderfully melt-in-the-mouth. When beating the mixture, you are looking for it to just come together, overworking the dough will give you a tough cookie, rather than a buttery, crumbly one.

½ cup plus 5 tbsp (200g) salted butter, softened, plus extra for greasing
½ cup (100g) sugar
2⅓ cups (300g) all-purpose flour
pinch of salt
powdered sugar, for dusting (optional)

1 | Preheat the oven to 350°F (180°C). Lightly grease an 8-in (20-cm) square brownie pan with butter and line the base with parchment paper.

2 | Beat the butter and sugar in a large mixing bowl with a wooden spoon until well combined—you're not looking to add air here, just to ensure the butter is smooth and well mixed with the sugar.

3 | Using a fine mesh strainer or sifter, sift the flour and salt into the creamed mixture, then beat until evenly combined and the mixture comes together into a dough, taking care not to overwork it. With clean hands, press the dough into the prepared pan in an even layer.

4 | Using a table knife, cut the shortbread into 18 rectangles in the pan, cutting through to the base to help remove it from the pan after baking. Prick the top of each rectangle a few times with a fork.

5 | Bake on the middle shelf of the oven for 18–20 minutes, until light golden. Let cool in the pan on a wire rack before turning out and dusting the top of each shortbread with powdered sugar. Store in an airtight container for up to 1 week.

Flavor variations

Orange & cardamom: beat the finely grated zest of 1 orange and the crushed seeds from 6 cardamom pods with the butter and sugar in step 2, then follow the recipe (above).

Double ginger: add 1 teaspoon of ground ginger and 3 tbsp finely chopped candied ginger to the shortbread dough with the flour in step 3, then follow the recipe (above).

Lemon & Earl Grey: beat 1 tablespoon of Earl Grey tea leaves and the finely grated zest of 1 unwaxed lemon with the butter and sugar in step 2, then follow the recipe (above).

DESSERTS

FRUIT

This journey into desserts starts with fruit. From the simple pleasures of a single juicy ripe peach or fruit salad to the more complex apple tart or layered mixed berry confection, fruit provides the cook with a multitude of dessert options (and savory ones too). These are not only in the way it is served but in the techniques used to create your fruity dessert, from puréeing and baking to grilling and stewing—the table (below) gives you a few ideas to set you on the way.

You'll find that some slightly sour fruits, such as rhubarb, gooseberries, and cooking apples, require the addition of sugar, while others require little or no additional sweetening, but this may also depend on the level of ripeness (a useful trick if your fruit is unripe is to put it in a bag with a ripe banana, which will help speed up the ripening process). Generally, the riper your fruit, the sweeter it tends to be, which also serves as a reminder to opt for fruit that is in season. It will have the best flavor and should also be cheaper to buy. If not buying fruit in season, frozen is always a great alternative and you have the added advantage of a regular supply with convenience and no waste.

Whether fresh or frozen, nutritionally, fruit is an asset to a healthy diet, providing a wide range of vitamins, minerals, antioxidants, and fiber. An all-around winner!

Storage

Depending on type, storage can vary. Orchard fruit, such as apples and pears, are best kept in a cool place, while more delicate fruit, including berries, benefit from being stored in the fridge. Frozen fruit can be used from frozen or defrosted first, depending on what you plan to do with it. Wash fresh fruit just before use to avoid it becoming soggy.

FRUIT	TYPE	COOKING METHOD	PERFECT IN ...
Orchard	Apples, pears	Bake, purée, stew, poach	Crumbles, sauces, compotes, pies, tarts, stuffings.
Stone fruit	Cherries, plum, nectarines, peaches	Bake, poach, grill, purée, stew	Crumbles, sauces, compotes, pies, tarts, preserving.
Citrus	Oranges, limes, lemons, clementines, tangerines, grapefruit	Stew, poach, juice, zest	Preserving, marmalade, tarts, sorbets, macerating/marinating.
Berries & currants	Strawberries, raspberries, blueberries, blackberries, black currants, red currants	Poach, purée, bake	Fruit salads, compotes, preserving, sauces, sorbets, ice creams, tarts, crumbles, pies.
Tropical	Bananas, mangoes, pineapple, melons, papaya	Grill, purée, bake	Fruit salads, fritters, sauces, tarts, ice creams, sorbets.

MACERATING & PURÉEING FRUIT

Two of the simplest techniques to use with fruit are maceration and puréeing, yet both can have quite a profound effect, changing the texture and, to a certain extent, the flavor of a fruit.

Macerated fruit is left to sit in sugar, alcohol, or an acid, such as vinegar or lemon juice, to encourage it to soften and release its juices. This could be as simple as dusting raspberries in powdered sugar until softened, soaking dried prunes in Armagnac until plump and tender, or immersing strawberries in balsamic vinegar until juicy (see p.380).

Puréeing not only alters the texture of a fruit (or vegetable), it can also concentrate and intensify its flavor. Both cooked and uncooked fruit (and vegetables) can be puréed, and it is an easy way to make a quick sauce. Firmer fruit, such as apples and pears, benefits from cooking first, especially if you're looking for a fine, smooth result. An electric blender, either an immersion blender or large one with a pitcher (or a mini food processor), makes easy work of both cooked and raw fruit and is a useful tool to have in the kitchen.

RASPBERRY COULIS

Prep 10 minutes

Cook 10 minutes

Serves 4–6

A coulis (meaning "strained" in French) is a simple, thick sauce made from puréed cooked or raw fruit which are then passed through a strainer to remove any skin or seeds. This raspberry version is great as a topping for pavlova, simply spooned over Greek yogurt for breakfast, or as a tangy sauce to complement the Panna Cotta (see p.404). Raspberries work well in a coulis because they break down readily, allowing you to retain the bright, fresh flavor of the fruit without having to cook it for too long (if at all).

1lb (450g) raspberries
juice of ½–1 lemon
3–4 tbsp powdered sugar, to taste

1 | Cook the raspberries in a small saucepan with the juice of ½ lemon and 3 tbsp of powdered sugar over low heat, stirring now and again, until the juices release and the fruit starts to collapse, about 5–7 minutes.

2 | Place a fine metal strainer over a medium mixing bowl. Add in the raspberries and any juices, then use the back of a spoon to press the fruit through the strainer. Scrape the underside of the strainer to remove any leftover coulis into the bowl and discard the seeds. Stir and taste the coulis, adding more lemon juice and/or powdered sugar, if needed. Pour the coulis into a serving dish, cover the surface, and chill in the fridge before serving. It will keep for up to 5 days or 3 months in the freezer.

Balsamic strawberries

Prep 5 minutes + macerating

No cook

Serves 4–6

The combination of strawberries and balsamic vinegar may sound unusual but it is a classic; the sweetness of the berries enhances the sweet tang of the balsamic, taming the sourness. The key here is to use the best-quality balsamic you can afford which will have a more balanced, rounded flavor. The process of marinating the strawberries in the balsamic is called maceration (see p.379) which is a fancy term for leaving the berries to soften slightly until they releases their delicious juices.

1lb (450g) strawberries
1 tbsp sugar
2–3 tbsp good-quality balsamic vinegar
vanilla ice cream or whipped cream (see p.402), to serve

1 | Using a small, sharp chef's knife, slice off and discard the green leafy part from each strawberry and cut the fruit vertically into ½-in (1-cm) slices. Place in a medium shallow serving bowl.

2 | Add the sugar and balsamic vinegar (using the full amount if you want a stronger flavor) to the bowl and gently fold using a wooden spoon, taking care not to crush the strawberries. Macerate at room temperature for 1–2 hours, until the strawberries soften and release their sweet juices.

3 | Serve the strawberries and any juices with vanilla ice cream or whipped cream.

TIPS

Use the balsamic strawberries as a filling for the Victoria Sponge (see p.355).

Strawberries work well with many seasonings, including black pepper, toasted fennel seeds, lemon juice, and even a splash of sherry.

Swap the strawberries for other types of berries, such as raspberries, or try peaches or cherries.

POACHING & STEWING FRUIT

These two methods are largely the same, although stewed fruit tends to be peeled and cut into smaller, similar-size pieces to ensure even cooking. Fruit can be stewed in a small amount of water and/or fruit juice with or without sugar, if needed. The addition of sugar is an excellent method of sweetening more sour types of fruit, such as rhubarb (below) and cooking apples, which become soft and unctuous, almost sauce-like, when stewed. Serve stewed fruit on its own with yogurt, custard, or cream, or use as a base for a fruit crumble, pie, or tart filling.

Poaching particularly suits whole or large pieces of fruit, such as halved pears, apples, and nectarines or whole plums and apricots, which are cooked gently until they soften, but still retain their shape. A sugar syrup, wine, or sweetened fruit juice make an excellent poaching liquid and this method is particularly good for softening slightly underripe fruit.

RICOTTA & ORANGE DOUGHNUTS WITH STEWED RHUBARB

Prep 10 minutes

Cook 40 minutes

Serves 4

Rhubarb is a wonderful ingredient when in season and transforms from a tart, vegetable-like stem to tender, bright pink pieces once stewed. There are two types: the bright pink forced variety grown in dark sheds and available at the end of winter and the slightly less pink (and green) rhubarb, which is grown outdoors and available from late spring. The forced variety is sweeter and brighter in color and works wonderfully with the orange-zest-infused ricotta doughnuts here. If not using forced rhubarb, increase the amount of sugar to taste. The small fritters are best served piping hot with room-temperature rhubarb for a pleasing contrast.

1lb (450g) forced pink rhubarb, cut into
   2-in (5-cm) pieces on the diagonal
⅓ cup (75g) sugar
juice of 1 orange

For the ricotta & orange doughnuts
8oz (250g) ricotta cheese
finely grated zest of 1 orange
2 large eggs, at room temperature
1 tsp vanilla paste or extract
1 cup (125g) all-purpose flour
2 tsp baking powder
3 tbsp sugar
¼ tsp salt
1–3 tbsp whole milk
vegetable oil, for deep-frying
6 tbsp powdered sugar

1 | Start by stewing the rhubarb. Bring the rhubarb, sugar, and orange juice almost to a boil in a medium saucepan. Turn the heat down to a simmer and cook over medium-low heat for 7–8 minutes, until the rhubarb is tender but still holds its shape. Let cool to room temperature. (Continued overleaf.)

2 | Make the doughnut batter. Add the ricotta to a large mixing bowl with the orange zest, eggs, and vanilla. Using a balloon whisk, beat together until smooth and combined. Add in the flour, baking powder, sugar, and salt and whisk again to a smooth, thick batter—it should have a dropping consistency, but still hold its shape. If it's too thick, add a splash of whole milk to loosen slightly.

3 | Fill a large saucepan one-third full with oil and heat over medium-high to 340°F (170°C) on a cooking thermometer or until a cube of bread browns in 30 seconds. If the oil becomes too hot, simply turn off the heat, let it cool for a few minutes, then test the temperature again. Preheat the oven to 325°F (160°C) and line a plate with paper towel and a baking sheet with parchment paper. Use 2 spoons to carefully slide a spoonful of the batter into the hot oil (one of the

spoons to scoop the batter and the other to slide it off the spoon). You should get 6–8 in the pan at a time, depending on its size. Fry for 2–3 minutes, turning halfway, until golden and crisp, then use a slotted spoon to scoop out the doughnuts onto the paper-towel-lined plate. Move onto the lined baking sheet and keep warm in the oven while you repeat with the remaining batter to make about 16 doughnuts in total.

4 | Put the powdered sugar into a shallow bowl, then toss each hot ricotta doughnut in the sugar.

5 | Spoon the stewed rhubarb onto four plates, then add the ricotta doughnuts. Finish with a dusting of powdered sugar to serve. Any leftover rhubarb will keep in the fridge in an airtight container for up to 1 week (or freeze for up to 3 months).

Cherry compote sundae

Prep 20 minutes

Cook 15 minutes

Serves 4

A compote is a cooked dessert/sauce made with whole or chopped fresh fruit. With any compote, the trick is to cook the fruit just long enough to soften and release its juices without it becoming too soft and mushy. Cherries are perfect because they are juicy, but have a fairly robust flesh and a good balance of sweet and sour. This is delicious spooned over the Black Forest Pavlova (see p.400).

For the cherry compote
2¼lb (1kg) black cherries
juice of ½ lemon (about 4 tbsp)
¾ cup (150g) sugar

For the sundae
1¼ cups (300ml) heavy cream
1 tbsp powdered sugar
8 scoops of ice cream, such as Vanilla (see p.408), salted caramel, or pistachio
1 handful of pistachios, roughly chopped, to serve

1 | First, remove the pits from the cherries. You can use a cherry pitter or cut the cherries in half and remove the pits with a teaspoon.

2 | Put the pitted cherries into a medium saucepan with the lemon juice, sugar, and ¼ cup (75ml) of water. Place the pan over medium-low heat and simmer for 15 minutes, stirring occasionally, until the cherries release their juices and the fruit softens while still holding its shape. Put the cherries into a bowl while you make the rest of the sundae.

3 | Follow steps 1–2 from Whipping Cream (see p.402) with the powdered sugar to soft peaks.

4 | Add 2 spoons of the cherry compote into the bottom of each of four sundae glasses. Top each one with 2 scoops of ice cream, then add another spoonful of compote before piling on the whipped cream. Drizzle with a little more compote and sprinkle over the pistachios, to serve. Any leftover compote will keep for up to 1 week, covered, in the fridge.

TIPS

For a thick compote, mix 2 teaspoons of cornstarch with 2 tablespoons of the water to a paste, then add to the pan with the cherries and simmer for 2 minutes, until thickened slightly. This makes a good base for a pie or crumble.

Add some spice—a cinnamon stick, cloves, star anise, or cardamom pods lend a wonderful warm flavor.

Freeze the compote for up to 3 months in a lidded container. Defrost in the fridge overnight or reheat from frozen in a microwave in a heatproof bowl on high in 30-second bursts, or in a small pan if serving warm.

BAKING & BROILING FRUIT

Both baking and broiling are a satisfying and simple way to cook many types of fruit, concentrating and intensifying the flavor by evaporating any moisture and caramelizing the sugars. The dry, intense heat also transforms the texture of fruit, taking it from crisp or firm to soft and unctuous. Baking is particularly good for slightly underripe fruit, such as peaches, apricots, plums, and nectarines because it has a softening and sweetening effect, but still allows the fruit to retain its shape.

Fruit can be baked whole, sliced, or cut into chunks, depending on how it is going to be served. Toss in sugar with a little water or juice, then bake in a roasting pan or wrapped in foil until softened and slightly caramelized. If the fruit is prone to discoloration after cutting, like apples or pears, toss it in a little lemon juice until coated to prevent it from turning brown.

Like baking, broiling suits most types of fruit, with the exception of berries perhaps, especially if you're looking for a deep caramelization and golden tinge; think slices or wedges of pineapple, watermelon, mango, peaches, or nectarine. Make sure the broiler is set to high and place the fruit, sprinkled with sugar, in a single layer on a baking sheet about 2¾ in (7 cm) from the heat source until starting to soften and turn golden in places. A grill pan or barbecue grill are equally good for cooking slightly firmer fruit, including pineapple, apples, and pears, and lend a distinctive smokiness.

SPICED APPLE OAT CRUMBLE

Prep 25 minutes

Cook 35 minutes

Serves 6

A traditional baked fruit dessert, a crumble has many iterations, although apple is the most classic. Look for a good cooking apple which will break down into soft, fluffy pieces. The trick is in cooking the fruit perfectly, while ensuring the top becomes crisp and golden. The three types of sugar all add something different to the crumble: brown sugar caramelizes the apples; the regular adds sweetness and lightness to the crumble mix; and demerara, along with the oats, gives a pleasing crunch to the top. .

2¼lb (1kg) cooking apples
juice and finely grated zest of ½ unwaxed lemon
⅔ cup (125g) packed light brown sugar
3 tbsp (50g) salted butter
½ tsp ground cinnamon
¼ tsp ground allspice
¼ tsp ground nutmeg

For the topping
5 tbsp (75g) cold salted butter, diced
1 cup plus 2 tbsp (150g) all-purpose flour
¼ cup (50g) sugar (or packed light brown sugar)
2 tbsp demerara sugar
2 tbsp old fashioned rolled oats
Crème Anglaise (see p.394), whipped cream, or Vanilla
    Ice Cream (see p.408), to serve

1 | Using a vegetable peeler, remove the skin from the apples, then cut them into quarters lengthwise. Remove the cores with a small, sharp chef's knife and cut into 1¼-in (3-cm) cubes. Put the apples in a bowl and toss in the lemon juice to prevent browning.

2 | Put the apples and any lemon juice into a medium saucepan and add the brown sugar, butter, lemon zest, cinnamon, allspice, nutmeg, and 3 tablespoons of water. Cook the apples on medium heat for 5 minutes, stirring regularly, until they start to soften. Put the apples into a 9 x 13 in (30 x 20 cm) baking dish and spread them into an even layer. Meanwhile, preheat the oven to 400°F (200°C).

3 | Make the topping. Using your fingertips, rub the butter into the flour and sugar in a large mixing bowl until the mixture resembles coarse breadcrumbs. Stir the demerara sugar and oats together in another small bowl.

4 | Sprinkle the crumble topping evenly over the apples, then sprinkle with the rolled oat mixture to give the top a good crunch. Bake for 30 minutes, until golden and crisp on top and the fruit is tender.

5 | Serve the crumble warm with the crème anglaise, whipped cream, or vanilla ice cream on top.

TIPS

This crumble will keep for 3 days in the fridge. To reheat, cover with foil and place in an oven at 350°F (180°C) for 15 minutes, until bubbling and piping hot. Alternatively, microwave in single portions for 1½ minutes, until warmed through.

The crumble is also delicious served cold for breakfast with a spoonful of Greek yogurt.

Broiled peaches with ice cream & maple pecans

Prep 10 minutes

Cook 20 minutes

Serves 4

It's best to choose peaches that are just ripe or even slightly under-ripe for this simple dessert—you want them to soften and caramelize under the broiler, but not fall apart when cooked. The hot fruit and cold ice cream combination is great, but if you have any leftovers the peaches would be equally delicious served cold from the fridge with yogurt. Nectarines and plums make a good alternative to peaches.

4 just-ripe peaches, cut in half and stones removed
few sprigs of thyme, leaves picked, plus a few
    extra to serve
2 tbsp light brown sugar
Vanilla Ice Cream (see p.408) or store-bought,
    to serve

For the maple pecans
½ cup (50g) pecan halves
3 tbsp maple syrup
large pinch of sea salt flakes

1 | To make the maple pecans, preheat the oven to 350°F (180°C). Line a small roasting pan with parchment paper, add the pecans, and toast in the oven for 5 minutes, turning halfway.

2 | Pour the maple syrup over the nuts and add a large pinch of sea salt flakes. Return the tray to the oven for a further 3 minutes, until the nuts are sticky and caramelized. Let cool, then break into pieces or roughly chop, if you prefer.

3 | Turn the oven to a high broiler setting. Lay the peaches, cut-side up, in a medium roasting pan and sprinkle over the thyme leaves and brown sugar. Slide the pan under the broiler, about 2¾ in (7 cm) below the heat source, and broil for 6–8 minutes, checking every 2 minutes and turning the pan around if there are any hot spots, until the peaches caramelize.

4 | To serve, place 2 peach halves on each plate with a scoop of ice cream and the maple pecans sprinkled over. Finish with an extra sprinkling of thyme leaves.

TIP

The maple pecans will keep for up to 2 weeks in an airtight container at room temperature. They are fantastic in savory salads with chunks of blue cheese or sprinkled on top of yogurt for breakfast.

FRYING FRUIT

Frying perhaps doesn't immediately spring to mind as a method for cooking fruit, yet slices of pineapple, apple, plum, peach, pear, or banana pan-fried in butter or a dairy-free alternative, make a simple, delicious dessert, especially with a drizzle of honey or maple syrup. The secret is to cook the fruit briefly on high heat until softened slightly and caramelized, too long and it will start to fall apart and turn mushy.

Fruit, particularly bananas, dipped in batter and deep-fried until golden is a popular dessert or snack the world over (below). These fritters also work well with apple and pineapple (right).

BANANA FRITTERS

Prep 10 minutes

Cook 20 minutes

Serves 4

From Southeast Asia and India to Africa and the Caribbean, banana fritters are hugely popular and it's easy to understand why—sweet bananas are sliced, then coated in a light batter and deep-fried until crisp and golden. You want the bananas to be yellow and ripe but not overly ripe or they will turn to mush when fried. The baking powder in the batter makes it super light.

¾ cup (100g) all-purpose flour
1 tsp baking powder
1 tsp baking soda
pinch of salt
1 tsp vanilla extract
1 large egg, at room temperature
⅔ cup (150ml) whole milk
4 medium-ripe bananas
vegetable oil, for deep-frying
powdered sugar, to dust, and whipped cream or ice cream (optional), to serve

1 | To make the batter, mix the flour, baking powder, baking soda, and a pinch of salt in a large mixing bowl. Add the vanilla and egg and slowly whisk in the milk with a balloon whisk to make a smooth batter, the consistency of heavy cream. Set aside until ready to use.

2 | Peel the bananas and cut each into 5 diagonal slices, about ¾ in (2 cm) thick.

3 | Fill a large, deep skillet, about 11 in (28 cm) in diameter with 1½ in (4 cm) of vegetable oil and heat over medium-high heat to 360°F (180°C) on a cooking thermometer or until a cube of bread browns in 20 seconds; this takes about 8–10 minutes. Working one piece at a time, dip a slice of banana into the batter to completely coat, allow any excess to drip off, then gently place in the hot oil, releasing away from you to avoid splashing.

4 | Cook the bananas in two batches for 2 minutes, turning halfway, until the batter is crisp and golden. Remove the fritters with a slotted spoon onto a paper-towel-lined baking sheet. Repeat with the second batch of banana slices. Dust the hot fritters with powdered sugar and serve with whipped cream or ice cream, if you like.

TIP

If the frying oil becomes too hot, simply turn off the heat, let it cool for a few minutes, then test the temperature again before starting to fry the fritters.

Fritter variations

Apple fritters: make the batter following step 1 from Banana Fritters (left). Peel and remove the core from 4 crisp apples, then cut into wedges or rings. Heat the oil following step 3 (left) and dunk the apple, one piece at a time, into the batter to completely coat. Gently place the apples in the hot oil, cooking them in batches, and deep-fry for 3–4 minutes, until crisp and golden. Remove the apple fritters with a slotted spoon, drain on a paper towel and serve dusted with powdered sugar.

Pineapple fritters: make the batter following step 1 from Banana Fritters (left). Remove the top and bottom of a fresh ripe pineapple. Cut away the skin and remove any eyes. Cut the pineapple into ½-in (1-cm) thick slices and remove the core with an apple corer or sharp knife. (Cut the pineapple slices in half if large.) Heat the oil following step 3 (left) and dunk the pineapple, one piece at a time, into the batter to completely coat. Gently place the pineapple rings in the hot oil, cooking them in batches, and deep-fry for 3–4 minutes, until crisp and golden. Remove with a slotted spoon, drain on a paper towel and serve dusted with powdered sugar.

CHOCOLATE

You can't have a chapter on desserts without including chocolate, otherwise known as the "food of the gods." This wonder ingredient, popular around the globe, is complex and fascinating. Each type of cocoa bean comprises different characteristics and flavor notes based on its variety, how and where it's grown, and how it is processed. That process includes fermentation, drying, roasting, and grinding of the cocoa beans, followed by conching and tempering until smooth and glossy. It is a Herculean effort for an ingredient that is often sold cheaply.

There are three basic types of chocolate: dark, usually sweetened with sugar to make it less bitter; milk, containing cocoa solids, sugar, milk solids, and vanilla; and white, which technically isn't chocolate at all, but a combination of cocoa butter, milk solids, sugar, and vanilla extract. In desserts, the more bitter flavor profile of dark chocolate comes into its own. Look for a bar containing at least 70 percent cocoa solids because the higher the cocoa content the more intensely chocolaty the flavor will be. Dark chocolate is often combined with fat (butter, eggs, and dairy) and sugar for sweetness to create some of our most loved indulgent desserts.

Storage
Chocolate is affected by temperature, particularly heat, so ideally keep it in a cool place.

MELTING CHOCOLATE

Prep 5 minutes

Cook 5 minutes

Makes 7oz (200g)

Melting chocolate is not difficult but it does require careful handling because it is sensitive to heat. Start by chopping or breaking the chocolate into evenly-sized pieces to ensure that it melts evenly. Low heat on the stove top or short bursts of heat in the microwave is preferable, making the melting process more controllable and reducing the likelihood of it seizing or splitting. Not all is lost, though, if your chocolate does seize, just follow the Tip on p.392 to help. Also, avoid allowing steam or any liquid to come into contact with the chocolate during melting.

7oz (200g) dark chocolate, about 70 percent cocoa solids, chopped or broken into evenly-sized pieces

Using a bain-marie: to melt the chocolate, bring 2 in (5 cm) of water to a gentle simmer in a small saucepan over low heat. Put the chocolate in a medium heatproof bowl and set it on top of the pan, making sure that the bottom of the bowl does not touch the water. Heat the chocolate, stirring occasionally with a spatula, for 3–4 minutes, until melted and smooth.

Using a microwave: to melt the chocolate, put it in a microwave-safe bowl and melt the chocolate on medium in 30-second bursts, checking and stirring each time with a spatula until melted and smooth.

Melting white chocolate
White chocolate melts at a much lower temperature because it has a higher sugar and fat content. To melt over a bain-marie, use the same method as left but keep a vigilant eye and once the sides and bottom begin to melt, turn off the heat under the pan and stir until fully melted.

If using a microwave, melt the white chocolate on medium heat at 20-second intervals, stirring each time.

Melt-in-the-middle peanut butter & jam chocolate cakes

*Prep 20 minutes
+ 24 hours
freezing*

Cook 20 minutes

Serves 6

These cakes use a different method for melting the chocolate than those on page 390. Here, the chocolate is melted with butter in a saucepan directly over low heat, which works because the butter stabilizes the chocolate, preventing it from splitting. The secret to the success of these molten center cakes is freezing them before baking so the middle (in this case peanut butter and jam) remains slightly runny and gooey when baked. If you prefer a simple molten chocolate cake, omit the peanut butter and jam (you still get that oozing center). You will need six 5oz (150ml) dome molds or ramekins for this recipe.

½ cup plus 6 tbsp (215g) salted butter, cut into cubes
3 tbsp cocoa powder, sifted
6oz (175g) dark chocolate, chopped or broken
    into evenly-sized pieces
¾ cup (150g) sugar

4 large eggs, at room temperature
2 large egg yolks, at room temperature
    (see p.32 on Separating Eggs)
¾ cup (90g) all-purpose flour
large pinch of salt
6 tsp crunchy or smooth peanut butter
6 tsp raspberry jam
whipped cream, ice cream, yogurt, or cold Crème
    Anglaise (see p.394), to serve

1 | Melt 2½ tbsp (40g) of the butter in a small pan. Using a pastry brush, grease your molds or ramekins with the melted butter, then dust each one with the cocoa powder. The easiest way to do this is to add a spoonful of the cocoa powder after greasing and tilt the mold until the sides and base are evenly coated, then tip out any excess.

2 | Melt the remaining butter, dark chocolate, and sugar in a medium saucepan over low heat, stirring occasionally with a spatula until rich, smooth, and glossy, and the sugar dissolves.

3 | Take the pan off the heat, let the chocolate mixture cool for 2 minutes, then add the whole eggs and the yolks and whisk well with a balloon whisk to combine. Whisk in the flour and a large pinch of salt to make a thick chocolate batter.

4 | Half-fill each mold with the chocolate batter, then add 1 teaspoon each of peanut butter and jam to the center. Top with the remaining chocolate batter. Cover each one with plastic wrap, then freeze for 24 hours (or up to 3 months).

5 | Once ready to serve, preheat the oven to 400°F (200°C). Put the frozen cakes on a baking sheet and bake for 15–18 minutes, until risen slightly and the mixture looks set around the edges but is still soft in the center. Rest for 1 minute (this will help the cakes release from the molds), then run a table knife around the inside of each mold and, with oven gloves, carefully turn out onto serving plates.

6 | Serve the molten chocolate cakes with your favorite creamy accompaniment.

Chocolate mousse
with cereal crunch

*Prep 20 minutes
+ chilling*

Cook 10 minutes

Serves 4–6

This chocolate mousse is simple to make but its success relies heavily on the quality of the ingredients. Use a bar of good-quality dark chocolate with a high percentage of cocoa solids, at least 70 percent, and be sure to choose high-quality eggs because the mousse is uncooked. The crunchy cereal topping adds a touch of fun, but feel free to skip, if preferred.

3 large eggs, at room temperature
4 tbsp sugar
7oz (200g) dark chocolate, about 70 percent cocoa
   solids, chopped or broken into evenly-sized pieces
large pinch of sea salt flakes

For the cereal crunch
1 cup (30g) honey-nut cornflakes
½ cup (100g) sugar

1 | Separate the egg whites and yolks into two medium mixing bowls (see p.32 on Separating Eggs). Add 2 tablespoons of sugar to each bowl.

2 | Using an electric hand mixer, beat the egg whites and sugar until opaque white, voluminous, and they hold their shape in medium-stiff peaks (see p.400 on whisking egg whites).

3 | Next, using the electric hand mixer (no need to clean in between), beat the egg yolks and sugar until doubled in volume, pale in color, and foamy.

4 | Follow steps 1–2 from Melting Chocolate in a bain-marie (see p.390), adding ⅔ cup (150ml) of tepid water to the chocolate just before it melts to ensure the mousse is light and fluffy. Let the chocolate cool for 1 minute.

5 | Briefly whisk the melted chocolate into the egg yolk mixture; you want it to be smooth, but not lose too much air.

6 | Using a metal spoon, fold the egg whites into the chocolate mixture. Start with a large spoonful of egg white and, using a figure-eight motion, efficiently and confidently fold it in before adding the remaining egg white and folding it again. You want to retain as much air as possible for a light mousse.

7 | Spoon the mousse into 4–6 ramekins or small bowls and chill, uncovered, in the fridge for at least 24 hours, until set.

8 | Meanwhile, make the cereal crunch. Line a small roasting pan with parchment paper. Add the cereal to the pan, pressing it tightly into an even layer in the center of the paper.

9 | Sprinkle the sugar evenly into a small skillet, making sure there are no large lumps, and place over high heat. Once the sugar starts to melt and darken in places in the pan, swirl the pan off the heat to combine the melted with the unmelted sugar and return the pan to the heat. Do not stir, or the caramel may crystallize, then repeat until the sugar melts and turns amber in color. Pour the melted sugar over the cereal and let cool. Once cooled and set, break into pieces or roughly pulse in a small food processor into smaller chunks.

10 | To serve, sprinkle a little sea salt on top of each chocolate mousse and finish with a few pieces of cereal crunch. The mousse can be made up to 3 days in advance, kept covered in the fridge. Add the topping just before serving so it keeps its crunch. The cereal crunch keeps for up to 2 weeks in an airtight container.

TIP

If your chocolate splits or seizes during melting, turning grainy, place 2 tablespoons of water in a small saucepan over very low heat. Gradually, whisking continuously with a balloon whisk, spoon in the seized chocolate, until smooth and melted.

EGGS
(IN DESSERTS)

The incredible qualities and versatility of eggs in savory dishes have been lauded earlier in this book (see pp.16–35), but it's their use in desserts that allows eggs to shine, from silky homemade custard (below) and creamy tarts and mousses to marshmallowy meringues. Their ability to multi-task is impressive, since they not only add richness and flavor but also help to bind, stabilize, and thicken, as well as act as a raising agent in cakes and other baked goods (see p.354).

Storage
See page 18 for guidelines on storing eggs. When buying eggs, try to choose high-quality organic ones if possible. This is especially important if using them raw in mousses, tarts, and fools.

CUSTARD
(CRÈME ANGLAISE)

Prep 5 minutes

Cook 15 minutes

Makes about 16fl oz (500ml)

Eggs not only play a part in thickening custard (or crème anglais as it's sometimes known), but they also add richness and stability to this custard, meaning it can be served hot or cold, or gently reheated if necessary. The custard thickens as the eggs cook, so you need to do this slowly and evenly while stirring to ensure a smooth, silky finish. The consistency will be thinner than store-bought custard, similar to that of heavy cream but much richer in taste. Use the best vanilla you can when making custard, it's a crucial flavoring so you want it to sing. Serve with the Spiced Apple Oat Crumble (see p.384) or anything you like.

⅔ cup (150ml) whole milk
⅔ cup (150ml) heavy cream
3 large egg yolks, at room temperature
   (see p.32 on Separating Eggs)
2 tbsp sugar
1 vanilla pod, split in half lengthwise and seeds
   scraped out, or 1 tsp vanilla paste or extract

1 | Bring the milk and cream to a simmer in a small saucepan over medium heat—it should be steaming hot with a little bit of movement on the surface, but no rolling bubbles.

2 | Whisk the egg yolks with the sugar and your choice of vanilla in a medium mixing bowl using a balloon whisk until combined. Pour in one-third of the hot milk mixture, whisking continuously. Whisk in another third and repeat with the final third of the hot milk mixture when combined.

3 | Wipe the pan clean with a paper towel, then pour the combined egg and milk mixture into the pan over low heat. Using a spatula, stir in a figure-eight motion, scraping the bottom of the pan, if needed, to avoid the egg scrambling or lumps forming.

4 | Continue to cook for 8–10 minutes, stirring constantly with the spatula, until the custard thickens to the consistency of heavy cream and coats the back of a spoon—it should be runnier than store-bought custard. Pour the custard into a serving dish and serve immediately or keep in the fridge for up to 3 days.

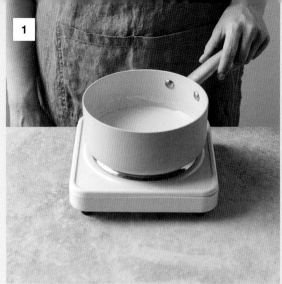

TIPS

If there are small lumps in the custard, pour the mixture through a fine mesh strainer to remove; this can happen if the heat is slightly too high or the custard isn't stirred enough.

If the custard has large lumps of egg, you will need to discard it and start again since even once strained, the custard will have a cooked egg taste.

If you're not serving the custard right away, cover the surface with plastic wrap or parchment paper to prevent a skin from forming as it cools.

CRÈME PÂTISSIÈRE

Prep 5 minutes
+ chilling

Cook 10 minutes

Makes about
24fl oz (700ml)

Otherwise known as pastry cream, crème pâtissière is a rich, creamy, vanilla custard that is thickened with cornstarch. Initially created to fill baked pastries, since it is more stable and doesn't spoil at room temperature as quickly as freshly whipped cream, crème pâtissière is perfect for filling Profiteroles and Eclairs (see p.340) or Mille Feuille (see p.346). It can also be flavored, see the suggestions (right).

2 cups (500ml) whole milk
1 vanilla pod or 2 tsp vanilla paste or extract
4 large egg yolks, at room temperature
   (see p.32 on Separating Eggs)
4 tbsp sugar
3 tbsp cornstarch

1 | Pour the milk into a small saucepan. If using a vanilla pod, cut it in half lengthwise with a small, sharp chef's knife, then scrape out the seeds running the length of the pod on each side. Add the vanilla seeds and pod to the milk. If using vanilla paste or extract, simply add it straight to the milk. Warm the vanilla milk over medium heat until just steaming, taking care that it doesn't boil.

2 | Meanwhile, whisk the egg yolks, sugar, and cornstarch in a medium mixing bowl with a balloon whisk until smooth and pale.

3 | Gradually pour the warm vanilla milk into the egg yolk mixture in the bowl, whisking continuously. It's important to keep stirring here so the yolks don't start to cook and become lumpy.

4 | Return the custard mixture to the pan over medium heat and cook for 3–4 minutes, whisking or stirring constantly and vigorously with a spatula until thickened—it should be the consistency of plain yogurt at this stage.

5 | Transfer the crème pâtissière to a medium bowl and cover the surface with plastic wrap to prevent a skin forming. Let cool at room temperature, then chill in the fridge for 2 hours to firm up and until ready to use. It can be made up to 24 hours in advance.

Flavor variations

Coffee: add 1 tablespoon of instant coffee powder to the warm milk and stir until it dissolves, then continue following the recipe (left), using 1 teaspoon of vanilla paste or extract.

Chocolate: replace the vanilla with 2 tablespoons of sifted cocoa powder, whisk it into the egg yolk, mixture, then continue following the recipe (left).

Citrus: replace the vanilla with the finely grated zest of 1 orange and 1 unwaxed lemon, heated with the milk. Strain the warm milk through a metal strainer before pouring it over the egg yolk mixture, then continue following the recipe (left).

TIPS

If your custard is looking a little lumpy, pass it through a metal strainer into a bowl to make it silky smooth.

Make the crème pâtissière the day before you want to use it and chill in the fridge. If it becomes a little thick, whisk again with a balloon whisk to loosen.

Use any spare egg whites to make the Black Forest Pavlova (see p.400).

Brown sugar custard tart

Prep 30 minutes + chilling

Cook 50 minutes

Serves 8–10

This tart has a silky-smooth, light custard filling with a rich caramel sweetness from the dark brown sugar topping. It features just a handful of ingredients, but there are a few techniques to nail here. Firstly, when caramelizing the dark brown sugar, you're looking to gently melt the sugar without stirring it initially to prevent it from crystallizing. Secondly, the crust (see p.328) should be flaky, crisp, and golden. And, finally, the custard should be baked until it is just set with the gentlest of wobbles in the middle. Let the tart cool at room temperature before chilling to prevent the top from cracking.

1 recipe quantity of Sweet Shortcrust Pastry (see p.328) or 9oz (250g) store-bought
scant 2 cups (450ml) heavy cream
1¼ cups (300ml) whole milk
1 cup plus 4 tbsp (225g) dark brown sugar
12 egg yolks (see p.32 on Separating Eggs)
½ tsp sea salt

1 | Follow steps 1–8 from Lining a Tart & Baking Blind (see p.330) using Sweet Shortcrust Pastry (see p.328), or store-bought pastry, and a 10-in (25-cm) loose-bottomed, fluted tart pan. Once the pie crust is cooling, turn the down oven to 275°F (140°C).

2 | To make the filling, gently heat the cream and milk in a small saucepan, stirring until it begins to simmer, then turn off the heat, leaving the pan on the burner.

3 | Meanwhile, heat the brown sugar in a large skillet over medium-high heat for 3 minutes, until the sugar starts to melt on the bottom, then start to stir with a spatula (don't be tempted to stir the sugar before this point). Continue to cook, stirring constantly, for 3–4 minutes, until melted and a rich brown color—it should have foamed up just a little, like very lightly whipped cream. Remove the pan from the heat.

4 | Carefully, pour the warm cream mixture into the melted sugar in the pan—take care because it will spit and bubble. Using a balloon whisk, mix for 2 minutes on low heat until a smooth, golden cream.

5 | Briefly whisk the egg yolks and salt in a large bowl until combined, then pour one-third of the hot cream mixture over the egg yolks, whisking continuously until combined. Whisk in another third and repeat with the final third of the hot cream mixture when combined.

6 | Working near the oven, pour the filling into the cooked pie crust, still on its baking sheet, and very carefully place it in the middle of the oven. Bake for 35 minutes, until the outer two-thirds of the custard is set but the middle still has a slight wobble. Let the tart cool on a wire rack. It will keep for up to 5 days in the fridge.

TIP

This recipe will leave you with plenty of leftover egg whites—divide them into handy portions, then freeze in airtight containers for up to 6 months.

Spanish flans

Prep 30 minutes + chilling

Cook 1 hour

Makes 6

These individual pots of classic baked vanilla custard are popular throughout Spain and Mexico. The creamy, silky custard is topped with a slightly bitter caramel that infuses the milky mixture as it sets and chills. The trick with any baked custard is to cook it gently—you want the egg mixture to have the perfect jiggle in the middle when taken out of the oven because it will continue to cook and set. You will need six 6oz (175ml) ramekins for this recipe. The flans can be made up to 2 days before serving, covered in the fridge.

1 recipe quantity of Caramel (see p.406)
3 large eggs, at room temperature
1 large egg yolk, at room temperature (see
   p.32 on Separating Eggs)
1 (14oz/396g) can condensed milk
1¼ cups (300ml) whole milk
2 tsp vanilla paste or extract
large pinch of salt

1 | Preheat the oven to 275°F (140°C). Follow steps 1–4 from Making Caramel (see p.406). Divide the caramel between the ramekins, spooning it in, then place the ramekins in a large, deep roasting pan, leaving a little room around each. Let the caramel cool and set for 15 minutes.

2 | Using a balloon whisk, beat the whole eggs with the egg yolk, condensed milk, whole milk, vanilla, and a pinch of salt in a large mixing bowl until smooth, making sure there are no streaks of egg white. Strain the egg mixture through a metal strainer, then divide evenly between the ramekins.

3 | Working near the oven, pour boiling water into the roasting pan until it comes halfway up the sides of the ramekins. Carefully place the roasting pan on the middle shelf and cook for 1 hour, until the sides are set but the centers have a slight wobble.

4 | Remove the pan from the oven and leave the flans in the water for 10 minutes, until cool enough to handle. Move the flans, still in their ramekins, onto a wire rack to cool for a further 20 minutes. Once cool, chill in the fridge, uncovered, for at least 4 hours but preferably overnight.

5 | When ready to serve, gently run a table knife around the edge of each flan. Put a small, upturned plate on top, then with one confident movement, flip the flan out onto the plate. Give both the flan and plate a gentle shake, you should feel it loosen in the ramekin. Carefully remove the ramekin, some of the caramel should flood out onto the plate. Repeat with the remaining flans, to serve.

TIP

Try adding different flavors to the egg mixture instead of vanilla, such as the finely grated zest of 1 orange, a shot of strong espresso, or 3 tablespoons almond or hazelnut liqueur.

BLACK FOREST
PAVLOVA

*Prep 35 minutes
+ cooling*

Cook 2 hours

Serves 8–10

A classic summer dessert, this pavlova combines the flavors of a classic black forest cake, including cherries, chocolate, and cream. A pavlova isn't as tricky to make as it looks if you follow the basic techniques for whisking egg whites (you want to incorporate as much air as possible), and the sugar is added gradually once they are whisked. Too quickly and you'll lose the air you've patiently whipped into the whites, or the sugar won't fully dissolve into the eggs. Both the cornstarch and vinegar give the meringue a slightly chewy, marshmallowy center with a crisp shell, which is just perfect for a pavlova.

6 large egg whites, at room temperature
   (see p.32 on Separating Eggs)
1¾ cup plus 4 tbsp (375g) sugar
1 tsp cornstarch
1 tsp white wine vinegar
½ tbsp cocoa powder
2½ cups (600ml) whipping cream
2 tbsp powdered sugar
1 tsp vanilla paste or extract
½ recipe quantity of Cherry Compote (see p.383)
3½oz (100g) dark chocolate, finely chopped into
   shards

1 | Preheat the oven to 250°F (130°C). Line a large baking sheet with parchment paper and mark it with an 11-in (28-cm) circle—this will be your template. Starting on low and gradually increasing the speed, whisk the egg whites in a large, clean, grease-free mixing bowl with an electric hand mixer, or in a stand mixer fitted with a whisk attachment, for 3–5 minutes, until they form soft peaks.

2 | Start to add the sugar, a spoonful at a time, whisking well for 30 seconds to 1 minute between each addition—the meringue will become more glossy, white, and stiff with each spoonful of sugar added.

3 | Once all of the sugar has been added, continue to whisk for 2 minutes, until smooth, glossy, and the mixture holds firm peaks. Spoon in the cornstarch and vinegar and whisk for another 20 seconds until everything is combined.

4 | Using a fine mesh strainer, sift the cocoa powder into the meringue mixture and then with a large metal spoon, make a couple of figure-eight motions to ripple it through the mix—you are looking for large streaks of cocoa powder.

5 | Spoon the meringue onto the marked circle on the baking sheet, keeping the sides high. Use the spoon to make peaks and troughs on the outer edge and a slight dip in the middle—this will hold the whipped cream, fruit, and other toppings. Bake for 2 hours, then turn the oven off and let the meringue cool in the oven for 1 hour. It shouldn't have browned or cracked, but will have a crisp shell. Remove from the oven and let cool completely.

6 | When you're ready to serve, assemble the pavlova (don't do this too far in advance or the meringue will become soggy). Using a balloon whisk, whip the cream, powdered sugar, and vanilla in a large mixing bowl to soft peaks (see p.402). Place the meringue on a large serving plate or platter. Spoon the whipped cream into the center, top with the cherry compote, then sprinkle over the chocolate shards. Cut into slices to serve.

TIPS

Make sure your mixing bowl is clean before making the meringue because any sign of grease will stop the eggs from whisking.

To make individual meringues, follow the same recipe, but omit the cornstarch and vinegar. Spoon into 4-in (10-cm) circles on parchment-paper-lined baking sheets and bake for 1 hour, then leave in the oven for another hour (above).

Save the egg yolks to use in the Crème Anglaise (see p.394), Crème Pâtissière (see p.396), or in the Caesar Salad Dressing (see p.431).

CREAM
(IN DESSERTS)

A key ingredient in many puddings, baked goods, and desserts (and not just poured over hot plum crumble, wonderful as it is), there are two main types of cream to choose from, each with its own characteristics. In order of viscosity, there's whipping cream and heavy cream, and each type is largely defined by its fat content (see p.56). It is this high fat-to-water ratio that gives cream its rich mouthfeel, which is perfectly suited to desserts, and also determines how it's best used.

Whipping cream: lower in fat than heavy cream but, as its name suggests, is good for whipping as well as used as a pouring cream. It can be heated.

Heavy cream: has a higher fat content than whipping cream, which makes it perfect for whisking into pillowy clouds (below). It can be folded into desserts to add lightness and richness, served as an accompaniment, and will withstand heat, so is perfect in creamy sauces and tarts.

Storage
Keep an eye on the use-by date because cream has a relatively short shelf life and, once open, lasts up to 3 days in the fridge.

WHIPPING CREAM

Prep 10 minutes

No cook

Makes 10fl oz (300ml)

Whipping cream is best done by hand (unless it's more than 4 cups (1 liter) or so, which is more demanding on the wrist) because this gives you greater control. You can also use a stand mixer or electric hand mixer—it's certainly faster—but be careful not to over-whip the cream, which can easily turn grainy and stiff. Heavy cream is used here but you can use whipping cream, if preferred, although it is slightly less stable. Both have a fat content high enough to suspend the trapped air. Cold cream whips the best, so keep it in the fridge until the point you need to use it.

1¼ cups (300ml) chilled heavy cream

1 | Pour the cream into a large mixing bowl. Holding the bowl firmly in one hand, between your body and arm, use a balloon whisk to start whisking the cream in a circular motion. After a few minutes, the cream will thicken enough to leave a ribbon trail on the surface, but it is still not thick enough to hold its shape.

2 | Continue to whisk for a few minutes until the cream holds soft peaks when you lift out the whisk but very gently and slowly collapses. This is the perfect cream for serving alongside desserts because it is soft and velvety but spoonable.

3 | Continue to whisk for another few minutes until the cream forms stiff peaks that do not collapse or soften. This is perfect for filling cakes because it is firm enough to hold the layers of cake without oozing out of the sides, and will cut cleanly when sliced.

TIPS

Whipped cream should be served immediately or can be kept covered in the fridge for up to 1 hour.

If your cream becomes too thick and a little grainy during whisking this could be a sign you've over-whipped it. To rescue it, add 1–2 tablespoons of cold whole milk and fold in with a spatula or large metal spoon. This should loosen the cream and bring it back together.

You can sweeten your whipped cream if serving with tarts, pies, and crumbles. Add a tablespoon of sifted powdered sugar and a splash of vanilla extract to the cream, then whip as instructed (left).

PANNA COTTA

*Prep 25 minutes
+ chilling*

Cook 5 minutes

Serves 4–6

Panna cotta is an Italian dessert of sweetened cream thickened with gelatin and left to set in the fridge, preferably overnight. Using the right amount of gelatin is crucial—too little and it will not set, while use too much and it will become bouncy and rubbery. Gelatin sheets are best for achieving a silky, smooth texture, but since it is an animal byproduct, this recipe is not suitable for vegetarians. Serve the panna cotta with the Raspberry Coulis (see p.379) spooned over the top. You will need four 5oz (150ml) or six 3½oz (100ml) ramekins or molds for this recipe.

3 sheets of fine leaf gelatin
1¼ cups (300ml) heavy cream
1¼ cups (300ml) whole milk
1 vanilla pod, split in half lengthwise and
　seeds scraped out
¼ cup (50g) sugar
Raspberry Coulis (see p.379), to serve

1 | Soak the gelatin sheets in a small bowl of ice-cold water for 10 minutes, until soft and floppy, then drain through a metal strainer, squeezing out as much water as possible. Set the metal strainer over the top of a bowl to continue draining.

2 | Warm the heavy cream, milk, vanilla seeds (save the pod, see Tip below), and sugar in a medium saucepan over medium heat, stirring occasionally with a spatula, until it comes to a low simmer (just above the point of steaming), then remove the pan from the heat.

3 | Add the drained gelatin to the warm cream mixture and stir with a spatula for around 1 minute until melted. Strain the cream mixture through the metal strainer. Let cool for 10 minutes, until thickened slightly.

4 | Put the ramekins on a baking sheet. Stir the cream mixture, then pour it evenly into the ramekins. Cover the tray with plastic wrap and chill in the fridge for at least 6 hours, preferably overnight, until the panna cotta sets.

5 | Once ready to serve, pour hot water from the faucet into a wide shallow bowl or roasting pan. Dip the bottom of each ramekin into the hot water for 10 seconds to loosen the panna cotta, then turn out onto serving plates, tapping the base with a teaspoon if needed. Serve with the raspberry coulis.

TIPS

Panna cotta can be made up to 3 days in advance of serving. Store covered in the fridge until ready to use.

Try substituting the vanilla with other flavorings, such as the finely grated zest of 1 orange or the crushed seeds of 6 cardamom pods.

Don't let the vanilla pod go to waste, you can use it to make vanilla sugar. Simply place it in the middle of a jar of sugar and let infuse for about 2 weeks.

MAKING CARAMEL

Prep 5 minutes

Cook 10 minutes

The base of many desserts and baked goods, golden caramel can transform the flavor profile of one-dimensional white sugar, adding depth and richness. Making caramel can be a bit daunting at first because it is prone to misbehaving and crystallizing in the pan, but the following method takes you through each step. Using a silver stainless steel pan is preferable, because it is much easier to monitor the sugar as it darkens in color and caramelizes so you can remove it from the heat at the perfect time. Caramel is also extremely hot, so be careful when handling it.

¾ cup (150g) sugar

1 | Put the sugar into a deep, stainless steel skillet, around 8–10 in (20–25cm) in diameter. Set the pan over medium heat and leave it for 2–3 minutes, until the sugar melts around the edges. It is important not to stir the sugar or move the pan during this stage or the sugar may start to crystallize.

2 | Once the sugar melts around the edges, lift the pan and gently swirl the sugar around the pan to help it melt evenly. Return the pan to the heat, then repeat.

3 | When the sugar has melted, cook for another 3–4 minutes over medium heat, swirling it now and again until caramelized and a deep amber color. It should smell similar to toffee, but not burned. Use the caramel as desired.

TIP

Liquid glucose stabilizes the sugar as it heats, making it less likely to crystallize. Swap ¼ cup (50g) of the sugar for the same amount of liquid glucose, adding it to the pan at the same time as the sugar.

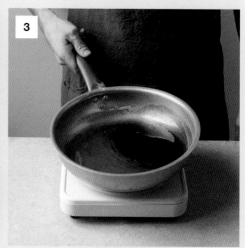

No-bake caramel cheesecake

*Prep 25 minutes
+ chilling*

Cook 15 minutes

Serves 8–10

The filling for this cheesecake is simply mixed together, then spooned onto the graham cracker crust—the fridge does the rest of the work for you. If you don't want to make the salted caramel sauce, swap it for 1 cup (200g) of store-bought instead.

For the salted caramel sauce
1 recipe quantity of Caramel (left)
2 tbsp (30g) salted butter
⅔ cup (150ml) heavy cream
large pinch of sea salt flakes

For the cheesecake
6 tbsp (100g) salted butter, melted, plus extra to grease
7oz (200g) graham crackers
8oz (250g) mascarpone cheese
9½oz (280g) full-fat cream cheese
1¼ cups (300ml) heavy cream
2 tsp vanilla paste or extract
2 cups (75g) caramel popcorn (optional)

1 | Follow steps 1–3 from Making Caramel (left). To make the salted caramel sauce, carefully add the butter to the caramel in the pan, followed by the heavy cream, carefully because it will spit. Put the pan on low heat and cook gently for 4–5 minutes, stirring until it comes together into a thick, smooth sauce. Stir in a large pinch of sea salt flakes, then pour it into a bowl, cover the surface with plastic wrap, and let cool.

2 | Lightly grease an 8-in (20-cm) springform cake pan with butter and line the base with a disk of parchment paper. To make the crust, put the graham crackers into a freezer bag and use the end of a rolling pin to bash into small, evenly-sized crumbs (or pulse in a food processor). Put the crumbs into a mixing bowl, add the melted butter, and mix until combined. Spoon the crust mixture into the pan, pressing it down with the back of the spoon into a firm, even layer. Chill for 1 hour.

3 | To make the filling, mix the mascarpone, cream cheese, and three-quarters of the salted caramel sauce in a large mixing bowl with a balloon whisk.

4 | Using a balloon whisk, whip the cream and vanilla in a large mixing bowl to soft peaks (see p.402). Fold the whipped cream into the mascarpone mixture with a metal spoon. Spoon the filling on top of the graham cracker crust, smooth the top, and chill for at least 4 hours or overnight.

5 | When ready to serve, run a small knife around the edge of the cheesecake, then unclasp the latch and remove the collar of the pan. Use the knife to loosen the crust from the bottom of the pan, then slide the cheesecake onto a serving plate. Pile the popcorn on top, if using, then drizzle over the remaining caramel sauce. It will keep for up to 3 days in the fridge.

TIP

Serve the salted caramel sauce spooned over Vanilla Ice Cream (see p.408) or swirled into the batter for the Salted Caramel Chocolate Brownies (see p.362) before baking.

FROZEN DESSERTS

There is something both satisfying and indulgent about a frozen dessert. The cold seems to temper the sweetness, leaving it to slowly wash over your palate instead of the instant sugar hit of some sweet treats. The three frozen desserts that follow cover all bases, from a classic vanilla ice cream to a simple no-churn version as well as a lip-smacking mango sorbet using tajin—a Mexican seasoning made from chili powder, salt, sugar, and lime. To enjoy them at their best, remove from the freezer 5–10 minutes before serving.

HOMEMADE VANILLA ICE CREAM

Prep 15 minutes
+ cooling, chilling
and freezing

Cook 15 minutes

Makes about
16oz (500ml)

Nothing compares to a scoop of vanilla ice cream on a hot summer day—or any day for that matter. Usually, ice cream is made up of two parts: first, you need to make a custard to give the ice cream a smooth, luxurious mouthfeel once frozen. Secondly, to prevent ice crystals from forming, you need to churn the ice cream as it freezes to keep it smooth.

¾ cup (200ml) whole milk
1¾ cup (400ml) heavy cream
2 vanilla pods, split in half lengthwise and seeds
   scraped, or 2 tsp vanilla paste or extract
6 large egg yolks, at room temperature
   (see p.32 on Separating Eggs)
½ cup plus 4 tbsp (125g) sugar
pinch of salt

1 | Follow steps 1–5 from Making Custard (see p.394). Let the custard cool for 1 hour, then move to the fridge and chill for another 3 hours. Remove and discard the vanilla pod (or wash and reuse, see Tip p.404), if using, then pour the custard into an ice cream machine and churn following the manufacturer's instructions until nearly frozen.

2 | Scrape the ice cream into a freezerproof container, cover with the lid, and freeze until firm. Remove from the freezer at least 5 minutes before serving. The ice cream will keep for up to 3 months in the freezer.

No-churn vanilla
ice cream

Prep 5 minutes
+ freezing

No cook

Makes about
1¾ pints (1 liter)

It is perfectly possible to make a delicious vanilla ice cream without a machine. This version utilizes the magic of condensed milk to create a stable, ice-free ice cream without the need for churning.

2½ cups (600ml) heavy cream
2 vanilla pods, split in half lengthwise and seeds
    scraped out, or 2 tsp vanilla paste or extract
1 (14oz/396g) can condensed milk

1 | Using a balloon whisk, whip the cream, vanilla, and condensed milk in a medium to large mixing bowl to soft peaks (see p.402). Alternatively, use an electric hand mixer or stand mixer, but be careful not to overbeat the mixture.

2 | Pour the creamy mixture into a freezerproof container, cover with the lid, and freeze for at least 4 hours, until firm.

3 | Remove the ice cream from the freezer at least 5 minutes before serving. It will keep for up to 3 months in the freezer.

TIPS

If unsure how to remove the seeds from a whole vanilla pod, turn to p.396 for instructions.

To flavor either the churned or no-churn ice creams, stir in chunks of your favorite chocolate with the Salted Caramel Sauce (see p.407); or for a traditional raspberry ripple, half-fold in the Raspberry Coulis (see p.379) to leave streaks of fruit. Continue with your choice of recipe to freeze the ice cream.

Mango sorbet
with tajin sugar

Prep 15 minutes
+ freezing

Cook 5 minutes

Makes about
1¾ pints (1 liter)

Mango is arguably the best fruit to use for sorbets. Its soft, sweet flesh blends super smooth, resulting in a sorbet with a silky, almost creamy texture, and an intensely fruity flavor. For simplicity, this recipe uses canned or frozen mango pulp, which is made from fruit ripened to perfection so there is no need to take a chance with fresh mango—and it also doesn't require an ice cream maker. Tajin is a Mexican seasoning made from sugar, salt, lime, and chili flakes and brings a salty-spicy complexity to the sorbet, but you can leave it out if you prefer.

¾ cup (150g) sugar
1 tbsp tajin seasoning, plus extra to serve
 (optional)
juice and finely grated zest of 1 lime
1lb 14oz (850g) canned or frozen mango pulp

1 | Heat the sugar and ⅓ cup (100ml) of water in a medium saucepan over medium heat. Stir and cook for 2–3 minutes, until steaming and the sugar dissolves into the water to make a light syrup.

2 | Remove the pan from the heat and stir in the tajin seasoning, if using, and the lime juice and zest. Let cool to room temperature.

3 | Using an immersion blender, blend the mango pulp with the sugar syrup to a smooth purée, then pour it into a 9 x 13 in (30 x 20 cm) freezerproof container and freeze for 20 minutes.

4 | Remove the container from the freezer and use a fork to stir the purée, scraping and crushing any icy bits into small pieces, then spread it out again and return to the freezer for another 20 minutes. Repeat this stirring and mixing for several hours until the sorbet is firm.

5 | Remove from the freezer at least 5 minutes before serving. Sprinkle with more tajin, if using, to finish. The sorbet will keep for up to 3 months in the freezer.

TIPS

If you have an ice cream machine, use it to churn the sorbet for an extra silky-smooth texture.

You can use fresh mango if preferred, but make sure it is nice and ripe. To prepare, hold the mango vertically on a cutting board, then use a sharp knife to cut away the flesh on each side of the stone. Make a criss-cross pattern into each piece of flesh, turn the skin inside out, and cut the cubes of mango away from the skin. Cut away any fruit still attached to the stone.

STOCKS,

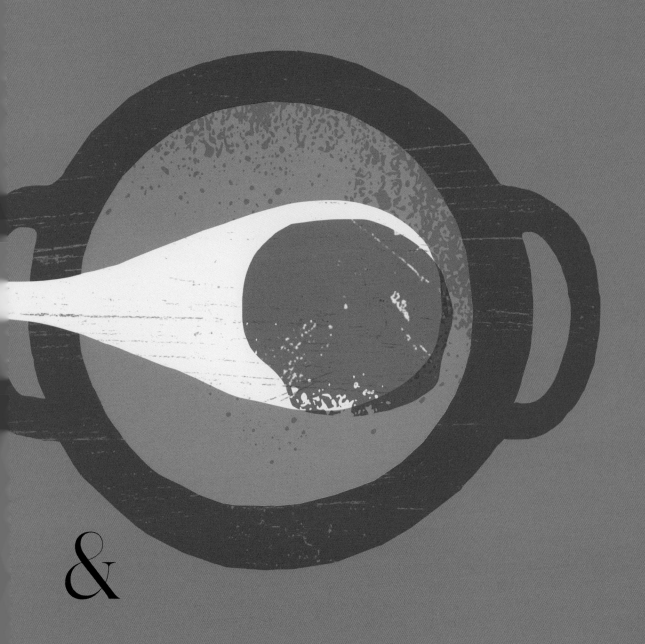

&

SAUCES

DRESSINGS

STOCKS

The best homemade stocks are all about the raw ingredients, their quality and freshness, and how you prepare them (see guide below). For meat, chicken, and fish stocks, you are looking to unlock the collagen found within the bones through low-and-slow cooking. This collagen gives body and a fatty richness to the flavor of your stock. When making a meat (brown) stock, you are additionally looking for caramelization (right). Roasting the meat bones at the start adds a good meaty depth of flavor and a rich appealing color to the finished stock.

Similarly, when making a good vegetable stock, roasting the veggies first adds color and depth to the final flavor—try to choose a mix of root vegetables, leeks, onions, mushrooms, and herbs (see p.436).

Storage
A homemade meat or chicken stock will last in a sealed container for up to 4 days; a vegetable stock 5 days; and fish stock 3 days in the fridge. All will keep for 3 months in the freezer. Store-bought stocks will last much longer and it's best to check the package.

STOCK	HOW TO MAKE ...
Chicken **Makes** **4½ cups** **(1 liter)**	Follow the meat stock recipe (right), replacing the meat bones with chicken wings, making the total quantity of wings 4–5lb (around 2kg).
Fish **Makes** **4½ cups** **(1 liter)**	Melt 2 tbsp (30g) of butter in a large saucepan and add 1 finely chopped fennel bulb with a pinch of salt. Cook gently for 10 minutes, until softened, then add 2¼lb (1kg) of clean white fish bones, such as cod, haddock, sea bass, sea bream, coley, or hake (do not use the bones of oily fish). Pour in 5 cups (1.25 liters) of cold water and 1 cup (250ml) of dry white wine, along with a few parsley stalks and a bay leaf. Bring to a simmer and cook for 30 minutes, skimming regularly. Strain through a metal strainer over a bowl, gently squeezing the bones for their liquid.
Shellfish **Makes** **4½ cups** **(1 liter)**	In a large, wide, deep skillet, heat 2 tablespoons of olive oil and sauté 1¼lb (500g) of cleaned shellfish shells (shrimp, langoustine, crayfish) for 10 minutes, until the shells turn pink and smell slightly nutty. Remove the shells and add a finely chopped onion, leek, fennel bulb, and 4 peeled, chopped garlic cloves. Add a pinch of salt and cook gently for 5 minutes. Add 2 tablespoons of tomato paste and cook for 2 minutes, then pour in ⅓ cup (100ml) of brandy. Using a match or long firelighter, carefully light the brandy to burn off the alcohol. Add the shells back to the pan, along with 6½ cups (1.5 liters) of cold water. Simmer gently for 2 hours, skimming regularly, then strain through a metal strainer into a bowl, using a ladle to squeeze out as much liquid from the shells as possible.
Vegetable **Makes** **4½ cups** **(1 liter)**	Preheat the oven to 425°F (220°C). Peel (if needed) and roughly chop 2 onions, 3 carrots, 2 leeks, 2 celery stalks, ¾lb (300g) of mushrooms, and 2 bulbs of fennel. Put them into a large roasting pan, spoon over 2 tablespoons of tomato paste, mix well, and roast for 40 minutes. Scrape everything into a large saucepan with 6½ cups (1.5 liters) of cold water, 1 teaspoon of black peppercorns, some parsley stalks, and a bay leaf. Bring to a boil, then reduce to a simmer and cook gently for 2 hours. Strain through a metal strainer over a bowl, using a ladle to squeeze out as much liquid from the vegetables as possible.
Dashi (light **Japanese** **stock)** **Makes 4½** **cups (1 liter)**	Put 6½ cups (1.5 liters) of cold water into a large saucepan and add a 1-oz (30-g) piece of dried kombu seaweed. Put the pan over medium heat and bring to a simmer, then remove from the heat and add 1oz (30g) of katsuobushi (dried bonito) flakes. Leave to stand for about 10 minutes, then strain through a metal strainer placed over a bowl.

MAKING A MEAT STOCK

Prep 15 minutes

Cook 7 hours

Makes 1¾ pints
(1 liter)

This is called "meat" stock since the recipe is flexible and works with fresh raw beef, pork, or lamb bones. The brown stock has a poultry base, specifically chicken wings, which provide plentiful amounts of collagen as well as a rich background flavor that is ramped up by the meat bones. Meat bones are often free, or at least cheap to buy, from a butcher, and need to be cut into roughly 4–6-in (10–15-cm) long pieces, ensuring all the goodness is unlocked from inside the bones, as well as making them easier to fit in the roasting pan or saucepan. It doesn't matter if there are bits of meat still on the bones, these add to the flavor of the stock, which can be used as a flavorful base for Gravy (see p.418; pan sauces, such as peppercorn sauce for steak (see p.114); or added to a soup or stew, including Beef Bourguignon (see p.120).

1½lb (750g) raw beef, pork, or lamb bones, cut
    into 4–6-in (10–15-cm) long pieces
2¼lb (1kg) chicken wings
1 onion, peeled and cut into wedges
2 carrots, peeled and cut into chunks
3 celery stalks, roughly chopped
1 whole garlic bulb, cut in half horizontally

2 tbsp tomato paste
salt and freshly ground black pepper
1 handful of thyme sprigs

1 | Preheat the oven to 425°F (220°C). Put the meat bones and chicken wings, chopped vegetables, garlic, and tomato paste into two large roasting pans and season well with salt and pepper. Sprinkle over the thyme and roast for 1 hour, turning halfway, until everything is caramelized and beginning to blacken in places.

2 | Put the contents of the roasting pans into your largest saucepan and pour in 12½ cups (3 liters) of cold water. Pour an additional 1 cup (200ml) of water into each roasting pan, then return to the oven for 3 minutes to loosen any crusty brown bits on the bottom. Using a spatula, scrape the bits from the roasting pans into the saucepan, discarding anything that is too burned. (Continued overleaf.)

3 | Put the pan over high heat and bring to a boil, skimming off any foamy scum that floats to the surface with a ladle and discarding. Once boiling, reduce the heat to a gentle simmer and cook for 6 hours, breaking up the chicken wings with a spatula during cooking, to help access all of their goodness.

4 | Place a large metal strainer over a large bowl. Using a ladle, carefully spoon out the bones and any flavorings and liquid into the strainer, using the back of the ladle to gently press and squeeze any liquid from the meat, bones, and vegetables.

5 | Leave the stock to settle for 5 minutes, then use the ladle to scoop off any fat or impurities that have risen to the top. The stock is now ready to use, or if not using it immediately, cover and leave to cool to room temperature, then chill or freeze.

Using leftover roast chicken for stock

The gift of a roast chicken (see p.69) is that it can be turned into multiple meals as well as a delicious stock. Once all the meat has been picked off (see p.70), put the carcass into a large saucepan with chopped carrot, celery, onion, and a bay leaf and cover with cold water. Bring to a boil, then simmer over medium heat for 3–4 hours. Strain the stock through a metal strainer into a container and discard the solids. It is now ready to use, or to reduce and concentrate the flavor of the stock, strain it into a medium saucepan and simmer over medium heat until reduced by two-thirds. The stock will keep in the fridge for up to 4 days or freeze for 3 months.

SAUCES

If the thought of making a sauce fills you with trepidation, fear not, you don't have to be a classically trained chef to learn the basics. You'll find a few classics in this chapter to help you get started, plus there are recipes for White Sauce (see p.40), Béchamel (see p.41), and Nut Sauces (see p.294) sprinkled throughout the book. The first rule to remember with any sauce is that its role is to enhance, complement, and support whatever it is served with, like meat, seafood, vegetables, eggs, pasta, or noodles. Choose your sauce with care and you can elevate your cooking to something new and special. The following pages include recipes for different types of sauces, from those that are served on the side as a condiment to others that are a fundamental part of the dish, such as a pasta sauce (see p.422), as well as those that will lift and excite the palate, like the Asian dipping sauces (see p.427).

Storage
The shelf life of a sauce varies depending on the type. It is best to check the individual recipe for guidelines.

SAUCE	VARIATIONS	PERFECT WITH ...
Butter sauces (see p.50)	White butter sauce, Brown Butter (see p.51), Clarified Butter/ghee (see p.50)	Vegetables, pan-fried fish or meat fillets/steaks, curries.
Herb sauces (see p.442)	Pesto (see p.442), Gremolata (see p.443), Persillade Sauce (see p.443), Chimichurri (see p.444)	Roast meat, fish and vegetables, pasta, pulses, pan-fried fish and meat fillets/steaks, steamed vegetables, potatoes.
Hollandaise (see p.33)	Hot Sauce Hollandaise (see p.33), mustard/herb/watercress hollandaise, béarnaise	Spooned over eggs, white fish, roast meat, steamed vegetables.
Mayonnaise (see p.420)	Aioli (see p.421), rouille (with chile), Tartar (see p.421), remoulade	Condiment, salads, fish stew, pan-fried fish, cold meats, boiled eggs, shellfish, roasted vegetables.
Nuts & seeds (see p.294)	Romesco (see p.294), Tahini (see p.302), cashew sauce, walnut sauce	Condiment, vegetables, pulses, eggs, fish, shellfish.
Pan sauces (see p.418)	Gravy (see p.418), Vegan Gravy (see p.419), wine (red and white) sauce, jus, stock-based sauces, Creamy Cider Sauce (see p.104), Peppercorn Sauce (see p.114)	Roast meat, vegetarian roasts, pan-fried meat and fish fillets/steaks.
Vegetables (see p.158)	Tomato sauce (see p.422), Mushroom Sauce (see p.423), Butternut Squash Sauce (see p.180), Baba Ganoush (see p.187), Salsa (see p.425), Sauce Vierge (see p.426)	Condiment, pasta, vegetables, fish, eggs, pan-fried meat and fish, roast meat and fish, as a dip, dressing.
White sauces (see p.40)	Béchamel (see p.41), Cheese Sauce (see p.41), parsley sauce	Baked pastas, vegetable casseroles, fish, savory pie fillings.

GRAVY & PAN SAUCES

A good gravy unites a meal, bringing the various components of the dish together in a harmonious way. The best example of this is perhaps a roast dinner. You can make perfectly crisp potatoes, light and fluffy Yorkshire puddings, succulent roasted meat or a flavorful nut roast, but without a good gravy holding everything together, it wouldn't be the same. Here are two great gravy recipes—one meat-based, the other vegan—to cover all bases. A meat gravy usually starts with the juices and crispy, caramelized bits found in the bottom of the roasting pan or in the pan after frying a steak or pork chop. These form the base, and the flavor is then built on with the addition of wine and/or stock, maybe herbs, and thickened, either by adding flour, cornstarch, a roux (flour/butter paste), or deglazing (cooking until reduced) to create a savory-tasting gravy or sauce. The Vegan Gravy (right) re-creates the caramelized roasted meaty undertones by cooking the vegetables in the oven first to lend a rich depth of flavor.

HOMEMADE GRAVY

Prep 10 minutes

Cook 20 minutes

Serves 4–6

This recipe utilizes two surefire tips for achieving amazing gravy. First, make sure you use all the crusty bits from the bottom of the roasting pan after roasting the meat—they're full of concentrated flavor and far too good to waste. Secondly, gravy is only as good as the stock you use to make it, so follow the guide for homemade Meat Stock (see pp.414–15) before you start this recipe.

2 tbsp all-purpose flour
⅔ cup (150ml) dry red wine
3½ cups (800ml) good-quality Meat (see p.415) or
    Chicken Stock (see p.414) or store-bought
2 tsp English mustard
salt and freshly ground black pepper

1 | Pour 2–3 tbsp of fat from the roasting pan into a saucepan. Put the pan over medium heat, stir in the flour with a spoon, and cook for 3 minutes, stirring, until slightly golden and the mixture smells nutty.

2 | Meanwhile, put the roasting pan over medium-high heat and pour in the wine. Scrape the pan to remove all the good bits stuck on the bottom and edges, and bring to a boil.

3 | Once the flour is golden, stir in the wine from the roasting pan to make a thick paste. Gradually stir in the stock and add the mustard. Season with salt and pepper and simmer for 15 minutes, until thickened. Pour any juices from the roasted meat into the gravy before reheating.

Vegan gravy

Prep 10 minutes

Cook 35 minutes

Serves 4–6

A good gravy can make or break a meal and this meat-free recipe uses slow-cooked, caramelized vegetables as a base, which are enhanced with store-bought flavor boosters.

2 tbsp extra-virgin olive oil
1 onion, peeled and finely chopped
2 celery stalks, finely chopped
2 carrots, peeled and finely chopped
8 dried shiitake mushrooms
3 vegetable bouillon cubes
6 garlic cloves, peeled and finely chopped
1 handful of thyme sprigs, leaves stripped
1 tbsp tomato paste
1 tbsp all-purpose flour
1 tbsp yeast extract, brewer's yeast, or
   nutritional yeast
1 tbsp soy sauce
1 tbsp apple cider vinegar

1 | Heat the olive oil in a medium saucepan or deep skillet over medium heat. Add the onion, celery, and carrots and cook for 20 minutes, stirring every 5 minutes, until the vegetables are really soft and lightly caramelized.

2 | Meanwhile, put the dried mushrooms into a large heatproof bowl with the vegetable bouillon cubes and top up with 3 cups (750ml) of boiling water. Stir to combine and let sit for 15 minutes, until the mushrooms soften.

3 | Add the garlic and thyme to the vegetables in the pan and cook for another 5 minutes, stirring regularly. Stir in the tomato paste and cook for 1 minute, then add the stock and rehydrated mushrooms to the pan and stir briefly until combined.

4 | Using an immersion blender, blend until completely smooth. Spoon in the yeast, soy sauce, and apple cider vinegar and simmer for a final 5 minutes, until reduced and thickened slightly. Serve immediately, or the gravy will keep in the fridge for up to 3 days.

TIP

Any leftover gravy can be frozen in an airtight container for 3 months. To defrost, simply reheat from frozen in a pan over low heat, then simmer gently for 5 minutes.

MAKING MAYONNAISE

Prep 20 minutes

No cook

Makes 12oz (350ml)

Homemade mayonnaise is very much the magic alchemy of sauce-making. The egg yolks and oil are whisked together until emulsified, and with a spritz of lemon transformed into a luscious, thick, creamy sauce. A simple mayonnaise is a great base for many recipes and its flavor can be taken in many different directions with the addition of herbs, garlic, spices, or capers, or see the suggestions opposite. It is crucial to use a neutral-tasting oil when making mayonnaise—you don't want the flavor of the oil to dominate. A mix of vegetable oil and light olive oil works well taste-wise and is also more stable than using the latter on its own.

⅔ cup (150ml) vegetable oil
⅔ cup (150ml) light olive oil
2 large egg yolks, at room temperature
  (see p.32 on Separating Eggs)
2 tsp Dijon mustard
pinch of salt
juice of 1 lemon
freshly ground black pepper

1 | Pour the two types of oil into a measuring cup. Place a kitchen towel on the work surface and a large mixing bowl on top—the towel stops the bowl from slipping when you are whisking. Add the egg yolks to the bowl with the Dijon mustard and a pinch of salt and use a balloon whisk to combine.

2 | Whisking continuously, very slowly pour the oil into the egg yolk mix. You want to start with a very small amount, around 1 teaspoon, and whisk until fully incorporated, then repeat adding more oil.

3 | Once you've done this 8–9 times, you will notice the egg yolks lighten and thicken slightly. You can now start to very slowly pour the oil into the egg yolks in a steady stream while whisking continuously. Continue until all of the oil has been added and it is a thick, glossy mayonnaise. Whisk in the lemon juice, then season to taste. Store the mayonnaise in a jar in the fridge and use within 2 weeks.

Rescuing curdled mayonnaise

If your mayonnaise curdles or splits, it may be because too much oil has been added too quickly, but this is easy to fix. Add an egg yolk into the mixing bowl. Whisking continually, very slowly add the split mixture. The curdled mixture will gradually incorporate into the egg yolk, resulting in a smooth mayonnaise.

TIP

Mayonnaise is also easy to make in a food processor. Follow the method (above) with the motor running on a low speed and slowly add the oil until incorporated.

Mayonnaise variations

Roasted garlic aioli: preheat the oven to 400°F
(200°C). Put a whole garlic bulb in a small piece of
aluminum foil, drizzle over some olive oil and season
with salt. Wrap the foil around the garlic to make a
parcel, place on a baking sheet, and bake for
40 minutes, until very soft. Allow to cool, then
squeeze the cloves from their skins into the
egg yolks and mustard before adding the oil.

Hot sauce mayo: make the mayonnaise as instructed
(left), swapping the lemon juice for 1–2 tablespoons
of vinegar-based hot sauce, depending on how spicy
you like it.

Tartar sauce: make the mayonnaise as instructed
(left), then mix in 10 finely chopped cornichons,
2 tablespoons of finely chopped capers, 1 peeled
and finely chopped shallot, and a handful of finely
chopped flat-leaf parsley leaves.

PASTA SAUCES

This book touched on how to pair pasta with the right type of sauce on p.224, so they both enhance and work together for the best-tasting dish. As with the choice of pasta shapes, the variety of pasta sauces to go with them is extensive—there are tomato-based ones, slow-cooked ragus and Bolognese, mixed seafood options, creamy béchamel, herby emulsions, or simply aromatic-infused olive oil, but this just scratches the surface. Here, are a few ideas to get you started, and once you have a few pasta sauces as part of your repertoire, you can take the flavors in many directions. Each sauce recipe, serves 2 with 2½–3½oz (75–100g) of dried pasta per person, cooked following the package instructions.

SIMPLE TOMATO SAUCE

Prep 5 minutes

Cook 40 minutes

Serves 4

This tomato sauce is so simple, but packs so much flavor. It is the epitome of something being more than the sum of its parts, and an essential in a cook's repertoire of recipes. Try to use the best-quality canned tomatoes you can afford.

4 tbsp extra-virgin olive oil
6–8 fat garlic cloves, peeled and thinly sliced
    (depending on how garlicky you like it)
1 (28oz/400g) can crushed tomatoes
salt and freshly ground black pepper
½ tsp sugar
½ tsp dried chili flakes (optional)
1 handful of basil, stalks and leaves

1 | Heat the olive oil in a large, deep skillet over medium heat. Add the garlic and cook gently for 4–5 minutes, until softened but not colored.

2 | Add the canned tomatoes with an extra quarter can of water. Season with salt and pepper and add the sugar, chili flakes, if using, and basil stalks.

3 | Using a potato masher or fork, crush the tomatoes to break them up. Bring to a gentle simmer and cook for 30 minutes, stirring occasionally, until the sauce reduces and the tomatoes break down. Check the seasoning, pick out the basil stalks, if preferred, and stir in the basil leaves before serving.

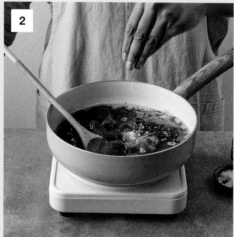

Pasta sauce variations

Garlic, chili & olive oil (aglio olio): heat 4 tablespoons of extra-virgin olive oil in a skillet over medium heat. Add 3 thinly sliced garlic cloves and cook for 2 minutes. Sprinkle in ¼–½ teaspoon of dried chili flakes, to taste. Using tongs, lift your cooked pasta (a long shape, such as spaghetti or linguine works well here) out of the cooking water straight into the skillet and toss together with a ladleful of pasta cooking water. Stir in a handful of finely chopped parsley.

Creamy mushroom: heat 1 tablespoon of olive oil and 2 tbsp (30g) of salted butter in a large skillet over medium-high heat. Add 8oz (250g) of sliced button mushrooms and sauté for 4–5 minutes, until any water has evaporated and the mushrooms are browned. Add 2 peeled and finely chopped garlic cloves and cook for 1 minute, stirring regularly. Pour in ⅓ cup (100ml) of dry white wine and let it bubble for 2 minutes before pouring in ⅓ cup (100ml) of heavy cream. Season with salt and lots of black pepper, then cook for 3–4 minutes, until reduced and thickened. Lift your cooked pasta (rigatoni and penne are great here) out of the cooking water straight into the skillet and toss together. Finish with ⅓ cup (30g) of finely grated Parmesan and a ladleful of pasta water to loosen the sauce, if needed.

Pesto: arguably the simplest sauce of them all. Cook the pasta (fun small shapes, such as spirals or shells work well) following the instructions on the package, then drain well, reserving a ladleful of the pasta cooking water. Put the pasta back into the pan and add ½ cup (50g) of fresh Basil Pesto (see p.442) or store-bought. Add 2–3 tablespoons of the pasta water and toss until you have a silky sauce. Stir in ⅓ cup (30g) of finely grated Parmesan to finish.

TIPS

For a velvety tomato sauce, blend with 2 tbsp (30g) of butter using an immersion blender until smooth, then stir in the basil leaves before serving.

To freeze sauces, let them cool and divide into portions in individual containers. The sauce can be frozen for up to 3 months. Reheat from frozen or defrost before use.

TAPENADES & SALSAS

The one thing tapenades and salsas have in common is that they both pack a punch when it comes to flavor. These uncooked condiments are great at multi-tasking too, working as a sauce, dip, or spread.

Fresh, zingy, and bright, a salsa (meaning "sauce" in Spanish and Italian) can lift the taste of a dish from the ordinary to the extraordinary. The secret to a good salsa is a balance of spice (usually from chiles), salt, and acid (from citrus juice or vinegar). A favorite in Mexican cooking, a classic combination is finely chopped tomatoes, fresh cilantro, chile, onion, lime juice, and a sprinkling of salt, but experiment with different combinations of flavorings, herbs, and fresh fruit and vegetables.

The tapenades and salsas that follow can be paired with other recipes in this book. All would be equally delicious served with grilled vegetables, steak, chicken, swirled through pasta, or as a side to a simple grilled fish fillet.

Olive tapenade

Prep 5 minutes

No cook

Serves 4

This Provençal sauce/spread/condiment is briny, bright, and packed with flavor. It's great with roasted meat and fish, such as the Pistachio & Coriander-Crusted Lamb Rack (see p.292).

6oz (175g) pitted Kalamata olives, drained
2 tbsp capers, drained
6 canned anchovy fillets in oil
4 tbsp extra-virgin olive oil
1 tbsp red wine vinegar
freshly ground black pepper

1 | Put the drained olives into the bowl of a small food processor, add the capers and anchovy fillets, and pulse to a rough paste.

2 | Pour in the oil and vinegar and briefly pulse to combine—it should be smoothish in texture. Season with pepper, there should be no need for added salt.

3 | Store the tapenade in an airtight container or lidded jar for up to 5 days in the fridge.

Flavor variation

Green olive & lemon: for a vibrant tapenade, swap the black olives for pitted green ones and the red wine vinegar for the same quantity of lemon juice. Instead of the anchovies, stir in 1 crushed garlic clove, 1 handful of chopped flat-leaf parsley, and ¼ cup (30g) finely chopped pine nuts. Season with salt and pepper to taste. This is a delicious side to fish, chicken, or with egg dishes.

Charred tomato & orange salsa

Prep 15 minutes

Cook 5 minutes

Serves 4

Cooking the tomatoes and chile very briefly in a searing hot pan until the outsides blacken and char is a great way to add a smoky flavor to this spicy, fruity salsa. Serve with the Chipotle Black Bean Burgers (see p.276) or as a dip with tortilla chips.

4 large vine-ripened tomatoes
1 large red chile
1 orange
3 green onions, green and white parts, finely chopped

juice and finely grated zest of 1 lime
2 tbsp olive oil
½ tsp ground cumin
1 handful of cilantro, stalks and leaves, roughly chopped
salt and freshly ground black pepper

1 | Set a medium, dry skillet over high heat. Once visibly hot and smoking, add the tomatoes and chile and cook, turning regularly with tongs, for around 3–4 minutes, until the outsides of both are nicely blackened and charred. They should still hold their shape, and the inside of the tomatoes remain uncooked. Put them in a bowl and leave to cool.

2 | Using a serrated knife, cut the top off the orange so it sits flat on a cutting board. Continue to make downward cuts around the orange, following the curvature of the fruit, to remove the peel.

3 | Once peeled, cut the orange into ½-in (1-cm) thick round slices, then into ½-in (1-cm) cubes and put into a medium serving bowl, along with any juices left on the cutting board.

4 | Cut the cooled charred tomato into similar-size cubes to the orange and add to the same bowl, discarding the seeds. Finely chop the charred chile, removing the seeds if you don't like it too spicy.

5 | Add the remaining ingredients to the bowl, stir and season the salsa with salt and pepper to taste before serving.

TIP

This salsa is best eaten within a couple of hours of making, otherwise it can become a little watery. If you want to work ahead, char the tomatoes and chile up to 1 day in advance, then leave, covered, at room temperature and chop when you're ready to serve.

Sauce vierge

Prep 5 minutes

Cook 10 minutes

Serves 2

This French sauce comes with a hint of citrusy warmth from the coriander seeds but mainly a nice acidity from the tomatoes and lemon juice, which help cut through rich, fatty meats, such as lamb. It's also delicious with seafood, like mackerel, tuna, or thick white fillets of hake or cod. Basil leaves add a fragrant lift but you can also use parsley, chervil, or chives. The sauce is served just warm or at room temperature, so is great for making slightly ahead of serving.

2 tsp coriander seeds
5 tbsp extra-virgin olive oil
3½oz (100g) cherry tomatoes, quartered
juice of ½ lemon
1 large handful of basil leaves,
  left whole
salt and freshly ground black pepper

1 | Put the coriander seeds into a small saucepan over medium heat. Toast for 2–3 minutes, tossing regularly, until the coriander smells fragrant. Put the seeds into a pestle and mortar and roughly crush.

2 | Pour the crushed coriander seeds back into the pan and add the olive oil and cherry tomatoes. Put the pan back on low heat until the oil has warmed through and the tomatoes have softened slightly.

3 | Remove the pan from the heat and stir in the lemon juice and basil leaves. Season with plenty of salt and pepper.

TIP

If you're making the sauce vierge ahead of time, don't add the basil leaves until you are ready to serve. Stir in the lemon juice, then keep the sauce covered at room temperature. Basil leaves are very delicate, so you only want them to lightly wilt and not discolor in the sauce.

ASIAN DIPPING SAUCES

These dipping sauces pack a punch—they are salty and savory and, in the case of the Vietnamese Nuoc Cham (below), spicy and sour too. Dumplings, grilled seafood, tempura, spring rolls, fritters, grilled vegetables, and more are all delicious on their own, but accompanying them with a dipping sauce adds a different dimension and flavor hit.

Nuoc cham

Prep 5 minutes

No cook

Makes 3oz (90ml)

This Vietnamese dipping sauce is the perfect balance of salty, funky, sour, sweet, and spicy. In Vietnam, you make it yourself at the dining table, adding more spice, acid, or salty fish sauce depending on your preference, so please feel free to taste and adjust the ingredients to how you like it. It is ideal as a dipping sauce for Grilled Squid (see p.140), or with an herby rice noodle salad, grilled pork, or even an Omelet (see p.28).

4 garlic cloves, peeled and finely chopped
1–2 bird's eye chiles, finely chopped
2–3 tbsp fish sauce
1 tbsp light brown sugar
juice of 2 limes

1 | Add the garlic, chiles, fish sauce, sugar, and lime juice to a small bowl and then whisk together until combined. The dipping sauce will keep for up to 2 weeks in a lidded jar in the fridge.

Soy & ginger dipping sauce

Prep 5 minutes

No cook

Makes 6oz (175ml)

This simple dipping sauce can be tweaked to your preference. The Chinkiang black rice vinegar lends a touch of acidity and sweetness to balance the saltiness of the soy, as well as adding more funky depth. Buy the best soy sauce you can—the better ones have lots of umami depth as well as bright, briny notes.

½ cup (120ml) soy sauce
3 tbsp Chinkiang black vinegar (or balsamic vinegar)
2-in piece of fresh ginger, peeled and shredded
2–3 tsp Crispy Chili Oil (see p.452) or store-bought

1 | Mix together the soy sauce and vinegar in a small bowl and divide between small dipping bowls. Add the ginger and chili oil, to taste.

DRESSINGS

The role of a dressing is to enhance the flavor profile of a salad, and its success relies on creating balance and complementing the ingredients it is served with, rather than dominating them.

Once you've tried the dressing recipes on the following pages, try experimenting with different types of oil and vinegar, both key ingredients. Wine vinegar (red and white) makes a sharp-tasting dressing, while sherry vinegar and apple cider vinegar are more rounded, and balsamic provides a touch of sweetness. Citrus juice can also be used in place of vinegar for a fresh flavor. When it comes to oil, extra-virgin olive oil is the most popular choice, but you can also try using cold-pressed canola oil, which has a slightly grassy, nutty taste, or there are distinctive nut and seed oils, such as walnut, hazelnut, and toasted sesame as well as the richly flavored avocado oil.

Storage
Homemade dressings will keep anywhere between 1 day to 2 weeks, depending on the type. It is best to check the individual recipe for guidelines.

From left, green goddess dressing, honey & mustard dressing, ranch dressing, and balsamic dressing.

FRENCH
DRESSING

Prep 5 minutes

No cook

*Makes about
3½oz (100ml)*

Making your own salad dressing is so simple and way cheaper than buying ready-made. This is a classic, and a useful one to have in your repertoire. It's roughly a 3:1 ratio of oil-to-vinegar, but your palate may enjoy more vinegar, so feel free to adjust according to taste.

1½ tsp Dijon mustard
large pinch of sugar
2 tbsp white wine vinegar
6 tbsp extra-virgin olive oil
salt and freshly ground black pepper

1 | Spoon the mustard into a small bowl. Add the sugar and vinegar. Whisk together with a fork or small balloon whisk until fully combined.

2 | Add the olive oil and whisk again until smooth and combined. Season with salt and pepper to taste, adding a pinch more sugar if your vinegar is particularly astringent. The dressing will keep in the fridge for up to 2 weeks and is best kept in a lidded jar, so you can just shake it to combine before use.

To serve: perfect tossed with a simple salad of mixed crisp greens. Finish with a sprinkling of Parmesan shards and a handful of crunchy Croutons (see p.311).

TIPS

Another way to make this dressing is to add all of the ingredients to a clean jar, tightly screw on the lid, and shake until fully combined—quick and easy. You can also store it in the jar.

Once you've mastered this dressing, try adapting the flavors, using red wine vinegar or sherry vinegar instead. Switch the sugar for a little honey or maple syrup and add some very finely chopped shallot, crushed garlic, or chopped herbs, if you like.

Balsamic dressing

Prep 5 minutes

No cook

Serves 2

Use the best balsamic vinegar you can afford for this recipe so it will have a balanced sweetness, rather than tasting harsh and sharp, while the splash of red wine vinegar adds a touch of acidity. The vinegars lightly "cook out" the raw taste of the garlic so it is more of a background hum. This is ideal spooned over a simple tomato and mozzarella salad (right).

2 tbsp balsamic vinegar
½ tbsp red wine vinegar
1 small garlic clove, peeled and crushed
   (optional)
4 tbsp extra-virgin olive oil
salt and freshly ground black pepper

1 | Using a fork, whisk all the ingredients together in a small bowl. Season with salt and pepper to taste. Alternatively, add all the ingredients to a jar, put on the lid, and shake to combine.

To serve: slice 4 large vine-ripened tomatoes into rounds and place on 2 plates, season with salt and pepper, then spoon over half of the balsamic dressing. Tear a 6oz (150g) ball of buffalo mozzarella into chunks and sprinkle over the tomatoes, then top with ½ of a finely sliced red onion, the remaining dressing, and a large handful of torn basil leaves, to serve.

Honey & mustard dressing

Prep 5 minutes

No cook

Serves 2

The wholegrain mustard adds little pops of mustard seeds to the dressing and is milder in flavor than Dijon or English equivalents so you can still taste the sweetness of the honey. It's perfect spooned over warm new potatoes, as a sticky glaze on oven-roasted sausages, and on the Beet, Feta & Lentil Salad (right).

2 tsp wholegrain mustard
1 tsp honey
2 tbsp apple cider vinegar
4 tbsp extra-virgin olive oil
salt and freshly ground black pepper

1 | Using a fork, whisk all the ingredients together in a small bowl. Season with salt and pepper to taste. Alternatively, add all the ingredients to a jar, put on the lid, and shake to combine.

To serve: defrost ½ cup (100g) of frozen peas, finely slice ½ cup (100g) of sugar snap peas and cut 4 ready-cooked beets into wedges. Add the veggies to a large salad bowl with 1½ cups (250g) of cooked Puy lentils, ¾ cup (100g) of crumbled feta, 2 large handfuls of spinach leaves, 2 tablespoons of toasted flaked almonds, and the honey & mustard dressing. Gently toss to combine and divide between two bowls.

TIP

These dressings will keep, covered, for up to 2 weeks in the fridge. Once chilled, they may separate, so whisk or shake the jar to emulsify and bring back together before serving.

CREAMY DRESSINGS

A creamy salad dressing is the perfect match for crispy, crunchy lettuce because the freshness of the salad is balanced by the richness of the dressing. Traditionally, creamy has meant a mayonnaise-, buttermilk-, or yogurt-based dressing, such as the classic Ranch (see p.432), but relative newcomer Green Goddess Dressing (see p.432) gets its silky smoothness from a combination of avocado and creamy tahini. All these dressings serve 2 people but can easily be doubled or tripled if needed.

CAESAR SALAD DRESSING

Prep 10 minutes

No cook

Serves 2

A homemade Caesar is worlds away from store-bought alternatives with its creamy, cheesy, citrus zing. Canned anchovies are traditional and provide a salty hit, but feel free to leave them out and season with extra salt instead. Since the dressing contains raw eggs to emulsify and thicken, use the freshest, best-quality ones you can. This is a hand-whisked version, but you could put all the ingredients in a blender or food processor to combine.

6 canned anchovy fillets in oil, drained
1 small garlic clove, peeled
pinch of sea salt flakes, plus extra to season
1 tsp Dijon mustard
2 large egg yolks, at room temperature (see p.32 on Separating Eggs)
⅓ cup (30g) Parmesan cheese, finely grated
4 tbsp extra-virgin olive oil
juice of ½ lemon
freshly ground black pepper

1 | Pound the anchovies and garlic with a pinch of sea salt in a large pestle and mortar to a paste.

2 | Add the mustard, egg yolks, and Parmesan and whisk with a fork until combined. Continue to whisk, adding the olive oil, 1 tablespoon at a time, until a creamy consistency.

3 | Finally, whisk in the lemon juice and season with lots of pepper. You shouldn't need salt. Use immediately or within 2 days of making, stored in the fridge. Loosen with a splash of water, if needed.

To serve: slice 1 Romaine lettuce and put it in a large serving bowl with 8oz (250g) of shredded or sliced cooked chicken (this is ideal for using up leftover roast chicken, see p.70), a handful of Croutons (see p.311), ⅓ cup (30g) of Parmesan cheese shavings, and the Caesar dressing. Toss the salad together to evenly coat it in the dressing to serve.

Ranch dressing

Prep 5 minutes

No cook

Serves 2

This creamy dressing uses a combination of mayonnaise and sour cream or buttermilk as its base, the latter adding a touch of acidity to the richness of the mayo. This classic dressing is great on a crisp lettuce leaf salad (right), as a marinade, or as a dip for crunchy crudités, with the freshness of the vegetables cutting through the richness.

¼ cup (50g) mayonnaise
¼ cup (50g) sour cream or buttermilk
1 tbsp apple cider vinegar
1 tsp Dijon mustard
1 handful of chives, snipped
½ tsp garlic powder
salt and freshly ground black pepper

1 | Using a fork, whisk all the ingredients together in a small bowl. Season with salt and pepper to taste. Use immediately, or the dressing will keep for up to 5 days, covered, in the fridge.

To serve: cook 4–6 slices of bacon to your liking. Follow steps 1–2 from Quick Pink Pickled Onions (see p.459)—you want half the quantity for this salad. Thaw 1½ cups (165g) of frozen corn and halve 3½oz (100g) of cherry tomatoes. Slice 1 small iceberg lettuce into 8 wedges and divide between two plates, spoon over the Ranch dressing, then top with the cherry tomatoes, corn, pickled red onions, crispy bacon, and some snipped chives, to serve.

Green Goddess dressing

Prep 5 minutes

No cook

Serves 2

This vegan dressing uses tahini and avocado to provide a rich creaminess that usually comes from mayonnaise and/or sour cream. It is a great example of how a creamy dressing can be plant-based, and is excellent for using up whatever fresh herbs you have in the fridge. Serve with the sweet potato salad (right) for a hearty vegan dish.

1 large ripe avocado, stone removed and flesh scooped out
3 tbsp tahini
juice and finely grated zest of 1 unwaxed lemon
1½ cups (30g) mixed herbs, stalks and leaves, such as flat-leaf parsley, dill, and basil
½–1 green chile, seeded and roughly chopped
salt and freshly ground black pepper

1 | Put all the ingredients in a blender or small food processor with 4 tablespoons of water and blend to a smooth, creamy dressing with the consistency of plain yogurt. If it's a little thick, add 1–2 tablespoons of water and blend again. Season with salt and pepper to taste. The dressing will keep for up to a day, covered, in the fridge but is best eaten immediately. Add a splash of water if it becomes too thick.

To serve: cut 2 medium unpeeled sweet potatoes and 1 large peeled red onion into similarly-sized chunks. Cut 8oz (200g) radishes in half. In a roasting pan, add the prepared vegetables, drizzle over 2 tablespoons of olive oil, and season with salt and pepper. Spread the vegetables out in an even layer and roast at 425°F (220°C) for 20–25 minutes, until tender. Once roasted, mix in a serving bowl with 4 cups (85g) of arugula leaves and ⅓ cup (50g) of toasted pumpkin seeds. Drizzle over the Green Goddess dressing to serve. For a more substantial dish, serve with some pan-fried tofu or, if not vegan, a couple of poached eggs or grilled chicken breasts.

TIP

This dressing is delicious stirred into cooked grains for a vibrant side dish. Turn to Cooking Grains (see p.210) for ideas.

WARM DRESSINGS

These are similar to regular oil-based salad dressings but supercharged, since the addition of heat allows you to add more complex flavors and textures. The dressing below, for instance, has a similar oily-piquant flavor to a regular vinaigrette but comes with crispy shallots and crunchy peanuts, while the Sauce Vierge (see p.426), is halfway between a sauce and a dressing. Serve warm dressings on roasted or steamed vegetables or with grilled meat or fish. Even humble lettuce leaves are improved with a spoonful.

CRISPY SHALLOT & PEANUT DRESSING

Prep 5 minutes

Cook 15 minutes

Serves 4

This Asian-style dressing is a real winner. It has crispy fried shallots, garlic, and ginger; crunchy salted peanuts; umami from the soy; sharpness from the lime; and spice from the chili. It is good served warm on almost anything, particularly Steamed Broccolini (see p.172).

4 tbsp vegetable oil
1 garlic clove, peeled and thinly sliced
1-in piece of fresh ginger, peeled and
   cut into matchsticks (see p.163)
1 shallot, peeled and thinly sliced into rings
juice of 1 lime
2 tbsp soy sauce
½ tsp dried chili flakes
1 handful of salted peanuts, roughly
   chopped

1 | Heat the vegetable oil in a small saucepan with the garlic and ginger over medium-high heat. Once sizzling, cook for 1–2 minutes, until crisp and golden, then scoop out the garlic and ginger using a slotted spoon onto a paper-towel-lined plate, spreading them out into an even layer. Set aside.

2 | Separate the shallot into individual rings, then add it to the hot oil. Sauté for 3–4 minutes, until golden and crisp, then use the slotted spoon to scoop them out onto the paper-towel-lined plate. As they cook, remove any that become too dark to prevent them from burning and turning bitter.

3 | Remove the pan from the heat and let the oil cool for 5 minutes. Squeeze in the lime juice, then add the soy sauce, chili flakes, and peanuts. Mix in the crispy garlic, ginger, and shallots and serve immediately.

HERBS,

&

SPICES

CHILES

HERBS

Herbs come into their own when fresh, but it's always useful to keep a few jars of essential dried herbs in the pantry for those times when a recipe calls for herbs and you don't have any fresh on hand. You can dry them yourself using the guide on p.439. Certain herbs dry better than others, such as oregano, thyme, bay leaves, and sage, but those with a more delicate leaf, such as basil, parsley, and cilantro don't fare so well. If going down the store-bought route, it's well worth checking out ready-made fresh pastes and frozen herbs too.

When it comes to flavor, most agree that fresh herbs taste brighter and, not surprisingly, fresher than dried, but look for bunches that have perky, green leaves and avoid those that are wilted or discolored. In most cases, both the leaves and stalks can be used to avoid waste. Finely chop the stalks to add to salsas, green sauces, salads, soups, stir-fries, and stews, while a sprinkling of leaves enliven all manner of dishes.

Storage

Fresh herbs are best bought as and when needed. Wrap the stalk end of the herbs in a damp paper towel and place in a sealable bag in the fridge for up to a week. Basil doesn't do well in the fridge because it dislikes the cold, so is best stored at room temperature. If you have any leftover herbs in the fridge, don't waste them, they can be frozen or dried (see p.439).

Dried herbs lose their flavor with time but will keep for up to 1 year, making them a convenient alternative to fresh. Store them in an airtight container or lidded jar in a cool, dark place.

STRIPPING FRESH HERBS

Prep 5 minutes

No cook

Makes ¾oz (20g)

Picking the leaves from the stalks of herbs can be laborious, particularly if you have a large quantity to do, but you don't have to pick each leaf off individually, here's how to save time ...

1½ cups (30g) fresh sprigs of herbs, such as mint, flat-leaf parsley, cilantro, thyme, or rosemary

1 | Take a single herb sprig in one hand and hold it at the top—this will be the thin end of the stalk with more tender leaves. Starting from the base, with your other hand, gently pinch your fingers together and carefully draw them along the stem, pulling the leaves off in one smooth movement. The herbs are ready to use or chopping (see p.438).

Clockwise, from top, mint, dill, flat-leaf parsley, basil,
rosemary, cilantro, thyme, and oregano (center).

CHOPPING FRESH HERBS

Prep 5 minutes

No cook

Makes 1½ cups (30g)

Fresh herbs are best chopped just before use to avoid wilting or discoloration, and to ensure they retain their flavor. There are two stages to efficiently chopping fresh herbs: first, gather the herbs into a bundle on a cutting board to slice, then use a rocking motion to evenly chop to your desired size.

1½ cups (30g) fresh herb leaves, such as flat-leaf parsley, mint, cilantro, thyme, or rosemary

1 | **To slice herbs:** gather the herbs into a neat, tight pile on a clean cutting board. Holding the herbs together tightly with one hand, use a large, sharp chef's knife in the other to thinly slice the herbs into strips. This technique, called a "chiffonade," is used to chop soft-leafed herbs, such as flat-leaf parsley, mint, basil, and cilantro.

2 | **To roughly chop herbs:** spread the sliced herbs out in a line on the cutting board. Move the hand that was holding the herbs together toward the tip of the knife blade. Using a rocking motion, chop down with the knife through the herbs, keeping the tip of the knife on the board and moving the handle end up and down and from one side to the other until all the herbs are chopped.

3 | **To finely chop herbs:** continue to chop the herbs, as in step 2, until you have an even, fine texture.

TIP

If you have a lot of herbs that need chopping it maybe easier to use a mini food processor, if you have one. Roughly chop the stalks beforehand to help them break down more evenly in the processor, then pulse for 15 seconds at a time until the herbs are chopped to the consistency you desire. This isn't recommended for basil because its soft, delicate leaves bruise easily.

FREEZING & DRYING HERBS

Prep 5 minutes + freezing or drying

These are both fantastic methods for saving any leftover or surplus herbs that you may have, perfectly preserving them to use at a later date. There are two ways to freeze herbs, depending on whether you have hardy or soft-leaved types. When it comes to drying herbs, you want to preserve their fresh flavor and vibrancy as much as possible, so this means drying them very slowly—you can't rush this. Traditionally, this would have been done by hanging the herbs in bundles from rafters and leaving them to dry over several weeks, or spreading them out in the sun to gently dry. Delicate soft herbs, such as parsley, cilantro, tarragon, and dill, benefit from both their stalks and leaves being dried, while fresh oregano and mint should be treated like woody hardier herbs, like rosemary, thyme, and bay, removing their stalks before drying the leaves.

1 | **To freeze hardy herbs:** remove the leaves from the bay stalks, if using, and place in a sealable freezer bag in the freezer. Thyme, oregano, rosemary, and sage leaves don't need to be taken off their stalks; they can be bagged and put straight into the freezer. You can use the herbs frozen or follow Stripping Fresh Herbs (see p.436) to remove the leaves from the stalks, if needed.

2 | **To freeze soft herbs:** follow steps 1–3 from finely Chopping Fresh Herbs (left). Pack 1 tablespoon of the herbs in each hole of an ice-cube tray, pour in 1 tablespoon of cold water, and mix until combined. Freeze until completely solid. Once frozen, transfer the herb ice cubes to a sealable freezer bag. To use, stir into stews, sauces, soups, and curries, straight from frozen, toward the end of the cooking time so they just melt and heat through for a fresh, herby hit.

3 | **To dry herbs:** preheat the oven to 180°F (100°C) or the lowest setting. Line a large baking sheet with parchment paper. Lay the herbs in an even layer on the parchment paper. Put the baking sheet in the oven for 3–4 hours, depending on the moisture content of the herbs, checking after 2 hours and then every hour until very dry and crumbly, but not burned. Crumble the herbs and store them in a lidded jar or container in a cool, dark place—they will keep for up to 3 months.

HERB OIL

*Prep 15 minutes
+ straining*

Cook 5 minutes

*Makes about
9oz (250ml)*

This is a great recipe for using up any leftover herbs you may have in the fridge. You can use the stalks along with the leaves, then simply blend them with oil into a fragrant, bright green condiment. The secret is to blend the herbs for a few minutes, no less, since the friction makes the blender hot, which helps release the chlorophyll in the herbs (hence the green color) into the oil. Leaving the herb oil to strain for 3–4 hours, preferably overnight if time allows, ensures you get every drop of green oil. You can make this flavored oil with just one variety of herb to let it sing or use a mixture for a more rounded herbaceous flavor. Herbs to consider include flat-leaf parsley, oregano, cilantro, basil, dill, chive, tarragon, and mint.

3 cups (50g) of a single herb or a mixture of soft green
   herbs, leaves and stalks
1 cup (200ml) vegetable oil

1 | Bring a pot of water to a boil in a medium saucepan over medium-high heat. Put a handful of ice cubes into a medium bowl and top it up with cold water, then place it next to the pan of boiling water. Lower the herbs into the boiling water and blanch, stirring, for 30 seconds.

2 | Using a slotted spoon, scoop out the herbs into the bowl of ice water. Let cool completely for a few minutes.

3 | Lift the blanched, cooled herbs out of the bowl with a slotted spoon and drain through a fine mesh strainer.

4 | Using clean hands, squeeze as much moisture as possible out of the herbs—they will condense into a small ball. Put the herbs into a high-powered blender with the oil and blend for 4 minutes, until a bright green, smooth purée (if you touch the sides of the blender pitcher, it will feel warm—this is fine).

5 | Set a metal strainer over a medium bowl and line the strainer with a large piece of cheesecloth. Pour the herb oil into the lined strainer—you should start to see it drip through into the bowl below. Put the bowl into the fridge and leave the herb oil to strain for 3–4 hours, preferably overnight.

6 | After straining, remove and discard the pulp left in the cheesecloth, then pour the bright green oil into a lidded clean jar or bottle. It will keep in the fridge for up to 1 week.

TIPS

To freeze, pour the herb oil into a clean ice-cube tray. Once frozen, move the cubes of herb oil into a freezer bag, seal tightly, then put them back in the freezer until needed. They will keep for up to 3 months.

You can reuse the cheesecloth for another batch of herb oil. Simply scrape off any herb residue, then wash.

Fresh basil pesto

Prep 15 minutes

No cook

Makes about 10oz (300g)

This herbaceous, nutty Italian sauce is great on almost anything, adding flavor, color, and texture. Traditionally made from pine nuts, fresh basil leaves, olive oil, and Parmesan, you can easily swap the pine nuts for other nuts, such as almonds or walnuts, or the Parmesan for pecorino. The sauce is great stirred through cooked spaghetti for a quick meal or used as part of a dressing, such as the Lemony Pesto Potato Salad (see p.170). If you prefer a chunkier, more rustic pesto, blend the mixture for less time.

⅓ cup (50g) pine nuts
1 large bunch of basil leaves, about 6¼ cups (100g)
1 garlic clove, peeled and chopped
2½oz (75g) Parmesan cheese, finely grated
juice and finely grated zest of 1 unwaxed lemon
½ cup (120ml) extra-virgin olive oil
salt and freshly ground black pepper

1 | Toast the pine nuts in a small, dry skillet over medium heat for 2–3 minutes, tossing regularly until lightly browned.

2 | Put the pine nuts into a mini food processor or blender and let them cool for 3–4 minutes. Add the basil, garlic, Parmesan, lemon juice and zest, and olive oil and blend until roughly chopped or smooth, depending on your preference. Season with salt and pepper to taste.

3 | Pour the pesto into a lidded jar or covered bowl and store in the fridge for up to 1 week.

TIPS

Parmesan is traditionally made with animal rennet. If you are vegetarian, it is possible to find suitable alternatives to the hard, salty cheese so check the label before buying.

Pesto is traditionally made with a pestle and mortar. To follow this method, put the toasted pine nuts, basil, Parmesan, and lemon zest and juice into a mortar, then crush with the pestle to a rough, chunky pesto. Continue to pound the mixture while slowly adding the oil.

Gremolata

Prep 5 minutes

No cook

Makes about 3oz (85g)

This Italian garlicky, herby condiment couldn't be simpler to make and adds freshness and zing. It's delicious spooned over the top of a classic Simple Risotto (see p.204), on the Mushroom Ragu with Soft Polenta (see p.219), or the Chicken, Preserved Lemon & Chickpea Soup (see p.72).

1½ cups (30g) flat-leaf parsley, leaves and stalks, finely chopped
1 small garlic clove, peeled and crushed or finely grated
juice and finely grated zest of 1 unwaxed lemon
4 tbsp extra-virgin olive oil
salt and freshly ground black pepper

1 | Put the parsley into a small bowl. Add the garlic, lemon juice and zest, and olive oil. Stir and season with salt and pepper to taste. The gremolata will keep for up to 3 days in an airtight container in the fridge.

Persillade Sauce

Prep 10 minutes

No cook

Makes about 5oz (140g)

A classic French accompaniment, this herby green sauce has a note of tangy sharpness from the capers and vinegar and is perfect for cutting through rich dishes. That said, it goes with most things, especially grilled meats, pan-fried fish, or vegetables. Try it with the Pan-Fried Hake (see p.148) or the Perfect Steak (see p.114).

1½ cups (30g) flat-leaf parsley, leaves and stalks, finely chopped
2 tbsp capers, drained, rinsed, and roughly chopped
1 small garlic clove, peeled and finely grated
1 tbsp Dijon mustard
2 tbsp red wine vinegar
4 tbsp extra-virgin olive oil
salt and freshly ground black pepper

1 | Put the chopped parsley and capers into a small bowl with the garlic, mustard, vinegar, and oil. Season with salt and pepper to taste and mix until combined. The sauce will keep covered in the fridge for up to 1 week.

TIP

For an even punchier persillade sauce, drain a 1oz/30g can of salted anchovies in oil and finely chop, then mix through the sauce before serving.

Chimichurri

Prep 10 minutes

No cook

Makes about 9oz (250g)

Originating from Argentina and Uruguay, this hot green salsa is traditionally eaten with grilled meat. It's herbaceous, a bit spicy, and zingy and can cut through the rich fattiness of any smoky meat cooked over fire. Chimichurri is also great with the Perfect Steak (see p.114) instead of the peppercorn sauce.

1 shallot, peeled and finely chopped
1½ cups (30g) cilantro, leaves and stalks, finely chopped

1 red chile, seeded and finely chopped
2 garlic cloves, peeled and very finely chopped
1 tsp dried oregano
5 tbsp extra-virgin olive oil
3 tbsp red wine vinegar, plus extra if needed
salt and freshly ground black pepper

1 | Mix together all the ingredients in a small bowl. Season with salt and pepper to taste, then add a splash more vinegar, if you like a bit more sharpness.

From left, zhoug, chimichurri, and mint sauce.

Fresh mint sauce

Prep 5 minutes

No cook

*Makes about
2½oz (75g)*

This mint sauce is miles away from the overly sweet store-bought alternative. It is fresh and vibrant and has the ability to cut through the richness of roasted meat, in particular lamb. Serve it with the Slow-Roasted Anchovy & Rosemary Lamb Shoulder (see p.106).

1½ cups (30g) mint, leaves picked
1 small garlic clove, peeled
3 tbsp red or white wine vinegar
3 tbsp extra-virgin olive oil
½–1 tsp sugar
salt and freshly ground black pepper

1 | Put the mint leaves, garlic, vinegar, and olive oil into a food processor or a pestle and mortar. Blend or pound until the mint and garlic are very finely chopped. Season to taste with the sugar, salt, and pepper. Store the sauce in a covered container at room temperature. Serve on the day of making.

TIP

The mint sauce can also be used as a punchy dressing for grain-based salads or sides. Loosen the sauce with an extra 1 tablespoon of olive oil and stir it into the warm cooked grains.

Zhoug

Prep 10 minutes

Cook 5 minutes

*Makes about
5oz (150g)*

This spicy green sauce originates from Yemen. It is fragrant and earthy from the fresh cilantro leaves and whole spices, with a slight hit of heat from the chile. The condiment enhances the flavor of many dishes, from chicken and fish to meat and vegetables. Try it spooned over a Fried Egg (see p.25), in the Grilled Chicken Sandwiches (see p.88), or as part of a veggie centerpiece, such as the Shawarma-Spiced Whole Baked Cauliflower (see p.177).

1 tbsp coriander seeds
1 tbsp cumin seeds
6¼ cups (100g) cilantro, leaves and stalks
1 medium-size green chile, roughly chopped, seeded if preferred
1 garlic clove, peeled
juice of 1 lemon
4–5 tbsp extra-virgin olive oil
salt and freshly ground black pepper
small pinch of sugar (optional)

1 | Put the coriander and cumin seeds in a small, dry skillet over medium heat. Toast for 2–3 minutes, until aromatic, then put into a blender or a mini food processor. Let cool for a few minutes.

2 | Add the cilantro leaves and stalks, chile, garlic, lemon juice, and 4 tablespoons of the olive oil, then blend to a smooth, vivid green sauce. If the sauce is a little thick, add the remaining 1 tablespoon of olive oil and blend again.

3 | Season to taste with salt and pepper and a small pinch of sugar to counteract any bitterness, if you think it needs it. Use immediately or store in the fridge in an airtight container for up to 3 days. Add a splash of water to loosen, if needed.

SPICES

The seeds, pods, bark, fruit, and buds of plants, spices may look unassuming but they have the ability to lift a dish, taking it from bland and uninteresting to complex, aromatic, and flavorful. Many of the recipes in this book make use of spices and it is a good idea to stock up on a few favorite individual ones and blends to enliven your cooking. Preferably buy spices in small quantities and whole, rather than as a powder, because they will have the best flavor and last longer. To lift both their aroma and taste, it's well worth toasting whole spices before adding them to a dish—it takes next to no time or effort (right). A spice grinder or pestle and mortar are both useful or grinding them after toasting. Alongside preparation techniques, there are also a few ideas in this chapter for spice blends which are used in some of the recipes in the book. They tend to have a superior fresh and robust flavor to the ones that you find in stores, but if more convenient, you can buy ready-made.

Storage

Spices are particularly vulnerable to light, air, and heat, so it pays to keep them in an airtight container or lidded jar in a cool, dark place. Once ground, spices lose their flavor with time and should ideally be used within 6 months.

From left, garam masala, za'atar, and Cajun spice mix.

TOASTING, CRUSHING & GRINDING SPICES

Prep 10 minutes

Cook 5 minutes

Toasting is a simple process that transforms the flavor of a spice. The heat unlocks the natural oils found in the spice, intensifying both its aroma and taste. For this reason, whole spices and their seeds are always best roasted before adding to a dish. This includes cloves, cardamom pods and seeds, star anise, cinnamon sticks, coriander seeds, cumin seeds, black pepper, and fennel seeds, which after roasting can be used whole or ground in a spice grinder or pestle and mortar. It's best to roast spices in small batches, as needed, because their "unlocked" essential oils can turn rancid and the flavor dull with time.

Once toasted, bruising, crushing, or grinding the spices will help release more of the natural oils and aroma into your dish. Toasting cumin seeds and then grinding them, for instance, will lend a much earthier profile to the dish than pre-ground cumin. When it comes to cardamom pods, lightly bruise or crush to split the pod open or remove the seeds completely before toasting and grinding, to give a stronger intensity of flavor than when left whole.

1 | **To toast spices:** put the whole spices of your choice into a dry skillet over medium heat, then toss the spices every 30 seconds or so to allow for even toasting. Cook for 1–3 minutes, until the spices release their aroma and slightly darken in color. Remove from the heat and put into a bowl, spice grinder, or pestle and mortar (depending on how you plan to use them). Let cool before bruising, crushing, or grinding (below).

2 | **To bruise/crush spices:** put the toasted spices (above) into a pestle and mortar. Once cooled, roughly bruise or crush to the desired consistency.

3 | **To grind spices:** follow the step (above) for bruising/crushing but continue to grind the spices in the pestle and mortar until you have a powder consistency. Alternatively, put into a spice grinder and grind to a powder.

Shawarma
spice mix

Prep 5 minutes

No cook

*Makes about
1¾oz (50g)*

Shawarma is a Middle Eastern spice mix traditionally used on rotisserie or grilled meat, and often refers to the whole dish itself. It's a blend of coriander, cumin, cinnamon, and other warm-flavored spices. Use this spice blend to coat the roasted Shawarma-Spiced Whole Baked Cauliflower (see p.177).

1 tbsp ground coriander
1 tbsp ground cumin
2 tsp sweet smoked paprika
1 tsp ground cinnamon
1 tsp ground turmeric
½ tsp ground ginger
4 cardamom pods, seeds removed and
   ground (optional)
½ tsp dried chili flakes
large pinch of salt
freshly ground black pepper

1 | Mix everything together in a small bowl, then season with a large pinch of salt and lots of pepper. Use for the Shawarma-Spiced Whole Baked Cauliflower (see p.177) or see the Tip (below).

TIP

Quadruple the quantity of the shawarma spice mix to make multiple recipes—it will keep in an airtight container in a cool, dark place for up to 6 months.

Garam masala

Prep 10 minutes

Cook 5 minutes

*Makes about
1¾oz (50g)*

This aromatic, ground spice blend is used widely across the Indian subcontinent and is generally added toward the end of cooking so it retains its flavor and aroma. The selection of spices used may vary in type and quantity, but it tends to be a finely balanced combination of warm spices, like cinnamon and cloves, and those with a slightly zesty note, such as coriander seeds. Use this garam masala in curries, dal, and to flavor tofu (see p.278).

30 green cardamom pods
2 tbsp cumin seeds
2 tbsp coriander seeds
1 tbsp fennel seeds
1 small cinnamon stick
10 cloves
2 tsp black peppercorns
1 star anise
½ whole nutmeg, finely grated

1 | Put the cardamom into a pestle and mortar and gently crush to break open the pods. Remove the green husks and discard. Put the black seeds into a large, dry skillet.

2 | Add the cumin, coriander, and fennel seeds to the pan along with the cinnamon stick, cloves, peppercorns, and star anise and follow the step from Toasting Spices (see p.447).

3 | Put into a spice grinder or pestle and mortar and follow the step from Grinding Spices (see p.447).

4 | Add the nutmeg to the toasted and ground spices and transfer to an airtight container or lidded jar and keep in a cool, dark place for up to 1 month.

Cajun
spice mix

Prep 5 minutes

No cook

*Makes about
1¾oz (50g)*

This spice mix is smoky, earthy, and herbaceous and works with everything from meat and chicken to vegetables and seafood. It makes a perfect spice rub: use 1 tablespoon to coat the skin of a salmon fillet before pan-frying (see p.148) or try on roasted vegetables or chicken thighs.

1 tbsp ground cumin
1 tbsp smoked paprika
2 tsp garlic powder
2 tsp dried oregano
1 tsp cracked black pepper
½ tsp cayenne pepper

1 | Mix all the ingredients in a small bowl until combined, then transfer to an airtight container or lidded jar and keep in a cool, dark place for up to 3 months.

Za'atar

Prep 5 minutes

Cook 5 minutes

*Makes about
1¾oz (50g)*

This Middle Eastern spice/herb mix is a mixture of dried herbs, sesame seeds, cumin, and the citrusy-flavored dried berry, sumac. The result is a delicious combination of spicy, herby, earthy, and zesty with a pleasing crunch. It can be used as a seasoning; sprinkled over a salad, such as the Marinated Pepper Fattoush (see p.188); as a topping for the Green Shakshuka (see p.24); or turned into a dip with olive oil for freshly baked flatbread.

1 tbsp cumin seeds
½ tsp sea salt flakes

3 tbsp dried thyme
1 tbsp dried oregano
1 tbsp sumac
1 tbsp toasted sesame seeds

1 | Follow the steps from Toasting & Grinding Spices (see p.447) to toast the cumin seeds.

2 | Put the toasted cumin into a lidded jar or airtight container with the salt, thyme, oregano, sumac, and sesame seeds and mix until combined. The spice mix will keep for up to 1 month in a cool, dark place.

Gingerbread spice mix

Prep 5 minutes

No cook

*Makes about
2oz (60g)*

This aromatic sweet spice mix is classically used in gingerbread but is very adaptable. Try sprinkling it over the Perfect Pancakes (see p.349) before serving, whisk a tablespoon into the eggs for the Crème Anglaise (see p.394) for a spice-infused custard, or add to the Gingerbread-Spiced Cookies (see p.373).

4 tbsp ground ginger
2 tbsp ground cinnamon
4 tsp ground allspice
1 whole nutmeg, finely grated

1 | Mix the spices together in a small bowl, then transfer to an airtight container or lidded jar. The spice mix will keep for up to 6 months.

CHILES

Lovers of chiles won't be surprised to find out they have been scientifically proven to be mildly addictive—something to do with the release of endorphins when eating a particularly spicy one! Although you are only likely to see a handful of different types of fresh and dried chiles to buy in stores, there are hundreds of varieties, ranging in size, color, heat, and flavor. Some of the most popular are red and green jalapeños, which are mild and fruity; the small, spicy bird's eye chile from southeast Asia; and the globe-like Scotch bonnet, which is similar to the Mexican habanero, which is both hot and fruity in flavor. As a general rule, larger chiles are less spicy than smaller ones, although, for a more thorough analysis of heat levels, the Scoville scale is used to measure the spiciness of a chile.

When buying fresh chiles, look for ones that have a smooth, taught, bright skin.

The choice of dried chiles available is equally diverse, ranging from the mild-tasting Indian Kashmiri, which imparts a deep red color to dishes, to the Mexican hot and smoky chipotle, and many more between. Dried chili flakes also make a convenient, ready-to-use option and similarly vary in heat levels, so it's worth adding gradually to dishes to avoid over-spicing.

Storage
Fresh chiles are best kept in the fridge, but can be frozen and dried for future use. Store dried chiles in an airtight container in a cool, dark place for up to 6 months.

CHOPPING CHILES & REMOVING THE SEEDS

Prep 5 minutes

No cook

Contrary to popular belief, it is the white pith (or ribs) on the inside of the chile and not the seeds that carry the heat, thanks to the active component capsaicin. To reduce this heat, remove the white part (and the seeds in contact with the pith) before use.

1 red or green chile of choice

1 | **To seed:** using a sharp chef's knife, remove and discard the top part of the chile with the stalk and cut it in half lengthwise. Scrape the white part and seeds out of each chile half with a teaspoon, leaving the flesh. Start from the pointed end and work your way down.

2 | **To thinly slice:** place the chile horizontally on a cutting board and use a sharp chef's knife to cut each chile half into thin slices.

3 | **To finely chop:** use a sharp chef's knife to cut each chile half lengthwise into thin strips. Turn the strips horizontally, then finely chop into small dice.

Toasting chiles

Roasting adds a deep umami smokiness to fresh chiles, and by charring the skin on the outside you also temper their spiciness. Turn your gas burner to high and place the chiles directly on top of the flame or hold them in place with tongs. Roast the chiles, turning every minute, for 4–5 minutes, until blackened.

Alternatively, put the chiles on a baking sheet under a high broiler, close to the heat source, and broil for 6–8 minutes, turning every minute until charred and blistered. You can do this on a barbecue grill too.

Homemade crispy chili oil

Prep 10 minutes

Cook 15 minutes

Makes about 16oz (500ml)

This chili oil is truly addictive! A combination of spicy, sweet, and salty, you will soon be topping everything with a spoonful, from eggs and noodles to stir-fries and grilled cheese sandwiches. A spoonful is perfect on top of the Soy-Marinated Egg Ramen (see p.21).

15 whole dried Kashmiri chiles or 4 tbsp dried chili flakes
1 tbsp cumin seeds
2 tsp black peppercorns
¼ cup (30g) salted peanuts, roughly chopped
½ tbsp sea salt flakes, plus extra to taste
1 tbsp light brown sugar, plus extra to taste
1¾ cups (400ml) peanut, sunflower, or vegetable oil
2 shallots, halved, peeled, and sliced into thin half-moons
8 garlic cloves, peeled and thinly sliced
2½-in piece of fresh ginger, peeled and cut into matchsticks (see p.163)

1 | If using whole chiles, use kitchen scissors to snip off the ends to remove and discard the stalks. Put the chiles and seeds into a spice grinder and pulse to the consistency of dried chili flakes. Put the ground chiles, or store-bought chili flakes, into a large, heatproof bowl.

2 | Follow the step from Toasting Spices (see p.447) to toast the cumin seeds and peppercorns in a small, dry skillet over medium heat. Toss the pan regularly for 3 minutes, until they smell toasted, then put them into the spice grinder or pestle and mortar and roughly crush (see p.447). Transfer to the bowl with the chiles and add the peanuts, salt, and brown sugar.

3 | Set a metal strainer on top of a medium heatproof bowl. Heat the oil in a small pan over medium-high heat and once it starts to shimmer, carefully add the shallots—they will splutter. Cook for 4–5 minutes, stirring regularly, until crisp and light golden brown. Carefully pour the shallot oil into the strainer-topped bowl. When drained, put the fried shallots into the bowl with the chili flakes, then carefully pour the oil back into the pan.

4 | Add the garlic and ginger to the pan, still over medium-high heat, and cook for 1–2 minutes, until the garlic is light golden (it will become bitter if too brown). Pour the hot oil, garlic, and ginger into the chili flake bowl—be careful, it will sizzle—then mix well. Let cool to room temperature, then check the seasoning and adjust with salt and extra sugar if needed.

5 | Spoon the chili oil into a sterilized 2-cup (500-ml) flip-top jar (see p.456) and seal. The chili oil is ready to use immediately; once opened, keep it in the fridge and eat within 2 weeks. Unopened it will keep for up to 3 months stored in a cool, dark place.

Turkish chili sauce

Prep 5 minutes

Cook 10 minutes

Makes about
14oz (400ml)

This is a fresh Turkish chili sauce, rather than a fermented one. The sauce is cooked briefly to give a balanced sweetness and to soften the harshness of the onion and garlic. Try your chiles before using to check how hot they are: cut a sliver off the pointed end and sample raw—some chiles are super spicy, while others taste more mild—then adjust accordingly. Serve with Falafel (see p.274) or over anything you like, especially Fried Eggs (see p.25).

1 red onion, peeled and roughly chopped
3 garlic cloves, peeled
2–3 red chiles, roughly chopped (depending on
    how spicy you like it)
1 (14.5oz/400g) can diced tomatoes
1 tbsp tomato paste
1 tbsp apple cider or white wine vinegar
2 tsp sugar
1 tbsp olive oil
salt and freshly ground black pepper

1 | Put the onion, garlic, chiles, diced tomatoes, tomato paste, vinegar, and sugar into the bowl of a large food processor and blend to a chunky sauce consistency—it shouldn't be completely smooth.

2 | Pour the mixture along with the olive oil into a large skillet over medium heat and cook, stirring regularly, for 8–10 minutes, until thickened to the consistency of ketchup and the raw onion and garlic have cooked a little so as not to overpower the flavor. Season with salt and pepper to taste.

3 | Let the sauce cool completely, then transfer it to a sterilized jar (see p.456), or airtight container if not serving immediately. Once in jars, keep in the fridge for up to 3 weeks and use as you like.

PICKLES

&

FERMENTS

PICKLES

Before the days of refrigeration, preserving was an essential way to ensure a steady supply of food for those times of the year, particularly the cold winter months, when fresh produce was hard to come by, as well as utilize and preserve summer gluts.

Pickling is an ancient method of food preservation that creates a hostile environment for bacteria or microbes, preventing growth and spoilage. Vinegar (or other acidic liquid) is key, and is often mixed with salt and sugar to make a pickling solution. A wide variety of foods are suitable, such as fruits, vegetables, nuts, fish ,and eggs, which are steeped in an acidic solution and then left for a period of time to preserve. Foods can be cooked, either lightly or completely, before pickling, and at other times, they are left raw. The pickling liquid not only preserves but also gradually softens the ingredients, which results in a pickle that develops in both flavor and texture with time.

If you have minimal time on your hands, you can still pickle. There are two recipes for speedy fresh pickles that don't require prolonged preserving but still result in a bright, vibrant, pop of flavor, see the Pink Pickled Onions and Quick Pickled Cucumbers on p.459.

Storage
If unopened, store bottles and jars in a cool, dark place. Opened pickles should be stored in the fridge; the keeping time will vary depending on the type.

STERILIZING JARS

Before you start, it's important to have super clean jars for your pickles and ferments to remove bacteria and avoid any likelihood of cross-contamination. The following steps show you how to sterilize glass containers before filling to ensure the contents don't spoil. If your jars or bottles have a rubber seal, remove them and boil them separately in a small pan of water for about 3 minutes. Always use new lids if reusing screw-top jars.

1 | Preheat the oven to 325°F (160°C). Wash the jars in hot, soapy water and rinse well. Put the washed jars, upside down into a large, clean roasting pan and place in the oven for 20 minutes, until completely dry.

2 | Remove the jars from the oven and allow to cool slightly for 5 minutes before filling and sealing immediately with a new lid.

PICCALILLI

*Prep 40 minutes
+ salting and
2–3 weeks
fermenting*

Cook 15 minutes

Makes 2¼lb (1kg)

Originally known as "Indian pickle", the first recipe for this vibrant vegetable pickle was seen back in the 1770s. Influenced by the Indian subcontinent, this interpretation features chopped vegetables and various spices in a pickling solution—its bright yellow color comes from the use of turmeric powder.

1 small cauliflower, leaves removed, florets and stalk
    cut into ¾-in (2-cm) pieces
1 small broccoli head, florets and stalk cut into
    ¾-in (2-cm) pieces
8oz (200g) radishes, quartered
8oz (200g) green beans, cut into ¾-in (2-cm) pieces
12 shallots, peeled and each cut into 6 wedges
2 tbsp sea salt flakes
2 tbsp mustard powder
1 tbsp turmeric powder
4 tbsp cornstarch
3 cups (750ml) apple cider vinegar
3 tbsp black mustard seeds
3 tbsp cumin seeds
¾ cup (175g) sugar

1 | Put all the chopped vegetables into a large nonmetallic mixing bowl and sprinkle in the sea salt. Mix well, cover, and refrigerate for 6 hours. The salt draws moisture from the vegetables, making them more crunchy and also preventing the piccalilli from turning watery.

2 | Drain the vegetables through a metal strainer and rinse well under cold running water to remove the salt, then drain well again. Follow steps 1–2 from Sterilizing Jars (left) using four 1-cup (250-ml) jars with lids. (Continued overleaf.)

3 | Put the mustard powder, turmeric, and cornstarch into a small bowl and pour in ½ cup (100ml) of the vinegar. Using a balloon whisk, mix everything into a smooth, runny paste.

4 | Put the mustard seeds and cumin seeds into a large pan and toast, stirring often, over medium-high heat for 2 minutes, until aromatic. Carefully pour in the remaining 2½ cups (650ml) of vinegar. Whisk the mustard and cornstarch mix again, then pour this into the pan. Continue to whisk until the mixture thickens.

5 | Add the sugar to the pan with the drained vegetables and ¾ cup (200ml) of cold water, then bring to a simmer and cook for 3–4 minutes, stirring constantly, until the vegetables just begin to soften.

6 | Remove from the heat and allow to cool for 10 minutes, then ladle the warm pickles into the sterilized jars, cover with the lids, label, and leave in a cool, dark place for 2–3 weeks, until ready to eat. It will keep unopened for up to 6 months, then store in the fridge once opened and eat within 2 weeks.

PINK PICKLED ONIONS

*Prep 5 minutes
+ pickling*

No cook

Serves 4

Quick pickling couldn't be more simple and is a surefire way to add a fresh tang and lift to your meals with very little effort. When pickled, red onion becomes a vibrant pink color. The key is to slice the onion very finely (see p.160) so it readily takes on the taste and softening effect of the lime juice. Serve sprinkled over Falafel (see p.274), as a zingy boost on Cochinita Pibil Tacos (see p.125), or spooned over the Broiled Sardines with Warm Nduja-Honey Dressing (see p.141).

1 red onion, peeled and very finely sliced
  (see p.160)
juice of 1 lime
large pinch of salt

1 | Put the red onion into a small bowl. Squeeze over the lime juice and season with the salt. Using clean hands, scrunch the onion, massaging in the salt and lime juice—this encourages it to soften and pickle.

2 | Let sit for 10 minutes or up to 30 minutes, to pickle. The longer you leave the onion, the softer and pinker it will become, but there's a fine line; don't leave it longer than a day or it will become soggy and unpleasant to eat.

Pickle variation

Quick pickled cucumber: cut a whole cucumber in half lengthwise, then into irregular, similarly-sized diagonal pieces. Put the cucumber in a metal strainer over the sink, season with a large pinch of salt and let sit for 10 minutes. Mix 4 tablespoons of rice wine vinegar, 1 chopped garlic clove, and 1 teaspoon of sugar together in a medium mixing bowl, until the sugar dissolves. Stir in the cucumber so it is evenly coated in the liquid and set aside for 10 minutes to allow it to take on the flavors of the pickle before serving. The cucumber pickle is best eaten immediately so it retains its crunch but will keep for an hour or two if kept covered in the fridge.

FERMENTS

With some methods of preserving, you want to remove the possibility of bacterial growth, so it is vital to encourage the good guys to flourish to get rid of the bad guys and extend the shelf life of your preserve. This is how lacto-fermentation works: you utilize friendly bacteria, or the good guys, to boost the hostile environment and encourage the fermentation process.

It may sound complicated but all you need is salt. The use of salt, either as a liquid in the form of a brine or sprinkled liberally over fruits and vegetables to encourage them to release internal moisture, initially inhibits and kills off any harmful bacteria, which in turn encourages the good bacteria present to flourish. This second stage occurs when lactose and other natural sugars present in the food are converted to lactic acid.

Through this process of lacto-fermentation a humble vegetable, for instance, is transformed into something more complex-tasting with a slightly sour tang and distinctive funky flavor. What's more, this type of preserve is said to have numerous health benefits, helping to boost immunity and digestion.

When making lacto-ferments, certain types of vegetables work best, such as carrots, cabbage, beets, cucumbers, green beans, radishes, and cauliflower. Lemons are good too (below). When making the recipes that follow, if your fruits and vegetables aren't completely covered by the brine you will need to top it up with extra—dissolve 1 teaspoon of salt in ⅓ cup (100ml) of just-boiled water, let it cool, then pour into the jar.

PRESERVED LEMONS

Prep 15 minutes
+ 2 days salting
+ 3 weeks fermenting

No cook

Makes 1lb 2oz (500g)

This classic North African preserve involves packing lemons in salt to draw out their moisture, encourage fermentation, and consequently extend their keeping properties. The salt also softens any harsh, bitter, sour notes of the lemons, mellowing them over a period of time, while the rind still adds a pop of citrus, but develops a deeper, more complex flavor. Used classically in tagines, preserved lemons are also great in pasta sauces, relishes, salad dressings, stews, grain salads, and soups, such as the Chicken, Preserved Lemon & Chickpea Soup (see p.72), where they add a citrusy umami hit. Try to buy unwaxed lemons whenever possible and give them a good scrub before use.

6 unwaxed lemons
6 tbsp sea salt flakes
4 fresh bay leaves
1 tsp black peppercorns
juice of 6 lemons

1 | Scrub the lemons well in cold running water and follow steps 1–2 from Sterilizing Jars (see p.456) using a large, 2-cup (500-ml) flip-top jar. Trim the top and bottom from each lemon, then cut a deep vertical cross into the top of each one with a large, sharp chef's knife, leaving ¾ in (2 cm) still attached at the base to hold it together.

2 | Put the lemons in a nonreactive, nonmetallic bowl and, one at a time, open up the cut and spoon in 1 tablespoon of the salt. Repeat for all the lemons.

3 | Pack the lemons into the sterilized jar, pressing to compact them together and scraping any salt from the bowl into the jar. Cut a small circle of parchment paper and sit this directly on top of the lemons. Put the jar in the fridge for 2 days.

4 | After 2 days, the lemons will have released some of their liquid. Remove the parchment paper circle, add the bay leaves and peppercorns, and pour in enough of the extra lemon juice to completely submerge the fruit in juice. Use water if needed to submerge the lemons in the jar. Mix well, cover with a clean parchment paper circle, and put on the lid. Let the lemons sit in the fridge for 3 weeks before eating. The preserved lemons will keep in the fridge for up to 6 months.

TIP

To use preserved lemons in your cooking, scoop out and discard the inner flesh and pith from the lemon, then finely chop the rind and add to dishes as instructed.

Sauerkraut

*Prep 15 minutes
+ 5–6 days
fermenting*

No cook

Makes 2lb (1kg)

This fermented cabbage is eaten all over Germany and Eastern Europe and is a perfect example of the transformative nature of fermentation. The humble cabbage is shredded, salted, and packed into jars, and then left to steep for about a month, turning it into a crunchy, sour accompaniment that's good with almost everything. When fermenting, you'll need to use 2 percent of salt per overall weight of the vegetable or fruit in the recipe (see step 2).

1 white cabbage, about 2lb (1kg)
about 1½ tbsp (20g) fine sea salt
1 tsp caraway seeds
1 tsp black peppercorns

1 | Follow steps 1–2 from Sterilizing Jars (see p.456) using a 4½-cup (1-liter) flip-top jar or four 1-cup (250-ml) jars with lids. Follow steps 1–3 from Shredding Cabbage (see p.162).

2 | Weigh the quantity of cabbage in a large nonmetallic mixing bowl. To calculate the amount of salt needed weigh your cabbage and add approximately 1½ tbsp of salt to 2lbs of cabbage.

3 | Sprinkle the sea salt over the cabbage, then with clean hands, knead and massage it in for about 5 minutes—the cabbage will start to break down and soften, releasing enough liquid to create a brine. When the cabbage has softened slightly, mix in the caraway seeds and black peppercorns.

4 | Pack the cabbage and spices into the sterilized jar(s) and pour in the liquid from the bowl, pressing the cabbage down so it is fully submerged in the liquid. Make an additional quantity of brine if there is not enough to cover the cabbage (see p.460). Top the cabbage with a small disk of parchment paper.

5 | Cover the jar with the lid and leave to ferment in a cool, dark place for 5–6 days, until it tastes slightly sour and funky, then chill. During fermentation, open the lid slightly once a day to release any built-up gases. Store in the fridge for up to 1 month.

TIP

You can make sauerkraut with almost any crunchy, watery vegetable, such as radishes, zucchini, cucumbers, carrots, peppers, turnips, or celery. You can also change the flavorings by adding garlic, ground turmeric, mustard seeds, dill, and/or sliced chile.

Fermented hot sauce

*Prep 20 minutes
+ 1 week
fermenting*

No cook

*Makes 1lb 2oz
(500g)*

Spicy, hot, sweet, and sour, this chili sauce comes with a real kick of umami funk from the lacto-fermentation process. For an even deeper fermented flavor, leave the chiles in the brine for an extra 7 days at room temperature (preferably somewhere cool and dark) before blending.

1½ tbsp (25g) sea salt flakes
4 tbsp light brown sugar, divided
3 Scotch bonnet chiles, stalks removed and
   cut in half
15 mild red chiles, stalks removed and cut
   in half
6 garlic cloves, peeled
2-in piece of fresh ginger, peeled and
   roughly chopped
3 tbsp apple cider vinegar

1 | Heat the salt and 2 tablespoons of the brown sugar with ⅓ cup (100ml) of water in a small pan over medium-low heat, swirling the pan until the sugar and salt dissolve. Pour in 1¾ cups (400ml) of cooled boiled water, stir, and let cool completely.

2 | Follow steps 1–2 from Sterilizing Jars (see p.456) using a 2-cup (500-ml) flip-top jar.

3 | Put both types of chile, the garlic cloves, and ginger into the jar and pour over enough of the brine to completely submerge everything. Cover the surface with a small disk of parchment paper and put on the lid. Leave at room temperature in a cool, dark place for 7 days, opening the lid a little every 24 hours to release any gas buildup, then closing it again.

4 | After 1 week, drain the chiles, garlic, and ginger in a strainer set over a large nonmetallic bowl, then put them into a high-powered blender with the vinegar, 4 tablespoons of the brine from the bowl, and the remaining brown sugar and blend until completely smooth. Taste and season with a little more sugar and/or vinegar if you like, stirring until the sugar dissolves, if using.

5 | Sterilize the jar again and pour in the chile mixture. Put on the lid and keep in the fridge for up to 1 month.

TIP

*As the sauce continues
to ferment, you'll need to
open the lid occasionally
to let out any built-up gas.*

KIMCHI

Prep 30 minutes + salting and 1–3 days fermenting

Cook 5 minutes

Makes 2¼lb (1kg)

The traditional kimchi is made from Chinese cabbage fermented with other vegetables, fish sauce, and gochugaru (Korean dried chili flakes). Available in Asian grocery stores and online, gochugaru provides a deep red color with a mild heat, slightly fruity taste, and hint of smokiness. The real knack here is judging when the kimchi has fermented sufficiently at room temperature—taste it once made and then every 12 hours or so until it develops a spicy, salty, sour tang and slight umami flavor.

2lb (1kg) Napa or Chinese cabbage
1 tbsp sea salt flakes, plus an extra pinch
1 tbsp white or brown rice flour
8 garlic cloves, peeled
2½-in piece of fresh ginger, peeled and chopped
2oz (60g) gochugaru (Korean dried red chili flakes)
4 tbsp fish sauce
8oz (250g) radishes (or Daikon radish or turnip), quartered, peeled, and thinly sliced
1 carrot, peeled and cut into julienne (see p.163)
6 green onions, cut into 1½-in (4-cm) long pieces

TIP

For a vegan and/or gluten-free kimchi, swap regular fish sauce with vegan fish sauce or use soy sauce or tamari.

1 | Cut the cabbage in half lengthwise, then each piece in half again lengthwise. Remove and discard the core from each wedge, then cut roughly into 3¼-in (8-cm) pieces and place in a large, nonmetallic mixing bowl. Sprinkle the sea salt evenly over the cabbage and mix well with your hands. Cover and chill for 3 hours, stirring every 30 minutes.

2 | Follow steps 1–2 from Sterilizing Jars (see p.456), using a 4½-cup (1-liter) flip-top jar or four 1-cup (250-ml) jars with lids. Rinse the cabbage under cold running water, then drain well and put back into the clean bowl.

3 | Put the rice flour into a small saucepan with ⅓ cup (100ml) of water, stir until combined, and cook over medium heat for 3–4 minutes, until a thick paste. This mixture boosts the fermentation process and gets everything going.

4 | Put the garlic and ginger into a pestle and mortar with a pinch of salt and pound to a smooth paste. Alternatively, use a mini food processor (you may need to add 1 tablespoon of cold water to help it blend). Mix the rice flour paste, garlic and ginger paste, gochugaru, fish sauce, and vegetables into the cabbage bowl, gently squeezing and massaging everything with clean hands to fully mingle and combine. You should notice the vegetables starting to release some liquid.

5 | Pack everything from the bowl into the sterilized jar(s), pressing the vegetables down so they are covered with the brining liquid, then cover them with a small disk of parchment paper.

6 | Leave in a cool, dark place at room temperature for 1–3 days (depending on how hot the room is), slightly opening the lid every 24 hours to release any gas buildup, then closing it again. When ready, the kimchi will be slightly sour, funky, and fizzy. Store in the fridge for up to 1 month.

COOKING TERMS & GLOSSARY

Al dente: Pasta, rice, and vegetables may be cooked until *al dente*, which is until just tender, yet still with a slight resistance when you bite into them.

Bake: To cook food in the dry heat of the oven.

Bake blind: To bake a crust without the filling. The pastry is lined with parchment paper or foil, then weighed down with pie weights, rice, or beans while in the oven to prevent it losing its shape and until the edge of the pastry is golden. The paper/foil and weights are removed and the crust returned to the oven to finish cooking the base.

Bain-marie: A "water bath" used to cook foods slowly and gently. A bain-marie can be a saucepan of simmering water over which a bowl is set, a double boiler, or a roasting pan, half-filled with water, and in which the dish being cooked is placed.

Baste: To spoon fat or liquid over food as it cooks to prevent it drying out and to add flavor.

Bind: To add eggs, flour, cornstarch, or fat to dry ingredients to combine and help hold them together.

Blanch: To immerse foods, such as vegetables, in hot water for a short time to slightly soften, remove the skin (from tomatoes), or dilute strong flavors.

Blend: To mix or combine ingredients together, either by stirring or in a food processor or blender.

Boil: To cook food in fast bubbling liquid, usually water or stock.

Braise: To cook meat, poultry, seafood, beans, or vegetables in a small amount of liquid, such as stock, wine, cider, or water, in a heavy-based pan with a lid, either on the stove or in the oven.

Broil: To cook food under the high heat of a heating element until browned and/or melted.

Butter: Both salted and unsalted butter are used in the recipes. If the recipe calls for "softened butter," then let it sit at room temperature until soft or malleable.

Buttermilk: Originally a byproduct of butter-making, today it is made by adding bacteria to milk to thicken and sour it.

Caramel: Sugar heated above 340°F (170°C) until it melts and becomes deep amber in color. It is used to sweeten desserts and drizzled over cakes, tarts, and ice cream.

Caramelize: To heat food (sweet and savory) until its surface sugars break down and turn golden brown.

Ceviche: A South American and Caribbean method of "cooking" seafood without heat. An acidic marinade made with citrus juice is used to partially "cook" thin slices of seafood.

Clarify: To skim or filter a liquid, such as melted butter, until it is clear and free of impurities.

Compote: Whole fruits poached in a sugar syrup, used for berries and soft fruit in particular.

Coulis: A thick sauce made from raw or cooked fruit.

Cream, to: To beat ingredients, such as butter and sugar, together until light and creamy when making a cake.

Crème anglaise: A thin, vanilla-flavored egg custard served warm or cold with/in many desserts.

Curdle: When milk, a sauce, or any mixture separates into a solid and liquid, such as with mayonnaise or a cake batter.

Cure: To add flavor and preserve meat, poultry, and seafood by drying, smoking, and salting or by marinating.

Dashi: A tuna and seaweed-based fish stock used in Japanese cooking.

Deep-fry: To cook food quickly immersed in a pan of hot oil until crisp and golden.

Devein: To remove the dark, thin vein that runs down the back of a shrimp.

Durum wheat: A hard wheat grain, with a high proportion of gluten, used to make dried pasta.

Egg wash: A glaze made from egg or egg yolk and water or milk, used for browning baked goods.

En papillote: Foods sealed in a package, such as parchment paper or foil, and gently cooked/steamed in the oven or a steamer to retain flavor, texture, and aroma.

Fermentation: The breakdown of a substance, food, or drink, by bacteria, yeasts, or other microorganisms. A process used to make kimchi, sauerkraut, yogurt, bread, and beer.

Fillet: A boneless piece of meat or fish.

Flour: All-purpose and bread flour usually made from wheat. All-purpose is most often used to make pastry or cakes, while bread flour has a high proportion of gluten and is perfect for breads and some pastries. Italian 00 flour is a finely milled, soft flour used to make pasta.

Fold, to: To stir a beaten or whisked mixture with a gentle lifting motion in a way not to lose any air, such as gently mixing flour into a cake mixture.

Garam masala: An Indian spice blend, usually added toward the end of cooking.

Gelatin: A setting agent available in powder or sheet form. Sheets of gelatin must be soaked in cold water to soften, and the powder dissolved before use.

Ghee: A clarified butter often used in Indian cooking and capable of being heated to a high temperature without burning.

Grill: To grill/cook food on a rack over a hot barbecue or in a grill pan on a stove.

Infuse: To immerse flavorings, herbs, and spices in hot liquid.

Macerate: To soak food, such as fruit, in liquid to soften it.

Marinade: A liquid for soaking or basting that adds flavor to food and protects it from drying out. If the marinade has an acidic component, such as lemon juice or yogurt, it can also have a tenderizing effect on meat, poultry, and seafood.

Marinate: To soak meat, poultry, seafood, or vegetables in a marinade (above) to add flavor and/or soften.

Meringue: A combination of egg whites and sugar whisked until light and fluffy, baked for a dessert or topping.

Mezze: A Middle Eastern combination of small plates and appetizers.

Miso: A (white, red, or brown) paste of fermented soy beans and other flavorings most often used in Japanese cooking as a condiment or flavoring.

Parboil: To partially cook in boiling water.

Pâtisserie: The art of pastry making and a collective name for cakes and pastries.

Pickle: To preserve foods, especially firm vegetables, in a brine or acidic liquid, such as vinegar.

Peel: To remove the skin from fruits or vegetables using a knife or peeler.

Pinch, a: A very small quantity of dry ingredient, held between thumb and finger, such as salt.

Poach: To gently cook or simmer in liquid, usually water, stock, or milk.

Pot-roast: To braise a whole chicken or joint of meat in a casserole dish or Dutch oven.

Pressure cooking: A method of cooking food under high pressure, ideal for soups, stews, and reducing the cooking time of slow-cooked dishes. Liquid is required, producing steam as it heats, creating increasing pressure in the cooker, thereby cooking the food in less time than conventional methods. Pressure cookers are also good for tenderizing cheaper cuts of meat or cooking dried beans.

Prove: The final rise of a bread dough before it is baked.

Pulses: Also known as legumes and includes dried and canned peas, beans, and lentils.

Purée: Fruit or vegetables blended using a blender or through a fine mesh strainer to a smooth consistency.

Quick bread: A bread made with an instant leavening agent, such as baking soda or baking powder, in place of yeast.

Roast: To cook meat, poultry, seafood, or vegetables in the high, dry heat of an oven.

Reduce: To boil or simmer a liquid or sauce in order to intensify the flavor or thicken.

Refresh: To cool down quickly under cold running water or in ice water. A way of stopping the cooking process for vegetables that have been blanched so they retain their texture and color.

Rehydrate: To add water to a food that has been dried, such as mushrooms, to reconstitute it.

Render, to: melt or clarify hard animal fat, such as that found in bacon, duck, or other meats, so it can be used for shallow-frying and roasting.

Rest: To allow meat or poultry to sit for a period after cooking to let the muscles relax and the juices redistribute, improving the taste and texture. Resting also refers to chilling pastry so it can relax or soften. A batter is rested before cooking so the flour can expand in the liquid.

Risotto: A rice dish from northern Italy in which hot stock is slowly stirred into short-grain risotto rice, such as arborio or carnaroli, until the grains are creamy, but still slightly firm and separate.

Roux: A cooked mixture of butter and flour used to thicken a white sauce, such as béchamel.

Rub in: To mix flour and butter together lightly with the fingertips until the mixture resembles breadcrumbs. Used in the first stage of pastry making.

Saffron: The dried red stigmas of the saffron crocus lend a golden color and a warm, musky flavor to dishes. Use in small quantities.

Sauté: To cook small pieces of food in fat, butter, or oil, shaking and tossing in a wide, deep-sided skillet over high heat.

Score: To make shallow or deep cuts into a food, such as the skin of a fish or cut of pork, so it cooks evenly and crisps up. Decorative cuts can also be made into pastry and bread doughs before baking.

Sear: To brown and seal the surface of meat or poultry by cooking in a skillet or saucepan over medium to high heat.

Semolina: The endosperm of durum wheat, available in a variety of grinds and primarily used to make pasta, or to prevent fresh pasta sticking together.

Shallow-fry: To cook in a small amount of oil in a skillet until browned and crisp.

Sift: To shake a dry ingredient, such as flour or powdered sugar, through a strainer to remove lumps and aerate.

Simmer: To cook food gently in liquid that bubbles lightly just below boiling point so the food cooks in an even heat without breaking up.

Skim: To remove fats and other impurities from a sauce or liquid using a spoon or ladle.

Soft peaks: Egg whites whisked until their peaks are still soft and barely hold their shape when the beaters are lifted.

Spatchcock: To remove the backbone from a chicken,

or other type of poultry, and then flatten so it cooks more quickly and evenly.

Spice rub: A dry marinade of spices used to coat meat, poultry, or seafood before cooking to impart flavor and texture.

Stew: To simmer gently in liquid in a heavy-based pan, with or without a lid. Perfect for vegetables, beans, less expensive cuts of meat, or chicken thighs, which should be immersed in a liquid, stock, or a sauce before cooking.

Stiff peaks: Egg whites whisked until their peaks are firm, stand straight up, and the tips don't bend when the beaters are lifted.

Stir-fry: To cook small pieces of food quickly in a small amount of fat, tossing continuously over high heat, usually in a wok.

Sugar syrup: Sugar and water cooked together to different temperatures to produce varying concentrations of syrup for cakes, desserts, candies, and ice creams.

Steam: To cook food in a steamer basket or perforated container set over a pan of boiling water (without direct contact with the water).

Tempeh: Made from fermented cooked soy beans, similar to tofu but with a firm, chunky texture and slightly nutty, mushroomy flavor.

Tofu: Also called bean curd, made from soy beans in a similar way to soft cheese. Tofu has a mild flavor and responds well to marinating, readily taking on stronger flavors. Used widely in Asian cooking and available in different types/textures: silken (soft), firm, and extra firm.

Unwaxed lemons: Some lemons (and other citrus fruit) are coated in a type of wax to increase their shelf life. Buy unwaxed fruit or, if hard to find, remove the wax by putting the fruit in a colander and pouring over boiling water or scrubbing it in a sink, then dry the fruit to remove the waxy residue.

Yeast: A fungus that uses the natural sugars in a mixture to release carbon dioxide to ferment bread. Yeast can be bought fresh or dried and sometimes needs activating in liquid before use. Dry instant yeast does not need to be pre-activated and can be used straight away.

Zest: The thin, colored, outer skin of a citrus fruit, such as lemons, limes, and oranges. Usually pared or removed with a small, sharp chef's knife or grated with a zester or over a fine-holed grater to separate it from the bitter white pith underneath.

CONVERSION CHARTS

LINEAR

3mm	($^1/_8$in)
5mm	(¼in)
1cm	(½in)
2cm	(¾in)
2.5cm	(1in)
5cm	(2in)
6cm	(2½in)
7.5cm	(3in)
10cm	(4in)
12cm	(5in)
15cm	(6in)
18cm	(7in)
20cm	(8in)
23cm	(9in)
25cm	(10in)
28cm	(11in)
30cm	(12in)
46cm	(18in)
50cm	(20in)
61cm	(24in)
77cm	(30in)

WEIGHT

10g	(¼oz)	550g	(1¼lb)
15g	(½oz)	600g	(1lb 5oz)
20g	(¾oz)	675g	(1½lb)
25g	(scant 1oz)	750g	(1lb 10oz)
30g	(1oz)	800g	(1¾lb)
45g	(1½oz)	900g	(2lb)
50g	(1¾oz)	1kg	(2¼lb)
60g	(2oz)	1.1kg	(2½lb)
75g	(2½oz)	1.25kg	(2¾lb)
85g	(3oz)	1.35kg	(3lb)
100g	(3½oz)	1.5kg	(3lb 3oz)
115g	(4oz)	1.8kg	(4lb)
125g	(4½oz)	2kg	(4½lb)
140g	(5oz)	2.25kg	(5lb)
150g	(5½oz)	2.5kg	(5½lb)
175g	(6oz)	2.7kg	(6lb)
200g	(7oz)	3kg	(6½lb)
225g	(8oz)	3.5kg	(7lb)
250g	(9oz)	4.5kg	(9lb)
300g	(10oz)	5kg	(10lb)
350g	(12oz)	6kg	(12lb)
400g	(14oz)	6.5kg	(13lb)
450g	(1lb)	8.5kg	(17lb)
500g	(1lb 2oz)		

VOLUME

METRIC (ML)	TSP, TBSP, CUPS	IMPERIAL (FL OZ/PINTS)
5ml	1 tsp	-
10ml	2 tsp	-
15ml	1 tbsp (equivalent to 3 tsp)	-
30ml	2 tbsp	-
45ml	3 tbsp	-
60ml	¼ cup	(2fl oz)
75ml	⅓ cup	(2½fl oz)
90ml	6 tbsp	(3fl oz)
100ml	6½ tbsp	(3½fl oz)
120ml	½ cup	(4fl oz)
150ml	⅔ cup	(5fl oz)
175ml	¾ cup	(6fl oz)
200ml	scant 1 cup	(7fl oz)
240ml	1 cup	(8fl oz)
250ml	1 cup plus 1 tbsp	(9fl oz)
300ml	1¼ cups	(10fl oz)
350ml	1½ cups	(12fl oz)
400ml	1¾ cups	(14fl oz)
450ml	scant 2 cups	(15fl oz)
500ml	generous 2 cups	(16fl oz)
600ml	2½ cups	(1 pint)
750ml	3 cups	(1¼ pints)
900ml	scant 4 cups	(1½ pints)
1 liter	4$^1/_3$ cups	(1¾ pints)
1.2 liters	5 cups	(2 pints)
1.4 liters	6 cups	(2½ pints)
1.5 liters	6¼ cups	(2¾ pints)
1.7 liters	7 cups	(3 pints)
2 liters	8½ cups	(3½ pints)

INDEX

Publisher's acknowledgments
DK would like to thank Scramble LDN for their contribution to the book, and Nicola Graimes and Claire Rochford for their contributions. Thanks to Katie Hardwicke for proofreading, Lisa Footitt for indexing, Ana Zaja Petrak for the illustrations and to the entire shoot team. Thank you to all those who agreed to contribute their own recipes: Riaz Phillips (p.84 and p.263), Karla Zazeuta (p.125), Verna Gao (p.173, p.244, p.246, p.283), Idy Osibodu (p.203, p.262) and Jodie Nixon (p.249).

Editorial Director Cara Armstrong
Project Editor Izzy Holton
Senior US Editor Megan Douglass
US Consultant Renee Wilmeth
Project Art Editor Jordan Lambley
Editorial Assistant Charlotte Beauchamp
Sales and Jackets Coordinator Emily Cannings
Senior Production Editor David Almond
Senior Production Controller Stephanie McConnell
Art Director Maxine Pedliham
Publishing Director Katie Cowan

Editorial Nicola Graimes
Design Claire Rochford, Sarah Snelling
Illustrator Ana Zaja Petrak
Photographer Luke Albert
Prop styling Hannah Wilkinson, Faye Wears
Food styling Adam Bush, Sonali Shah, Caitlin MacDonald
Food styling assistants Maria Gurevich, Sophie Pryn, Caitlin MacDonald, Sadie Albuquerque

First American Edition, 2024
Published in the United States by DK Publishing,
a division of Penguin Random House LLC
1745 Broadway, 20th Floor, New York, NY 10019

Copyright © 2024 Dorling Kindersley Limited
24 25 26 27 28 10 9 8 7 6 5 4 3 2 1
001–341724–Oct/2024

A catalog record for this book
is available from the Library of Congress.
ISBN: 978-0-5938-4431-1

Printed and bound in Slovakia

www.dk.com